POSTMODERNISM AND CHRISTIAN PHILOSOPHY

American Maritain Association Publications

General Editor: Anthony O. Simon

Jacques Maritain: The Man and His Metaphysics
Edited by John F. X. Knasas, 1988
ISBN 0-268-01205-9 (out of print)

Freedom in the Modern World: Jacques Maritain, Yves R. Simon, Mortimer J. Adler
Edited by Michael D. Torre, 1989, Second Printing 1990
ISBN 0-268-00978-3

From Twilight to Dawn: The Cultural Vision of Jacques Maritain
Edited by Peter A. Redpath, 1990
ISBN 0-268-00979-1

The Future of Thomism
Edited by Deal W. Hudson and Dennis Wm. Moran, 1992
ISBN 0-268-00986-4

Jacques Maritain and the Jews
Edited by Robert Royal, 1994
ISBN 0-268-01193-1

Freedom, Virtue, and the Common Good
Edited by Curtis L. Hancock and Anthony O. Simon, 1995
ISBN 0-268-00991-0

Postmodernism and Christian Philosophy
Edited by Roman T. Ciapalo, 1997
ISBN 0-8132-0881-5

POSTMODERNISM AND CHRISTIAN PHILOSOPHY

Edited by

Roman T. Ciapalo

With an Introduction by

Jude P. Dougherty

American Maritain Association

Distributed by The Catholic University of America Press

Library of Congress Cataloging-in-Publication Data

Postmodernism and Christian philosophy / edited by Roman T. Ciapalo ;
with an introduction by Jude P. Dougherty.
    p.   cm. — (American Maritain Association publications)
    Includes bibliographical references and index.
    ISBN 0-8132-0881-5 (pbk. : alk. paper)
1. Postmodernism. 2. Neo-Scholasticism 3. Postmodernism—Religious
aspects—Christianity. 4. Christianity—Philosophy.
    I. Ciapalo, Roman T. (Roman Theodore), 1950-   . II. Series.
B831.2.P676 1997
149.97—dc21   96-49919
                                                         CIP

Manufactured in the
United States of America

American Maritain Association
Anthony O. Simon, Secretary
508 Travers Circle
Mishawaka, Indiana 46545

Distributed by The Catholic University of America Press
Washington, D.C. 20064

To Nancy

Contents

Acknowledgments

I am indebted to a variety of individuals for their contributions to the publication of this volume. I am very grateful to Deal W. Hudson, Anthony O. Simon, and Curtis L. Hancock for their suggestions and advice regarding the preparation of this volume, and to David J. McGonagle, Director of The Catholic University of America Press, for his advice on the technical aspects of its layout and design, and to Joseph Pappin III for his assistance during the early stages of its compilation.

Of course, it is to the authors of the contributed articles that I am most grateful, for the ultimate value of this volume is due to the depth and breadth of their scholarship and to the clarity of the expression of their insights. In particular, I am indebted to Jude P. Dougherty, for writing such a lucid and provocative *Introduction,* and to Curtis L. Hancock, for contributing a fitting *Epilogue*, one which is both frank and, at the same time, optimistic in its assessment of the theme of the volume.

In addition, I would like to pay particular tribute and express my profound gratitude to Jonathan Raymon, a Philosophy major at Loras College and a veritable magician with a computer, for his tireless, patient, cheerful, and extremely skillful preparation of the typescript for publication and imaginative design of the front and back covers. His contribution was invaluable. I am also most appreciative of the material and moral support provided by Jim O'Brien, by my Philosophy Department, particularly by Joe Magno, Chairperson; Gladys Fitzpatrick, department secretary, and by the administration of Loras College, especially Ken Kraus, Academic Dean, and Joachim Froehlich, President.

Finally, I would like to thank my wife, Nancy, for her understanding, never-wavering support, and cheerful optimism throughout the preparation of this volume.

Introduction

Nova et Vetera:
Maritain as Critic

Jude P. Dougherty

In the second year of his pontificate, Leo XIII promulgated the encyclical, *Aeterni Patris*, August 4, 1879, endorsing a fledgling Thomistic movement which was to enlist some of the best minds of the following generation. That encyclical was followed by the founding of philosophical institutes at Louvain and Washington for the purpose of making available the thought of St. Thomas as an antidote to the then dominant positivisms and materialisms. The *Institut Superieur de Philosophie* under the direction of Desiré J. Mercier came into being in 1891; the School of Philosophy at The Catholic University of America under the direction of Edward A. Pace in 1895. The *Institut Catholique de Paris* was already twelve years old when Leo became Pope and the *Institut* in due course was to play an important role in the Thomistic revival. Jacques Maritain was to be offered a professorship there in 1914.

Leo recommended to the Catholic world the study of St. Thomas because of the perceived value of his philosophy in meeting "the critical state of the times in which we live." Leo saw that the regnant philosophies of his day not only undercut the faith but were beginning to have disastrous effects on personal and communal life. Succinctly he says in *Aeterni Patris*, "Erroneous theories respecting our duty to God and our responsibilities as men, originally propounded in philosophical schools, have gradually permeated all ranks of society and secured acceptance among the majority of men."[1]

By any measure, the 19th century was no less an intellectually tumultuous one for Europe than the 20th. Dominated in the intellectual order by the Enlightenment, Anglo-French and German, Europe underwent a systematic attempt on the part of the intelligentsia to replace the inherited, largely classical

---

[1] Maritain reproduces this encyclical in his *St. Thomas Aquinas: Angel of the Schools,* trans. J. F. Scanlon (London: Sheed and Ward, 1948), 134-154.

1

and Christian learning, by a purely secular ethos. The Napoleonic wars in their aftermath added materially to the destabilization, eradicating many institutional structures, economic, and social as well as religious.

Startling advances in the physical sciences reinforced the Enlightenment's confidence in natural reason. In retrospect we can see that the ideas which formed the secular outlook of the 19th century were the product of two major intellectual revolutions. The first is associated with the biological investigations of the period and with the names of Spencer, Darwin, Wallace, Huxley and Haeckel. Their work employed the vocabulary of "evolution," "change," "growth" and "development" and led to the worship of progress. The effect of the new biological studies was to place man and his activity wholly in a materialistic setting, giving them a natural origin and a natural history. Man was transformed from a being with a spiritual component and a transcendent end, elevated above the rest of nature, into a purely material organism forced to interact within a natural environment like any other living species.

The second revolution resulted from advances in physics that were taken to be a reinforcement of the fundamental assumptions of a mechanistic interpretation of nature. Convinced that all natural phenomena can be explained by structural and efficient causes, the disciples of Locke and Hume discarded any explanation invoking the concept of "purpose" or of "final cause."

The convergence of these concepts in physics and in biology made possible the resurgence of a purely materialistic concept of human nature with no need for the hypothesis of a creative God or of a spiritual soul. The foremost symbol of the new outlook became Darwin's *Origin of the Species* (1859). For an intellectual class it codified a view which had been germinating since the preceding century. Darwin confidently marshalled evidence and systematically formulated in a scientific vocabulary ideas already available, but the spontaneous acceptance of his doctrine of evolutionary progress was possible only because the philosophical groundwork had been laid by the Enlightenment Fathers.

Leo XIII was not alone in his assessment of the situation. On both sides of the Atlantic various philosophical idealisms were created in a defensive effort to maintain the credibility of religious witness. Challenged by purely naturalistic interpretations of faith, many found the rational support they needed as believers in a post-Kantian idealism. *The Journal of Speculative Philosophy*, the first journal of philosophy in the English language, was founded at St. Louis, Missouri in 1867, the same year that the *Institut Catholique de Paris* was created, for the dual purpose of making available the best of German philosophy and of providing the Americans with a philosophical forum. In the first issue of the journal, William Torrey Harris gave three reasons for the pursuit of speculative philosophy. According to Torrey, speculative philosophy provides, first, a philosophy of religion much needed at a time when traditional religious teaching and ecclesiastical authority are losing their influence. Secondly, it provides a social philosophy compatible with a communal outlook as opposed to a socially devastating individualism. Thirdly, while taking cognizance of the startling advances in the natural sciences, it provides an alternative to empiricism as a philosophy of knowledge. Speculative philosophy for Harris is the tradition beginning with Plato, a tradition which finds its full expression in the system of Hegel.

II

Jacques Maritain was born just three years after *Aeterni Patris*. By the time Maritain discovered St. Thomas, the Thomistic movement was well under way. It was a movement that not only nourished his searching intellect, but one which he substantially enriched. He came to Thomas, he would say, already a Thomist without knowing it. Maritain's influence eventually extended worldwide, notably to Italy, to Latin America, especially Argentina, and to North America.

The convert early on placed his intellect in the service of the church. He knew first hand the contemporary intellectual milieu and shared Leo's assessment of the dominant philosophies, philosophies clearly at odds with the Catholic faith. "If I am anti-modern, it is certainly not out of personal inclination, but because the spirit of all modern things that have proceeded from the anti-Christian revolution compels me to be so, because it itself makes opposition to the human inheritance its own distinctive characteristic, because it hates and despises the past and worships itself . . ."[2]

Maritain's critique of Luther, Descartes and Rousseau and his early critique of his mentor, Henri Bergson, display an intellect fully aware of the impact of ideas and philosophical systems on the practical order. Much of that early work would not today withstand professional scrutiny, largely because of its apologetic character but also because it was often marred by a vagueness and imprecision which his critics easily exploited. Furthermore, Maritain did not in practice always keep clear the distinction between philosophy and theology. It made him later an easy target for American philosophers, such as Sidney Hook and Ernest Nagel, who were schooled in the prevailing pragmatic naturalism. It also hurt his chance for an appointment at the University of Chicago. Robert M. Hutchins, as chancellor of the University of Chicago, three times tried to get Maritain appointed to its faculty of philosophy. The department blocked the

---

[2] *Ibid.*, ix-x.

appointment each time, even when Hutchins offered to pay his salary from non-departmental funds, because in the words of one member of the department, "Maritain is a propagandist." Hutchins shot back, "You are all propagandists." On another occasion Hutchins sent an emissary, probably John Nef, to the chairman of the department, a well known positivist. The response to Hutchins was, "Maritain is not a good philosopher." The emissary then asked, "Do you have any good philosophers on your faculty?" The answer, "No, but we know what a good philosopher is."[3] The faculty at that time was led by George Herbert Mead and James Hayden Tufts. Ironically, one would have to be a specialist in the history of American philosophy to know their names, whereas the achievement of Jacques Maritain as a philosopher is acknowledged throughout the West.

One must concede that the chairman of the philosophy department at the University of Chicago may have had it right when he said, "Maritain is an apologist." He was one all of his professional life. But Maritain was philosophizing within a Thomistic framework where philosophy in the service of theology loses nothing of its integrity. In fact, as Maritain consistently affirmed, the philosopher himself may gain insight by his association with a theological perspective which thrusts new problems and demands greater precision. Maritain maintains that philosophy in the abstract is pure philosophy and can never be "Christian," but concretely it is always pursued within a social setting which in providing a milieu for reflection, gives it color, if not direction. In *Existence and the Existent* he writes, "We do not philosophize in the posture of dramatic singularity; we do not save our souls in the posture of theoretic universality and detachment from self for the purpose of knowing."

As a critic of modernity Maritain was at times violent and cutting. Raïssa was to say of his style, "As for the men whose ideas he criticized, he certainly respected them personally, but they were for him scarcely more than vehicles for abstract doctrines."[4] Étienne Gilson, when asked by a journalist to comment on the difference between his method and that of Maritain, characterized Maritain's as one that sets bare ideas in juxtaposition, submerging the individuality of the philosophers who espoused them. Speaking of his own technique, Gilson said, "It is more important to try to understand ideas through men . . . in order to judge in a way that unites . . . Pure ideas, taken in their abstract rigor are generally irreconcilable.[5] But Maritain

---

[3] Cf. Milton Mayer, *Robert Maynard Hutchins: A Memoir* (Berkeley: University of California Press, 1993), 118.

[4] *Memoirs*, 353, as quoted by Donald and Idella Gallagher, *The Achievement of Jacques and Raïssa Maritain*, (Garden City, New York: Doubleday and Co., 1962), 12.

[5] Laurence K. Shook, *Étienne Gilson* (Toronto: Pontifical Institute of Medieval Studies, 1984) 194.

was not put off. His response: "It is not psychology, but the critique of philosophers which brings truth to light." Where truth is concerned there can be no compromise. One ought to be tenderhearted and tough-minded, not hardhearted and softheaded. Yet Maritain could say, "I am content to owe something to Voltaire in what concerns civil tolerance, and to Luther in what concerns nonconformism, and to honor them in this." In *Theonas* he acknowledges a respect for Comte insofar as he seeks the realization of human order, for Kant for the restoration of the activity of the knowing subject, and for Bergson for the recognition of the spiritual.[6]

III

It is commonly acknowledged that Maritain's best work in the area of social and political philosophy was accomplished during his years in America. What gives that work power, however, is its grounding in a solid metaphysics of being and in a realistic epistemology. Maritain the metaphysician is at his best in his *A Preface to Metaphysics* and in his *Existence and the Existent*. As a theorist of knowledge he produced *The Degrees of Knowledge*, *Philosophy of Nature*, and *Creative Intuition in Art and Poetry*. With the exception of the last mentioned, those works formed the background to his political philosophy, a political philosophy that had considerable influence on important thinkers such as Mortimer J. Adler, John Courtney Murray, and Yves R. Simon and on more than one generation of Thomists who staffed the then flourishing Catholic colleges and universities in the United States. Many students were first exposed to philosophy through his clearly written *Introduction to Philosophy*.

It is Maritain's recognition of the practical effects of the materialisms and empiricisms of his day and his critique of the Enlightenment spirit which determine his life's work. One of his earliest books sets the tone for much that is to come. The myth of "necessary progress" as found in philosophers like Condorcet and Comte is one of his major targets in *Theonas*, a dialogue first published in 1921. He quotes Condorcet, "There will then come a moment upon this earth when the sun will shine on none but free men who recognize no other master than their reason; when tyrants and slaves, priests and their stupid hypocritical instruments, will exist no more save in history and on the stage."[7] And Auguste Comte, "To re-establish the Catholic order it would be necessary to suppress the philosophy of the eighteenth century, and as this philosophy proceeds from the Reformation, and Luther's Reformation in its turn was but the result of the experimental sciences introduced into Europe by the Arabs, it

---

[6] *Theonas*, trans. Frank J. Sheed (New York: Sheed & Ward, 1933), 172.
[7] *Ibid.*, 117.

would be necessary to suppress the sciences."[8] Maritain, through the character Philonous, responds to Comte as follows: "That surely is a perfect text, I know it by heart: and it illustrates as clearly as the historico-economic synthesis of Karl Marx—What havoc the myth of progress can work in the mind of an intelligent man."[9]

As Maritain characterizes it, "the law of progress" demands the ceaseless changing of foundations and principles inherited from the past; but if foundations can change, that which rests on them must also change. The movement of humanity towards the better, according to Comte and his disciples, implies the repudiation of all previous gains. The progressivists, Maritain suggests, fail to recognize that there are types of change. Some change can be constructive as Thomas appropriating Augustine or the Copernican revolution incorporating Ptolemaic astronomy. To use a homey example, the production of a plant is bound up with the corruption of the seed. "There is no destruction," he argues, "that does not produce something, no production that does not destroy some existent thing. The whole question is to know whether it is the production or the destruction which is the principal event."[10] Judgment is required. The conservative takes newness to be a sign of corruption; the mystics of revolution take all newness for a newness of achievement. Placed in perspective, the myths of "humanity," "the city of the future," "revolution" and "necessary progress" are but secular substitutions for Christian ideas such as the "church," the "heavenly Jerusalem," "regeneration" and "providence." "When men cease to believe in the supernatural," Maritain says, "the Gospel is reduced to the plane of nature."[11]

Although Maritain's early targets are Bergson and the three reformers, his real enemy is Immanuel Kant. In Maritain's judgment, Kant's critical philosophy is born of the convergence of the three intellectual currents represented 1) by Luther's revolt in theology, 2) by Descartes' in philosophy and 3) by Rousseau's in ethics. Kant represents a lack of confidence in the intellect's ability to metaphysically grasp being. Bergson similarly underestimates the intellect, but Maritain is willing to commend Bergson for attacking the anti-metaphysical prejudices of 19th century positivism. Still, in Maritain's judgment, Bergson's notion of intuition and his theory of conceptual knowledge leads, not unlike Descartes, to a subjectivism and irrationalism. In retrospect, Maritain may be seen to have more in common with Bergson than not; he nevertheless saw the difficulty of maintaining an objectivist metaphysics and even natural science on Bergson's somewhat anti-intellectualist epistemology. In Maritain's judgment, both Bergson and Kant give too large a role to the activity of the experiencing subject in constituting the known. Maritain's conviction that the realism of

---

[8] *Ibid.*, 126.   [9] *Ibid.*, 126-27.   [10] *Ibid.*, 137.   [11] *Ibid.*, 139-40.

Aristotle and Aquinas is perfectly in accord with common sense and with modern science finds full expression in his mature work, *The Degrees of Knowledge* (1932).[12]

Maritain provides this insightful notion of how philosophies differ. "Modern philosophies" he writes, "grow out of what has gone before, but rather by way of contradiction; the Scholastics by way of agreement and further development." The result is that philosophy in our day is like a series of episodes simply stuck end to end, not like a tree where each is organically related to each and all to the roots.[13] "The labor of the mind, by its very nature demands a collaboration running through the years." There is such a thing as a *philosophia perennis;* though its source is in antiquity, it is forever open-ended.

IV

In the closing years of his life Maritain returned to themes which he first approached as a young convert grateful for the insight provided by his newly acquired faith. In the last decade of his life, the old philosopher equipped with both the faith and years of experience reflects at length on the condition of his beloved Catholic Church. Between 1966 and 1973 he produced three books. One may view these simply as works of apologetics, but one may also find in them profound philosophical insight. The most widely noted was his *Le Paysan de la Garonne* published shortly after the close of the Second Vatican Council when Maritain was eighty-four years of age. *On the Grace and Humanity of Christ* appeared in 1969; *On The Church of Christ* followed four years later.

Acknowledging that he was writing in a "troubled historical moment," Maritain presents *On the Church of Christ* as a reflection of a philosopher on the faith, a faith accorded him through the instrument of the Church. The book, he proclaims, is not a work of apologetics; "It presupposes the Catholic faith and addresses itself above all to Catholics, (and) to our nonseparated brothers who recite the Credo each Sunday."[14] It addresses itself to others to the extent that they "desire to know what Catholics believe even if the latter seem sometimes to have forgotten it."[15]

The last is not an idle remark. In Maritain's judgment, Vatican II unleashed a subversive movement in the Church which constitutes, perhaps, an even greater

[12] Jacques Maritain, *The Degrees of Knowledge*, trans. Gerald B. Phelan (New York: Charles Scribner's Sons, 1959).

[13] *Theonas*, 5.

[14] *On the Church of Christ*, trans. Joseph W. Evans (Notre Dame, Indiana: University of Notre Dame Press, 1973), vi.

[15] *Ibid.*

threat to her integrity than the external modernist attack of the 19th century. "The modernism of Pius X's time," he writes, was "only a modest hay fever" compared to the sickness which besets the intellectuals today.[16] In *Le Paysan*, he speaks of an "immanent apostasy." The new theologians through an exhausting work of "hermeneutic evacuation" have emptied our faith of every specific object and reduced it to a "simple sublimating aspiration." "The frenzied modernism of today is incurably ambivalent. Its natural bent, although it would deny it, is to ruin the Christian faith."[17] Ironically, Maritain says, the leaders of our neo-modernism declare themselves Christian, even though they have separated themselves from its basic tenets. In a way, their attitude is a backhanded compliment to Christianity itself, since they still cherish their identification with the Church.

Responding to a frequent claim, Maritain asks, "if divine transcendence is only the mythical projection of a certain collective fear experienced by man at a given moment in history," then why should an observer faithful to the tradition "be astonished that so many modernists believe they have a mission to save a dying Christianity, their dying Christianity for the modern world."[18] Simply put, modernism and Christianity are incompatible.

A Greek confidence in the human intellect and in the intelligibility of nature is the cornerstone of Maritain's philosophy of being. It led him, on first acquaintance, to an appreciation of the realism of St. Thomas whom he came to venerate both as a person and as a philosopher/theologian. Even before the end of the Second Vatican Council, Maritain sadly detects a drift away from St. Thomas on the part of Catholic theologians. Disparaging references to St. Thomas and the Scholastics and the call to de-hellenize Christianity, he is convinced, is usually a repudiation of philosophical realism and the first step toward a subjectivism which reduces the revealed word of God to mere symbols for truths accessible to human reason. He finds this regrettable not only because it marks off the repudiation of a great teacher but because of its implications for theology as a discipline. Theology, heretofore, was thought of as "rational knowledge." The new approach, by contrast, when it does not reduce the faith to *praxis*, seems to adopt a fideistic starting point; Christ is the way, if one is inclined to adopt Him as a guide.

In an aside, Maritain notes, "some of our well bred contemporaries are repelled by the vocabulary of Aquinas." Yet it is hard to believe that men who understand Hegel, Heidegger and Jean-Paul Sartre should be terrorized by

---

[16] Jacques Maritain, *The Peasant of the Garonne*, trans. Michael Cuddihy and Elizabeth Hughes (New York: Holt, Rinehart and Winston, 1968), 14.

[17] *Ibid.*, 17.   [18] *Ibid.*, 19.

scholastic rigor. They should know perfectly well that every science has its technical vocabulary.[19] Their difficulty lies much deeper, in the skepticisms they have unwittingly embraced, skepticisms which deny the intellect's ability to reach being in knowledge and in speech. The only way we can logically and clearly express many of the truths of the faith is by appropriating the language of ontology. If we cannot know reality in itself but only as it appears to us, what are we to make of the teachings of Chalcedon, i.e., that Jesus Christ is one person with two natures, one divine and one human? What are we to make of the doctrine of the Eucharist?

V

Speaking of method, Maritain says, the teaching of Aquinas "is not the doctrine of one man, but the whole labor of the Fathers of the Church, the seekers of Greece, . . . the inspired of Israel"[20] and the scholars of the medieval Arabic world. Far from reaching a dead-end, the Thomistic corpus "is an intelligible organism meant to keep on growing always, and to extend across the centuries its insatiable thirst for new prey. It is a doctrine open and without frontiers; open to every reality wherever it is and every truth from wherever it comes, especially the new truth which the evolution of culture or science will enable it to bring out."[21] It is, too, a doctrine open to the various problematics it may see fit to employ, whether created from within or adopted from without. Because it is an open doctrine, it is indefinitely progressive. Those who adopt the philosophy of St. Thomas recognize that their master does not require subservience. "The philosopher swears fidelity to no person, nor any school— not even if he be a Thomist—to the letter of St. Thomas and every article of his teaching."[22]

Josiah Royce saw this more than a half century earlier. Writing as an outsider, he was convinced that the neo-scholastic movement endorsed by Leo XIII was an important one, in Royce's words, "for the general intellectual progress of our time." The use of St. Thomas, he says, entails growth, development and change. He even uses the word "progress." "Pope Leo, after all, 'let loose a thinker' amongst his people—a thinker to be sure, of unquestioned orthodoxy, but after all a genuine thinker whom the textbooks had long tried, as it were to keep lifeless, and who, when once revived, proves to be full of the suggestion of new problems, and of an effort towards new solutions."[23] But Royce was

---

[19] *Ibid.*, 155.   [20] *Ibid.*, 153.   [21] *Ibid.*   [22] *Ibid.*, 161.

[23] *The Boston Evening Transcript* (July 29, 1903), reprinted in *Fugitive Essays* (Cambridge, Massachusetts: Harvard University Press, 1925), 422-23.

also fearful that a resurgent Thomism might give way to the Kantian legions and their demand that the epistemological issue be settled first. In Maritain he would have found a kindred spirit.

The key to Maritain's conception of philosophy, his love for St. Thomas, and his chagrin at contemporary drifts in theology is grounded, as I said, in his doctrine of being. "To maintain . . . that the object of our intellect is not the being of things but the *idea* of being which it forms in itself, or more generally that we apprehend immediately only our ideas, is to deliver oneself bound hand and foot to skepticism."[24] Maritain's controlling principle can be stated simply: being governs enquiry. There are structures apart from the mind which can be objectively grasped. Or put another way, being is intelligible, and not only being, but being in act is intelligible. The senses bring us into contact with a material, changing world, but in the flux of events there are identifiable structures which control enquiry. Although the senses are limited to the material singular, there is more in the sense report than the senses themselves are formally able to appreciate. The intellect's ability to abstract enables it to grasp the universal, the intelligible nature, the "whatness" of the thing. Those things which are not self-intelligible need to be explained by means of things other than themselves.[25] Acknowledging the principles of substance and causality, Maritain avoids the phenomenalism of Locke and the empiricism of Hume. So equipped, he is able to reason to an immaterial order and to the existence of God, *ipsum esse subsistens*. Maritain's defense of the first principles of thought and being in his little book, *A Preface to Metaphysics*, is difficult to surpass.

Philosophies which fail to achieve a doctrine of being will inevitably be subjective in tone. Methodologically, they will be cut off from the transcendent source of being itself. Oddly, philosophy seems to entail a theology whether it reaches God or not. "When Feuerbach declared that God was the creation and alienation of man; when Nietzsche proclaimed the death of God, they were the theologians of our contemporary atheistic philosophies."[26] They define themselves and their projects against a tradition they hope to supersede, but one in which their own roots are planted. "Why are these philosophies so charged with bitterness," Maritain asks, "unless it is because they feel themselves

[24] Jacques Maritain, *Elements of Philosophy,* trans. E.I. Watkin (New York: Sheed and Ward, 1930), 186.

[25] Jacques Maritain, *Existence and the Existent,* trans. L. Galantiere and Gerald B. Phelan (New York: Pantheon Books, 1948), Chap. I, 10-46; *A Preface to Metaphysics* (New York: Sheed and Ward, 1948), Lectures II-IV, 43-89.

[26] Jacques Maritain, *Existence and the Existent,* 137.

chained in spite of themselves to a transcendence and to a past they constantly have to kill."[27] Theirs is, in fact, a religious protest in the guise of philosophy.

VI

The essays which constitute this volume are the fruit of the 1993 Annual Meeting of the American Maritain Association. The reader should not seek a unity of outlook among the contributors. There are almost as many starting points, assumptions and methodological tacks as there are contributors. Certainly not all contributors can be called disciples of Maritain or even of St. Thomas. There are almost as many references to Heidegger as there are to Maritain. Many of the essays succumb to the contemporary vice of taking ill-defined abstractions seriously, abstractions such as postmodernism, deconstructionism, feminism and Thomism. Yet in common with Maritain all the authors, without exception, have an appreciation for classical learning; all write from a "realistic" perspective; all recognize that ideas have consequences in the practical order.

One can believe that if Maritain were writing today his assessment and critique of so-called "postmodernism" would not be substantially different from that taken by the contributors to this volume. If anything he would likely be more pugnacious and cutting. Having lived through the modernist period he could only view postmodernism as the *reductio ad absurdum* of the former.

[27] *Ibid.*

The End of Philosophy
and the End of Physics:
A Dead End

Benedict M. Ashley, O.P.

Heidegger announced the "end of philosophy," i.e., the completion of the philosophical enterprise as the Greeks conceived it. This has been echoed by deconstructionists, who say that philosophy is merely literature expressive of personal attitudes, and by Marxists, critical theorists like Theodore Adorno, and pragmatists like Richard Rorty, who see it as a form of self-serving rhetoric. Now physicists are predicting a "Theory of Everything" which will be a "Final Theory" which will complete the history of physics. Stephen Weinberg has even suggested that this "Final Theory" will eliminate the need to determine any "initial conditions" for the universe and thus show that the universe as it actually exists is not only the only one possible but an absolutely necessary existent. This carries the Pythagoreanism of Plato to its ultimate conclusion.

Moreover, the consequences of relativity and quantum theories and the postulation by many scientists of the Anthropic Cosmological Principle in one or another of its various forms,[1] seems to some to make the existence of the universe dependent on the human observer, and thus eliminate the empirical realism of science. Thus the crisis of postmodernism is extended beyond the humanities to the hard sciences.

While this would seem to present Thomists with a grand opportunity for a hearing, in the twentieth century they have isolated themselves in various ways

[1] J.D. Barrow and F. J. Tipler, *The Anthropic Cosmological Principle* (Oxford: Oxford University Press, 1988). For a discussion see Errol E. Harris, *Cosmos and Anthropos: A Philosophical Interpretation of the Anthropic Cosmological Principle* (Atlantic Highlands, New Jersey: Humanities Press International, 1991). For some cautions see Stanley L. Jaki, *God and the Cosmologists* (Edinburgh: Scottish Academic Press, 1989), 189-192.

from the findings of the physical sciences, and left the field to the Whiteheadians. This withdrawal rests on certain mistakes in Thomistic exegesis.

There is a need to return to a more serious study of Aquinas' philosophy of nature understood in its own proper terms, and not merely as subject to metaphysical reflection. Central to such a study is the question of the knowability of the essences of material things, which is defectively treated in many accounts of St. Thomas' thought.

Steve Weinberg in a chapter on philosophy in his *Dreams of a Final Theory*[2] has also said that philosophy has done more harm to science than good, and cites the bad scientific notions spawned by mechanism, Marxism, Kantianism, positivism, sociologism and cultural relativism. "I know of *no one* who has participated actively in the advance of physics in the post-war period whose research has been significantly helped by the work of philosophers." (168f.). After quoting remarks of Wigner on the "unreasonable effectiveness of mathematics" in science, Weinberg says "I want to take up the other equally puzzling phenomenon, the unreasonable ineffectiveness of philosophy." (169) "Even when philosophical doctrines have in the past been useful to scientists, they have generally lingered too long becoming of more harm than ever they were of use." (169).

What Weinberg takes for granted is that science is not philosophy. Historically, however, the great scientists up to the eighteenth century all regarded themselves as natural philosophers. What Weinberg is calling "philosophy" is precisely those systems of philosophy which separated themselves from scientific practice and then worked to infiltrate science with alien ideas, whose influence, coming as it did from non-scientific sources, could only be harmful to science.

Before the eighteenth century natural philosophers, i.e., scientists, all aimed to understand the *reality* of the world accessible to our senses. They distinguished sharply between mathematical hypotheses about the universe which merely "saved appearances" but which might be only remotely related to the real state of affairs, for example the Ptolemaic system of epicycles, and genuinely physical theories that dealt with real entities and causes. The former type of knowledge was for them merely instrumental and provisional to achieving the latter kind of real knowledge.

It was with Descartes' "turn to the subject" in the seventeenth century and David Hume's reaction to Descartes in the eighteenth that some philosophers began to deny to science the possibility of achieving a knowledge of physical reality as such.

For Descartes what we know is our thinking selves and the bridge to

---

[2] (New York: Pantheon, 1992), Chapter VII, "Against Philosophy," 166-190.

physical reality becomes problematical. For Hume what we know is only our stream of consciousness and what produces that stream of impressions is unknowable.

Finally, Immanuel Kant profoundly influenced the whole of modern culture, including the way science is philosophically understood, when he defended Newtonian science against Hume. Kant conceded to Hume that the *Ding an Sich*, the real thing, is unknowable, but maintained that, nevertheless, we can impose an order on our stream of consciousness, although this order is rooted not in things but in the necessities of our own thought. Thus Newton's laws are valid because they supply a self-consistent way of imposing on sense data the categories of space and time inherent not in things but in our own minds. Since Kant assumed that all human minds have the same structure, he was assured that this "turn to the subject" would not reduce science to mere relativism.

In our century, however, this assurance has been shattered by cultural pluralism, so that today philosophers are conning scientists into believing that scientific theories are simply culturally conditioned paradigms for giving some order to our chaotic experiences.

In this essay I want to raise the question whether the pre-Humean notion that science is able to understand, however imperfectly, something of the reality of things, of their *essences,* does not better correspond to the actual praxis of scientists than do Kantian interpretations of science. It is worth noting here that the term "essence" is from the infinitive *esse* of the Latin verb meaning "to be" (i.e., to be "real," to exist independent of what we think about it, so that when we think about it, it measures the truth of our thinking, not vice versa.)

IS THE UNIVERSE THE ONE REAL THING?

There is no sense asking about the essence of something unless we first know what thing it is whose essence we are trying to know.

Much scientific talk today makes it hard to identify what we are trying to understand, because it denies that the "things" of ordinary experience are independent realities. Rather it is asserted that the only real thing is the universe as a whole, of which all other entities are simply parts. A part of something cannot have an essence, because it exists only as a part of some larger whole, and it is this whole which has the essence that explains the part. If all the things of our experience are simply parts of a universe which as a whole transcends our experience, it seems futile to seek its essence in the empirical ways on which science depends. That is the problem with some recent cosmologies which propose to become a "Final Theory" or "A Theory of Everything." How can they ever be tested empirically, since they seek to explain all the parts of universe by some primordial event which took place under conditions that cannot be experienced or repeated?

Those who believe the universe is a single thing, or in the language of ancient science, one "substance" of which the things of experience are merely parts, present us with the following picture.

The universe is a largely empty space which is growing more and more empty as the matter within it disperses into particles, stars, galaxies, supergalaxies moving farther and farther from each other. But these material bodies in space are actually not distinct from the space in which they exist since their presence modifies that space gravitationally and they fill it with waves of energy which pass through it in all directions. Thus, all space is, as it were, in a state of more or less intense agitation and matter is only those volumes of space that are most intensely agitated. Thus, the universe is like one great ocean in which the "things" we experience are simply parts where waves become most evident. To know reality, therefore, will be to discover the essence or fundamental law which will state why this vast ocean is agitated in various ways in its various parts.

ARE THERE MANY REAL THINGS?

This picture of the universe as one great thing is becoming more and more popular today and is replacing its opposite, which was formerly so uncritically accepted, namely, the *reductionist* view of physical reality. [3] According to this view, the universe is a collection of many things, but these things are in turn only collections of many smaller things, and so on down to the elementary particles, which are then resolved into quarks, and so *ad infinitum*. If that were the whole truth, of course, essences would again escape us, since every essence would turn out to be a mere conglomeration of other essences, and we could never reach any knowledge of what is really real.

Perhaps it is in reaction to this reductionism, that the fashion has now turned toward holism, and the picture of the universe as one great, evolving thing, which I have just described. No doubt science seeks to understand the universe as a whole, but is it not a big leap to say that we now know the universe so well that we are sure it is one single thing, rather than a more or less interacting

---

[3] One version of this trend which is especially interesting but in my opinion excessively organicist is the notion of an "implicate order" in which all parts of the universe are "enfolded" in each other, advocated by the distinguished physicist David Bohm. See his essay "The Implicate Order: A New Approach to the Nature of Reality" in David L. Schindler, ed., *Beyond Mechanism: The Universe in Recent Physics and Catholic Thought* (Lanham, Maryland: University Press of America, 1986), 13-37, with the reflections of the other contributors.

collection of things? Recently, a so-called "Gaia Hypothesis" has been proposed and become popular among activists in the ecological movement according to which our earth is a single organism.[4] We have no proof of that hypothesis. An ecological system is not necessarily a single organism, any more than our solar system is a single body, rather than an accidental but interacting system of bodies which have been unified to a degree by the presence of one body, the sun, which holds them together by its superior gravity, and floods them with its superior energy. In an ecological system living things have adapted to their environment and to each other, but they have not become parts of each other, the way our organs are part of our body. We must not force the analogy to an organism of the solar system or an ecological system to the point of failing to see that their kinds of unity are of very different orders.

Can we, then, identify any real things that are not mere collections of other collections *ad infinitum* splintering into unknowable small bits, or which are not mere parts of one vast whole transcending our knowing powers? Is it not more scientific to begin with some objects of our experience which we can ascertain have an intrinsic unity, stability, and independence of existence which distinguishes them from mere collections or even collections that form systems? I would propose that according to present knowledge these are atoms, molecules, organisms. I think it is clear enough that the plant and animal organisms of ordinary experience have a distinct existence from the ecological environment in which they exist. It is true that a bamboo grove is the optimum environment for a panda, as a proper flow of blood is the right environment for the brain, and that the panda will die without bamboo, and the brain without blood; but this is a mere analogy, the sorts of unity between the panda and the forest, and between the brain and the body are of different orders, just as my unity as a person is of quite a different order than the unity of the family or the society of which I am a member. To read these analogies literally is to end in totalitarianism.

Why can we say that at least atoms, molecules, and organisms are real things? What about elementary particles? As I see it, atoms have a relative stability and capacity to maintain their independent existence against outside forces which is of different order than the existence of elementary particles. When these particles exist in the atom they exist not as things, but as part of the atom. When massive particles become separate from the atom their existence is transient and can be understood more as temporarily existing fragments, which are very soon incorporated in other atoms and become transformed as their parts. When the particles are photons, neutrinos, quarks, gravitons, "virtual"

---

[4] J. E. Lovelock, *Gaia: a New Look at Life on Earth* (Oxford: Oxford University Press, 1987). This is also discussed in Harris, *Cosmos and Anthropos*, 93-101.

particles, they can be understood rather as the action (energy exchange) of atoms on other atoms, or of one part of an atom on another part. In any case, they seem not to have the claim to be "things" that atoms have.

But what about the "empty" spaces that exist between the parts of the atom and among the atoms? In the space among the parts of our solar system and among the stars and even more among the galaxies the atoms are widely scattered and most of the universe is sheer space. The notion of "empty" space is one of the useless notions imposed on scientists by the mechanist philosophy of which Weinberg complained, and which Newton reintroduced into science, after even Descartes had seen its folly. How can we call space "empty" when it is always filled with waves of energy? While Einstein eliminated the notion of a mechanical ether, he replaced it with a space "curved" by the presence of matter, and eliminated the Newtonian notion of absolute space and time.

We need also to reject the reductionist view, another relic of mechanism, that atoms are composed of discrete particles, that molecules are simply a collection of atoms, and that organisms are collections of molecules. In each of these cases, when the lesser unit enters into the larger unity it is so modified that it becomes a part of, dependent for its existence in that form on, the whole. A atom incorporated in a molecule or a molecule in an organism is no longer identical with the atom or molecule before its incorporation or after the death of the organism.

Thus I would say that the relatively stable realities which science studies are atoms, molecules, and organisms in their coming to be, their interactions with one another, and their ultimate dissolution. In doing so it also studies their parts and the instruments of their interactions; and also their collection into larger systems, such as planets, stars, galaxies, the universe.

WHAT ARE THE ESSENCES OF THESE THINGS?

Now that we have identified at least some real things, we can ask whether it is possible to know their essences, i.e., not only *that* they are, but *what* they are, and perhaps even *why* they are? As I have said, the term "essence" simply refers to independent existence, to thingness. To know an essence of a thing is to understand its unity and stability. This requires us to know two facts.

1) We have to be able to isolate a thing in its independence. For example, To understand the atomic element gold, or the molecular compound water, I must obtain a pure sample. To study an organism, I must get a mature, healthy specimen and I must observe it reacting in a variety of situations, not merely when it is dormant or hibernating. In philosophical terms this means to

distinguish its nature or essence from the accidental circumstances or modifications resulting from its environment.

Thus, to understand human nature, we have to survey human history and the variety of human cultures, to find what is common and perduring for the human species everywhere and always. That this process of isolating the essential character of any particular kind of thing is sometimes difficult and subject to error does not mean that it is impossible. Who doubts that gold is really an element and not a mixture or compound, that water is H_2O, or that it is possible to classify the species of living things? The theory of evolution, of course, has led some to say that the differences between species of organisms is merely a matter of degree, but most evolutionary biologists admit that in any cross-section of the historical evolution of organisms, the organic world is made up of distinct, discontinuous species defined by the incapacity of closely related species to interbreed.

2) We have to determine the essential properties of the thing, once isolated from merely superficial, accidental modifications. For example, we must determine the properties of gold, water, or a particular species of organism. By a property we mean some observable aspect of the thing which it always has and which if lost means its destruction as a thing, and by which we can identify every other individual which we classify with it as of the same species. For example, gold has an atomic weight not possessed by any other metallic element, and a transformation of gold that would deprive it of this atomic weight would mean its transformation into some other kind of element. Water has a characteristic way of freezing not found in any other compound; an elephant has a kind of trunk not possessed by any other organisms, and so on. There are, of course, many qualifications to what I have just said. In organisms some properties are apparent only in fully mature species and only at certain times. Water exists as a gas, a liquid, and solid and exhibits some properties in one of these states that it does not in another. But ultimately it is possible to say that each of these kinds of things has proper characteristics.

3) We have to discover the inter-relation of these properties, and ultimately that property which is most fundamental and in which the other properties are rooted. For example, we now know that the color, malleability, melting point, weight, chemical activity and stability. of the element gold are all grounded in its unique atomic number, which reveals the composition of its nucleus and planetary electrons. Thus, gold is not just a random collection of properties, these properties form an ordered set that expresses its most profound characteristics. We also know that the properties of water can be understood in terms of its chemical structural formula and the bonding between its compounded

atoms which this expresses. In the case of organisms we are dealing with a vastly more complicated set of properties, anatomical, physiological, and in the case of animals, psychological. Yet even here it is obvious that there is an orderly relation among the properties. For example, in a cat or any of the members of the feline genus, its highly specialized carnivorous way of eating explains many features of its anatomy and physiology. Finally, in the most privileged case of all, our human species, it has long been understood that it is our intelligence, our capacity to think symbolically, and thus to be able to create a culture, which marks us off from all other living organisms, and which explains why we have the most complex of brains, and how the rest of our nervous system and the physiology and general human anatomy has been modified in the service of our brain.

4) We now come to a fourth and final step. After we have discovered the properties of a thing, and found which of these properties is the most fundamental, we need to view the thing not merely as an ordered collection of properties but as a whole, in its entire structure and unified function, in its unique way of existing as an independent thing. To know the thing in this unified way is what has always been meant when philosophers talked about knowing a thing's essence: knowing it essentially and profoundly, not merely superficially. The essence is not some hidden core concealed within the phenomena by which the thing is known to us. Rather it is the thing taken as a whole in its reality but understood in a fundamental way. Thus, to say that we know the essence of Mr. Smith is not to know something secret about Mr. Smith, but to know Mr. Smith as he really is, in all his complexity, but precisely as he is human, a member of that species whose whole life is permeated by the capacity to think. Similarly, to know the essence of water, is to know so much about water and the interrelation of its properties that we begin to understand water in a truly profound way in all its uniqueness, and what it would mean to our planet and therefore to the universe if our planet were as dry as the moon or Mars.

DO WE KNOW THESE ESSENCES EXHAUSTIVELY?

Let me hasten to say that this kind of essential knowledge is never complete or perfect. We know ourselves as human in a uniquely deep way, yet to say that "man is a rational animal" is not to know ourselves thoroughly. Although "rational" is the supreme and defining human property that reveals our essence, we only know very imperfectly what that term "rational" means. To know it perfectly we would first have to be able to see it as the root of all the observed properties of the human being, which would mean a perfect understanding of our special kind of animality, i.e., our anatomy, physiology, and psychology. We know a great deal about such things, but not everything, and never will know everything.

We would then have to understand what it is to think in a human way, and this too we only imperfectly understand.   But to say that we know the human essence incompletely and imperfectly does not mean that we do not know it at all.   When it comes to the rest of things, it has been common in neo-scholasticism to say that our essential knowledge goes no further than the broad genera: atoms, molecules, plants, animals.

Some have said that this is what divides philosophy from science, that philosophy has essential knowledge, science does not. This is a false distinction. It is true that we can state the distinction of the aforesaid genera of things with considerable precision, but it is not true that our essential understanding goes no further.   As I have already indicated modern chemistry has developed a taxonomy of elements and compounds and physics explains this taxonomy with a high degree of precision and thus we have some degree of essential understanding of the non-living world. Similarly, biologists have developed a remarkable taxonomy of the species of living things, not only in our present time, but also throughout much of evolutionary history. For a long time, however, this taxonomy although accurate in distinguishing species did so on the basis of relatively superficial anatomic differences. To give a positive understanding of a species it is necessary to know its living behavior: how a plant nourishes and reproduces, how an animal does these things and also acts by instincts and learning in unique ways. We are yet pretty far from a taxonomy of organisms based on behavior. The present study of genetics seems to open a way to explain the connection among the properties of living things, but until we can relate genetics to behavior and not merely to anatomy and physiology, we will not have gone very deeply into an essential knowledge of living things.

DOES MATHEMATICS YIELD ESSENTIAL KNOWLEDGE?

Physicists understand that mathematics is one thing, while physics, for all its use of mathematics, is another. Natural scientists, even physicists who most depend on mathematics, know that their interests and ways of thinking are quite different than that of pure mathematicians. Why then is mathematics, as Wigner said, so "unreasonably effective" in understanding physical reality? The Pythagoreans and Plato actually thought that the essences of material things were numbers, but this cannot be so, since the essence of material things is dynamic, while numbers belong to a realm utterly unchanging. But if Plato was wrong and mathematics cannot attain to the essence of any physical thing, why has it proved so immensely helpful in coming to know essences?

We can answer this question, I believe, if we remember that the properties of a thing through which we come to know its essence are not all of one kind but pertain to various categories. They are qualities, actions, relations, timings, spatial orderings, etc. But in a physical body all other categories of properties presuppose a characteristic quantity of parts and their spatio-temporal relations. Thus, in an atom of gold, the number of particles and their interrelations in space and time are the fundamental essential properties of the thing. Similarly, in a human being nothing about humanity can be understood without knowing our gross and fine anatomy and chemical composition. This does not mean that the other properties can be reduced to quantity, but only that they presuppose it as form presupposes matter, a whole the parts. Consequently, all science must rest on a quantitative understanding of a thing, and quantitative relationships are most clearly expressed and easy to manage in human thinking when we treat them abstractly in the discipline of mathematics.

Yet in using mathematical abstraction to help us arrive at an essential knowledge of things, we must not forget the following. (a) The application of mathematical abstractions to real quantities is always approximate. We can be certain that what is mathematically impossible is not physically possible, but we can never be sure that what is mathematically possible, is in fact the way things really are physically. Thus, to arrive at an essential knowledge of things that is truly certain, and not merely hypothetical, we must do so in terms of the observation of physical quantities and not merely mathematical models. (b) We must not fall into reductionism, by thinking that when we understand the quantitative relations in a thing, its measurements, we have an essential understanding of it until we can also understand it in physically *causal* terms. Thus, to tell us the range of normal human height and weight, or the gross size of the human brain is not very illuminating until we understand how these measured quantities are related to human physiology and function. (c) Quantity expresses the parts of a whole, not the unity of the whole, and essential knowledge must attain to an understanding of the unity of a thing. To know the parts of human anatomy does not tell us why all these parts work together and produce various kinds of behavior. (d) Mathematics abstracts from change, reducing time to a static geometry, and the dynamism of change and causality to timeless functional relationships. A mathematical picture of the world, therefore, is essentially static, while reality is dynamic. Thus, natural science is not merely an effort to invent mathematical models whose self-consistency and beauty is not contradicted by the facts of the real world, but is a genuine philosophy that more and more reveals the real world to us, and ultimately an understanding of our own selves as human, thinking, scientific organisms.

Thus, the reason for insisting that we do in fact have essential knowledge of physical things is that this interpretation of science overcomes the dichotomy that has so troubled human culture since the seventeenth and especially the eighteenth century, the split between philosophical, humanistic knowledge, and scientific knowledge, the "Two Cultures" that C.P. Snow made famous,[5] with the resultant split between values and facts. Once we see that science is not limited to a superficial, reductionistic understanding of the world, but that science has in fact deepened our essential knowledge of reality, and opened the way, therefore, to deal with all the greatest problems that trouble humanity, our culture will be delivered from its present confusion.

---

[5] *The Two Cultures, And a Second Look,* 2nd ed. (Cambridge, Massachusetts: Cambridge University Press, 1964).

Catholic Philosophy, Realism, and the Postmodern Dilemma

Don T. Asselin

I. THE POSTMODERN DILEMMA

By "modernism" let us signal a complex of doctrines that crystallized in the nineteenth century and whose late ramifications include egalitarian and libertarian liberalism. The tentacles of modernism, so defined, reach us at this moment. The majority of free democracies in the West embrace one or the other of the liberalisms just mentioned. We would not recognize the democracies without modernism. Similarly, as concerns theory of knowledge, the confidence with which modern philosophy began, whether in classical empiricism or rationalism, have, with only recent and still few exceptions, long since yielded to pragmatism and analysis and their offspring in Anglo-American circles and to existentialism and its affiliates on the Continent.

However oxymoronic the term "postmodernism" seems, yet postmodernism is a reality. The reason, known to all and openly celebrated by many, correlates with observations already made: the foundations of liberalism, egalitarian or libertarian, have collapsed under the weight of repeated attack. A progression of sallies have been made against these foundations, and, to simplify matters, we shall mention only two. It came to be realized that modernism depended upon an elaborate structure of contingent historical circumstances and processes. This is a fact to which J. S. Mill himself points when confronted with the question of what background is necessary for the utilitarian concept of humane rationality to work.

The answer: On condition of the liberalism that Mill tried to take in an increasingly progressive, reformist direction.[1] But this condition traces modernism beyond its halting first steps in the Renaissance and Enlightenment, back to the Middle Ages when superstition reigned. Thus one sortie made against modernism would force admission that modernism is not modern enough. From this perspective, postmodernism includes the belief that just as modernism rid us of religion, so postmodernism will destroy its epigone, morality; and that just as modernism attacked hierarchicalized order, whether theoretical or practical, so postmodernism will develop both epistemology and ethics non-hierarchically.[2] In the latter day, however, came a second wave. It attacked modernism for being too modern. These attackers would extract the concession that meaning and truth in the practical or theoretical order arises only from highly particularized, traditional canons of rationality and humaneness. Despite their opposing points of departure, the attacking parties agree that liberalist modernism has exhausted its moral and intellectual capital.

But alas, the institutions of liberalism remain in place in the West, and no sane person would tear them all down; hence today arise liberal reformers on the model of J. S. Mill, such as Martha Nussbaum and Amartya Sen and Derek Phillips.[3] The same goes for the church and us philosophers in her embrace, no less than for latter day modernists and postmodernists. Today and indeed for centuries, the Catholic moralist and the church he serves would directly interfere with the state only when there arises a question of sin. Otherwise, the church expects no treatment beyond what is given to the denominations and to non-Christian religions, although she reserves the orthodox belief that she is the mother church. Against the modernist backdrop, the church has grown and prospered; or at the very least, she has suffered little more than in ages past. So, only on likelihood of grave harm to religion itself or to the whole civil order will she interfere with the modern regime. Nor would it be prudent to forego modernism's palpable advantages, at least not if wholesale postmodernism is the only alternative.

---

[1] As in Chapter II of Mill's *Utilitarianism, Liberty, and Representative Government*, where Mill tries to overcome the objection that utilitarianism is a crass hedonism. In his answer, Mill acknowledges a debt to the whole of the Western tradition of civil order and rational discourse that enables him to reform it.

[2] We use "hierarchy" here only to stress order indexed from a privileged first principle. "Non-hierarchical" thus encompasses both (a) the holism inaugurated with Quine's net analogy for knowledge and (b) epistemological or moral anarchism.

[3] Martha Nussbaum's thought more and more has followed this trajectory since her review of Allan Bloom's *Closing of the American Mind* in "Undemocratic Vistas," *The New York Review of Books* v. 34, n. 17 (November 5, 1987). See also Derek Phillips, *Looking Backward* (Princeton: Princeton University Press, 1993), 175-96; Amartya Sen, *Inequality Reexamined* (Cambridge: Harvard University Press, 1992), esp. Ch. 9, 129-52; Susan Moller Okin, *Justice, Gender, and the Family* (New York: Basic Books, 1989), 14.

Accordingly, the postmodern dilemma presents itself to the Catholic philosopher as follows. Either accept the collapse of modernism's foundations and commit oneself to an as yet uncertain and, in many ways unfriendly, postmodernism; or, in a postmodern setting, accept so much of a weakened modernism as does not compromise Catholic wisdom.

Accepting Horn A, i.e., the outright admission of modernism's bankruptcy and an unqualified embrace of postmodernism, should not worry us long. Under this alternative, it is hard to see what attitude the Catholic philosopher could assume to the faith besides the Modernism or the Traditionalism condemned by the First Vatican Council. Similarly, Horn B, i.e., an unqualified commitment to defective infrastructures for knowledge and values, hardly commends itself. The example and precept of Catholic tradition is to perfect existing structures, to heal what is sick; so it would be presumptuous to imply that, under the care and guidance of the vicar of Christ, the moral and intellectual foundations of civil order cannot be renewed, reformed, reconstructed. Nor is an attempt to go around the horns of this dilemma promising. This approximates a Catholic triumphalism out of step with the Second Vatican Council. The remaining alternative is to grasp both horns of the dilemma. And this all raises the question, in what manner and to what extent may we accept postmodernism, for the time being still superimposed upon modernism, without compromising the wisdom that as Catholic philosophers we ought to preserve? For convenience, let us call this the postmodern dilemma.

II. PHILOSOPHICAL REALISM STEPS INTO THE BREACH

Because it is a human dilemma and not a parochially Catholic one, the dilemma may be generalized. One example will suffice for now. The debate on physician assisted suicide rages about us in Europe and North America. The practice, or to be more precise, the belief that one has a moral right to its legalized practice, manifests the Hobbesian and Lockean strains of modern liberalism; whereas progressive liberals counsel protection of the vulnerable. Perhaps it is no surprise, then, that a perfectly liberal argument against legalizing physician assisted suicide can be generated from modernism's resources as well as an argument in favor of it. If one wishes to avoid the paradox altogether, one may take libertarian liberalism a bit further. One might protest that, over time, there should be fewer laws enacted on the basis of moral principles. But this answer will not hold still for long. Its reach extends to a political anarchy, a sinister element of postmodernism.

The dilemma thus generalized over a well known crisis of knowledge and values, the Catholic instinct is to repair to philosophical realism. Well and good, but to which philosophical realism? No one can have failed to notice that because of the postmodern dilemma just described, today a few so called mainstream Anglo-American philosophers themselves have repaired to philosophical realism, one that defies so called classical or Aristotelian or Thomistic realism.

We refer to what is perhaps the most well known version of this new realism, the internal realism of Hilary Putnam. Passing momentarily its definition, let us notice the generic similarity between this new realism and the old one, as well as the profoundly humane and rational interests the new form represents. Declining to follow two paths that realism has taken—one, what we might call classical realism [and Putnam calls metaphysical realism], and two, positivism— Putnam still champions a first philosophy, a unity of knowledge and value. Thus

> [W]e should recognize that *all* values, including the cognitive ones, derive their authority from our idea of human flourishing and our idea of reason. These two ideas are interconnected: our image of an ideal theoretical intelligence is simply a *part* of our ideal of total human flourishing, and makes no sense wrenched out of the total ideal, as Plato and Aristotle saw.[4]

Under this broad theme of the unity of knowledge and value, Putnam insists that his is a genuine realism. Indeed, he makes a foray into what I shall later call radical realism, when he criticizes Richard Rorty for being unable to deny that even he, Rorty, is a "metaphysical realist." For Rorty does not recognize that (in *Philosophy and the Mirror of Nature*) his picture is only a picture, but believes that in some deep pre-theoretic sense his picture is the way the world is.[5] But Putnam, for his own part, truly is a realist: truth is a property independent of justification or probability.[6] A review of the ethical and social and religious directions of his late work[7] would show that Putnam embraces both horns of our postmodern dilemma. Fully aware of the weakness of modernism's foundations but distrusting a Rorty-type irrationalism, Putnam defends philosophical realism. It is a realism within a postmodern setting. Given the postmodern dilemma, Putnam instinctively repairs to philosophical realism, too.

---

[4] Hilary Putnam, "Beyond the Fact/Value Dichotomy," in *Realism with a Human Face* (Cambridge: Harvard University Press, 1990), 141.

[5] Hilary Putnam, "A Defense of Internal Realism," 32.

[6] *Ibid.*

[7] See, for example, Putnam's *Renewing Philosophy* (Cambridge: Harvard University Press, 1992), 180-200; *The Many Faces of Realism* (LaSalle, Illinois: Open Court, 1987), esp. Chs. II-IV; and *Meaning and the Moral Sciences* (London: Routledge, 1978), 83-94.

III. THE DOCTRINE OF INTERNAL REALISM

Yet as everyone knows, Putnam denies the validity of classical or Aristotelian or Thomistic realism, let us now call it simply classical realism. It is a realism that, *ceteris paribus*, Putnam thinks has been propounded in nearly every age. For Putnam, it is not this extravagant realism, but, instead, what he calls internal realism, that is valid. It will be helpful, first, to see what Putnam thinks internal realism is not, viz., metaphysical realism.

Responding to critics of his *Reason, Truth, and History* (1981), Putnam says that the metaphysical realist accepts all three of these principles: (1) the world consists of a fixed totality of mind-independent objects; (2) there is exactly one true and complete description of the way the world is; and (3) truth involves some sort of correspondence.[8] Wary Thomists might protest the *ceteris paribus* clause uttered a moment ago. For "metaphysical realism 2" smacks of classic foundationalism, and especially the rationalist, Cartesian sort, whereas classical realism is nothing of the kind. True enough, Maritain, Gilson, and many other Thomists categorically disown Cartesian foundationalism. Their point, however, is ontological: the fact of human knowledge is a contingent fact. This ontological point in no way requires that knowledge, e.g., true philosophy or true science, in some meaningful sense is not a true and complete description of the way the world is. (Let us allow for a benign incompleteness entailed by the ongoing discovery process at any time.) "Metaphysical realism 3" might be disowned, because classical realism propounds an identity theory of knowledge, not a correspondence theory. This objection also pertains to the ontology of knowledge. Putnam's point, however, is more modest. Whatever the ontology of knowledge be, the notion that metaphysical realism, and so, in this context, classical realism, does not require correspondence would make classical realism vacuous. Indeed, what do we suppose that we mean, when we affirm "metaphysical realism 1," if not this: the sentence, the world consists of a fixed totality of mind-independent objects, corresponds to the way the world is? Thomas himself developed the nuance of classical realism that truth is something completed by the mind: truth, in the proper sense, occurs in the synthetic act of judgment. To be sure, the matter is more subtle and complex than this. But in terms of our analysis so far, it remains true that classical realism, *in its life as a theory*, must presuppose correspondence. If the way out of the impasse is to demonstrate that realism cannot mean, unqualifiedly, that truth is itself theoretical and linguistic, well and good. But the move is premature just now. The corresponding charge will have to be made to stick against Putnam, too.

---

[8] Hilary Putnam, "A Defense of Internal Realism," 30.

Putnam's internal realism begins by saying that metaphysical realism makes sense only in a tradition of metaphysical discourse. Thus, if one accepts a definite set *I* of individuals of which the world consists, then the metaphysical realism corresponding to that *I* makes sense. Metaphysical realism, then, is always internal to a particular metaphysical discourse. By parity of reason, any realism worthy of the name is an internal realism. Putnam states internal realism as follows.

> What I believe is that there is *a* notion of truth, or, more humbly, of being right, which we use constantly and which is not at all the metaphysical realist's notion of a description which corresponds to the noumenal facts. . . . From the point of view of the notion of being right that does actual work in our lives and intellectual practice, a mathematical theory which takes sets as primitive and a mathematical theory which is intertranslatable with the former, but which takes functions as primitive, may . . . both be right.[9]

Immediately following this, Putnam introduces his concept of truth.

> In my picture, objects are theory-dependent in the sense that theories with incompatible ontologies can both be right. Saying that they are both right is not saying that there are fields out there as entities with extension and (in addition) fields in the sense of logical constructions. It is not saying that there are both absolute space-time points and points which are mere limits. It is saying that various representations, various languages, various theories, are good in certain contexts.[10]

The doctrine of internal realism thus accepts ontological relativity as concerns a theory. To recall the postmodern dilemma, however, Putnam insists that he is no relativist: neither moral nor general conceptual relativism attracts him in any way. Rather, reviving and revitalizing the realistic spirit is the important task for a philosopher at this time.[11]

Having jettisoned metaphysical realism and correspondence and justification, and having embraced ontological relativity, Putnam would rescue truth. He would do so from the generically realist motive already sketched. But how? Here Putnam rings a change upon the theme of warranted assertability. Generally, defenders of this concept think of truth not through causal theories of knowledge (classic Empiricism); not through causal theories of reference (physicalist metaphysical realism); and again not through theories of justification worked out relativistically (on which account, Putnam says, even Rorty must be a metaphysical realist)—generally, exponents of warranted assertability think of truth as the quality of knowledge that entitles reliable proponents of a doctrine to affirm something. Putnam calls his specific version,

---

[9] *Ibid.*, 40.   [10] *Ibid.*, 41.   [11] *Ibid.*, 42.

idealized warranted assertion. It means that what is supposed to be "true" be warrantable on the basis of experience and intelligence for creatures with "a rational and sensible nature."[12]

What sorts of truths does Putnam think meet this criterion? What indeed, if not many truths that anyone with a rational and sensible nature—so not only qualified experts—are warranted in affirming on the basis of experience and intelligence? "Talk of there being saber-toothed tigers here thirty thousand years ago, or beings who can verify mathematical and physical theories we cannot begin to understand (but who have brains and nervous systems), or talk of there being sentient beings outside my light cone, is not philosophically problematic for me. But talk of there being 'absolute space-time points,' or of sets 'really existing' or 'not really existing,' I reject."[13]

Thus Putnam would rescue truth. And thus he also would overcome a certain pathology that Edward Pols has called the dogma of the empirical impotence of philosophy. [14] We trust that this, too, heartens realists among us. In Putnam's realism, so called truth-talk ranges widely. At one end are the findings of common sense, and at another, the most sophisticated, empirically grounded scientific theories. Somewhere in between is truth-talk that realism so desperately wants to recover from the postmodern dilemma. It is empirical talk of middle-sized objects and this from a philosophical, namely, non-reductive, point of view. We mean talk of morals and art and religion, even of philosophy itself. Let us go further and suggest that Putnam is generous enough that he would engage the fair minded among us who think we are entitled to the term, realism, too.

IV. THE DILEMMA OF INTERNAL REALISM

In this event, devotees of the dogged Detective Columbo might recall the line, Oh, just one more question . . . When we open up truth-talk to this wide range of middle-sized objects, and when we do so from a realist philosophical perspective, there is one more question we should ask, before going far. The question is, what of this truth-talk we enter and exercise and participate, as we widen the philosophical horizon?

In truth, that dogged detective always had several one more questions. Not being his match, we can only develop the question raised just now. Is the talk wherein we talk about and develop internal realism; is the talk whereby we criticize

---

[12] *Ibid.*, 41.   [13] *Ibid.*

[14] In Edward Pols, *Radical Realism* (Ithaca, New York: Cornell University Press, 1992), 62-64. By this term, Pols imputes to his opponent the view, which he calls a dogma of the linguistic consensus, that philosophy has no empirical function; we accept it in this sense and note, too, that in his own way, Putnam would restore philosophy's empirical function.

other theories, including other realisms; is the talk wherein we would engage fellow realists; is the talk used to express dissatisfaction with postmodernism and to embrace, however reluctantly, corrupted foundations of modernism—is all this talk, internal to internal realism, true itself? If it is, then Putnam himself would insist that it must be talk warranted on the basis of experience and intelligence of a creature with a sensible and rational nature.

Nor do we lack evidence of the questions to which these qualities of warranted assertion extend. They extend to the issues of value and knowledge that realists wish to reconstruct in our day.

Thus we come to the internal realist dilemma. On one horn, we would internalize internal realism itself. To the question, is the discourse of internal realism true?, those who seize the one horn must answer: Yes, it is true, but internally to internal realism. A moment's reflection reveals the fallacy of this move. Internal realism now becomes internal, internal realism. Asking about its truth, we beget another internal realism; and so on, *ad infinitum*. On this first horn, the question whether internal realism is true is a non-starter, or it loses its sense.

True enough, Putnam acknowledges that his view, too, is only a picture; he also acknowledges a debt to pragmatism in his own reconstruction of realism.[15] A soft version of the first horn thus comes into view. Accordingly, Putnam might plead that to internalize internal realism is unavoidable, yet far superior to the non-realist alternatives. But Putnam's criterion of truth pinches somewhere right about here. For if truth is what is warrantedly assertible in his idealized sense, there surely are few people of experience and intelligence, having a sensible and rational nature, who would hasten to affirm that the very talk of internal realism itself is true only in an internal-to-theory sense, this being better than non-realism. It is hard to think of anything that people of experience and intelligence, having a rational and sensible nature, should shrink from affirming, if not this. At any rate, they should not affirm it of the very talk wherein they formulate the truth of internal realism![16]

---

[15] Hilary Putnam, "A Defense of Internal Realism," 40-41.

[16] In another study in the same work, Putnam faces this charge pretty squarely. In his context, he asks whether his views commit him to realism, small "r," or to Realism. The common ground between this context and our charge is noted by Putnam himself: If saying what we say and doing what we do is being a "realist," then we had better be realists—realists with a small "r." This equates with our charge that in saying what we say about realism, we just are realists *simpliciter*. Then Putnam talks about object relativity for a page or so, and concludes: What I am saying is that elements of what we call "language" or "mind" *penetrate so deeply into what we call "reality" that the very project of representing ourselves as being "mappers" of something "language-independent" is fatally compromised from the very start* (italics in original), "Metaphysics" in *Realism with a Human Face*, 26, 28. But to repeat, if truth is what

If the first horn of the dilemma of internal realism leads to an infinite regress, the second approximates internal realism to classical or Aristotelian or Thomistic realism. Here, the word, approximate, is all-important. Yes, the internal realist might say, I really mean to affirm realism; if we do not get the truth, surely we approximate it. We either come close to it, or we accumulate truths. Either way, realism is distinctive because of this approximation idea. That is why I would rescue science from conceptual relativists and metaphysical realists and justificationalists like Rorty; it is what I mean by rescuing the objectivity of morals and art and religion; it is what I mean by rescuing even philosophy itself from mere justificationalist schemes and conceptual relativism and reductionist physicalism. Internal realism, accordingly, is like the old realism: if it does not attain the truth, it comes so close that we ought to breathe life back into the pursuit of truth and, above all, put philosophy back to work.

But the approximation horn of the dilemma remains incomplete. That we ought to put philosophy back to work, in a manner internal to internal realism, completes the thought. This horn, it seems to us, either makes Putnam's criterion of truth ambiguous between (a) internal, internal realism and (b) classical realism, or it makes the criterion vacuous.

Setting off philosophers again on the pursuit of truth, we surely can expect that, before going far, they check their compass. It registers the sensibleness and rationality of what they are doing. The compass is reason, reasoning about itself and its own activity. Thus if Putnam's criterion of truth works as to internal realism itself, then what he tells us about internal realism is true, approximately.

How should one judge the approximation? Putnam tells us that you do not judge it according to philosophical consensus. Idealized warranted assertability points not merely to what qualified members of the philosophic community say—and for science, not what its consensus says, and so on. It is this, but more; it is what is true. The "more" comes in the approximation to the truth,

is warrantedly assertible in Putnam's idealized sense, then who would hasten to affirm that the sentence in our first quotation above implicates truth, but only internally to internal realism? Doing so, one encounters again the regress problem. If, on the other hand, one wishes to situate ontological relativity alongside realism, the second quotation above comes into view. In this scenario, often several viewpoints can be true. But if so, then by the gravity of the realism that Putnam commends, one must be coming very close to the truth that Realism seeks, or at least accumulating truths. In either event, one begets an approximation to truth thesis, despite Putnam's avowal to the contrary. In what immediately follows, we seize this approximation thesis. First, it approximates internal realism to the old or classical realism, at least insofar as saying what we say and doing what we do in developing internal realism is concerned. Second and in consequence, the basic claims about the truth of internal realism, so construed, cannot be true only internally.

and Putnam would overcome the consensualist problem that weakens other versions of warranted assertibility.[17]

Immediately, though, we turn to the doctrine of internal realism itself, and we uncover a damaging ambiguity. If the statement internal realism is approximately true, is true only internally to itself, then we lose the extra-consensual sense of approximate truth. Indeed, we encounter the regress problem again. If, however, we wish to retain a strong sense of approximate truth about the doctrine of internal realism, i.e., extra-consensual, approximate truth, we are on a slippery slope. At the bottom is classical realism. But if not this, then Putnam's criterion of truth seems vacuous. For if it were meaningful, then at least these points must be more than approximately true: that we know what we are doing when we exercise talk of realism, that it is really true that we know ourselves as rational agents, and so our talk of internal realism is the truth.

V. THE META-LANGUAGE COUNTER-OBJECTION

On the other hand, now we may be pressed to explain why our talk of internal realism is not simply meta-talk. Here, meta-talk of internal realism might fail to represent the linguistic domain of Putnam's concept of truth. Addressing the general issue of self-referential discourse, Putnam raises the objection against himself:

> [We are brought] to a philosophically important possibility: the possibility of denying that our informal discourse constitutes a language. . . . According to this position, the informal discourse in which we say Every language has a meta-language, and the truth predicate for the language belongs to that meta-language, not the language itself is not itself part of any language, but a speech act which is *sui generis*.[18]

The *sui generis* clause troubles Putnam. We have been assuming that whatever differences might exist between (a) discourse of realism and (b) discourse about realism, they are not such that (a) is possible directly, whereas (b) is possible only in a strange meta-sense. So for Putnam, and then some. He rejects even the possibility that we can engage discourse about realism without using the concept of truth. His basic move is to collapse the distinction between saying and showing. Thus the things that we are shown when the meta-language objection is explained to us are shown by being said. "The idea that there are

---

[17] Putnam vigorously denies that realism commits one to the belief that scientific or philosophic theories approximate, bring us ever closer, to The Truth (our term); on whether he is entitled to deny this, see immediately preceding note.

[18] Hilary Putnam, "Metaphysics," 14.

discursive thoughts which cannot be 'said' is just the formalistic trick . . . I don't understand."[19]

So Putnam seems committed to truth-talk of realism and of internal realism as unavoidable, as though elements of it cannot be gainsaid. This is all we have been presuming all along. It might also be pointed out that the meta-language objection bears a family resemblance to the regress problem already discussed; to the extent they are similar, the regress problem afflicts the meta-language problem, too. Finally, the same strategy pursued so far was generalized by Jerrold Katz. He argues that any attempt to exclude so called folk semantics from scientific semantics must either collapse of its own weight or become dogmatic.[20] The meta-language counter-objection suffers the same fate, and Putnam is fully aware of the fact.

VI. THE PARADOX OF RADICAL REALISM

Passing over further intricacies of the second dilemma, we turn to a mere paradox. Once or twice in the immediately preceding discussion, we called the realism used to analyze Putnam's internal realism, classical realism. The term has been used on occasion until now, on the presumption that most readers would follow its trajectory. It is a vexing term. This is so not only because the term sometimes refers to thinkers of importantly different persuasions in anthologies and monographs and articles in epistemology. Nor has it seemed necessary till now to track closely the meaning Putnam attaches to it. For he thinks it refers to the antique forms of metaphysical realism, the classical realism of Aristotle or Aquinas. We have used it quite loosely so far, only to suggest a wide spectrum of issues that to many classical realists includes the doctrine of the intellect's knowledge of itself.[21]

The better term for this aspect of realism is radical realism. It is Edward Pols' term from his recent book of the same name.[22] By "radical realism"

[19] *Ibid.*, 15.

[20] Jerrold J. Katz, *The Metaphysics of Meaning* (Cambridge: Massachusetts Institute of Technology Press, 1990). For a brief discussion along these lines, see 29-34.

[21] Here, the parasitic nature of knowledge of the thinking self in Aristotle and Aquinas raises only a false problem. If one thinks there is a critical reason for affirming the doctrine, that is fine. We have been stressing only that the thinking mind can know itself directly. "Parasitic" and "direct" are not contradictory opposites in the Aristotle-Aquinas axis. If they were, then "parasitic" would mean "indirect." But this would require that the self knew itself, actually through another intelligible, which is what the doctrine rather obviously denies.

[22] See Pols, *Radical Realism*, ix-x, for the most primitive statement of his thesis. There, he recalls an incident in which he came to know something about knowing: What I enjoyed was

here, in general, we refer to meaningful, true discourse about reason, reasoning (though this involves only part of the term's range as Pols uses it). Or to break the term down: "realism" signals empirical discourse about middle-sized objects that is unavoidable and undeniably true; within this range, we embrace Putnam's criterion of truth as that which persons of experience and intelligence and having a sensible and rational nature would affirm. "Radical," in the special context of much of our discussion so far, indicates a direct realism about reason itself. The part of classical realism that we take radical realism to be often has been overlooked. Perhaps the reason is that it leans a bit on subjectivism, an element we stress in order to draw attention to the directness of self-knowledge. And it seems to us that radical realism is indispensable in setting philosophy about its business again, more or less as Putnam would have things be.

What, then, of the paradox of radical realism? A while back, we raised the possibility that Putnam's criterion of truth is a vacuous element of his realism. This is true only in a qualified way—that is, if it is true at all. For it does seem possible that in time the approximation thesis will deliver Putnam to radical realism, deliver him from wholesale internal realism. In the meanwhile, however, internal realism and its truth criterion are not in any unqualified way vacuous. Nor should they be. The paradox of radical realism is connected with its radicalness. For however necessary radical realism might be to set classical realism aright, the former does not move very far in the grooves of the latter. Pols himself virtually admits that radical realism needs to accommodate what we should call internal realism—what many now also call antirealism. His admission primarily concerns ongoing scientific investigations. Pols thinks that we are entitled to treat—no, he thinks that we must treat—some, and perhaps many, of them as antirealisms, i.e., internal realisms.[23] This is a necessary condition of getting realism started in science, when we consider the abstractness and the immense detail of most physical or mathematical or biological theories; their sheer number, as well as the many and complex interrelations of *grand* and *petit* versions of many of them, must also be kept in mind. For scientific

---

a rational awareness (as I now call it) of ordinary things, but a rational awareness suddenly qualified and heightened by a surge in the intensity of the reflexive feature that is always native to it. And what that surge brought me was the assurance that we, the knowers, do not endow the thing known with the structure that comes through to us in our knowing it , ix-x. For his own adaptation of this radical realism, this direct knowing, to the sort of problem before us in this paper, see *Ibid.*, 143-44.

[23] Pols discusses this issue in *Radical Realism*, 156-60. The accommodation to internal realism is transferred, not without remainder, to the important, related context of direct knowing in religion. See Pols "Is There Religious Knowledge?" manuscript in progress, draft of April 16, 1993 cited with permission of author, 32-34.

investigation, radical realism assures the scientist of the rationality of what he does. As a science becomes more developed, it reaches a point from which it may discover enough of the truth that it is radically realist in some of its results. In the vast intermediate range where most science gets done, however, radical realism is overcome by an operational internal realism. This is the paradox of radical realism.

VII. CLASSICAL REALISM AND THE PARADOX OF RADICAL REALISM

Does this paradox bear consequences for the realism in philosophy that we gather to exercise and to appreciate and to develop? Let us turn briefly to one issue, though many issues would underscore the point urged in relation with it. The issue is a controversy that raged in neo-Thomist circles some years ago. Ralph McInerny reopened it not long ago, handling it with insight and elegance. It is the question of Christian ethics and some of the premises it seems to need. The reasons for choosing this issue are two. First, the controversy tacitly requires the concession before us at the moment; second, it will return us shortly to the postmodern dilemma and realism's place in it.

The negative thesis of McInerny's *The Question of Christian Ethics*[24] is that the Thomist revival inaugurated by Leo XIII has foundered, because of its inability to demonstrate the existence of a valid, purely philosophical ethics. The affirmative thesis distinguishes between ethical theories that (a) tell us the truth and (b) a false expectation of ethical theory, viz., that it enable us to love the good appropriately. McInerny shows how Aristotle and Thomas give us the former; then he argues that they never intended to give us the latter. Along the way, McInerny rejects the conclusions of Maritain and Gilson on this question. This all suggests a benign manner in which classical realism leans on internal realism. No truth integral to the theory itself was ever jeopardized.

The question of Christian ethics, however, implicates classical realism and internal realism in a more serious, more interesting manner. At one point in his argument, McInerny suggests that the doctrine of natural immortality is necessarily part of the picture of the philosophical ethics that he elaborates.[25] Given limitations of space, let us forget whether the concept of immortality itself is an ethical one. Rather, let us concede its importance, especially to a philosophical ethics wherein (a) the moral life in historic time and (b) personal relation with God in eternity are mutually implicated. Nor does space allow a

---

[24] Ralph McInerny, *The Question of Christian Ethics* (Washington, D.C.: The Catholic University of America Press, 1993).

[25] *Ibid.*, 59.

rehearsal of all the reasons that the commitment to a purely philosophical demonstration of natural immortality is over-confident.[26] For the moment, the name of Cajetan recalls a classical realist, whose credentials otherwise are impeccable, who demurred on this point.

Happily, Professor McInerny's translation and commentary of Thomas's *De Unitate Intellectus contra Averroistas* also has appeared lately.[27] If we rightly read McInerny reading Aquinas, something like Cajetan's suspicion remains plausible.[28] If so, we find a deep and substantive controversy within philosophical (classical) realism: whether one doctrine, purely philosophical, depends upon another, true *ex suppositione fidei*. Here, internal realism or theory or antirealism is indispensable to classical realism. Either Cajetan's view is a realism internal to classical realism, or the standard approach to immortality is. We chose this issue, because of its profound interest and importance, but the results that pertain to it could be generalized over many other instances. In this and similar cases, what else besides internal realism annexed to classical realism can settle the matter? Indeed, what else raises the question?

VIII. RADICAL REALISM AND THE POSTMODERN DILEMMA

A question so profound as immortality and its connection with the moral life thrusts us back into the postmodern dilemma. Plainly enough, the question is consigned to metaphysics—and so to Hume's flame—by many or most modernist perspectives. Postmodernism, the setting of Putnam's realism, is far more generous. If Putnam would rescue realism; and if he also would rescue truth in philosophy and art and morals and religion, the question of immortality and many more compelling ones may be raised anew. To all this, radical realism settles the question of reason's birthright, as Pols sometimes calls it. Philosophy, art, religion, and morals all may go about their business, assured of the realism of reason itself. On certain questions, say as in McInerny's argument on behalf of a valid philosophical ethics, or perhaps Pols' own similar argument—both of which, at some level of generality, Putnam affirms—the birthright of reason

[26] For a treatment of one central problem, see our "A Weakness in the Standard Argument for Natural Immortality," forthcoming in a volume to be published by the American Maritain Association.

[27] Ralph McInerny, *Aquinas Against the Averroists: On There Being Only One Intellect* (West Lafayette, Indiana: Purdue University Press, 1993).

[28] The most important claim in this context is that this human being understands, *ibid.*, 205-11. This true assertion does not entail individual, natural immortality of soul, unless the relations between (a) the soul's being the form of the body, (b) the soul's potentially knowing all things, and (c) its being a subsistent intellect is one of either natural or absolute necessity. But what line of implication, and what sort of necessity, runs between these items?

seems secured, even as concerns philosophy herself. Along the way, however, internal realism enters the discovery process. This is what, to Putnam, makes realism so especially vital: it is the very soul of investigation, whether scientific or philosophic or religious or artistic or moral.

This is all to urge that we seize both horns of the postmodern dilemma. It would be foolish to ask for a wholesale revision of the practices of modernism. More important, presently we anticipate a useful reconstruction of modernism. Postmodernism has drawn attention to the discourse of realism once again. The time is ripe to follow Leo XIII, Maritain, Gilson, Simon, McInerny, *et al.* Embracing the postmodern dilemma, we gain a keener view of (a) the narrow, though radical, realism of philosophy at the outset, and (b) realism's complex dependence upon theory or internal realism or antirealism at the end. This view becomes keener as we engage our opponent in a manner that, we trust, in some small way follows the example of the common doctor.

Heidegger and Aquinas on the Self as Substance*

Michael Baur

The thought of Martin Heidegger has been influential in postmodernist discussions concerning the "death of the subject" and the "deconstruction" of the metaphysics of presence. In this paper, I shall examine Heidegger's understanding of Dasein in terms of care and temporality, and his corresponding critique of the metaphysics of presence, especially as this critique applies to one's understanding of the human knower. I shall then seek to determine whether Aquinas' thought concerning the human knower falls prey to the Heideggerian critique. My purpose in elucidating the Heideggerian and Thomistic conceptions of the human discloser is to begin opening up some possible spaces for further dialogue between students of these two thinkers.

I. HEIDEGGER ON DASEIN, CARE, AND TEMPORALITY

The central task of Heidegger's *Being and Time*, and of his thought in general, is to unfold "the question concerning the meaning of Being."[1] According to Heidegger, the meaning of something is "that wherein the intelligibility of something maintains itself."[2] Thus to ask about the meaning of Being is to ask about that wherein the intelligibility of Being maintains itself; it is to ask about the horizon wherein something like Being can be intelligible to us in the first place. Accordingly, the uncovering of the meaning of Being ". . . is tantamount to clarifying the possibility of having any understanding of Being at all—an understanding which itself belongs to the constitution of the being called Dasein."[3] The question concerning the meaning of Being thus seeks to illuminate the possibility of our having any

---

* Reprinted with permission of the *American Catholic Philosophical Quarterly* 70.3 (Summer 1996).

[1] Martin Heidegger, *Sein und Zeit* (Tubingen: Max Niemeyer Verlag, 1986), 1.
[2] *Ibid.*, 151.   [3] *Ibid.*, 231.

understanding of Being at all. For Heidegger, an understanding of Being belongs intimately to Dasein, the being which each of us is. In fact, "Being 'is' only in the understanding of those beings to whose Being something like an understanding of Being belongs. . . . There is a necessary connection between Being and understanding. . . ."[4] Because Being and Dasein belong together, it is possible to ask about the meaning of Being (the horizon within which Being is intelligible), only if one also asks about Dasein, the being to whom an understanding of Being belongs. Thus: "The very possibility of ontology is referred back to a being: Dasein, i.e., it is referred back ontically."[5] According to Heidegger, "Dasein's Being reveals itself as *care*."[6] The structure of care, in turn, is rooted in temporality. Thus, for Heidegger, Dasein's understanding of Being must be explained ultimately in terms of temporality:

> If an understanding of Being belongs to the Existenz of Dasein, then this understanding of Being must also be grounded in temporality. The ontological condition of the possibility of the understanding of Being is temporality itself. Thus that out of which we understand something like Being must be taken from time.[7]

In the first section of this paper, I shall seek to explain how Heidegger characterizes Dasein's Being in terms of care, and how care, in turn, is rooted in temporality.

Care, for Heidegger, is not a simple phenomenon, but is characterized by the threefold structure of existentiality, facticity, and fallenness. According to Heidegger, the structure of care is complex, but it is not composite; that is to say, it is not a structure built up out of elements. The fundamental ontological characteristics of Dasein's Being—existentiality, facticity, and fallenness— "are not pieces belonging to something composite, one of which might sometimes be missing;" instead, these characteristics are "woven together" in a "primordial context" which constitutes the totality of Dasein's Being.[8] For Heidegger, the structural unity of care is not something which is "constructed" from within experience, but is in fact an "existential-*apriori*" unity which precedes, and even makes possible, all of Dasein's comportments within experience: ". . . care lies existentially-*apriori* 'before' every factual 'comportment' and 'position' of Dasein. . . ."[9]

Given the aims of Heidegger's "fundamental ontology," it is no wonder that

---

[4] *Ibid.*, 183; see also, 212 and 230.

[5] Martin Heidegger, *Gesamtausgabe*, gen. ed. Friedrich-Wilhelm von Hermann (Frankfurt am Main: Vittorio Klostermann, 1975), vol. 24, 26.

[6] Martin Heidegger, *Sein und Zeit*, 182.

[7] Martin Heidegger, *Gesamtausgabe*, vol. 24, 323.

[8] Martin Heidegger, *Sein und Zeit*, 191.   [9] *Ibid.*, 193.

the unitary structure of care must be demonstrated as an "existential-*apriori*" unity, in contrast to any kind of unity which is "constructed" out of elements derived from experience. After all, Heidegger intends to show how Dasein's understanding of the Being of beings—an understanding which belongs essentially to Dasein—is rooted in temporality. Thus if Heidegger's investigation is not to be viciously circular, he cannot begin by articulating the unity of Dasein's Being simply in terms of those "categories" which are derived from our experience of beings; Heidegger's aim is to illuminate the horizon of time insofar as it makes possible our experience of beings *as* beings in the first place. This also explains why Heidegger's fundamental ontology is different from any empirical investigation of the human knower. From the point of view of fundamental ontology, any appeal to the empirical characteristics of the human being would be essentially question-begging. Unlike all empirical investigations, fundamental ontology does not seek to explain one kind of being, or ontic presence, in terms of another. Fundamental ontology seeks rather to articulate the *apriori* conditions of the possibility of our understanding of beings *as* beings in the first place. Fundamental ontology seeks to articulate the non-empirical or non-present horizon for the presencing of beings as such.

Since Dasein is the kind of being that has an understanding of Being, it follows that our own kind of Being affords us access to the question of the meaning of Being itself. But conversely, a failure to understand our own unique kind of Being as Dasein can block access to the question of the meaning of Being. For this reason, Heidegger objects to any kind of characterization of Dasein in terms of "substance" or "reality." For Heidegger, these terms are borrowed from beings which have the character of presence-at-hand or ontic presence. By contrast, Dasein's Being is nothing like presence-at-hand or ontic presence. Dasein's Being, as characterized by temporality, must be understood in terms of a kind of non-presence which allows for the presencing of ontic presences in the first place. Thus ". . . beings with Dasein's kind of Being cannot be conceived in terms of reality and substantiality."[10] As Heidegger later tries to show, Dasein's tendency to misinterpret its own Being in terms of categories (such as "substantiality" and "reality") borrowed from beings other than itself is perfectly explicable on the basis of its own unique kind of Being as care. We now turn to the three-fold structure of Dasein's Being as care: existentiality, facticity, and fallenness.

The meaning of Dasein's existentiality is indicated by the claim that Dasein is a being for which its very own Being is always an issue. Because of this,

---

[10] *Ibid.*, 212.

Dasein is fundamentally "projective:" all of Dasein's "factual" activities and involvements are what they are only as self-projections of Dasein upon its own potentiality-for-Being. It is by virtue of this kind of projection that Dasein is always "ahead-of-itself:"

> The phrase "is an issue" has been made plain in the state-of-Being of understanding—of understanding as self-projective Being-towards its ownmost potentiality-for-Being. . . . But ontologically, Being towards one's ownmost potentiality-for-Being means that in each case Dasein is already *ahead* of itself in its Being. Dasein is always "beyond itself," not as a way of behaving towards other beings which it is *not*, but as Being towards the potentiality-for-Being which it is itself.[11]

A crucial point here is that Dasein's Being-ahead-of-itself is not merely an empirical or factual kind of Being-ahead-of-itself. All empirical or factual kinds of Being-ahead are grounded in a more primordial, "existential-*apriori*" kind of Being-ahead. According to this more primordial notion of Being-ahead, Dasein is not merely "ahead" or "out towards" actualities which are other than itself, or which may even be identified with itself (e.g., some future, yet-to-be-actualized factual state which one can imagine about oneself). Dasein's Being-ahead-of-itself is not a Being-ahead towards anything "actual" at all (whether other than oneself or identifiable with oneself); Dasein is existentially-*apriori* ahead of itself towards nothing other than its own potentiality-for-Being. This is what is meant when Heidegger tells us that Dasein's very Being is always an issue for it. Finally, Dasein's existentiality—indicated by terms such as "is an issue," projection, understanding, and Being-ahead—is not an isolated feature or characteristic of Dasein which arises only from time to time. Rather, "this structure pertains to the whole of Dasein's constitution."[12]

An equally primordial and essential structural characteristic of the Being of Dasein is its facticity; Dasein's facticity means that Dasein "has in each case already been thrown *into a world*."[13] As Heidegger continually emphasizes, the "world" into which Dasein is "thrown" does not refer to a collection of things (no matter how "complete") or to a factual state of affairs. Accordingly, Dasein's primordial thrownness does not mean that Dasein is thrown into a factual state of affairs; it means rather that Dasein is thrown into its own "state" of having a world where its own Being is an issue for it. One might say that all of Dasein's factual comportments and involvements are instances of its own self-projection; but the one thing that cannot be a result of Dasein's self-projection is the fact *that* all of its factual comportments and involvements are

---

[11] *Ibid.*, 191-192.   [12] *Ibid.*, 192.   [13] *Ibid.*

such self-projections, i.e. the fact that its very own Being is always an issue for it. Just as Dasein's Being-ahead-of-itself is not a Being-ahead towards anything "actual" but only towards its own potentiality-for-Being, so too Dasein's primordial thrownness is not a thrownness into any "factual" state of affairs but only into its own way of Being. On the basis of this, one can see already that the projective character of Dasein, Dasein's Being-ahead-of-itself, bears an intrinsic relation to its thrownness: "'Being-ahead-of-itself' means, if we grasp it more fully, '*ahead-of-itself-in-already-being-in-a-world*'."[14] Accordingly,

> ... the constitution of Dasein, whose totality is now brought out explicitly as ahead-of-itself-in-Being-already-in . . . , is primordially a whole. To put it otherwise, existing is always factical. Existentiality is essentially determined by facticity.[15]

It would be wrong to think of Dasein as something which is first of all projective and which then looks to the "world" as some kind of arena within which it can exercise its projective capacity (e.g., an arena where its projections can be either satisfied or frustrated). In this misconception of Dasein, facticity, or thrownness, is understood as an empirical determination which can offer resistance to an otherwise unlimited projective capacity. In this misconception, the ontological or *apriori* unity of existentiality and facticity is overlooked in favor of a merely factual or empirical relatedness. Contrary to this misconstrual, Heidegger wants to argue that even if there is no resistance at all from things within the "world," Dasein remains fundamentally "thrown" in the ontological sense. Thrownness into a world does not refer to the possibility of factual resistance or coercion, but rather to fact that—regardless of the factual state of affairs which surrounds Dasein—Dasein is thrown into its own kind of Being such that it must always take up its own Being as an issue.

This brings us to the third structural feature of Dasein's Being as care: fallenness. Dasein's existentiality and facticity belong together in a manner which is qualified as "fallen:"

> Dasein's factical existing is not only generally and without further differentiation a thrown potentiality-for-Being-in-the-world; it is always also absorbed in the world of its concerns.[16]

Because Dasein's own Being is always an issue for it, Dasein is always involved with things in the world, things which Dasein projects against its own potentiality-for-Being and for the sake of its potentiality-for-Being:

> That very potentiality-for-Being for the sake of which Dasein is, has Being-in-the-world as its kind of Being. Thus it implies ontologically a relation to beings within-the-world.[17]

---

[14] *Ibid.*   [15] *Ibid.*   [16] *Ibid.*   [17] *Ibid.*, 194.

Far from hovering above the things in the world, Dasein is so involved with them that for the most part it interprets itself in terms of the things in the world. To the extent that Dasein understands itself not out of its own [*eigen*] self, but out of things in the world, it is fallen or inauthentic [*uneigentlich*]. However, Dasein's fallenness or inauthenticity is not something which happens to Dasein through an external state of affairs, or which afflicts Dasein only from time to time. Dasein's fallenness is itself a primordial structural characteristic of care.

Dasein's Being is articulated in terms of the three-fold structural unity of care. In turn, the meaning of (or that which makes possible) Dasein's Being as care is temporality. This thesis has been implicit already in the preceding discussion; for Dasein's existentiality (its Being-ahead-of-itself) bears an implicit reference to futurity, and its facticity (its Being-already-thrown) bears an implicit reference to pastness. From the unity of the future and the past there can emerge something like the present, and it is only through the present that Dasein can be alongside the beings which it encounters within the world. In other words, the presencing of beings becomes possible only by way of the *apriori* unity of the temporality which constitutes Dasein's Being. These claims now have to be set forth in more detail. The meaning of—i.e., that which makes possible—Dasein's existentiality or Being-ahead-of-itself is the future. Dasein's existentiality is nothing other than its

> ... *Being towards* its ownmost, distinctive potentiality-for-Being. This sort of thing is possible only in that Dasein *can, indeed,* come towards itself in its ownmost possibility, and that it can put up with this possibility as a possibility in thus letting itself come towards itself—in other words, that it exists. This letting-itself-*come-towards*-itself in that distinctive possibility which it puts up with, is the primordial phenomenon of the *future as coming towards.*[18]

Thus "... *the primary meaning of existentiality is the future.*"[19] As Heidegger emphasizes, the "future" as it is meant here can have nothing to do with the coming-towards us of now-moments which have not yet "transpired" (or the coming-towards us of actualities which are qualified by such now-moments). The "future" here means a coming-toward in which Dasein comes towards its own self. Dasein's coming-towards itself, however, is a coming-towards its ownmost potentiality-for-Being; accordingly, that which Dasein approaches primordially in its futurity is nothing "actual" at all.

The meaning of—i.e., that which makes possible—Dasein's facticity or Being-thrown is the past. Thus "the primary existential meaning of facticity lies in the character of 'having been.'"[20] Once again, the past here is not to be understood

---

[18] *Ibid.*, 325.   [19] *Ibid.*, 327.   [20] *Ibid.*, 328.

as any kind of now-moment which is no longer present (or any actual state of affairs which might be qualified by such a now-moment). To take over one's thrownness authentically means to "choose" one's own Being as a burden which cannot be lightened by, or blamed on, anything "actual."

Dasein can take over its facticity or thrownness authentically only in virtue of Dasein's existentiality or Being-ahead-of-itself, and this is for two related reasons. First of all, Dasein can be related authentically to itself only to the extent that it is related to itself as to its own potentiality-for-Being; and Dasein's relatedness to its own potentiality-for-Being is possible only insofar as Dasein is ahead of itself, or futural: "Taking over thrownness is possible only in such a way that the futural Dasein can *be* its ownmost 'as-it-already-was'—that is to say, its 'been.'"[21] Thus Dasein is able to "choose" itself authentically only by being ahead of itself or futural. But secondly, that which is chosen in this kind of authenticity is not any actual thing which one simply is or was, but rather one's thrownness into potentiality-for-Being, i.e., one's thrownness into futurity. Thus Dasein can be authentically related to its pastness only insofar as Dasein is futural.

Conversely, Dasein can come authentically towards itself futurally only in coming back to itself as having been; once again, this coming back to itself is not to be understood as a coming back to any past event or state of affairs; this coming back is simply Dasein's coming back to itself as having-been thrown into existentiality: "Dasein can come towards itself futurally in such a way that it comes *back*, only insofar as Dasein *is* as an 'I-*am*-as-having-been.'"[22] To be authentically futural is to be authentically as having-been, and *vice versa*; both "moments" of authentic temporality mutually imply and require one another. By contrast, Dasein is inauthentic to the extent that it takes refuge in interpreting itself in terms of actual things encountered within the world, whether these be actualities approaching from the "future" or disappearing into the "past."

Although not defined in terms of anything "actual," Dasein's futural pastness or past futurity is not a free-floating structure which somehow hovers above the "actual" world. The structural unity of Dasein's futurity and pastness makes sense only as the structural unity of Dasein's caring Being-in-the-world. Because Dasein's Being is always already an issue for it (because of Dasein's futural pastness), Dasein is fundamentally involved with beings within the world. In fact, Dasein "needs" beings for the sake of its own Being, i.e., for the sake of the Being which is always the "*apriori*" issue for itself:

> Dasein exists for the sake of a potentiality-for-Being of itself. In existing, it has

---

[21] *Ibid.*, 325-326.   [22] *Ibid.*

been thrown, and as something thrown, it has been delivered over to beings which it needs *in order to* be able to be as it is—namely, *for the sake of* itself.[23]

Moreover, Dasein as thrown projection (past futurity) is not only necessarily related to beings (as present) within the world; the very structure of Dasein's past futurity makes possible the presencing of beings within the world in the first place:

> The present arises in the unity of the temporalizing of temporality out of the future and having been. . . . Insofar as Dasein temporalizes itself, a world *is* too. In temporalizing itself with regard to its Being as temporality, Dasein *is* essentially "in a world."[24]

This is not to say that Dasein's temporal structure creates the beings themselves; but Dasein's temporality is the horizon which makes possible Dasein's openness to the presencing, or the Being, of the beings. As Heidegger writes, "There is [*es gibt*] Being—not beings—only insofar as there is truth. And truth *is* only insofar as and as long as Dasein is."[25] Thus the presencing, the Being, of the beings is given only through the futural pastness of Dasein:

> The character of "having been" arises from the future, and in such a way that the future which "has been" (or better, which "is in the process of having been") releases from itself the present.[26]

With this, Heidegger shows not only that temporality is the meaning of care, but also that it is the horizon which makes possible the presencing of beings; temporality is "the unity of a future which makes present in the process of having been."[27] Beings can be made present *as* beings only through temporality: "the present is rooted in the future and in having been."[28] More specifically, something can be encountered *as* a being only in the unity of Dasein's temporality, through Dasein's futural pastness and past futurity. That which "gives" us our understanding of Being is nothing other than temporality. But as Heidegger explains in a lecture course of 1927-28, primordial temporality is not "ontically creative:" it does not create the beings themselves. Nevertheless, it is in a sense "ontologically creative:" it provides the horizon for our *apriori* understanding of Being, without which there could not be beings *as* beings.[29]

That which allows us to encounter beings *as* beings is our primordial temporality, our futural pastness. In other words, "primordial and authentic temporality temporalizes itself in terms of the authentic future and in such a way that in having been futurally, it first of all awakens the present."[30] Dasein's primordial temporality means that Dasein is always in a world and open to beings

---

[23] *Ibid.*, 364.   [24] *Ibid.*, 365.   [25] *Ibid.*, 230.   [26] *Ibid.*, 326.
[27] *Ibid.*   [28] *Ibid.*, 360.   [29] Martin Heidegger, *Gesamtausgabe*, vol. 25, 417.
[30] Martin Heidegger, *Sein und Zeit*, 329.

within the world. In fact, one can say that Dasein, in its thrown projection, or in its futural pastness, is for the most part delivered over to the world:

> In seeking shelter, sustenance, livelihood, we do so "for the sake of" constant possibilities of Dasein which are very close to it; upon these the being for which its own Being is an issue has already projected itself. Thrown into its "there" every Dasein has been factically submitted to a definite "world"—its "world."[31]

But although Dasein is essentially delivered over to its world, the crucial point is that Dasein is fundamentally different from those beings which it encounters within the world. Dasein's Being is not to be understood on the basis of those beings which are present to it; on the contrary, the presencing of these beings must be understood in light of the fact that Dasein's Being must always already "first" be an issue for it, i.e., in light of Dasein's past futurity. It is Dasein's unique concern about its own Being which "first" makes possible its Being-encountered-by beings which are other than itself.

The aim of fundamental ontology is to show how the presencing of beings is possible. Thus Heidegger cannot simply begin with Dasein as something "present," but must seek to show the conditions of the possibility of any presencing whatsoever. As it turns out, Dasein is not the kind of being which can be made present at all; indeed, it is precisely in virtue of its non-presence (its caring Being-outside-of-itself) that Dasein is the "there" ["Da"] for the presencing of any beings whatsoever. The temporality which constitutes Dasein's Being "is not a being at all,"[32] but is rather "the primordial 'outside of itself'"[33] which makes possible the presencing of beings.

II. PROBLEMS WITH THE METAPHYSICS OF PRESENCE

By virtue of its existentiality, Dasein is always ahead of itself, projecting itself upon its own potentiality-for-Being; and as factical, Dasein is always thrown into the kind of Being (potentiality-for-Being) that it is. It is through its thrown projection, or past futurity, that Dasein is always an issue for itself; and it is because it is an issue for itself that Dasein can be open to, and concerned with, the Being of beings other than itself. But in being concerned with other beings for the sake of itself, Dasein tends to become absorbed in such beings and thus tends to forget its own Being-an-issue for itself.

Dasein is not any kind of ontic presence, but is rather the non-present locus or transparency for the presencing of ontic presences. However, in its fallen

---

[31] *Ibid.*, 297.   [32] *Ibid.*, 328.   [33] *Ibid.*, 329.

self-forgetfulness, Dasein tends to interpret itself as a kind of ontic presence among others. According to Heidegger, it is this tendency towards self-forgetful fallenness that underlies traditional metaphysical interpretations of the human knower in terms of substantiality, reality, causality, form and matter, and so forth. For Heidegger, the problem with traditional metaphysics is not simply that one tries to conceive of Dasein, or the human discloser, as an object-like or thing-like kind of being. The problem is that one tries to conceive of Dasein in terms of *any* kind of presence or actuality:

> Even if one rejects the "soul substance" and the thinghood of consciousness, or denies that the person is an object, ontologically one is still positing something whose Being retains the meaning of what's present-at-hand, whether it does so explicitly or not.[34]

As we have seen, the Heideggerian unfolding of the question of the meaning of Being required an *apriori*-existential analysis of Dasein's authentic Being (in terms of care and temporality) as the non-present locus for the presencing of ontic presences. For Heidegger, then, the traditional metaphysical interpretation of Dasein in terms of ontic presence (e.g., in terms of substance, reality, or something else) essentially blocks access to a proper unfolding of the question of the meaning of Being.

In addition to blocking access to the question of the meaning of Being, the traditional metaphysics of presence also has other deleterious ramifications, according to Heidegger. For example, the traditional metaphysics of presence also stands in the way of a proper understanding of Dasein's own finite freedom. This can be seen if we first consider what is implied by the Heideggerian understanding of Dasein's "thrown projection." Insofar as Dasein is projective, or ahead-of-itself towards nothing other than its own potentiality-for-Being, it is free; in other words, Dasein is "free" insofar as Dasein's Being does not receive its definition or determination from any pre-given presences or actualities. But Dasein is finite in this freedom insofar as Dasein does not choose its own freedom, but is rather "thrown" into it. To say that Dasein is characterized by thrown projection is tantamount to saying that Dasein is characterized by finite freedom. As we have already seen, Dasein's projection makes sense only as thrown (and *vice versa*), and so Dasein's freedom makes sense only as finite. The key here is that Dasein is finite, but not because it comes upon some empirical limit which it discovers as an obstacle within experience. Dasein is finite, but not because it is limited by any being or ontic presence outside of it. Rather, Dasein's finitude is written into its very ontological constitution, even "before" Dasein can experience any beings which can ostensibly limit its

[34] *Ibid.*, 114.

activities.

In contrast to this existential-*apriori* determination of Dasein's finite freedom, the inauthentic metaphysics of presence sees Dasein as one kind of ontic presence among others. According to the metaphysics of presence, the finitude of Dasein's freedom consists in the fact that there are empirical limits to Dasein's otherwise unimpeded activity; Dasein is finite to the extent that, in its self-assertion, it must contend with resistances or limits imposed upon it by the beings, or ontic presences, surrounding it. According to this view, of course, Dasein's freedom is potentially infinite; on this view, Dasein's finitude can be overcome through the progressive removal of obstacles to Dasein's willing. By contrast, Heidegger wants to argue that Dasein is delivered over to its own potentiality-for-Being in a non-empirical manner; and thus Dasein remains finite through and through, whether or not it experiences obstacles to its self-assertion.

In addition to blocking access to the question of the meaning of Being and misconstruing Dasein's finite freedom, the traditional metaphysics of presence also falls prey to what for Heidegger is perhaps the greatest threat to Western thinking; this is the threat of nihilism, whereby the highest values become devalued and "nothing is sacred" anymore. Indeed for Heidegger, the traditional metaphysics of presence plays right into the hands of nihilism (in spite of its own anti-nihilistic intentions). This can be seen if we consider the typical anti-nihilistic strategies employed by the metaphysics of presence. Typically, the metaphysics of presence seeks to combat nihilism by appealing to some kind of ontic presence or actuality which is supposed to serve as an obstacle to the otherwise limitless and arbitrary power of human willing. For Heidegger, this appeal to ontic presences is doomed to fail. After all, the putative limit provided by an ontic presence is, in principle, always surmountable, both in theory and in practice. In theory, we can always explain one ontic presence in terms of some further ontic presence: secondary qualities may be explained in terms of primary qualities; and these supposedly "primary" qualities, in turn, can always be explained in terms of some further, more fundamental, primary qualities. In the realm of theoretical enquiry, then, there is no *prima facie* reason why we should respect the immediate limits imposed upon us by beings as ontic presences. The progress of science has shown us that such ontic limits in the realm of theory are always only temporary and relative to our ever-expanding disclosive power as enquirers. This has potentially disastrous implications, since, as Nietzsche pointed out, to explain is to de-mystify, and to de-mystify is to de-sanctify.

The same kind of trend is at work in the area of practice. Modern technology has shown us that any ontic presence or resistance can, in principle, be overcome by more powerful and efficient technology. Ontic presences or beings which we encounter within the world can in themselves never provide an adequate boundary or limit to the seemingly limitless practical orientation of the human being. In principle—though perhaps not yet in actuality—human beings can bring any given being or ontic presence within their control.

For Heidegger, the problem with the metaphysics of presence is not that it tries to identify limits to the seemingly unlimited manipulative power of the human being; the problem is that it seeks such limits in the *ontic* givenness of beings. Insofar as such ontic, or empirical, limits are surmountable in principle, the metaphysics of presence plays into the hands of nihilism; as long as the limits are located on the ever-receding ground of ontic presence, the metaphysics of presence is vulnerable to the nihilistic counter-claim that there really are no limits at all. Like the metaphysics of presence, Heidegger wants to argue that there are limits to the power of human willing and that the human being is finite in its knowing and doing; but unlike the metaphysics of presence, Heidegger argues that this finitude and these limits are determined by the *ontological* givenness of Being as such, and not by the (ever-surmountable) *ontic* givenness of beings. For Heidegger, an adequate limit to the power of human willing is to be provided, not by the resistance of beings or ontic presences, but by "the prior resistance of Being" as such [*die vorgängige Widerständigkeit des Seins*].[35] Stated differently, Dasin's indebtedness and finitude are properly determined, not by ontic givenness, but only by the ontological givenness of Being itself. Dasein can always in principle overcome the limits provided by beings or ontic presences, but can never outstrip Being or presencing as such, over which we do not have any control. Indeed, all of Dasein's theoretical and technological success is inevitably indebted to the givenness of Being. Dasein's understanding and manipulation of beings would not be possible apart from the prior givenness of Being as such.

III. AQUINAS ON THE HUMAN KNOWER

At first glance, it may seem that Aquinas' thinking on the human knower is a classic case of the inauthentic, or merely ontic, kind of self-interpretation which Heidegger rejects. After all, Aquinas does speak of the human knower as a kind of substance or actuality, and he refers to the intellect as a kind of "thing" (a *res*).[36] In spite of first appearances, however, a strong argument can be made in

---

[35] Martin Heidegger, *Kant und das Problem der Metaphysik* (Frankfurt am Main: Vittorio Klostermann, 1973), 70.

[36] St. Thomas Aquinas, *Summa Theologiae* (Rome: Leonine Commission, 1882), I, Q. 82, a. 4, ad. 1.

favor of the claim that what Thomas means by the substantiality or actuality of the human knower has little to do with the ontic, or entitative, view which Heidegger rightfully criticizes.

In the following pages, I will try to show that Aquinas' thought on the human knower is indeed compatible with Heidegger's understanding of Dasein. My demonstration of this will have a negative side as well as a positive side. On the negative side, I will try to show that Aquinas' Aristotelian background leads him to view the human knower as a kind of being which—unlike beings within experience—can never be made immediately present. On the positive side, I will try to show that Aquinas understands the human knower as a kind of substance which exhibits such a high degree of immateriality that it retains no entitative obstinacy of its own, and thus is a sheer openness of the kind that Heidegger describes. The openness of the human knower, in turn, has implications for a Thomistic account of the human being's finite freedom. We begin, then, with the negative side of our discussion.

No contemporary Thomist can deny the Aristotelian roots of Aquinas' thought. Some Thomists, however, may not fully realize that Aquinas' Aristotelianism leads him to a position which sounds very much like Heidegger's own position: the human discloser can never find itself as a simple presence among other presences within experience. We can explicate this further by referring to Aristotle.

According to a fundamental Aristotelian principle, nothing is intelligible except insofar as it is in act. The intellect is in act only insofar as it is actually understanding something, and so when it is not actually understanding something, the intellect is not actually intelligible. From this it follows that the intellect cannot know itself by virtue of itself alone, or by an act of direct introspection; such direct self-understanding would be possible only if the intellect were already intelligible by virtue of itself, apart from its being actualized in the knowing of something other than itself. Thus for Aristotle and for Aquinas, the intellect can come to know itself only through its understanding of something other than itself.[37]

According to another Aristotelian principle, the knowing and the known are one. The intellect can come to know itself only through its understanding of something other than itself; but in this self-understanding through the other, the intellect does not find itself as an object to be known alongside the other object being known. For such a duality of objects would violate the Aristotelian principle that the intelligible in act is one with the intelligent in act. If, in knowing itself through the other, the intellect knew the other as one object and itself as another

[37] See *ST*, I, Q. 87, a. 1

object, then there would not be an identity of the intelligible and the intelligent. Thus for Aristotle and Aquinas, as for Heidegger, the human discloser does not know itself as something present within experience or as something alongside other objects which are known. Rather, the human discloser is fundamentally "outside" of itself and comes to know itself *as* a discloser only insofar as it returns back to itself "out of" the objects which it knows within experience. Along these same lines, Aquinas recognizes in the human knower a tendency very similar to what Heidegger calls the tendency towards inauthenticity or fallenness. According to Aquinas, material beings are the proper objects of the human intellect.[38] Since the proper object of the human intellect is material being, there always remains the danger that the human knower will misinterpret itself in terms of those material beings which it knows most directly.

This brings us to the positive side of our discussion of Aquinas. If the human discloser, for Aquinas, does not find itself as an ontic presence among other presences within experience, then how are we to conceive of the Being of the human discloser? Aquinas does refer to the human knower as a kind of substance, but he also says other things about the knower's substantiality which make clear that his own "substantialist" understanding of the human knower comes rather close to Heidegger's conception of Dasein. According to Aquinas, a material substance is determined by both form and matter. The greater degree of formality or immateriality possessed by a substance, the greater is that substance's capacity for immanently-grounded unity; and the more immanently unified a being is, the greater is that being's capacity to withstand external threats to its own existence:

> The mode of a thing's being is according to the mode by which it possesses unity. Hence each thing repulses, as much as it can, division, lest by this division it should tend towards non-being.[39]

A naive reading of this passage would suggest that, for Aquinas, a being which is more immaterial and thus more resistant to threats to its own existence must also be more cut off from other beings. But for Aquinas, just the opposite is the case: it is by virtue of its immateriality that a being can be cognitive; and to be cognitive is to be open to the Being of other beings.[40] But how can this be, if a greater degree of immateriality implies a greater degree of self-subsistence in the face of external threats to a being's existence?

---

[38] See *ST*, I, Q. 84, a. 7

[39] St. Thomas Aquinas, *Summa contra gentiles* (Rome: Leonine Commission, 1882), I, 42.

[40] St. Thomas Aquinas, *Summa Theologiae*, I, Q. 14, a. 1.

Paradoxically, the knower's greater degree of immateriality and self-subsistence in the face of otherness makes it essentially ecstatic, open, and directed towards the intelligibility of beings other than itself. It is because of the knower's high degree of immateriality and self-subsistence that the knower does not regard the other as simply "other." We can illustrate this by contrasting two different formal principles, the nutritive and the intellectual. On the level of nutrition, the living being withstands and overcomes the alien-character of other beings by destroying the other being in its otherness (i.e., by consuming it). On the level of intellectual cognition, the intellect withstands and overcomes the alien-character of other beings, not by destroying the other in its otherness, but by preserving the other in its otherness. The intellect does this by *becoming* the other. Because of its greater degree of immateriality, the intellect can become the other while still remaining itself. The other loses the character of sheer otherness, not because it is destroyed (as in consumption), but because the knower *qua* knower does not stand opposed to the other as other; it is rather open to the other in its otherness. This is possible because the intellect perfects itself—and indeed truly *becomes* itself—only by becoming the other.

The intellect truly becomes itself only in becoming the other, and it can do this because it has no pre-given entitative obstinacy of its own. It can do this, in other words, because the intellect *qua* intellect is not already an ontic presence with entitative determinations of its own. The intellect's becoming-other is not self-destructive (as it would be for more material beings) since the intellect is nothing actual apart from its knowing of beings other than itself. By virtue of its immateriality, the intellect has no pre-given entitative actuality of its own, and thus it is nothing other than an openness for the presencing of beings other than itself.

For Aquinas, as for Heidegger, the human knower's openness to other beings implies something about the human knower's freedom. As Heidegger argues, Dasein's freedom means that Dasein's Being as a discloser is not determined or defined by any pre-given ontic presences or actualities within its world. In a similar vein, Aquinas argues that the human being's intellectual knowing is not caused directly by the material objects which are present and knowable within the world. This is so, according to Aquinas, since there must be a fundamental commensurability between recipient and what is received; accordingly, intellectual knowledge, which exhibits a fundamentally immaterial mode of being, cannot be caused in us by material objects alone. Our intellectual knowledge has an essentially immaterial manner of being, and thus cannot be caused immediately and directly by the material things which are the intellect's proper objects. Because of this, Aquinas argues for a two-fold mediation:

It is not in the nature of the intellect to receive knowledge from sensible things immediately, but by means of sensitive powers, since it is necessary for there to be a certain fittingness between recipient and received. Species, however, existing in the senses have a certain agreement both with the intellect in so far as they are without matter, and with material things in so far as they have the conditions of matter. Whence sense fittingly receives from material things and the intellect from the senses. The intellect, however, does not receive immediately from material things.[41]

The first mediation, then, has to do with the senses: the senses exist in material organs and can thus be affected by material objects. Sense knowledge is particular, and thus it comes with the conditions of matter, but it is immaterial insofar as it is also a kind of knowledge. As immaterial, sense knowledge is available to the intellect.

But while sense knowledge is available to the intellect, it alone cannot suffice for the kind of knowledge which we have through the intellect. Sense knowledge, which is particular, must be transformed into intellectual knowledge, which is universal. Accordingly, there is required a second kind of mediation; this mediation takes place through the act of abstraction which the agent intellect performs upon the sensible phantasm. The phantasm, however, is not simply given as already intelligible; the phantasm is only potentially intelligible in itself, and must first be made ready for the act of abstraction by the knower's own faculties, including the cogitative sense. In turn, the knower's own faculties, including the cogitative sense, may be directed by the enquiring orientation of the intellect.

With this notion of abstraction, Aquinas affirms something similar to what Heidegger discusses under the rubric of Dasein's projective character. We will recall that, for Heidegger, we are open to the presencing of beings because of our projective orientation: in projecting ourselves upon our own potentiality-for-Being, we are open to the presencing of beings other than ourselves. The potentiality-for-Being towards which we project ourselves, however, is nothing already actual or present for us. In a similar vein, Aquinas would argue that the intellect *qua* intellect does not simply find itself existing amongst a collection of actualities or presences which already happen to be present for it, apart from its own activity. After all, the beings-to-be-known become actually intelligible for the intellect only to the extent that the active intellect supervenes upon the not-yet-intelligible phantasm and makes that phantasm actually intelligible. Since the proper object of the intellect is the intelligible *qua* intelligible, the not-yet-intelligible phantasm is, from the point of view of intellectual knowledge, "nothing" at all; and to that extent, the intellect is open to the

---

[41] St. Thomas Aquinas, *Scriptum super libros Sententiarum,* liber IV (Rome: Leonine Commission, 1882), d. 50, q. 1, a. 1.

presencing of beings only if it projects itself upon that which is simply not yet "there" for it. Insofar as the intellect's activity is not determined or delimited by pre-given presences, it is free in its projective, disclosive activity.

For Aquinas, as for Heidegger, the human knower is essentially free in its disclosive activity; however, this freedom does not imply any kind of arbitrariness. The human knower, for Aquinas as for Heidegger, is essentially finite in its freedom. The knower is finite, however, not because of any putative limits imposed by the pre-givenness of beings, but rather because of the pre-givenness of Being itself. As Aquinas affirms in his commentary on Aristotle's *Metaphysics* (lec. 6, 605), Being is the first object of the intellect, and ". . . nothing else can be conceived unless Being is understood." No ontic or entitative presences can be given to the intellect except by virtue of the *apriori* givenness of Being itself. Thus while the human knower can outstrip the temporary limits imposed by any given ontic presence, it can never outstrip its dependence upon the presencing of Being as such. Thus the human knower remains finite in its disclosive activity.

The non-ontic, ontological basis for the knower's finitude becomes clearer if we consider Aquinas' discussion of the sensory powers. The human knower is finite and limited, but not because the knower has an otherwise infinite intellect which happens to be restricted by its dependence on sensory organs. As Aquinas suggests, the sensory organs exist for the sake of cognitive powers which are already finite in their very Being: "the powers are not for the organs but the organs for the powers."[42] By extension, we can say that the knower is not finite because it is dependent on the sensory organs; rather the human knower has sensory organs because the human knower is "already" finite in its knowing. The human knower is finite in its very Being, even "before" it must contend with the ontic or empirical limits imposed upon it through its dependence on sensory organs. By the same token, Aquinas can affirm that angels are finite in their Being, even though their knowing is not restricted by the ontic limits of sensory organs. Borrowing from Heidegger's terminology, we might say that the human knower is finite because it is thrown, in a non-empirical way, into the kind of Being that it is.

Just as we might say that Aquinas' human knower is thrown non-empirically into the finite kind of Being that it is, so too we might also say that Aquinas' human knower exists as Being-ahead towards its own potentiality-for-Being. This, to be sure, is not Thomistic terminology; however, this terminology is not inappropriate if one understands how the human knower exists as Being-ahead. Aquinas would say that the human knower exists out towards its own perfection. The knower *qua* knower achieves its perfection in the act of knowing, and thus

---

[42] St. Thomas Aquinas, *Summa Theologiae*, I, Q. 78, a. 3).

in *becoming* (cognitionally) the object-to-be-known. But how does the human knower, as potential knower, exist out towards its own perfection? It cannot do so by comporting itself towards some actual being which it already knows to be there for it; after all, insofar as the knower is merely out towards its own perfection, it is not yet perfected in the act of knowing, and thus does not yet know the object as something actual towards which it could comport itself. Accordingly, the enquiring human knower cannot relate to its own perfection as it would relate to any kind of ontic presence or actuality which is already there for it. As with Heidegger's Dasein, Aquinas' human knower maintains itself authentically in its Being by projecting itself out towards its own perfection, a perfection which, precisely insofar as the knower is characterized by enquiry, is nothing yet actually present for it.

IV. CONCLUDING REMARKS

My analysis of Heidegger and Aquinas here differs from the well-known analysis by John Caputo in two important respects. First of all, I disagree with Caputo's claim that ". . . the essential issue in the confrontation of Heidegger and Aquinas is centered in the later Heidegger."[43] I agree, of course, that a full confrontation between Heidegger and Aquinas must take the later Heidegger into consideration; however, Caputo's prioritizing of the later Heidegger is, to my mind, one-sided. As I have tried to show throughout this paper, some of the central points at issue between the two thinkers can be addressed through a comparison of Aquinas and the early Heidegger, insofar as both Aquinas and the early Heidegger focus on the Being of the intellectual knower. Caputo himself seems to acknowledge this, in part, when he writes: "The genuine point of contact [betweeen Aquinas and Heidegger] is opened up by consideration not of *esse* but of *intellectus*."[44]

Secondly, I believe that Caputo is wrong to think that the only genuinely Heidegger-friendly elements in Aquinas' thought are to be found outside of Aquinas' metaphysics, and in his personal, religious life instead. Concerning those elements in Aquinas' thought which approach the thought of Heidegger, Caputo writes:

> I would look for the unspoken horizon of St. Thomas' thought outside metaphysics, in a certain kind of non-metaphysical experience, of which the metaphysics is an objectivistic conceptualization and toward which it tends. I would look for the unspoken horizon of St. Thomas' thought in the mystical-

---

[43] John Caputo, *Heidegger and Aquinas: An Essay on Overcoming Metaphysics* (New York: Fordham University Press, 1982), 217.

[44] *Ibid.*, 266.   [45] *Ibid.*, 249.

religious experience of life which animates his works. . . ."[45]

Contrary to Caputo's claim here, I have tried to show that there are, even within Aquinas' metaphysics of the human knower, elements which sound remarkably like Heidegger himself. This is not to suggest, however, that we can recover the "Heideggerian" elements of Thomas while still remaining completely true to the explicit intentions of Aquinas himself. As Caputo is right to insist, it is not possible to adhere to the "historical actuality" of Aquinas, while also demonstrating his philosophical affinity with Heidegger:

> So long as we remain on the level of the Thomistic text in its historical *actuality*, on the level of what St. Thomas himself actually said and intended to say, of the actual metaphyscial doctrine which he developed in the Scholastic mode, then we shall never be able to bring Heidegger and Aquinas into living relationship with one another.[46]

Here, Caputo is quite right to stress something that Heidegger himself stresses: "higher than actuality stands *possibility*."[47] With regard to our interpretation, this means that we should never content ourselves with thinking that the meaning of a thinker like Aquinas has been explained and "made actual" once and for all. The thought of any thinker from the past always contains new and unforeseeable possibilities for us today, and the revelation of these new possibilities is just as much a function of our own confrontation with Being today, as it is a function of an earlier thinker's confrontation with Being in the past.

In this paper, I have tried to suggest the possibility of a dialogue between Heidegger and Aquinas because I believe that a Heideggerian reading of Aquinas can unlock and release some of the existential-ontological possibilities of Aquinas' rich thought. For too long, many of these possibilities have been overlooked and even repressed by certain currents in neo-Thomism which seek to turn Aquinas' thought into a set of techniques for the purpose of combatting what some fear to be the incipient nihilism of contemporary philosophy. However, if we have learned anything from Heidegger, we should realize that such attempts to fasten onto the ontic presence of rigid techniques only play into the hands of nihilism itself.

Finally, if a Heideggerian reading of Aquinas can unlock some of the possibilities of Aquinas' thought, then, conversely, a return to Aquinas might serve as a corrective to Heidegger's thinking. In his affirmation of the radical discontinuity betweeen the Being of Dasein and other ways of Being, Heidegger may have unwittingly bought into those Enlightenment dichotomies

---

[46] *Ibid.*, 246. [47] Martin Heidegger, *Sein und Zeit*, 38.

which he sought to undermine: the dichotomies betweeen autonomy and heteronomy, inside and outside, self and other. In the long run, it may turn out that Aquinas demonstrates the distinct advantage of being able to affirm a certain kind of continuity between knowing substances and non-knowing substances, yet without misconceiving the knowing substance as a kind of ontic presence among others.

Reflections on "Negative Theology" in the Light of a Recent Venture to Speak of "God Without Being"

David B. Burrell, C.S.C.

A Maritain gathering which took its theme from the title of Josef Pieper's monograph, *The Silence of Saint Thomas*, seemed a timely occasion to try to take the measure of a book which has only recently appeared in English by Jean-Luc Marion, a French philosopher quite decidedly Catholic: *God Without Being*. Anyone who has made the effort necessary to discover the riches of Aquinas' understanding of *being*, notably in his semantic *tour de force* in uniquely identifying God as the One whose essence is simply to-exist, could only be aggravated by such a title, even if titles are meant to arrest our attention. Yet a quick perusal could put that same person's mind at rest, for in a few pages Marion quickly concludes that the only reasonable way to interpret Aquinas on this elusive subject is to understand what he says about *ens* as Scotus does: "the result of a concept first nested in our apprehension, which remains univocal for 'God' as well as all other beings."[1] (I shall be citing from the French, with English pagination following, since his prose is so evocative that it seemed better to risk my own misunderstandings than to trust the interpretations of a translator.) If that's the way it must be, then better have God without such *being*. And this would hardly be the place to contest Marion's jejune reading of Aquinas—one which he himself abjures in a Preface to the English edition. Yet once arrested, one's attention cannot but help being drawn to other dimensions of his work, even if he has not succeeded in throwing down the gauntlet to those who have endeavored to sound out Aquinas on the uniqueness

---

[1] 112-20, citation at 120, taken from the "Quadrige" French edition, *Dieu sans l'être* (Paris: Presses Universitaires de France, 1991), while the work was initially published by Fayard in 1982. The English edition was published by The University of Chicago Press in 1991.

of divine being as a singularly opportune way to characterize the all-important "distinction" of God from the world.[2]

For if that very "distinction" is in question, then we will need all the help we can get to grasp it, for it is only "glimpsed "on the margin of reason," as Sokolowski would have it, indeed "at the intersection of faith and reason"(39). And Jean-Luc Marion is very interested in that intersection, as his other writings, as well as the theological appendices to this work, make abundantly clear. Moreover, his argument is not with Aquinas' *being* anyway; the few pages devoted to Aquinas reduce him to Avicenna, and seem intended to parry any thrusts from a Thomist quarter. The focal polemic is rather with Heidegger's *Sein* and his "ontological difference," which we shall see has little to do with that underscored by Kierkegaard or articulated by Sokolowski's "distinction." For Marion's training had been with a group of French philosophers quite taken with Heidegger, and he has written extensively on Descartes as well. All this emerges quite clearly in his earlier *L'idole et la distance* (Paris: Grasset, 1977). For that work opposes *idol* to *icon* in the interest of formulating the relation of God to the universe, of predication which does duty in this world to that which will be needed if we propose to speak of the One from whom all-that-is derives. It is in this work that he initially takes the measure of Heidegger's "ontological difference (*Sein/seiende*) and of Lévinas' "Other" whose constituent otherness comes to be rendered *differance*.

For it is Marion's contention that these linguistic contortions are in the service of seeking a source that can still be assented to, even without being actively "present." In fact, it is the *absence* of this source which he intends to capture in his own formulation: *la distance*. This source will not be an explanation or a cause, since our understanding of both of these intellectual maneuvers is quite similar: what explains (or causes) can only be shown to do so in virtue of a framework which comprehends both *explanandum* and *explanans*. Yet he will be more patient with pseudo-Dionysius' fascination with *aitia*—a Greek term regularly rendered "cause"—since that writer uses it to gesture towards a fecund origin whose relation to what it originates is not itself categorizable. But since that is precisely the kind of move which Aquinas intends to make by identifying God as *ipsum esse* ("existing itself"), and many concur that he also found pseudo-Dionysius to be a fruitful inspiration for his unique synthesis, it would be best now to examine more closely the quarrel which Marion has with "being."

It seems that *being* periodically comes on hard times. For positivists it was

---

[2] Notably Robert Sokolowski in *The God of Faith and Reason* (Notre Dame, Indiana: University of Notre Dame Press, 1982)—a work which appeared the same year as Marion's.

meaningless to speak of "being *qua* being," for Heidegger the challenge had been to think *being* in contrast to beings, and to do so in a not very implicit polemic against the One whom Jews, Christians, and Muslims designate as creator. For it was the faith-assertion that the universe was freely created by the One God which stimulated medieval philosophers to turn Aristotle's identification of *two* fundamental questions—what is it?, is it?—into a fruitful strategy for opening his universe to the activity of a creator, and for spawning the question: why is there something rather than nothing? These thinkers were captured by Aristotle's insistence that there was no way of getting around speaking of a thing's being, yet understood this claim in the richly analogous manner in which he made it. *Being* is not to be conceived as a floor, a basic stuff, a substratum. Indeed, that temptation has already been dismissed by Aristotle in his treatment of the paradigmatic realization of being, substance, in the *Metaphysics*.

The question of *being* reduplicates and intensifies when one directs it towards the source of what-is, indeed, of all-that-is. For when that question is posed, one may first ask (in imitation of Aristotle's actual practice): why pose it that way? Yet if we do, then we are constrained to attempt to articulate the relation of that unique source with all-that-is. (So it is that the question reduplicates.) Here is where Josef Pieper's contention (in the essay inspiring this essay): that creation is the hidden element in the philosophy of Saint Thomas, gives us specific purchase on the inquiry. For it followed, for Aquinas, that "the beginning and end of all things and of reasoning creatures especially"(ST 1.2.Prol) could not itself be one of those being, indeed, could not be "a being": "it is plain that God does not belong to the genus of substance"(ST 1.3.5.1). Yet what such a One does do, in freely calling forth all-that-is, is to inscribe in those who can recognize their existence for the gift it is, an impulse to return it. (That impulse Marion very much wants to elicit, yet will attempt to do so by the sheer category of *gift*, with no reference at all to what is given.)

To continue with Aquinas for a moment: in individuating this God as *ipsum esse* ("existing itself"), he expressly indicates that such a One does not instantiate a concept of *being* (as chipmunks do chipmunkhood), but that the activity which is existing defies any essential characterization, much as Aristotle's attempt to lead us to grasp *act* from a series of examples of becoming (*potency*). So if the primary effect of the creator (for Aquinas) is the very existing of things, the primary intent is the "order of the universe," the *telos* which existing builds into things. So speaking of *good* is not adding anything to discourse about *being*, but rather calling attention to the *telos* inherent in that act of existing which creatures derive from their creator. To speak of "the good," then, is to call attention to the *eros* of being. Now if all this makes eminent sense, why should some pious Catholic philosophers contend that "love alone has nothing to do with being;" and that "God loves without being"(195/138)?[3] What is going on?

Marion's presumption seems to be that human discourse introduces categories, and that the true God must transcend such categories. As a way of gesturing at this, he introduces his own category—*la distance*—which intends to name the "logical space" correlative to God. It is to this space that the language of praise directs itself, so such linguistic practices must detach themselves from assertion just as loving (though an act) is purportedly "beyond being." Again, the presumption seems to be that *being* is a kind of floor, to call attention to which cannot help but supplant—in our ways of proceeding intellectually—God's own proper manner of acting or of being present. The further presumption is that *all* of our ways of trying to speak of God have been undone by God's revelation in Jesus. Or they ought to be undone if we are to understand that act properly, and hence relate ourselves to the true God. If I have properly identified the operative presumptions, we have here a decisive question of method: are Christians (and other believers) to press the articulation of human speech as far as possible, allowing ourselves to be led by revelation to articulate as best we can the God in whom we believe?[4] Or are such believers to presume that human discourse is an inherently finite project, which if adopted will inevitably constrict (and so falsify) our attempts to articulate divinity? If the latter, as Jean-Luc Marion apparently believes, then theologians of these faiths will be constrained to limit themselves to thematic elaborations of a revelational story. Put in medieval terms, the question is whether or not *theologia* can be a *scientia*: whether theological inquiry can itself be a way of knowing, or not? Chenu's coy title for his exploration—*Théologie comme science au XIIIème siècle*—underscores the difficulty while resolving it in one direction. Marion takes the opposite tack, or tries to do so.

He makes extensive use of both Heidegger and Lévinas to prose ways of detaching discourse about God from *being*, that is, from ordinary predication schemes, substituting his own category of *distance*. Working through Heidegger's "ontological difference" (*Sein/seiende*) and Lévinas' "Other" and Derrida's *differance*, he finds them all inadequate, so tries to make a case for "la distance"—*not* as a category but as a *name* for matters divine, as "love"

---

[3] 'God' in this passage is rendered with a cross atop it to call attention to the revelation of the true God in the death and resurrection of Jesus; otherwise 'God' is placed between double quotes ("God") to show that he is referring to non-believers' attempts to name (falsely) the One.

[4] That is the contention of my *Freedom and Creation in Three Traditions* (Notre Dame, Indiana: University of Notre Dame Press, 1993).

and *"Verbum"* can be used as names as well, after the manner of pseudo-Dionysius. Indeed, he avers, the best we can do is to name God, better with the names which God gives to us in Scripture. Here he praises pseudo-Dionysius for his focus on names (and on "the Good" rather than on *being*), and critiques Aquinas for having placed a conceptual limit on the use of divine names by interposing his discussion of divine simpleness (ST 1.3-11) before his question treating of "divine names"(ST 1.13). Yet of course questions 3-11 in the *Summa* speak not of attributes, strictly speaking, but rather delineate "formal features" of divinity: rules for using divine names properly so that they will not be thought to be predicated in any ordinary sense of an ordinary subject.[5]

Understood in that way, Aquinas is actually protecting divine names for their use in praising God, and doing so by proposing God as a unique subject of knowledge while at the same time seeing to it that our assertions about God will not turn their subject into an ordinary object. Is not that something which Marion himself wishes to do? Indeed the fruit of such a focus on *being*, concentrated in the act of existing (*esse*), is to allude to an activity constitutive of and present to all things: "the act of existing is the ultimate actuality of everything, and even of every form"(ST 1.4.1.3); indeed, "existence is more intimately and profoundly interior to things than anything else"(ST 1.8.1). We are then led, by the grammar of the matter, to see God's unique being (where essence = to-be) as the source of all-that-is, and so of all perfections, so that all of the given names can be used to praise God and to mean something in doing so. The language of praise cannot be equated to the language of assertion, yet it does (and must) assert! Or better, properly instructed by the metaphysical grammar of the introductory questions (ST 1.3-11), we can use the language of praise to assert truthfully of God what we praise God for.

How can we do that? Here is the dimension which Aquinas left almost entirely implicit and which principally concerns Marion. How can Christians (or by extension, other believers) speak authentically of God?[6] Can it suffice that they praise rather than predicate? What would that be like? Those who praise God, Aquinas avers in responding to Maimonides (ST 1.13.2), want to speak in such a way as to reveal their understanding, their inner appreciation of the *inadequacy* of such terms to articulate divinity properly. To speak properly, their discourse must incorporate a judgment regarding the manner of predication that is going on here, for it is not a simple apprehension that can warrant our

---

[5] See my *Aquinas: God and Action* (Notre Dame, Indiana: University of Notre Dame Press, 1979).

[6] See my "Ghazali and Aquinas on the Names of God," *Literature and Theology* 3 (1989) 173-80; as well as *Al-Ghazali on the Ninety-Nine Names of God*, trans. David B. Burrell and Nazih Daher (Cambridge: Islamic Texts Society, 1992).

using such terms of God, but using them properly involves an analogous use of language which *use* incorporates a differentiated judgment on the part of the one praising.

The presence of such a judgment is shown in what is said and what is left unsaid, in the implications drawn or not drawn in the course of, say, a homily or in speaking to someone of the loss of a loved one. Such use of language does assert while it renders praise, displaying at once God's distance from our way of understanding things, as well as God's intimate presence to us. How do we come to make such judgments? How do we learn to subordinate our learned sense of the coherence which belongs to statements to a yet more exigent coherence: that of the one making the statement with the faith-statement one makes? Jean-Luc Marion calls this "the final rigor" and in the concluding supplementary essay of *God without Being* develops its logic with the help of J.L. Austin's performativity of discourse as well as a penetrating reflection on the interchange of subject and predicate in a true statement. He comes in this way to an understanding of the activity of professing one's faith quite similar to that of George Lindbeck (in his *Nature of Doctrine*): that the marauding crusader's cry "God is great!" is a travesty and a falsehood.[7]

Yet the attitude involved in a truthful confession (which in turn renders my uttering it truthful) must itself be appropriate to the realities involved. And if that can only be assured, as Marion insists, by my conversion to a life of *agape* (charity), that life is true because it imitates that of Jesus and thereby reflects a proper relation to the source of all. Yet let us try to articulate, with the help of Aquinas' onto-logical stretching of language, how this free creator relates to creatures. It cannot be by way of simple opposition, as Kathryn Tanner has so carefully ruled out in her *God and the Doctrine of Creation*, for God cannot be thought of as "a being" alongside of the universe which emanates from God.[8] Indeed the very terms 'emanation' and 'participation,' as Aquinas uses them, can only be metaphors in this case. God "differs differently;" "the distinction" is hardly an ordinary one. While monism is ruled out by that very "distinction," one might be tempted to invoke a form of "non-dualism" (celebrated in Vedanta): *otherness* must be asserted, but in no ordinary way. The revelation of God in Jesus offers an image here: creatures are related to the creator by an extension of God's loving self-expression in the Word. And once that creating Word becomes an invitation to respond wholeheartedly to the free gift of creation— as it does in the giving of the Torah, the Word's becoming human in Jesus, or made Arabic in the Qur'an—then we can properly understand creation for the

---

[7] Philadelphia: Westminster Press, 1987; 64.
[8] Oxford: Basil Blackwell, 1988; 45-48.

gift that it is.[9] And this brings us back to the intent of Jean-Luc Marion, shorn of the polemic and bereft of the need for his non-categorical "category," *distance*,

In a key chapter (in *God Without Being*) entitled "La croisée de l'étre/The Crossing of Being," he seeks to do to *being* what he had earlier proposed for 'God': to submit the name 'God' to the dialectic of self-emptying that is the cross of Christ, our paradigm for love (*agape*), and so help us to make the effort to think such a God—beyond Heidegger's "ontological difference" or "the question of being"(73/46-7). Beyond these two, since (as we shall see) Heidegger's "ontological difference" succeeds in occluding the universe as a personal gift, while the Hellenic legacy of *being* obscures the ontological difference which Marion wants and which he tries to capture in the evocative notion of "distance." The sign that the Hellenic legacy does just that is to hear its best proponents (like Thomas Aquinas) endorse Avicenna's insistence that "*ens* is that which first occurs in human intellectual conception"(119/80). For Marion, that means that "*ens* is defined as the first *object* apprehended by the human mind"(120/81) so that, in any event, anyone (Thomists included) who begins with *being* has no choice but to accept it as the univocal floor proposed by Scotus. For proof of that, consider how Aquinas' treatment in the *Summa Theologiae* evacuates his own presentation of the divine names as analogical (ST 1.13) by "grounding it" in God as "*ipsum esse* and thus an [essential] names taken from *ens*"(120/81). The presumption throughout, in fashioning this polemical springboard, is that *being* is (or must be) a univocal concept, so that tying the Christian treatment of God to *being* will inevitably falsify the God revealed in Jesus Christ under the name of *agape* (123/82). A not unfamiliar polemical springboard, be it with some sixteenth-century reformers or with twentieth-century "process theologians;" and if the project is to "liberate God from [that conception of] Being, *tant mieux!*

His way of doing that can be shown by having recourse to three scriptural texts: Romans 4:17 sq, 1 Cor 1:28 sq, and Luke 15:12-32. His isogesis of these texts will falter somewhat on alternative translations of the original text (which he is careful to reproduce in Greek), but the first focuses on Paul's description of Abraham's faith in a God who "calls forth beings as though non-beings"

---

[9] Aquinas puts it nicely in ST 1.32.1.3: "knowledge of the divine persons [i.e., the triunity of God] was necessary for us . . . for the right idea of creation. The fact of saying that God made all things by His Word excludes the error of those who say that God produced things by necessity. When we say that in Him there is a procession of love, we show that God produced creatures not because He needed them, nor because of any extrinsic reason, but on account of the love of His own goodness." See my *Freedom and Creation* . . . 19-22, and Nicholas Lash, *On Believing in One God Three Ways* (Notre Dame, Indiana: University of Notre Dame Press, 1992) ch. 2.

["who . . . calls into existence what does not yet exist" JB]. What would ordinarily be taken as an allusion to God's creative prowess Marion reads as "everything becoming indifferent in the face of the *differance* which God marks with the world"(130/88). Faith in this call "makes [the difference between being and nonbeing] appear indifferent, yet for all that leaves it intact"(131/88). One might have thought that this difference was utterly crucial to Paul's celebration of Abraham's faith, which cannot be without allusion to the call to sacrifice his own son, God's special gift and bearer of the promise (Gen 22).

The next text is the celebrated opposition between the wisdom of this world and God's wisdom. Here one is directed to the active intervention of God, who "chooses things scorned by the world, even nonbeings, to annul things which are, precisely so that nothing fleshly may glorify itself before God"(132/89). Here Marion opposes *agape* to *eros*, revelation to human inquiry, insisting on the quasi-legal term 'annul' to call attention to how God can "cancel out" what is, thereby turning the "wisdom of the world" into foolishness by determining the being (or nonbeing) of things without recourse to Being, so not only making the difference between life and death (ontic difference) indifferent, but also the "ontological difference" (*Sein/seiende*) (135/91). How so? The decision regarding whether this thing will be or not does not depend on philosophical categories, nor upon Being disseminating itself à la the "ontological difference," but on the *distance* which separates the limit between "the world" (of 1 Corinthians) and the call of God who makes things live. That "distance" is epitomized in the fact that this "world" grounds itself in its own works and pretends to glorify itself before God (Rom 4:29) (138/94). So Marion attempts to make metaphysical hay out of Paul's poignant contrast between what we might name *ego* and *self*: between the world as turned in on itself and thus falsifying its relation to its creator, and that same world opened to become its true self through acknowledging and receiving the saving action of the Word made flesh.

In the the final text, the parable of the two brothers, Marion pursues his intention of moving us "beyond Being" in our attempt to conceive the relation of creatures to a gracious creator, by focussing on the unique use of the word *ousia* in the gospels: "Father, give me my portion of the *substance* that is coming to me." Citing Heidegger's Marbourg lectures for an admittedly tangential sense of 'substance,' he proposes that the word *ousia* is here being used to denote "a possession that it is in one's power to dispose of"(141/96). That would parse the prodigal's conversion as his recognizing (1) that "the substance that was coming to him" really came to him "by a gracious concession"(142/97), and (2) that he had "had to fracture his very sonship to obtain the *ousia* as his possession"(144/98). It was, of course, his Father's receiving him that restored his sonship by reminding him that all was gift. A brilliant isogesis, certainly, and indicative of the kind of use to which Marion's theological wit can put the scriptures, yet hardly amounting to a "ploy which, indifferent to the 'ontological difference,' thereby detaches a being from Being and gives it the name of 'gift'."(146/100). For to see the universe as gift may well detach one from the intent of Heidegger's distinction, but it can hardly be proposed as liberating beings from Being—unless, of course, those very terms remain caught in a Heideggerian web of meaning.

The import of these three isogeses is to arrive at the One who can bestow the world as gift (146-48/100-02), and so liberate God to be God—from the impersonal "ontological difference" of *Sein/seiende* or the pretended conceptualizing of divinity as *ipsum esse*. So the polemic here is again primarily with Heidegger, where the *given* [*es gibt/il y a*] dispensed with any need for a giver, yet also with attempts to conceptualize God as *ousia*, and so falsely overcome the appropriate ontological difference, or otherness, which he names *la distance*. That *difference* is offered to us as "*agape* in Christ"(154/107), and only when we have so "crossed" 'God' can we "begin again to speak—but this time with joy and jubilation: offering praise"(154-55/107). But could one not also say—in fact, don't we need to if this One is to be the source of all that is?— that the One who *is*, whom no concept can capture, who has no essence except *to-be* and so "does not even belong to the genus of substance [*ousia*]"(ST 1.3.5.1); that such a One alone can give without gaining anything from the gift. Thus *agape*, and the praise that is the return appropriate to such a gift, is displayed in the One who is, and founded on the predication: God is the One who is— that name of names (ST 1.13.11). That name cannot be an idol, any more than *being* can be a concept, so it must be (in Marion's terms) and icon.

In short, the God who is portrayed for us in Robert Sokolowski's *God of Faith and Reason* by means of what he dubs "the distinction," or by the rules of discourse formulated by Kathryn Tanner in her *God and the Doctrine of Creation*, is utterly open to being "crossed" by the cross of Christ, but without thereby severing the connection with a free creator whose intrinsic mode of activity would have to be gift, since such a One could gain nothing from the transaction. Furthermore, so linking one's philosophical theology to that mode of inquiry natural to the human spirit will allow us to explore the intrinsic intelligibility of the ultimate gift of God in revelation. Far from releasing us to recognize that gift, by refusing to name the gift of creation as our very existence we are left hanging as to the meaning of the gift of redemption—left only with the name "gift." That move limits our theological inquiry to a biblical "positivism" which allows us only to thematize the texts of Scripture and prohibits us from exploring their interaction with the fruits of an inquiring reason. Martin D'Arcy, in his trenchant critique of Anders Nygren showed how disastrous it can be to human transformation to oppose *agape* to *eros*, yet that is in effect what Jean-Luc Marion is inviting us to do.[10]

---

[10] *Mind and Heart of Love* (London: Faber and Faber, 1945), responding to Anders Nygren, *Agape and Eros* (New York: Macmillan, 1939). I am indebted to several interlocutors at the American Maritain Association meeting in Irving, Texas, 5-7 November 1993, for improvements in this attempt at interpretation, notably to Merold Westphal. I can only hope that this final version reflects some of their perspective. Finally (June 1996) Marion's recent "Saint Thomas d'Aquin et l'onto-théo-logie," *Révue Thomiste* 95 (1995) 31-66, addresses the substance of this critique so thoroughly as to render it redundant *as* critique: Aquinas is recovered for who he is!

Quid Sit Postmodernismus?

John Deely

Early in his career Maritain wrote a book whose title haunted him through the remainder of that career: *Antimoderne*.[1] This was actually quite an interesting book, but the rhetoric of its title proved more than sufficient to defeat its message. More than half a century later, Brooke Williams posed the question in terms of *Jacques Maritain: Antimodern or Ultramodern?*, demonstrating that Maritain himself considered himself, in his own terms, the latter rather than the former.[2] But what does all this mean?

Contemporary philosophy considers itself not modern but postmodern, at least in what concerns the essential questions of ontology and epistemology, which is to say, in what concerns philosophy itself as transcending "fads and fashions," in what concerns whatever is perennial. What I would like to explore in this paper is the extent to which Maritain's "antimodernity" and "ultramodernity" meet the requirements of postmodernism in philosophy, and how postmodernism might be seen to relate to the Latin sources on which Maritain consistently drew.

1. WHICH LATIN SOURCES?

We face a problem concerning the sources right at the outset, and it is one on which each of us must make up our minds. When it comes to the understanding of St. Thomas Aquinas, is it to be allowed that there are even to be such a thing as sources other than the writings of Thomas himself? And if it is a question of philosophy in the writings of Aquinas, how serious are we to take St. Thomas' own injunction that authority is the weakest form of philosophical argument?

---

[1] Jacques Maritain, *Antimoderne* (Paris: Revue des Jeunes, 1922).

[2] Brooke Williams, *Jacques Maritain: Antimodern or Ultramodern?* (New York: Elsevier, 1976).

1.1. AQUINAS' TEXTS AS BOUNDARY:
THE GILSONIAN MODEL FOR AN AUTHENTIC THOMISM

The first of the two questions just posed is so extreme as to call into question the very possibility of a doctrinal tradition stemming from St. Thomas. You all recall the saying of Leibniz which serves as the best summary or maxim for the spirit of classical modern philosophy: "Monads have no windows." Monad was Leibniz's term for what Aristotle called rather substance. Each monad, of course, is alive (there are no inorganic monads); but the germane point is that each monad is enclosed in its own universe of representations and has no way beyond them.

My attention was first directed to this quintessentially Cartesian and solipsistic approach to St. Thomas by none other than Étienne Gilson himself, through a correspondence of some dozen or so letters we exchanged between 1968 and his death in 1978. Gilson himself, of course, did not call his approach Cartesian or Leibnizian, and would probably have been repelled by the suggestion. Yet his blindness on this point reveals him to be more modern than he realized, a point that will be germane to the upshot of our discussion.

To be fair to Gilson on this point, I would have to say that he adopted his approach not so much as a philosopher, but as an historian, and indeed one need not have personally met the two men, as I was fortunate enough to have done, in order to realize from reading them that in Maritain and Gilson we confront not only two great minds, but also two temperaments showing a constant bent or preference, the one for doctrine and philosophical development as such, the other for concrete textual expressions and circumstantially unique boundaries that enable us to place an idea not only in time but in culture as realized in the individual author of a given text. There is no question but that both men had philosophical minds of an exceptional caliber; but there is also no doubt that, within that philosophical bent, caution of historical scholarship characterized Gilson as typically as speculative daring characterized Maritain.

What safer route can there be to the thinking of a dead author than his very own words? This was the point that most struck Gilson. The nineteenth century revival of the study of St. Thomas Aquinas by Leo XIII translated into a concern in Gilson's mind to demonstrate the thought of Thomas Aquinas by using his actual vocabulary as a criterion of purity. Such practice would exclude from consideration work of later Latins who departed from that vocabulary, never mind that such departure would be perforce, inasmuch as there could be no way to apply philosophical principles to new questions (and new emphases on old questions) generated within their own social and cultural contexts *except* by sometimes an evolution and sometimes a creation of new vocabulary. In our correspondence, Gilson put it this way (letter of 10 July 1974): "I myself, who have lived in the familiarity of St. Thomas Aquinas, have not continued reading [John of St. Thomas] when I realized that he was not using the same language as that of our common master."

If our sole or even dominant concern is historical purity so far as that can be attained, it is hard to fault this approach. But if this attitude of linguistic limitation is adopted rather as a philosophical principle of interpretive methodology in its own right, we are on the road to a hermeneutic cul de sac, or perhaps I should say a hermetic hermeneutic. The Thomists of Gilson's school—and Maritain's own language of an "intuition of being," though I think it can be defended, is not without fault on this point—have applied to the matter of interpreting Aquinas a method in effect Cartesian: there is but a single optic, discovered only in our day, which allows for a correct reading of the Aquinian corpus. Viewed through this optic, each of the commentators of the period of Classical Thomism[3]— Capreolus (c.1380-1444), Thomas de Vio Cajetan (1468-1534), Ferrariensis (c.1474-1528), Francisco Vitoria (1492/3-1546), Dominic Soto (1494-1560), Melchior Cano (1509-1560), Domingo Bañez (1528-1604), and John Poinsot (1589-1644)—appears (or is claimed to appear) to be an unreliable interpreter, either because the commentator fails to stress to the modern reader's satisfaction the centrality of *esse* as became the fashion of the Thomistic revival (limited exception on this point is made for Bañez), or because, as has been said, the commentator, in dealing with problems beyond the purview of Aquinas' focal concerns in any given text, perforce introduces terminology not to be found in the master and therefore suspect.

In a letter of 28 August 1968, Gilson wrote to me in this regard that "'A thomist' of whatever brand should find it superfluous to develop a question which Thomas was content to pass over with a few words," because

> it is very difficult to develop such a question with any certitude of doing so along the very line he himself would have followed, had he developed it. If we develop it in the wrong way, we engage his doctrine in some no thoroughfare [dead-end], instead of keeping it on the threshold his own thought has refused to cross, and which, to him, was still an assured truth.[4]

---

[3] I have explained the designation "Classical Thomism" in an article titled "Metaphysics, Modern Thought, and 'Thomism'" written for *Notes et Documents* (Rome), which, unfortunately, was published from uncorrected proofs, but provides nonetheless a sound outline of what is at issue.

[4] In 1940, Mortimer J. Adler published a volume he proposed to be the first in a series of "Problems for Thomists," namely, *The Problem of Species* (New York: Sheed & Ward, 1940). He followed this book with an article, "Solution of the Problem of Species," *The Thomist* 3 (April), 279-379, in turn followed by two further discussions, "The Hierarchy of Essences," *The Review of Metaphysics* VI (September), 3-30 and "The Philosophers Give All the Answers

Gerald McCool, in writing his study *From Unity to Pluralism. The Internal Evolution of Thomism*,[5] had no access, as far as I know, to this correspondence. He did not have to. The attitude in question permeates the writings of the Gilsonian school. The fine line between a historical principle of methodological

---

and Establish None," in *The Difference of Man and the Difference It Makes* (New York: Holt, 1967), Chap. 4. In all of this, Maritain was an intimate participant, both through his "Foreword" to the original publication, his defense of the work against hostile reviewers titled "Solution of the Problem of Species," *The Thomist* 3 (April), 279-379, and through correspondence with Adler on the question of species which I was able to read during my tenure (1969-1974) as a Senior Research Fellow at Adler's Institute for Philosophical Research in Chicago. Through my own study under Raymond J. Nogar, author of *The Wisdom of Evolution* (Garden City: New York: Doubleday and Co., 1963) and later work with him—John Deely and Raymond Nogar, *The Problem of Evolution* (New York: Appleton-Century-Crofts, 1973)—I had myself become interested in the question of species in the context of Aristotelian and Thomistic natural philosophy, and had occasion to address the problem at length in a work which had the full benefit of Maritain's and Adler's earlier reflections on the problem, "The Philosophical Dimensions of the Origin of Species," *The Thomist* 33 (January and April 1969), Part I, 75-149, Part II, 251-342.

In a series of letters—beginning with mine of October 21, 1969, sending my article to Gilson, followed by his two-page reply of November 3, my seven-page sequel of November 7, and five more pages from Gilson dated November 14—Gilson and I discussed various aspects of the problematic. In his last letter of the series, toward the end, Gilson returned to what seems always to have been his central point (italics added): What is to you the main issue of your paper is one on which I have no definite opinion at all. *I mean: I do not know what St. Thomas would say were he living in our times.*"

Later Gilson, in a series of three lectures delivered at Toronto (1972), put his own hand to the question which, for him, Shook, in his biography, *Étienne Gilson* (Toronto: Pontifical Institute of Mediaeval Studies, 1984), 387, tells us "turned out to be particularly intractable." Indeed it is, but, given his manner of reliance on the medieval text, the intractability would have to prove terminal. And so it did. He wrote to Armand Maurer, in a letter dated August 20, 1971 (cited in Shook, *ibid.*): "I have suffered 'aches and pains' reading and rereading Adler and Deely on the subject. . . . What they say is irrelevant to the authentic thought of St. Thomas."

When I first read these lines the year the Shook biography appeared, I still had not grasped the "Aquinas' texts as boundary" concept under which Gilson constantly labored in philosophy, and remember feeling both somewhat hurt and glad that I had not turned over to Shook my full correspondence with Gilson, since already my experience with the "Gilsonians" as such had led me to distrust their attitude toward the work of Poinsot ("John of St. Thomas"), and the context for refuting their prejudices, which I intended to create through the publication of the *Tractatus de Signis* and related works, did not yet exist.

Now that I better understand the genius and the methodological limits of Gilson's approach, his dismissal of Adler's and my work in the area, which was as much a dismissal of Maritain himself, appears in its proper perspective and can be regretted without any need for disappointment. It is simply a fact that, for Gilson, there could be no "problems for Thomists" in the sense Adler proposed and Maritain pursued.

⁵ Gerald McCool, *From Unity to Pluralism. The Internal Evolution of Thomism* (New York: Fordham University Press, 1992).

purity and a philosophical principle of textual interpretation McCool crosses roughshod in his analysis of "The End of the Neo-Thomistic Movement:"

> St. Thomas' great contribution is his metaphysics of the act of existence which no other scholastic, including the great Thomistic commentators, really understood.
> Therefore Cajetan, Bañez, and John of St. Thomas had all lost their grip on St. Thomas' own philosophy. . . . the authentic philosophy and theology of the Angelic Doctor has not been transmitted to modern Thomists in the systematic philosophy and theology of his great commentators, and it could never be found there. *Although Gilson never said so explicitly, according to his criteria,* the Thomism of *The Degrees of Knowledge* is not authentic Thomism. *The true philosophy and theology of the Angelic Doctor can be found only by the individual historian and the philosopher who bypasses the commentators and approaches St. Thomas directly in the texts of his own theological works. Therefore there is no such thing as a Thomist movement. There is no such thing as the authentic transmission of St. Thomas' thought through a 'doctrinal tradition.' . . . The only true Thomists are the individual philosophers who discover him for themselves in the original sources of this thought and then become his disciples. The Thomists can have only one master,* St. Thomas himself, and, as philosophers, they have yet to find a better one. . . .[6]

If I needed an interpretant to assure me of what seemed to me years ago the dubious implication of Gilson's letters, McCool has provided it. I doubt that McCool has thought through the implications of his assessment, for it means that, as far as there is a question of understanding St. Thomas, reading McCool is perforce as much a waste of time as reading Cajetan or Maritain or, for that matter, Gilson. There can be no teachers in the world of authentic Thomism, only the individual philosopher, bypassing all commentators, who approaches the texts of St. Thomas directly. Never mind that there are also other individuals who have undertaken the task of mastering these texts. They must be disregarded completely—and so, for consistency, must the individual interpreter himself by all other would-be interpreters. A community of inquirers is ruled out from the start and in principle. That there has been a historical handful before us who had developed an intimate acquaintance with the complete range of Aquinas' writings and made this acquaintance a common reference point, along with reason itself, in the evaluation of theoretical issues in philosophy is to count for nothing. In the universe of authentic Thomism so conceived, there is only the text of Aquinas and the individual reading that text for himself or herself, that is

---

[6] Gerald McCool, *From Unity to Pluralism,* 226-7, italics added.
[7] "Why don't we quietly enjoy truth as we see it in the light of the authentic texts of Thomas Aquinas? I detest controversy," is how Gilson put it to me in a letter of 14 January 1973.

all. Every man his own Thomist, so to speak. A monad without windows; that is to say, a quintessentially modern interpreter.[7]

Of course this model becomes, at a certain point, preposterous. But no less so than was the original modern presumption of Descartes to shrive his mind of all influence from society and history an illusion (a transcendental one at that, inasmuch as it contained within itself the clues of previous—by definition historical—influences, as Gilson was to demonstrate in his doctoral work published in 1913). When we speak of postmodernism, we are confronting here the *type* of presupposition that is being abandoned.

Moreover, in dealing with the literature of the Gilsonian school, we will find this over and over again: methodological principles, faultless in themselves *ad hoc*, elevated to the status of hermeneutic principles. Let me mention the main one. McCool mentions "the Thomistic philosophy which had come into being in the seventeenth-century" (where did he do his 14th, 15th and 16th century history?), practitioners of which "had extracted their 'theses' from *both* St. Thomas' theological works *and* his commentaries on Aristotle." By contrast, Gilson restricted "the historical sources of St. Thomas' philosophy to the Angelic Doctor's theological works" and "to the descending theological order in its exposition," and "he held firmly to both practices in his exposition of medieval Christian philosophy."[8]

Again, Gilson's practice is methodologically faultless *ad hoc*. But as an exceptionless hermeneutic principle it is equally indefensible. For in fact the so-called "schools" in question hardly came into being in the 17th century. In the case of Maritain's sources, the 17th century commentator in question was the successor at Alcalá to Dominic Soto after a hundred years, and Soto himself as a graduate student had come to Alcalá fresh from the University of Paris where Thomas himself had been professor less than three centuries earlier. The history of the early generations of "authentic Thomists"—no monads they—is much more tangled than the Gilsonians would give us to understand, for reasons I cannot discuss here but go over in the forthcoming book, *New Beginnings*. If the commentators of the period of classical Thomism drew *both on* the theological works of St. Thomas *and* on his commentaries on Aristotle, it was hardly because of their "error" in equating "the philosophy of St. Thomas with the philosophy of Aristotle," as McCool reiterates,[9] but rather because, being men of the period, they fully understood that philosophy, even "Christian philosophy" (a complex term concerning which Maritain came to have his

---

[8] Gerald McCool, *From Unity to Pluralism. The Internal Evolution of Thomism* (n. 5 above), 170.

[9] *Ibid.*, 169.

reservations, as Korn points out),[10] could not be "identified with the speculative element contained within medieval theology itself."[11]

Being men of the period, themselves involved in the enterprise, Thomas's Latin commentators better understood than McCool or Gilson the literary genres proper to the expression of the thought of the times. And if they drew on the commentaries of Aquinas on Aristotle in interpreting the thought of Aquinas *as well as* on the theological writings, it was because they knew full well that the commentaries explained Aristotle no less *ad mentem commentatoris* than *ad literam textus commentati*. No doubt the thought of Aquinas is purest in his theological writings. But that does not mean that a purity of thought proper to him is absent in his commentaries on Aristotle; it is only more subtly expressed at worst. Being near contemporaries, it was not as difficult for the early Thomistic authors to differentiate expressions proper to the two genres as it is for us today after centuries of desuetude have separated us from all the Latin sources in question. As a methodological tool for gaining a first approximation of the thought proper to Aquinas in his own right, the approach of Gilson is faultless. As a principle of philosophical hermeneutics ruling out the text of the commentaries once and for all in the understanding of Aquinas' thought, the approach is indefensible.

1.2. AQUINAS' TEXTS AS CENTRE:
THE MARITAINIAN MODEL FOR AN AUTHENTIC THOMISM

Maritain, it is true, relied from the first on an author anathema to the *ad hoc* hermeneutic principles of Gilson. He told us so himself, both early[12] and late.[13] McCool constantly refers to "the Thomism of Cajetan and John of St. Thomas on which Maritain depended," as though the two were on equal footing in the

---

[10] "Pour parler de la philosophie considérée en son état existentiel qui est celui de la raison en régime chrétien, Jacques Maritain a souvent employé le terme de 'philosophie chrétienne.' Si aujord'hui il propose de la désigner par un autre mot, c'est d'abord parce que le nom de philosophie chrétienne évoque trop l'idée d'une philosophie non pas libre, mais liée par on ne sait quelles convenances d'ordre confessionelle. Il y a cependant une raison plus profonde pour changer le vocabulaire sur ce point. C'est que le term de 'philosophie chrétienne' risque de masquer aux yeux de notre esprit que nous avons affaire ici, non plus à la philosophie prise comme simplement telle, mais à la philosophie parvenue à sa pleine maturité, à la *philosophie comme plénièrement telle*. Dans le fond, ce qui est en jeu ici est bien plus qu'un changement de vocabulaire." (Ernst R. Korn, the pen name of Heinz R. Schmitz, one of Maritain's three literary executors, in his "Préface" to Maritain's 1973 work, *Approches sans Entraves*).

[11] *Ibid.*, 170.

[12] Jacques Maritain, *Antimoderne* (Paris: Revue des Jeunes, 1922).

[13] Jacques Maritain, *The Peasant of the Garonne; an Old Layman Questions Himself about the Present Time* (New York: Holt, Rinehart and Winston, 1968), 149.

thought of Maritain. But they were not. Cajetan Maritain knew and respected; but Poinsot was the principal source of his epistemology, and for a very good reason.

If we look to St. Thomas for the theory of knowledge, we do not find a finished, in the sense of integrated, theory, although we find indeed all the basics: an irreducible variety of nature, power, act, and product, all essential to the understanding of the subjectivity of the knower in its possibility as a finite knower. But how these pieces fit together is not settled in Aquinas, and it is useless to pretend otherwise. In the texts of Aquinas himself there are loose ends that need to be tied up, and this is no less true whether we approach his texts with the help of others familiar with its turnings or "on our own" *à la* the monads of authentic Gilsonian Thomism reduced to its extreme in McCool's book.

In this context it is ironic to find one of Gilson's principal disciples, in a work sponsored by Gilson himself, criticizing Occam on the ground that he has "no signs or likenesses whose whole function is to lead to a knowledge of something else, and which are not themselves direct objects of knowledge."[14] The irony is heightened by Gilson's own identification of Occam's notion of concepts as "natural signs" as "the only difficulty there is in understanding Ockham,"[15] a difficulty compounded by the almost exceptionless use of these notions under the designation "formal sign" by the contemporary Thomists determined, alongside Gilson and Maritain, to vanquish idealism from the philosophical arena (e.g., Simon, Wild, Veatch, Adler).

For neither are signs in the requisite sense found unequivocally in the work of Aquinas himself. Only one thinker in the long history of these questions actually undertook to systematize the multi-faceted writings of Aquinas himself on this particular point and reduce them to a thematic unity, and he did so not *in vacuo*, but precisely as a respectful student of those before him who had studied Aquinas as well as of the texts of Aquinas himself, and also as a rational animal confronted with data of experience in the light of which the texts of anyone, Aquinas included, need above all to be evaluated if it is to be a question of philosophy.

That thinker was John Poinsot, a man of Portuguese education and birth principally introduced to Aquinas as a graduate student at Louvain by a Spanish Dominican, and thereafter devoted to the exposition and rationalization of

---

[14] Armand Maurer, *Medieval Philosophy* (New York: Random House, 1962), 285, being Volume II of a projected 4-volume *History of Philosophy* under the general editorship of Étienne Gilson.

[15] Étienne Gilson, *History of Christian Philosophy in the Middle Ages* (New York: Random House, 1955), 491.

Thomistic thought for the remainder of his life. To this thinker Jacques Maritain turned principally for illumination in reading the texts of Aquinas on the subject of knowledge and epistemology generally. And what illumination he found!

Many and devoted as the students of Maritain are, there are few who have viewed his work in the light principally of his Latin sources. Those few who have done that have uniformly recognized, whether with chagrin or interest, that Maritain's epistemological theorizing follows step-by-step in the footsteps of John Poinsot as an interpreter of Aquinas on the subject of knowledge, in particular as regards the necessary product of the activity of finite knowing in order to achieve correlation with an object as terminus of that activity, namely, the production of a concept in the most generic sense as including, over and above the level of bare sensation prescissively considered as such, *phantasiari* and *intelligere*, or, as we would be inclined today to say, perception, imagination, and understanding.

One of the earliest theoretical confrontations between Gilson and Maritain came precisely in this area of knowledge and its relation to objects. In this debate neither of the two ever really gave ground. Maritain summarized his own point of view in the section of *The Degrees of Knowledge* titled "Critical Realism."[16] This summary was preceded in that work by a most remarkable statement,[17] wherein Maritain qualified his commitment to a philosophy "ordered to a knowledge of things" by dismissing the "unreasonable prejudices" which led those under their sway to proceed "as if a philosophy of being could not also be a philosophy of mind" ("comme si une philosophie de l'être ne pouvait être aussi une philosophie de l'esprit"). Later[18] he would say further that "looking at things" is "not as simple as might appear" ("ce qui n'est pas si commode que ça"); but this was because his model for an authentic Thomism took seriously not only the texts themselves of Aquinas—all of them, and not just the theological writings—but equally, and, in the end, especially, reason and experience itself as hermeneutic principles in the light of which all texts, including those of Aquinas, must be read and through which alone we are assured of contact with our contemporaries and historical situation vis-à-vis being itself.

Neither historical principles of methodological purity nor hermeneutical principles of textual exegesis separately or combined define the boundaries of Maritain's model for an authentic Thomism as "the only philosophy that claims to face the universality of the extramental real without at the same stroke

[16] Jacques Maritain, *Distinguish to Unite, or The Degrees of Knowledge*, trans. from the 4th French ed. under the supervision of Gerald B. Phelan (New York: Scribner's), 71ff.

[17] *Ibid.*, 66.

[18] Jacques Maritain, *The Peasant of the Garonne*, 137/203.

[19] Jacques Maritain, *Distinguish to Unite, or The Degrees of Knowledge*, 66.

pretending to absorb all knowing into itself."[19] How stark does his model contrast with that we have seen McCool derive from Gilson:[20]

> Given a chance to reveal its own nature, Thomistic philosophy exhibits the gait and demeanor characteristic of all philosophy; a demeanor and gait fully at liberty to confront the real. *The philosopher swears fidelity to no person, nor any school—not even, if he is a Thomist, to the letter of St. Thomas and every article of his teaching. He is sorely in need of teachers and of a tradition, but in order for them to teach him to think when he looks at things* (which is not as simple as all that), and not, as is the case with the theologian, so that he can assume the whole of this tradition into his thought. *Once this tradition has instructed him, he is free of it and makes use of it for his own work.* In this sense, *he is alone in the face of being; for his task is to think over that which is.*

1.3. WHICH MODEL?

We see in the end how different are the models of Thomism implicit in the work of Gilson and explicit in the work of Maritain. The Gilsonian Thomist is alone before the texts of Aquinas. The Maritainian Thomist confronts the texts of Aquinas in the company of all those before him—they are not all that many—who have similarly undertaken to view these texts in their totality, and not simply *to use them* here and there. The Thomist in Maritain's view is from the first a member of a community of inquirers, virtual and open-ended in time; and he is not only a part of that community, he is also an individual thinker with his own experiences and insights to render in the service of truth and humanity. As such, he is alone only before being, the adequate object of understanding considered as such, which it is his responsibility to articulate according to his best lights and interests as these relate to the truth about things. St. Thomas is a first among equals, but still himself a thinker before being.

Perhaps in the end the choice is no more than the choice between a historian's philosopher and a philosopher's philosopher, between taking responsibility for a thought in the past or for the future of thought so far as the future depends on us.[21] There is room for both, and both are necessary, but for any individual, at least at any given time, one or other must predominate.

---

[20] Jacques Maritain, *The Peasant of the Garonne*, 137. Italics added.

[21] "Your friend Jacques Maritain has left us in possession of a very remarkable book of nearly 600 pages, *Approches sans Entraves*. I regret very much not to have read it in its entirety thirty years ago. It would have made me understand the true nature of his attitude towards Thomas Aquinas, as well as the true nature of what he considered my historicism. . . . There is at least one thing I can say: during my whole life, I have misunderstood his true intention. "If you come to Paris next spring, and if I am still in Paris, please reserve me the

2. WHICH INSIGHTS?

The end of modernity is no tragedy for a Maritainian. Indeed, it is a relief. The coils of modernity oppressed Maritain from the moment he discovered Thomism. A philosophy of being thrives ill in a milieu which conceives of consciousness itself as a closed whole providing its own objects under the provocation of a stimulus unknowable in principle and in itself. All of his energies as a philosopher, practically speaking, Maritain devoted to bringing down the edifice of modern idealism, to demonstrating the illegitimacy of Descartes' patrimony. For him, as for Gilson, it seemed that the best and only way to achieve this was through a vindication of realism, a way he found in the end "not as simple as all that," and for good reason, as Heidegger best pointed out.[22]

He had not yet realized, I think, at least not as fully as the overthrow of modernity in philosophy requires, the reality of experience in its own right as the medium though which things are revealed in the first place and finally, only sometimes, known.[23] In this regard, it is necessary to go beyond Maritain, in the

---

pleasure of a luncheon with you at the Relai de Sèvres. . . . I hope you will then have read the book of Jacques and tell me if you have always understood him better than I have. I trust you did, for I did not understand him at all. He was right in reproaching me with sticking to history when it was a question of understanding the true meaning of Thomism. I still cannot think differently; but I quite agree that, till now, the great Thomists have always felt free to interpret it in their own ways. Including Poinsot!" — letter of 4 January 1974.

[22] Martin Heidegger, *Sein und Zeit* (7th ed.; Tübingen: Niemeyer, 1963), trans. John MacQuarrie and Edward Robinson as *Being and Time* (New York: Harper & Row, 1962), paginated to the German in the margins. "As compared with realism, *idealism*, no matter how contrary and untenable it may be in its results, has an advantage in principle, provided that it does not misunderstand itself as 'psychological' idealism. If idealism emphasizes that Being and Reality are only 'in the consciousness', this expresses an understanding of the fact that Being cannot be explained through entities. But as long as idealism fails to clarify what this very understanding of Being means ontologically, or how this understanding is possible, or that it belongs to Dasein's state of Being, the Interpretation of Reality which idealism constructs is an empty one. . . .

"If what the term 'idealism' says, amounts to the understanding that Being can never be explained by entities but is already that which is 'transcendental' for every entity, then idealism affords the only correct possibility for a philosophical problematic. If so, Aristotle was no less an idealist than Kant." Nor was Aquinas! See Vincent Guagliardo, "Being-as-First-Known in Poinsot," *American Catholic Philosophical Quarterly*, 68.3 (Summer 1994), 363-393.

[23] John Deely, "Philosophy and Experience," in *ACPQ* LXVI.3 (Summer, 1992), 299-319. But, see also Brooke Williams, *Jacques Maritain: Antimodern or Ultramodern?* (New York: Elsevier, 1976); Brooke Williams, "The Historian as Observer," in *Semiotics 1982*, ed. John Deely and Jonathan Evans (Lanham, MD: University of America, 1987), 13-25; Brooke Williams, "History as A Semiotic Anomaly," in *Semiotics 1983*, ed. Jonathan Evans

direction indicated by his own sources, the epistemological theory of St. Thomas as thematized in the work of John of St. Thomas, John Poinsot.

2.1. THE MEANING OF POSTMODERNISM

Postmodernism is a concept in search of a definition. There is no hurry. Definitions are unavoidable, and tend to take care of themselves over time. One of the defining elements of postmodernism that has already made itself unmistakable, however, is the idea that the work of philosophy must proceed through a study of history in order to achieve its best results, and this aspect of postmodernism is most congenial to the followers of Gilson and Maritain alike, albeit in different ways. It is ironic that while it was Gilson who established the analogy according to which history provides for the philosopher what the laboratory provides for the scientist, namely, the arena in which the consequences of ideas are played out,[24] he left it to Maritain to verify the application of this analogy to the understanding of the texts of Aquinas himself through a judicious consultation with the commentators as well.[25]

---

and John Deely (Lanham, MD: University Press of America, 1987), 409-419; Brooke Williams, "Foreword" (Collingwood in Relation to Semiotic) to Russell 1984: vii-xx; Brooke Williams, "What Has History To Do with Semiotic?," *Semiotica* 54.1/2, 267-333; preprinted in revised monograph form with index and historically layered bibliography under the title *History and Semiotic* (Victoria College of the University of Toronto: Toronto Semiotic Circle Number 4, Summer 1985); Brooke Williams, "Challenging Signs at the Crossroads," prefatory essay to Thomas A. Sebeok, *Contributions to the Doctrine of Signs* (Sources in Semiotics IV; uncorrected reprint edition of 1976 original; Lanham, MD: University Press of America, 1985), xv-xlii; Brooke Williams, "History in Relation to Semiotic," reprint with modest revisions of 1983 above in Deely, Williams, and Kruse 1986: 217-223; Brooke Williams, "Introducing Semiotic to Historians," paper presented in the first AHA History and Semiotics session, at the One Hundred Second Annual Meeting of the American Historical Association, Washington, DC, 27-30 December 1987; available on microfilm or in xerographic form as part of the *Proceedings of the American Historical Association, 1987*, reference #10485 (University Microfilms International, Ann Arbor, MI); Brooke Williams, "Historiography as a Current Event," in *Semiotics 1987*, ed. John Deely (Lanham, MD: University Press of America, 1988), 479-486; Brooke Williams, "Opening Dialogue between the Discipline of History and Semiotics," in *The Semiotic Web: 1987*, ed. Thomas A. Sebeok and Donna Jean Umiker-Sebeok (Berlin: Mouton de Gruyter, 1988), 821-834; Brooke Williams and William Pencak, Special Issue on History, *Semiotica* 83.3/4, and William Pencak, *History, Signing In* (New York: Peter Lang, 1993).

[24] Étienne Gilson, *The Unity of Philosophical Experience* (New York: Charles Scribner's Sons, 1937).

[25] ". . . Brentano, Husserl, and others *ejusdem farinae*, mean nothing to me. I say nothing of Poinsot because I do not know him well enough. All I can say is that I feel perfectly satisfied with Aristotle and Thomas and I can find no continuous thread that goes from them to

What Maritain did alone and as a pioneer in this regard I think is soon to become a staple of the curriculum in philosophical studies, namely, to view the early modern development—the influence of Descartes and Locke—not teleologically with regard to the mainstream growth of classical modern philosophy but contextually both in retrospect and in prospect: in retrospect with an eye to what of Latin developments modern philosophy obliterated in the area of epistemology especially, and in prospect of our current situation as finally become aware of the ubiquity of signs as the means whereby and medium wherein alone knowledge of whatever sort is acquired, developed, and communicated.

2.2. CYCLOPEAN THOMISM

No one among the Thomists save only Maritain's principal teacher on these points went as far as Maritain in understanding the semiotic nature of knowledge and the consequent priority of relation over substance in the constitution of objects of experience as such. Experience is not of things first of all but of objects which are only partially and not in all aspects things. Hence being as experienced, what Aquinas called *ens ut primum cognitum* or the *ens quod primum in intellectu cadit*, is not first of all real being only but being as objective, that is, as Thomas himself makes quite clear once one has been clued to the problem,[26] being as an irreducible admixture of mind-dependent and mind-independent relations constituting at their intersections the objects of everyday life, such as judges and policemen, doctors and teachers, classmates and strangers, etc. It is true that within this experience of an objective world there is a privileged moment when it is realized that not all objects reduce to our experience of them, and that, consequently, objects reveal to us not only themselves and their sign-linkages to other objects, but an act of existence which is exercised on the side of things in themselves in their contrast with objects as reducible to experience. This intuition of being, if we want to use Maritain's expression for it, is of the first importance for metaphysics, and is of a piece with understanding as a mode of consciousness distinctive of the human among

---

Cajetan and on, till the epistemology of our contemporaries. Nor do I experience any need to connect them in any way. I simply have no philosophical use for what is not plain realism and empirical method of Aristotle. I am not writing in order to convince others, but to achieve a clear awareness of what I think. I am not too successful even in doing that, and I very much admire the friends who, like Jacques Maritain and yourself, are trying to convert the Gentiles; but that kind of work is not for me." — letter from Gilson of 18 April 1973.

[26] See Aquinas, *De Veritate* q.1, art. 1 *corpus*, glossed in John Deely, *The Human Use of Signs* (Lanham, MD: Rowman & Littlefield, 1994) Part IV.

animals. But it is a mistake to see in metaphysics, as the neo-Thomists were wont to do, nothing more than the explication of this notion. For alongside it, and of a piece with it, there is *also* given the notion of a non-being essential to the existence even of things not in their own being but in their being for us as experienced or known in the first place.

Maritain knew this, though it was only late in his life that he began to realize its importance for the contemporary situation and, I would say, what would become its centrality for the emergence of postmodernism. "Once one has become conscious of non-being and of its formidable role in reality," he wrote,[27] one begins to see that "the paths of non-being are as difficult as those of being," and require of Thomism that it "open onto the avenues of non-being windows as large as those open onto the avenues of being." In making those remarks, Maritain was developing *ex professo* a seminar on the problem of human freedom and evil in the universe. He criticized his masters in this regard[28]—naming Bañez, Poinsot, and the Carmelites of Salamanca (harking back to the time of *Antimoderne*)—not for being "rigid" but for being "'Cyclopean' Thomists because they had their eyes fixed solely on the perspective of being."

But Maritain himself had been guilty of the Cyclopean approach, along with Gilson and the Gilsonians, to such an extent that he himself had missed an early and probably best opportunity to get beyond the rigid opposition of realism to idealism by transcending the modern problematic from the outset. Maritain prided himself from the first in being *antimoderne*. What too few of his readers realized and what he himself was not always successful in clarifying is that this did not constitute a call for a return to an early perspective already established and finished, say, in the texts of St. Thomas himself, still less in those of the great commentators. The problem was not to go backwards but forwards, to get beyond modernity, and for this outcome the strategy he shared in common with Gilson of vindicating realism was not adequate.

Modernity had mired itself in idealism because it had misunderstood the nature of knowing and of concepts as the means of knowing. Realism cannot address this question directly, because to address it directly requires the adoption of a perspective which is prior to the positions of realism and idealism alike and defines their prior possibility *as* positions that can be adopted in the first place. Being as first known—*ens ut primum cognitum seu quod primum cadit in intellectu*—provides a principle according to which the requirements of

---

[27] Jacques Maritain, *Dieu et la permission du mal* (Paris: Desclée de Brouwer, 1963) English trans. by Joseph Evans, *God and the Permission of Evil* (Milwaukee: Bruce, 1966), 32. Three seminars given in Toulouse (May 1962). Page references in the present essay are to the Evans trans.

[28] *Ibid.*, 14.

experience can be sorted out, but it puts us in touch not only with real being but with real being wrapped up with nonbeing through objectivity and the being of experience as the milieu within which alone objects, including those which are also things, exist as known.

2.3. BEFORE REALISM AND IDEALISM

In his own analysis of the problem of thing and object,[29] true to the Cyclopean concern of Thomism to vindicate the mind's capacity to grasp within objects being exercised independently of the knowing, Maritain concentrated on the fundamental Thomistic point that external sense, prescissively distinguished from internal sense and understanding, makes no use of concepts and images but places us in a direct predicamental or categorial relation with the material substances of the environment not, indeed, as substances, but as existing here and now through their action upon the senses. When it came to the concept itself, however, carefully as he studied the texts of St. Thomas and perused the tying up of textual loose ends by John of St. Thomas,[30] and though he achieved a profundity of analysis in the area of knowing unmatched by any other among the Thomists of modern times, Maritain yet missed a point in his masters that pointed a way directly beyond the problematic of modernity and established at a stroke a postmodern situation for a philosophy of being and knowledge. This was the point made by Poinsot in opening his *Tractatus de Signis*,[31] the point

---

[29] For example, in Jacques Maritain, *Distinguish to Unite, or The Degrees of Knowledge*, 90ff.

[30] Aquinas had qualified in passing in a number of contexts but never thematized the point that the classical definition of sign from Augustine is too narrow to cover the function of concepts as *aliquid stans pro alio*, a point that would be taken up fiercely by later Parisian doctors. In commenting on these various contexts spanning the professorial career of Aquinas—c.1254-1256: the *Commentary on the Sentences of Peter Lombard*, Book IV, dist. 1, q. 1, quaestiunc. 2; c.1256-1259: the *Disputed Questions on Truth*, q. 4. art. 1 ad 7, q. 9. art. 4 ad 4 and ad 5; c.1269-1272: the *Questions at Random*, q. 4, art. 17; c.1266-1273/ 4: the *Summa theologiae* III, q. 60, art. 4 ad 1—and synthesizing their import, Poinsot is able to conclude only that "in sententia S. Thomae probabilius est signum formale esse vere et proprie signum, atque adeo univoce cum instrumentali" (*Tractatus de Signis*, Book II, Question 1, "Utrum sit univoca et bona divisio signi in formale et instrumentale," 225/11-14), nicely illustrating Maritain's observation, in his "Preface" to the translation by Yves R. Simon *et al.*, *The Material Logic of John of St. Thomas* (Chicago: The University of Chicago Press, 1955), vi, that "Men like Cajetan and John of St. Thomas set such an example of exacting respect for the genuine thought of Aquinas that their guidance is a most effective protection against the risk of ignoring the historical evolution of problems."

[31] John Poinsot, *Tractatus de Signis. The Semiotic of John Poinsot*, ed. John Deely, in consultation with Ralph A. Powell (Berkeley, California: University of California Press, 1985), 181/1-14.

most central to the analyses to come and, at the same time, most presuppositioned
by the analyses of relation that preceded that treatise: "loquimur hic de relatione
secundum esse . .. quia loquimur de signo in communi, prout includit tam
signum naturale quam ad placitum, in quo involvitur etiam signum quod est
aliquod rationis . . . iuxta doctrinam D. Thomae 1. p. q. 28. art. 1. . . . quod solum
in his, quae sunt ad aliquid, invenitur aliqua relatio realis et aliqua rationis. . . ."[32]

---

[32] "Primo arguitur loco illo D. Thomae satis noto, sed difficili, 1. p. q. 28. art. 1., ubi dicit,
quod solum in his, quae sunt ad aliquid, inveniuntur aliqua secundum rem et aliqua secundum
rationem. Quae verba multis difficilia visa sunt. Nam vel loquitur D. Thomas de relatione
praedicamentali vel de relatione, prout abstrahit a reali et rationis. Si primo modo, falsum est in
relatione praedicamentali inveniri relationes rationis, vel falso diximus ad relationem
praedicamentalem requiri, quod sit realis. Si secundo modo, verum est in relatione sic abstracta
utramque reperiri, scilicet realem et rationis, sed falsum est hoc solum reperiri in relatione.
Nam etiam in substantia potest aliquid ficte concipi, quod dicetur substantia rationis, sicut
chimaera, hircocervus et similia, et in quantitate spatium imaginarium et similia in aliis generibus.
Ergo non in sola relatione invenitur aliquid rationis. Et auget difficultatem responsio Caietani
ibidem, quod relatio peculiariter hoc habet, quod esse in ratione non est conditio diminuens,
sed est vera relatio illa, quae est rationis; constat enim, quod si esset vera relatio, vere faceret
referre subiectum et non ficte, atque adeo neque per apprehensionem, sed realiter.

"Haec difficultas occasionem praebuit multis sinistre intelligendi Divum Thomam aut minus
bene philosophandi de relatione. <Quidam> enim existimant relationem realem partiri in duos
conceptus, scilicet in conceptum accidentis, quem vocant in, et respectum, quem vocant ad; et
primum esse realem, secundum rationis vel abstrahere a reali et rationis. <Alii [notably Suarez
in his *Disputationes Metaphysicae* disp.47, sect. 3, par. 5]> existimant solum voluisse D.
Thomam significare, quod potest aliquid excogitari per rationem ad instar relationis
praedicamentalis. <Alii> denique, quod loquitur de relatione, ut abstrahit a reali et rationis.

"Sed <primi> veram realitatem in praedicamento relationis, si id, quod est proprium talis
praedicamenti, scilicet respectus et ratio ad, non realizatur. <Secundi>^15 non dicunt aliquid
peculiare relationis, ut S. Thomas ponit, quia etiam possunt aliqua entia rationis formari ad
similitudinem aliorum generum, v. g. ad instar substantiae et quantitatis etc.

"Quare <tertia> expositio quantum ad unum verissima est, scilicet quod D. Thomas loquitur
de relatione in tota sua latitudine, ut abstrahit a reali et rationis. Neque enim dixit S. Doctor,
quod in praedicamento Ad aliquid inveniuntur aliqua secundum rationem, sed absolute dixit
'in his, quae sunt ad aliquid', ut significaret se non loqui de relatione, ut determinate est genus,
sed absolute secundum se. Quod deberent aliqui attendere, qui minus sollicite legunt S.
Doctorem. Itaque loquitur Divus Thomas de relatione sub formalissimo conceptu ad et significat,
quod ex illa parte, qua consideratur ad terminum, et positive se habet et non est determinate
realis forma, sed permittit, quod sit ens reale vel rationis; licet ad praedicamentale et fundatum
reale sit. Et ita non voluit D. Thomas significare, quae relatio sit realis vel quae rationis, sed ex
qua parte habet relatio, quod possit esse realis vel rationis, scilicet ex parte, qua est ad terminum;
licet enim ibi realitatem habere possit, non tamen inde. Quod expressit S. Doctor in 1. ad
Annibaldum dist. 26. q. 2. art. 1. dicens, 'quod relatio potest dupliciter considerari, uno modo
quantum ad id, ad quod dicitur, ex quo rationem relationis habet, et quantum ad hoc non habet,
quod ponat aliquid, quamvis etiam ex hoc non habeat, quod nihil sit; sunt enim quidam respectus,
qui sunt aliquid secundum rem, quidam vero, qui nihil. Alio modo quantum ad id, in quo est,
et sic quando habet eam in subiecto, realiter inest'. Sic D. Thomas.

When you come to think of it, this is actually a rather dramatic point. John of St. Thomas is tracing the basic insight of his doctrine of signs as accounting for the origins and structure of experience as irreducible to subjective being, whether physical or psychical, to Aquinas' treatment of the Trinity as a community of persons, through the interpretation of the notoriously difficult text in his *Summa Theologiae* wherein St. Thomas says that the Persons of the Trinity are able to subsist as purely relative beings because of what is unique to relation among all the modes of physical being, namely, that it exists suprasubjectively according to a rationale—the rationale of "being toward"—which is indifferent to the fact of being exercised independently of being cognized or known.

In other words, every physical being which exists either in itself or in another exists subjectively and must, as such, exist whether or not it is known to exist by some finite mind, that is to say, whether or not it exists objectively as well as

---

"Quomodo autem hoc sit peculiare in relatione et in aliis generibus non inveniatur, dicimus ex eo esse, quia in aliis generibus ratio propria et formalissima eorum non potest positive intelligi, nisi entitative etiam intelligatur, quia positiva eorum ratio est ad se tantum et absoluta, et ideo non intelligitur positive nisi etiam entitative, quod enim est ad se, entitas est. Sola relatio habet esse ens et ad ens, et pro ea parte, qua se habet ad ens, positive se habet, nec tamen inde habet entitatem realem. Sed aliunde relationi provenit realitas, scilicet a fundamento, aliunde positiva ratio ad, scilicet ex termino, ex quo non habet esse ens, sed ad ens, licet illud ad vere reale sit, quando fundatum est. Quod ergo aliquid possit considerari positive, etiamsi non entitative realiter, proprium relationis est. Et hoc solum voluit dicere Caietanus cit. loco, cum dixit relationem rationis esse veram relationem, non veritate entitatis et formae informantis, sed veritate obiectivae et positivae tendentiae ad terminum. Neque Caietanus dixit, quod in relatione praedicamentali ipsum ad est aliquid rationis; expresse enim dicit, quod vere realizatur.

"Quando vero <instatur,> quod etiam alia genera possunt hoc modo dici aliquid rationis, sicut substantia rationis erit chimaera, quantitas rationis spatium imaginarium, et sic de aliis: Respondetur, quod, ut supra dictum est [in] Praeambulo Primo art. 1., non dicitur ens rationis illud, ad cuius instar formatur; formatur enim ens rationis ad instar entis realis, sed dicitur ens rationis illud non reale, quod ad instar realis entis concipitur. Non datur ergo substantia rationis nec quantitas rationis, quia licet aliquod non ens concipiatur ad instar substantiae, v. g. chimaera, et aliquid ad instar quantitatis, v. g. spatium imaginarium, non tamen ipsa substantia vel aliqua substantiae ratio concipitur per rationem et formatur in esse ad instar alterius entis realis. Et ideo illa negatio seu non ens chimaerae, et illud non ens spatii imaginarii dicetur ens rationis. Sed hoc est ens rationis, quod vocatur negatio, non autem erit substantia rationis, cum non ipsa substantia ut ens rationis ad instar alicuius realis concipiatur, sed negationes seu non entia ad instar substantiae et quantitatis. At vero in relativis non solum aliquod non ens concipitur ad instar relationis, sed etiam ipsa relatio ex parte respectus ad, cum non existit in re, concipitur seu formatur ad instar relationis realis, et sic est, quod formatur in esse, et non solum id, ad cuius instar formatur, et ratione huius datur relatio rationis, non substantia rationis" (*Treatise on Signs*, Second Preamble, Article 2, from the "Resolution of Counter-Arguments," 93/16-96/36).

physically. But relation, in order to be what it is, exists not subjectively but as a suprasubjective nexus or mode, and for this it *makes no difference* whether *the relation* obtains physically as well as objectively or only in the community of knowledge. In either case—whether it exists only as known or physically as well as objectively—it exists in exactly the same way: suprasubjectively. By contrast, substance and accidents exist subjectively only when they are not pure objects of apprehension. Indeed, purely as objects apprehended, they are not subjective existents but relative objects *patterned after* what are not relative, namely, physically existent substances with their accidents, which, Poinsot points out, is precisely why there are mind-dependent relations but not mind-dependent substances or mind-dependent accidents other than relations.[33]

In other words, as *isolated* in this or that respect, physical being is determinately subjective; but in whatever respect reality enjoys *communion*, in that respect it is determinately *intersubjective* and as such can be maintained in cognition alone, in physical being alone, or in physical being and in cognition alike. Hence in the case of the Trinity, Aquinas argues, a diversity of Persons subsistent as *relations* is consistent with the unity of God as pure existence subsistent in itself, *ipsum esse subsistens*; hence too, "Comme particularité de

---

[33] Poinsot, *Tractatus de Signis*, Second Preamble, Article 2, "Quid requiratur, ut aliqua relatio sit praedicamentalis," 96/1-36: "When one insists that, as a matter of fact, other kinds of being too can in this way be said to be something mind-dependent—as a mind-dependent substance will be a chimera, a mind-dependent quantity an imaginary space, and so on for the other categories: *The response is* that, as was explained in our First Preamble on mind-dependent being [57/26-30], that on whose pattern a mind-dependent being is formed is not called mind-dependent; for mind-dependent being is formed on the pattern of mind-independent being, but that unreal being which is conceived on the pattern of a mind-independent being is called a mind-dependent being. There is not therefore mind-dependent substance nor mind-dependent quantity, because even though some non-being may be conceived on the pattern of a substance—for example, the chimera–and some on the pattern of quantity–for example, imaginary space–yet neither substance itself nor any rationale of subjectivity is conceived by the understanding and formed in being on the pattern of some *other* mind-independent being. And for this reason that negation or chimerical non-being and that non-being of an imaginary space will be said to be a mind-dependent being. But this [i.e., any unreal object whatever conceived as being a subject or a subjective modification of being] is the mind-dependent being which is called negation, yet it will not be a mind-dependent substance, because substance itself is not conceived as a mind-dependent being patterned after some mind-independent being–rather, negations or non-beings are conceived on the pattern of substance and quantity. But in the case of relatives, indeed, not only is there some non-being conceived on the pattern of relation, but also the very relation conceived on the part of the respect toward, while it does not exist in the mind-independent order, is conceived or formed on the pattern of a mind-independent relation, and so that which is formed in being, and not only that after whose pattern it is formed, is a relation, and by reason of this there are in fact mind-dependent relations, but not mind-dependent substances."

la doctrine de Jean de Saint-Thomas, il faut noter encore qu'il place le constitutif formel de la deité dans l'intellection actuelle de Dieu par lui-même."[34]

In the case of the *doctrina signorum*, the application of Aquinas' point about the being proper and unique to relation as a mode of being is much humbler and, philosophically, quite independent of the theological doctrine that the interior life of God consists in a communion of three persons.

By all accounts, Poinsot points out, signs are *relative* beings whose whole existence consists in the presentation within awareness of what they themselves are not, *aliquid stans pro alio*. To function in this way the sign in its proper being must consist, precisely and in every case, in a relation uniting a cognitive being to an object known *on the basis of* some sign vehicle. What makes a sign formal or instrumental simply depends on the sign vehicle: if it is a psychological state, an idea or image, the sign is a formal sign; if the sign vehicle is a material object of any sort, a mark, sound or movement, the sign is an instrumental sign. But whether the sign be formal or instrumental (this traditional terminology is not without its problems[35]) is subordinate to the fact that, as a sign, the being whereby it exists is not the subjective being of its vehicle (psychological or material, as the case may be) but the intersubjective being of a relation irreducibly triadic.[36]

Many centuries later, Peirce would resume this point under a clearer terminology: every sign, in order to function as a sign, requires an object and an interpretant, and hence consists in a triadic relation. But the point itself, that the *doctrina signorum* has for its subject matter a unified object of investigation in the being of relation as indifferent to provenating from nature or mind, debated intensely among the Latins in the forgotten centuries separating Aquinas from Descartes, is found thematically established in Poinsot, and established precisely on the basis of a careful reading, reflection upon, and taking together of the principal texts of Aquinas on the matter of signs and relations.[37]

---

[34] Santiago Ramirez, "Jean de Saint Thomas," *Dictionnaire de Theologie Catholique* (Paris: Letouzey, 1924) vol. 8, 803-808.

[35] See John Deely, "How Does Semiosis Effect Renvoi?," the Thomas A. Sebeok Fellowship Inaugural Lecture delivered October 22, 1993, at the 18th Annual Meeting of the Semiotic Society of America, forthcoming as a journal article in *The American Journal of Semiotics* and as a monograph publication through the SSA Secretariat.

[36] *Tractatus de Signis*, Book I, Question 3, "Utrum sit eadem relatio signi ad signatum et potentiam," 154/28-30: "unica relatione signi attingitur signatum et potentia, et haec est propria et formalis ratio signi."

[37] For the first time, a definitive resolution is effected in the *Tractatus de Signis* of Poinsot of "the possibility," originally suggested by Augustine, "of resolving . . . the ancient dichotomy between the inferential relations linking natural signs to the things of which they are signs and relations of equivalence linking linguistic terms to the concept(s) on the basis of which some

2.4. THING AND OBJECT

The problem of thing and object takes on a quite different visage once it is realized that the objects of experience in their constitution as objects are networks of sign relations, connecting not only common with proper sensibles and concepts with their objects, but objects with one another in a four-dimensional net or web whose lattice is precisely the relations through the intersection of which objects are constituted as experienced and known.

Let me give you a simple example. If I had come before this audience wearing a high-necked black cape, with my hair dyed black and slicked back, perhaps adding for good measure two long incisors, each of you would think at once of Dracula, a creature who, some think, does not exist. A perceived pattern is what constitutes an object of experience, not an existing thing. Our experience consists in the building up of a structure or network of cognitive and cathectic relations which constitute an objective world. This world partially includes aspects of the physical environment, to be sure, but it includes such elements according to its own plan and without reducing to them. If we consider the environment to be the world of things, then the objective world is constructed according to a quite different plan, and divisions in the one world vary relatively independently of divisions in the other world. Moreover, each world extends beyond the other's boundaries: not all things are known to us, and not all objects known to us are things.

Think of a kind of geodesic sphere the interior of which as well as its surface

---

thing 'is'—singly or plurally—designated," Umberto Eco, Roberto Lambertini, Costantino Marmo, Andrea Tabarroni, "Latratus Canis: or The Dogs' Barking," *Frontiers in Semiotics*, ed. John Deely, Brooke Williams and Felicia Kruse (Bloomington: Indiana University Press, 1986), 65.

"The conclusion," Poinsot explains (1632: 270/38-271/12), "derives from that distinguished doctrine in Cajetan's *Commentary on the Summa theologica*, I, q. 1, art. 3, that the differences of things *as things* are quite other than the differences of things *as objects* and in the being of an object; and things that differ in kind or more than in kind in the one line, can differ in the other line not at all or not in the same way. And so, seeing that the rationale of a sign pertains to the rationale of the knowable [the line of thing as object], because it substitutes for the object, it will well be the case that in the rationale of object a mind-independent natural sign and a stipulated mind-dependent sign are univocal signs; just as a mind-independent being and a mind-dependent being assume one rationale in their being as object, since indeed they terminate the same power, namely, the power of understanding, and can be attained by the same habit, namely, by Metaphysics, or at least specify two univocally coincident sciences, as for example, Logic and Physics. Therefore in the being of an object specifying, stipulated and natural signs coincide univocally.

"So too a cognitive power is truly and univocally moved and led to a thing signified by means of a stipulated sign and by means of a natural sign."

consists of a series of intersecting lines. Each intersection is an object, each line a relationship. Lines radiate outward from the center to the surface of the sphere, and lines extend also crosswise, intersecting the radii at the center of which each of us stands. The radii lines represent relations between ideas and objects, the intersecting lines represent relations between objects, and the intersections themselves the objects. Thus, the objective world is the sphere of an individual's experiences built up out of relationships, and the internal constitution of this sphere is precisely that of a web the various intersections of whose strands present to us the objects according to the meaning of which we lead our lives. At the center of such a three-dimensional spider's web, by maintaining and elaborating it, we live our lives.

The physical environment impinges upon our bodies, and according to their intrinsic constitution we respond to those impingements. Of most of the impingements we are sublimely oblivious; of a small subset we become aware. All the impingements establish relationships between us and the physical surroundings, but only the impingements of which we have an awareness transform the physical surroundings insofar into objective surroundings.

Take the simple case of the classical "external senses": the eye objectifies only colors, the ear only sounds, the tongue only flavors, the nose only odors, the touch only textures and temperatures. All five have in common that they reveal the surrounding environment only insofar as it here and now acts upon our organs of sense. That is to say, all five have in common that they reveal things of the environment not according to the subjective constitution of those things as such, but according as that subjective constitution is here and now affecting our own subjective constitution as organisms. In other words, all five senses have in common that they reveal things not as they are independently but partially as they are bodies here and now in interaction with our bodies, an "interested intersubjectivity," as we might say. We may regard the cognitive relations whereby each sense aspectually objectifies the body or bodies immediately acting upon it as basic radii in the construction of the geodesic sphere of experience, which guarantee that the sphere will always include objectively elements of the physical surroundings as such, and so will remain at its surface always a virtual intersection or interface between nature and culture, no matter how elaborate the sphere subsequently becomes on the ideal side of its construction.[38]

However, radii connecting eye with colors, ear with sounds, taste buds

---

[38] This is the point of the difficult analyses of Book III, Questions 1 and 2 of Poinsot's *Tractatus de Signis*. See the discussion in Michael Raposa, "Poinsot on the Semiotics of Awareness," *American Catholic Philosophical Quarterly* 68.3, 395-408.

with flavors, nose with odors, and touch with textures and temperatures are far from the whole story of sensation. Along with colors are conveyed shapes, movements and positions, as also along with touch. Hearing too directionalizes and localizes its stimuli, as does smell and, to a much lesser degree, taste. Thus, between the direct objects of the external sense, right from the start, a series of lateral relations are also given, relations which depend on the direct or proper objects, to be sure, but which are given simultaneously with those objects and as giving to those objects an incipient or nascent objective contour and structure: the color is not only a color, but a color with certain contours and a relative position, whether moving or at rest. In other words, the radii relations at this primitive level already present to the sense organs something that the sense organ itself is not, namely, its object, and so are sign relations; but, besides, the proper objects are involved in relations which further convey what they themselves are not, such as shapes, movements, positions, and the like, and so are themselves sign-vehicles right from the start. Already you see the beginning structure of the interior of the sphere take form: radii relations forming objects at the surface of the sphere, and between these objects other relations which further structure the objects themselves and interrelate them. The relations between the objective elements give rise to further objectification: the sound is not only heard, it is heard from behind me and as moving away, etc. Both the radii relations and the relations interconnecting them are, thus, sign relations.

Memory, imagination, and estimation of interest build upon these sensory elements, both by adding new radii and further intersections. Thus the sensory strands of the sphere are further woven into a *perceptual* network of ever more complex objects and objectifications, in which not only here and now physical environmental influences are at work, but objective influences from the past as well, and subjective influences from the needs and interests of the organism, both as arising here and now and entering into the objective world through the same cognitive and affective relational network by which the objective world exists in the first place, and as filtering what from the past is brought to bear on the here and now structure of objectivity.

Thus far the three-dimensional web of experience exists as tied to the biological type of the organism experiencing. Each species lives in its own species-specific objective world or (as von Uexküll termed it) *Umwelt*. This is also true of the human animal: its objective world is a biological *Umwelt* first of all, populated by objects that don't exist in the physical environment as such and objects that, while aspectually manifested indeed physically, exist otherwise in the Umwelt than they do in the physical environment as such.

But the human animal becomes aware of what the other animals do not, namely, the relational strands which constitute the web and structure the objects, and can now begin to play with those strands in their own right, as Maritain singularly observed, especially in his sustained reflections on the sign.[39] At that moment, language in the species-specifically human sense is born, only later to be exapted into the communication system we call speech.[40] At that moment also the strict proportion between biological heritage and objective world is transcended, and the possibility of reconstruction of the Umwelt along radically alternative lines of objectification opens up—such as "the environment as it appears through the eye of a fly." It is in this way, for example, that legal systems are devised, distributing, say, property, not along biological lines of species territoriality, but according to an abstract plan of objective boundaries imposed upon the physical environment as identified with this or that of its features—for example, the Mississippi River as separating Iowa from Illinois for a certain stretch. The way is also opened to science, in the sense of an investigation into the subjective dimension of physical objects according to their intrinsic constitution. Maritain's intuition of being belongs to this realization of contrast between objective world and physical environment, wherein the intellect "in its most perfect function," as Maritain remarks,[41] "seizes upon existence exercised by things."[42]

Thus, the sphere of human experience, unlike a purely perceptual objective world, does not remain completely closed unto itself but is able both to be restructured from within and to draw within itself, through the radii of sensations-intellectually-elaborated, increasingly remote and alien parts of

---

[39] Jacques Maritain, "Sign and Symbol," trans. Mary Morris for the *Journal of the Warburg Institute* (1937-1938), 1-11; "Signe et Symbole," *Revue Thomiste* XLIV (April 1938), 299-330; "Le Langage et la Theorie du Signe," Annexe au Chapitre II of *Quatre essais sur l'esprit dans sa condition charnelle* (nouvelle edition revue et augmentee; Paris: Alsatia), 113-124, and "Language and the Theory of Sign," originally published as Chapter V of the anthology *Language: An Enquiry into Its Meaning and Function* edited by Ruth Nanda Anshen (New York: Harper & Bros.), 86-101, is reprinted with the addition of a full technical apparatus explicitly connecting the essay to Maritain's work on semiotic begun in 1937 and to the text of John Poinsot, *Tractatus de Signis* (1632) on which Maritain centrally drew, in John Deely et al., *Frontiers in Semiotics* (Bloomington: Indiana University Press, 1986), 51-62, to which reprint page references are keyed.

[40] *Cf.* Thomas Sebeok, "A Origem da Linguagem," trans. by Fernando Clara for *Semiótica e Linguística Portuguesa e Românica. Homenagem a José Gonçalo Herculano de Carvalho*, ed. Jürgen Schmidt-Radefeldt (Tübingen: Gunter Narr Verlag), 3-9, and "Language: How Primary a Modeling System?," in *Semiotics 1987*, ed. John Deely (Lanham, MD: University Press of America, 1988), 15-27.

[41] Jacques Maritain, "On Human Knowledge," *Thought* XXIV.93 (June), 232.

[42] *Cf.* Jacques Maritian, *Existence and the Existent*, Engish version by Lewis Galantiere and Gerald B. Phelan (New York: Pantheon Books, 1948), 15-19.

the physical universe itself made objects of understanding and indirect experience. Questions can also be raised from within about being in its totality, its ultimate causes and first principles.[43]

Inasmuch as all our knowledge is tied to sensation and, through sensations, to the physical environment in *its* own being here and now acting upon and containing our bodies as parts of itself, things now appear as those particular and particularly fundamental objects or aspects of objects which do not reduce to our experience of them but have a constitution of their own—a *subjective* constitution, that is—prior to and relatively independent of their objective being. The being of objects as such is thoroughly relational, but the being of objects as things has a physical, subjective constitution which is what it is independently of the experience of it.

One of the particularly penetrating analyses Poinsot makes is based upon St. Thomas's division of purely objective being, *ens rationis*, into relations which are patterned after predicamental relations and relations which are patterned after physical individuals ("substances") and subjective characteristics of such individuals ("accidents"), which relations, since, *as* purely objective *relations* they *are not* what their patterns *are*, are called "negations".[44] The patterns of relations which weave sensory elements into objects and objective structures, thus, can be both physical and objective or only objective, without the difference in the two cases being always or even readily apparent. This relational structure of cognitional being as such explains the prevalence of error in human experience, all right, but also the possibility of truth, since objective relations according to their intrinsic structure can perfectly duplicate or *coincide and correspond with* physical relations, as well as diverge from them in constituting structures of objectivity which have no reality apart from human experience.

The refinements on the notion of causality that the relative constitution of objects requires for intelligibility is one of the greatest achievements of the later Latin Thomistic authors. Although it is impossible to expound it here in a

---

[43] "The fact that the Being-question stands out initially against the horizon of totality despite the fact that we never comprehend the totality in an actual way . . . has been designated by St. Thomas in . . . the 'contraction' of being into the predicaments . . . ." John Deely, "Finitude, negativity, and Transcendence: The Problematic of Metaphysical Knowledge" *Philosophy Today* XI.3/4 (Fall, 1967), 185.

[44] That objective relations which are and are not patterned after physical relations as such exhaustively divide the order of mind-dependent being according to Aquinas is set forth by Poinsot in the First Preamble to his *Treatise on Signs*, Article 1, "Quid Sit Ens Rationis in Communi et Quotuplex," notably 53/8-45 and 54/29-55/6; that in particular negations are themselves relations in what they have of actual cognitive existence is further explained in the same place at 56/35-57/17, 57/18-28, and also in the Second Preamble "On Relation," Article 2, esp. 96/1-36.

form sufficiently brief to the available time, I can at least refer you to a schematic historical treatment[45] of the division of both final and formal cause into intrinsic and extrinsic, and of the latter into ideal (or "exemplary") and objective (or "specificative"), and an extended theoretical treatment of how signs work that addresses the issue of the last and most fundamental of these distinctions—extrinsic formal causality as specificative—in depth.[46]

What I do want to do here is raise in passing the matter of *esse intentionale*, which plays so large a role in the analyses of Maritain and in some of my own earlier work[47] which relied heavily on Maritain, including the publicly unresolved dispute I had over this issue with Mortimer Adler.[48] Gilson alerted me in a letter of August 28, 1968, to his suspicion that the "bare fact" that St. Thomas never "made any extensive use of it" (i.e., the notion of *esse intentionale*) suggests "that the modern importance attached to that notion, reinforced by the wish to humor idealist Husserl, betrays the presence of a stream of thought foreign to the genuine doctrine of Thomas Aquinas." That was just a little before I began work on Poinsot's *Tractatus de Signis*. Since Maritain had drawn his epistemology especially from Poinsot, and since Poinsot was also the one on whom Gilson principally pinned responsibility for placing *esse intentionale* at the center of noetic, one would expect to find this notion as a dominant theme in Poinsot's presentation of the doctrine of signs and especially of the concept

[45] John Deely, "Semiotics and Biosemiotics: Are Sign-Science and Life-Science Coextensive?," in *Biosemiotics. The Semiotic Web 1991*, ed. Thomas A. Sebeok and Jean Umiker-Sebeok (Berlin: Mouton de Gruyter, 1992).

[46] John Deely, *The Human Use of Signs* (Lanham, MD: Rowman & Littlefield, 1994).

[47] John Deely, *The Tradition via Heidegger. An Essay on the Meaning of Being in the Philosophy of Martin Heidegger* (The Hague: Martinus Nijhoff, 1971).

[48] My own last word on this dispute is in note 43, p. 272, of the "Editor's Introduction: A Morning and Evening Star" to the *American Catholic Philosophical Quarterly* 68.3 (Summer, 1994). For the background, see John Deely, Review of Mortimer J. Adler's *The Difference of Man and the Difference It Makes*, in *The Thomist* 32 (July 1968), 436-439; "The Immateriality of the Intentional as Such," *The New Scholasticism* XLII.3 (Spring 1968), 293-306; "The Ontological Status of Intentionality," *The New Scholasticism* XLVI (1972), 220-223; "The Two Approaches to Language," *The Thomist* 39.4 (October 1974), 856-907, and "Reference to the Non-Existent," *The Thomist* 39.2 (April 1975), 253-308. Of this last essay Gilson wrote me (18 April 1973): "I have been looking from afar to your 'Reference to the Nonexistent' while I was trying to recover from a bout of sciatica, a disease that little favors metaphysical speculation. Finally I braced myself up and read it with the feeling of fear and admiration I usually experience when I feel dragged by powerful hands out of my natural element, the Thomism of Thomas Aquinas"—but this last, unfortunately, meant only *the theological texts as such* of St. Thomas, a rather limited horizon in the end, for, as Gilson commented in a 1957 letter to Gerald B. Phelan (cited in Laurence Shook, *Étienne Gilson*, 338): "We are too far now from Thomas to make people accept him as he was."

as a formal sign. This expectation is not realized. Instead, one finds that, in Poinsot's *Tractatus*, relation in the very sense that eluded even Maritain[49] holds the center stage throughout. *Esse intentionale*, far from being the predominant notion, appears rather as a secondary phenomenon the possibility of which is itself explained rather by the peculiar indifference of relation as such to its subjective provenance or ground than postulated as a fundamental datum in its own right.

The "doctrine that would be common to Aquinas and Poinsot," which Gilson believed "one cannot present to readers" through a doctrine of intentional being regarded as primary,[50] turned out to be instead, as I explained above, the doctrine of relation as a suprasubjective mode indifferent to the subjective ground of its realization. So I have come to think, on quite other grounds, that Gilson's suspicions of the doctrine of *esse intentionale* as regards its fundamentality for Thomistic thought had a good point to deliver. And it is ironic that it should have been Poinsot, contemned by Gilson, but Maritain's principal teacher beside St. Thomas himself, who taught me the true substance of what Gilson had only suspected.

2.5. HISTORICAL LINKAGES

In a certain way, I think it is not too much to say that the Latin era, understood in its true dimensions and extending, in what concerns Thomism, from Thomas to John of St. Thomas, concludes on one of the very points with which the postmodern era begins, the centrality of relation to the understanding of experience and knowledge. Charles Peirce stands in this regard in a position analogous to the position occupied by Augustine as last of the Western Fathers and first of the medievals. Peirce, with his doctrine of signs consisting in irreducibly triadic relations as a new foundation and beginning for the philosophical enterprise as a whole, is at once the last of the moderns and first of the postmoderns. For what I see in postmodernism, before all else, is the possibility of a philosophical response to the shortcomings of the modern paradigm, a response which at once remedies those shortcomings and retrieves for philosophy its lost history in the context of—and as supremely relevant to—the postmodern period which all agree we are entering without much

---

[49] See John Deely, "Semiotic in the Thought of Jacques Maritain," *Recherches Sémiotique/ Semiotic Inquiry* 6.2 (1986), 112-142.

[50] "I never agreed with Jacques Maritain on that point," Gilson wrote me (10 July 1974), following up on his earlier avowal (18 April 1973) that "I am not even sure there is a 'doctrine' of intentionality in Thomas Aquinas. To him, intentionality is of the essence of intellectual knowledge, and even of knowledge in general."

agreement on how it is to be defined. This lost history is the period from Occam—or even Aquinas, really—to Descartes,[51] when the first florescence of semiotic consciousness occurred in the Iberian peninsula, involving not only Poinsot but such other distinguished Thomistic authors as Soto and Araújo, predecessors to Poinsot's synthesis.[52] In the approach of these thinkers is found the adumbration of a way to deal with Heidegger's original and abiding central concern with the unity of being prior to its division into categories, as with Peirce's central concern with the nature of semeiosis. In a word, among these Thomistic authors, as neglected today as for the three centuries of modernity (but perhaps not for so much longer[53]), is found the anticipation of central themes of postmodernity.

No doubt my way of viewing the situation amounts to a retrieve in the Heideggerean sense of the very term "postmodernism." Against the fashionable literary/sophistic attempt to eviscerate rational discourse in philosophy and label the results "postmodern," the argument here is to make sense of the term by juxtaposing it philosophically—not ideologically—to the internal dimensions of the classical modern paradigm, to establish a philosophical sense of the term "postmodernism" defined historically and used to link contemporary requirements of speculative understanding to late Latin themes omitted from the repertoire of analytic tools developed by modernity. Following the example of Maritain, and building on his model of an authentic Thomism, we see thus how the insight into *esse* uniquely achieved in the metaphysics of St. Thomas is only one beginning of the Thomistic story, and far from the whole of it. There are other insights unique to Aquinas not reducible to this one, and not trivial alongside it. There is a community of inquirers familiar with Aquinas' texts from whom there is much to be learned, and the determined attempt to dismiss them heralded most recently in McCool's book is a misguided transformation of useful heuristic historical tools into obstacles on the path of inquiry. That Thomism can be, in Maritain's sense, a *living* philosophy requires that it be concerned with the past not in its unchangeable aspect, but rather with the past in its eminently changeable aspect, namely, our intellectual perception of it, and concerned with how that perception affects present and

---

[51] See John Deely, "What Happened to Philosophy between Aquinas and Descartes?" *The Thomist* 58.4 (1994), 543-568.

[52] Mauricio Beuchot, "La doctrina tomista clásica sobre el signo: Domingo de Soto, Francisco de Araújo y Juan de Santo Tomás," *Critica* XII.36 (México, diciembre 1980), 39-60.

[53] See Jorge Gracia, "Hispanic Philosophy: Its Beginning and Golden Age," *The Review of Metaphysics* 46 (March 1993), 475-502; John Deely, *New Beginnings: Early Modern Philosophy and Postmodern Thought* (Toronto: University of Toronto Press, 1994), and "What Happended to Philosophy between Aquinas and Descartes?" (n. 51 above).

future thought. Such a reshaping of our perception in particular of the modern past and its relations to Latinity as bearing on the future course of contemporary thought should be counted as among the ultimate portents of the work of Jacques Maritain and his model for an authentic Thomism.

CONCLUSION

The title of my presentation was carefully chosen. It is not "Quid est 'Postmodernism'?," a bastardized conflation of Latin indicative and English jargon. It is a purely Latin construction in the subjunctive mood, "Quid sit postmodernismus?," designed to express some wonder as to what might be possible in the wake of modernity: What might postmodernism turn out to be? What are its possibilities?

I think it might become the very era in philosophy Maritain worked the hardest to introduce, an era in which not only St. Thomas but also those who have taken St. Thomas seriously might be given a hearing in their own right and in the name of philosophy. If workers are not wanting—and they need not be many—the postmodern era shows every chance of realizing the velleity expressed by Maritain in his November 1, 1953, letter *Preface* to the translation of Poinsot selections by Yves R. Simon:[54]

> It is good to be alive at the time when to read John of St. Thomas seems almost as natural as to read Berkeley or Leibniz. Twenty-five years ago we could not even have dreamt of such a victory over age-old prejudices. . . .
>
> Of course it would be a great mistake not to scrutinize eagerly St. Thomas' text itself, and its inexhaustible riches. But it would be no less a mistake to neglect the invaluable contribution made by his great commentators, whom I would prefer to call his continuers. To do so would be to disregard the fact that Thomism is a living philosophy, which will never cease developing in time.
>
> Philosophy lives on dialogue and conversation, and it is a mark of any great philosophy that it can manifest constantly new aspects in a conversation which is pursued through centuries . . . with organic consistency. A philosopher finds reason for melancholy in realizing that the conversation about his own ideas (assuming that he is worthy of it) will begin only when he is dead. . . . To continue the conversation with congenial and clear-sighted companions of the stature of Cajetan, Bañez, and John of St. Thomas is a privilege of the genius of Thomas Aquinas and of his grace-given mission.
>
> The development of St. Thomas' doctrine in the works of the commentators is a fascinating process to which not enough attention has been given. The greater our familiarity with the writings of St. Thomas, the better we realize that

---

[54] Yves R. Simon *et al.*, *The Material Logic of John of St. Thomas,* (n. 30 above), v.

. . . to read St. Thomas well, the help of genius is needed and gratefully welcome. Our John is the latest and the most mature of the geniuses who explained St. Thomas.

"His thought has always been moving on and on; I am sure it still is," Gilson wrote me of Maritain (14 January 1973). Well, that is fitting. For it describes what Maritain thought of Thomism itself, that great conversation in philosophy today—now that we have survived modernity—which has the texts of St. Thomas as a center rather than as a boundary. This is something the historians among us need to better understand, "this fascinating process to which not enough attention has been given," and for which the works of Maritain stand as a sign at the boundary of modernity and postmodernity.

Feminism, Postmodernism and Thomism Confront Questions of Gender

Rosalind Smith Edman

Feminism will shape our future as a people and whether it does so
for good or ill entails a heavy responsibility.

Elizabeth Fox-Genovese[1]

Neither feminism nor postmodernism lends itself to clear definition. Both
encompass a broad spectrum of theories. Feminism may be liberal, Marxist,
radical or postmodern. Postmodernism defies definition, perhaps even
description. In its deconstructive form (the form of most interest to feminism),
it is anti-foundational and skeptical of any form of certainty. The various
theories which are drawn together under the umbrella of postmodernism all
have in common a repudiation of early modernism.

A number of feminist theorists within the past decade have found that they
hold much in common with postmodernists. ". . .Both [feminism and post-
modernism] have sought to develop new paradigms of social criticism which
do not rely on traditional philosophical underpinnings."[2] Yet, not all
feminists would espouse a marriage between feminism and postmodernism.
Some fear that postmodernism's repudiation of the subject would eliminate

---

[1] Fox-Genovese, Elizabeth, *Feminism Without Illusions: A Critique of Individualism* (Chapel
Hill, North Carolina: University of North Carolina Press, 1991), 10.

Ms. Genovese explores the positive and the negative effects of the feminist movement,
criticizing particularly feminism's total acceptance of the absolute rights of the individual so
idealized in our contemporary society.

[2] Nancy Fraser & Linda J. Nicholson, "Social Criticism Without Philosophy: An Encounter
Between Feminism and Postmodernism," in *Feminism / Postmodernism*, ed. Linda J. Nicholson
(New York: Routledge, 1990), 19.

feminism as a social-political power—there would be no subject "woman" and consequently no "woman's movement."[3]   Others find the postmodern "death of the subject" quite compatible with the feminist agenda. After all, the "subject" has always been conceived of as *male*.

The concept of gender has long been central to feminist thought. However, its evolution over the past twenty years has resulted in a growing consensus among feminist theorists that gender relations need not correspond to anatomy. Postmodernism with its denial of universalist and transcultural identities such as gender or woman has impacted even further upon the desexualization of gender for those feminist theorists who subscribe to postmodern thought. Gender need not, in fact, be related at all to anatomical sex. Arguing that not only gender, but sex as well is culturally constructed, Judith Butler suggests that "[w]hen the constructed status of gender is theorized as radically independent of sex, gender itself becomes a free-floating artifice, with the consequence that *man* and *masculine* might just as easily signify a female body as a male one, and *woman* and *feminine* a male body as easily as a female one."[4]   The social and ethical implications and ramifications of the desexualization of gender are significant.

Meanwhile, some philosophers and theologians are recognizing that there are affinities to be found between Thomism and postmodernism, particularly in the rejection of the Cartesian splits between mind/matter, body/spirit, and subject/object, as well as between Thomist and postmodern emphases upon bodiliness and the constitution of the individual self in and through social and cultural relations.[5] Can we bring feminism, postmodernism and Thomism into conversation with one another in such a way that the positive insights of each might further the great strides that have been made by feminist theorists in establishing the equality of men and women; in such a way that "feminism will shape our future as a people . . . for good?" What follows is necessarily only an overture to such an ambitious task.

POSTMODERN FEMINISM

Nicholson and Fraser, argue that feminism should adopt a "carefully constructed" postmodernism, taking the best aspects of each. They point out

[3] Susan Hekman provides a lucid discussion of the postmodern and feminist critiques of the subject in "Reconstituting the Subject: Feminism, Modernism, and Postmodernism," *Hypatia*, Vol 6, no. 2 (Summer 1991), 44 - 63.

[4] Judith Butler, *Gender Trouble: Feminism and the Subversion of Identity* (New York: Routledge, 1990), 6.

[5] See, for example, J. A. DiNoia, O.P., "American Catholic Theology at Century's End: Postconciliar, Postmodern, Post-Thomistic," *The Thomist* 54, no.3 (July, 1990), 499-518.

that postmodernism provides feminism with a critique of feminism's foundationalism and essentialism, while feminism provides postmodernism with feminism's strength as social criticism.[6]

One advantage of such a "carefully constructed" postmodern feminism is that categories such as the "modern, restricted, male-headed, nuclear family" would be understood to be "historically specific institutional categories" which would take precedence over "ahistorical, functionalist categories like reproduction and mothering."[7] Furthermore, a "carefully constructed postmodern feminism" would avoid any type of universalisms such as early feminist attempts to find one universal explanation of sexism that would be cross-cultural and cross-generational—what Nicholson and Fraser call "quasi-metanarratives" or "god's eye-views."[8] A "carefully constructed postmodern feminism" would embrace the "death of the subject." Rather than a universalist notion of "woman" or "feminine," social identity would be a multi-strand conception including class, race, gender, ethnicity, sexual orientation, age, etc.[9]

Jane Flax, writing as therapist, philosopher, feminist, and political scientist, approaches gender from the vantage point of "gender relations." Why should feminist theory analyze gender? Because gender relations have for the most part been simply relations of domination.[10] Flax describes gender relations as:

> Differentiated and (so far) asymmetrical divisions and attributions of human traits and capacities. Through gender relations two types of persons are created: man and woman. Man and woman are posited as exclusionary categories. One can be only one gender, never the other or both.[11]

If gender relations are not to continue to be relations of domination, then gender itself needs to be problematized. One must question the relationship between gender and sex. Why? Because, says Flax, " [i]f gender is as natural and as intrinsically a part of us as the genitals we are born with, it would be foolish, (or even harmful) to attempt either to change gender arrangements or not to take them into account as a delimitation of human activities."[12] But is gender a "natural"—pre-social—fact? No, according to Flax. Rather, gender

---

[6] Nicholson and Fraser, 19-20.   [7] *Ibid.*   [8] *Ibid.,* 29.   [9] *Ibid.,* 34-35.

[10] Jane Flax, "Postmodernism and Gender Relations in Feminist Theory," in *Feminism / Postmodernism*, ed. Linda J. Nicholson (New York: Routledge, 1990), 45. Flax describes herself as philosopher, therapist, feminist and political scientist in her own work *Thinking Fragments: Psychoanalysis, Feminism, and Postmodernism in the Contemporary West* (Berkeley, California: University of California Press, 1990), 3. *Thinking Fragments* is also a more developed presentation of the ideas found Flax's contribution to *Feminism / Postmodernism*.

Flax does not subscribe to a wholly postmodern feminism; however, she does believe that aspects of postmodernism can certainly advance the feminist cause.

[11] *Ibid.,* 45.   [12] *Ibid.,* 49.

results from three things:

1. social conditions, which are rapidly changing.
2. male dominance.
3. equation of sex and gender (sex being the anatomical
   differences between male and female.[13]

Like Nicholson and Fraser, Flax eschews Enlightenment essentialisms and universalisms. She, too, finds that "[f]eminist notions of self, knowledge, and truth are too contradictory to those of the Enlightenment to be contained within its categories."[14]   She suggests that both sex and gender find their origin in social relations, rather than in a natural or essential difference in being.

Judith Butler, best illustrates the postmodern feminist position with regard to gender. She is profoundly influenced by the thinking of Michel Foucault, especially in regard to the "death of the subject" and the theory of the body. In agreement with Nicholson and Fraser, but contrary to Flax, Butler questions the assumption that there is a subject—woman.[15]   In fact, the notion of the decentered self is essential to her postmodern critique of gender.   The consequences which follow from a thoroughly postmodern feminist theory of gender become most apparent in Butler's work.

Citing Foucault's idea that "juridical systems of power *produce* the subjects they subsequently come to represent," she notes the importance of the question of the subject for politics in general, but even more for feminist politics. "To what extent," she asks, "does the category of women achieve stability and coherence only in the context of the heterosexual matrix?"[16]

Her argument, following Foucault, is that the body comes into being as a function of discourse.[17] The fact that the body becomes sexualized as "naturally"

---

[13] Jane Flax, *Thinking Fragments*, 22.   [14] *Ibid.*, 183.

[15] "My suggestion is that the presumed universality and unity of the subject of feminism is effectively undermined by the constraints of the representational discourse in which it functions." See note 4 above.

Flax, on the other hand makes the point that "those who celebrate or call for a 'decentered' self seem self-deceptively naive and unaware of the basic cohesion within themselves that makes the fragmentation of experiences something other than a terrifying slide into psychosis." *Thinking Fragments*, 218-19.

[16] Judith Butler, *Gender Trouble: Feminism and the Subversion of Identity*, 4-5.

[17] Foucault says, "The body is the inscribed surface of events (traced by language and dissolved by ideas), the locus of a dissociated self (adopting the illusion of a substantial unity), and a volume in perpetual disintegration." McNay notes that Foucault is not denying the materiality of the body, only that the materiality or corporeality of the body can be known apart from its "cultural significations." Quoted by Lois McNay, in "The Foucauldian Body and the Exclusion of Experience," *Hypatia*, Vol. 6, No.3, Fall, 1991, 125-139.

One of Foucault's most important contributions to feminist theory, according to McNay, is

or "essentially" male or female is simply the effect of power relations which inscribe gender upon the surface of the body. These power relations are those of the heterosexual culture.

Gender ought not to be construed as a stable identity or locus of agency from which various acts follow; rather, gender is an identity tenuously constituted in time, instituted in an exterior space through a *stylized repetition of acts*.[18]

These acts give the "illusion of an abiding gendered self." The body performs or acts out what the dominant heterosexual culture determines to be normative for one sex or the other. In this way the dominant heterosexual culture conceals the fact that gender is performative and that it need not be limited to those acts which the dominant culture determines to be normative—heterosexual acts.[19] For the fact is, "the gendered body has no ontological status apart from the various acts which constitute its reality."[20]

Does Thomism have anything to say to postmodern feminism? *Yes*, inasmuch as Thomism shares postmodern feminism's rejection of the Cartesian dichotomies of mind/matter, body/spirit, subject/object, as well as its rejection of rationalist closed-systems of knowledge; *yes*, inasmuch as Thomism speaks to the embodiedness of the person; and *yes*, inasmuch as Thomism gives priority to existence over essence. Hence, to speak of the nature or essence of woman is not to deny the individual woman who exists in this historical, contingent moment, suffering oppression from the social, cultural, and linguistic biases of sexism and domination in its various forms.

THOMISM—A CORRECTIVE

At the outset, we must grant that one would not generally consider turning to the writings of Aquinas to support feminism in its attempts to eliminate male domination. One could cite passages from his writings which would

---

to have provided the possibility of speaking of a sexualized body (thus enabling continued reflection on the oppression of women which has been based in sexual difference) while at the same time denaturalizing sex, seeing it as clearly a cultural construct.

[18] Judith Butler, *Gender Trouble: Feminism and the Subversion of Identity*, 140.

[19] *Ibid.*, 141.   [20] *Ibid.*, 136.

[21] Citations from St. Thomas Aquinas are taken from *Summa Theologica* (3 vols.). Translated by Fathers of the English Dominican Province (New York: Benzinger Brothers, Inc., 1947-48).

Those sections in which Thomas Aquinas does treat of women are not likely to be the source of much fruitful conversation with feminism or postmodern feminism. A few choice comments follow:

"It was necessary for woman to be made, as the Scripture says, as a *helper* to man; not indeed as a helpmate in other words, as some say, since man can be more efficiently helped by

provoke a ballistic response from most feminist quarters![21]   However, in Thomas' defense, his reflections on women and the relations between male and female were influenced by Aristotelian physiology, by the cultural practices of his time, which he accepted as "given," and by his own reflections upon Genesis and the writings of Paul, without benefit of contemporary biblical exegesis. Furthermore, Thomas never problematized issues of male dominance or gender. How then might we bring Thomism into conversation with postmodern feminism? I suggest that we do so by way of the writings of Pope John Paul II (Karol Wojtyla) regarding the human person.

Rooted in the metaphysics of Aquinas, and influenced by French personalism and the phenomenology of Max Scheler, Karol Wojtyla further developed Aquinas' anthropology.[22] Wojtyla's reflections on the person include reflections on the person as subject, as embodied, as gendered, and as equal—male and female. All of these topics are core issues for postmodern feminism; thus, the appropriateness of employing Wojtyla as an interlocutor between Aquinas and postmodern feminism.   The focal point for this interlocution is the doctrine of the *imago Dei*.

Aquinas concludes that male and female are equal in regard to the image of God which dwells in the rational soul. They differ only bodily. However, this bodily difference becomes the basis for woman's subordination to man on the basis of Thomas' reading of Genesis 1-3 and of Paul's assertion that "man is the

---

another man in other works; but as a helper in the work of generation." (emphasis added) *ST* I, 92, 1

or

As regards the individual nature, woman is defective and misbegotten, for the active force in the male seed tends to the production of a perfect likeness in the masculine sex; while the production of woman comes from some defect in the active force or from some material indisposition, or even from some external influence; such as that of a south wind that is moist; as the Philosopher observes."*ST*. I, 92, 1, 1

or

"It was right for the woman to be made from a rib of man. First, to signify the social union of man and woman, for the woman should neither *use authority over man*, and so she was not made from his head; nor was it right for her to be subject to man's contempt as his slave, and so she was not made from his feet . . ." (emphasis added) *ST* I, 92, 4

For a comprehensive study of the nature and role of woman in the writings of both Augustine and Aquinas see *Subordination and Equivalence: The Nature and Role of Woman in Augustine and Thomas Aquinas*, Kari Elisabeth Borresen, Translated from the revised French original by Charles H. Talbot (Washington, D.C.: University Press of America, 1981) .

[22] For a brief summary of the origins of Pope John Paul's philosophical thinking, see Robert Modras, "The Moral Philosophy of Pope John Paul II," *Theological Studies* 41 (December 1980), 683-97.

glory of God, while woman is the glory of man." Aquinas distinguishes between the spiritual, intellectual soul (on the basis of which *both* man *and* woman are equally in *imago Dei* and destined for beatitude) and the body (woman's body, not man's!).[23] According to Genesis, woman's body was made from man. Thus, for Aquinas, based on the analogy between God as the beginning and end of the universe, man is the beginning and end of woman. Apart from her body, woman shares in being in the image of God and is equally destined for Beatitude. But, unlike man, who, as embodied, is made in the image and likeness of God, woman cannot, in her embodied state, be in the likeness of God. Why? Because her body is imperfect, dependent upon man's and thus not as perfect a likeness of the Divine. Furthermore, woman, according to Aquinas is weaker of intellect—again due to the difference in body.[24] The difference and the "defect" in woman's body is due to its end, which is to be a helpmate to the male in generation. In the male, both soul and body are ordered to the same end—intellectual operation—Beatitude. Woman, on the other hand is divided. While her soul is ordered to intellectual operation and Beatitude, her body is ordered to her role in reproduction. As Borresen points out, woman's subordinate role in Aquinas is "rooted exclusively in her reproductive role."[25]

Again, it must be remembered that Aquinas was thinking within the constraints of Aristotelian physiology and an unquestioned subordination of women to men which was rooted in the culture of his time. If we remind ourselves that at no point in his writings did he actually problematize either gender or the subordination of women, then perhaps we can free ourselves from some of his inadequate concepts regarding women and actually find the basis for dialogue with postmodern feminism.

Pope John Paul II (Karol Wojtyla) has taken Aquinas' metaphysical bases and applied a corrective derived in part from Scheler's phenomenology.[26] The

[23] *ST* I, 93, 4; 6, ad 2.

[24] "Now the proximate end of the human body is the rational soul and its operations; since matter is for the sake of the form, and instruments are for the action of the agent. I say, therefore, that God fashioned the human body in that disposition which was best, as most suited to such a form and to such operations. If defect exists in the disposition of the human body, it is well to observe that such defect arises as a necessary result of the matter, from the conditions required in the body, in order to make it suitably proportioned to the soul and its operations." *ST* I, 91, 3,

"But man is yet further ordered to a still nobler vital action, and that is intellectual operation. Therefore there was greater reason for the distinction of these two forces [active and passive powers of generation] in man; so that the female should be produced separately from they male; . . ." *ST* I, 92, 1.

[25] Borresen, *Subordination and Equivalence: The Nature and Role of Woman in Augustine and Thomas Aquinas*, 178.

[26] See note 22 above: Modras, 685.

result is an emphasis which sees sexual differences as *accidental* on the level of substance or nature, as Aquinas would have it, but as *necessary* on the level of *person*.[27]

For Wojtyla, person and nature are integrated, but they remain distinct.[28] The concept of a static human "nature" or "essence" which is so eschewed by postmodern feminism is, in Wojtyla's anthropology, dynamized by its integration in the person.[29] The person becomes manifest, both to self and others, through the body, which is thus *essential* to the person. Not just self-consciousness and self-determination, but the body itself is essential for the human being to be a subject. It is the activity of the body which gives expression to the person.[30]

Herein lies Thomism's corrective to postmodern feminism. One need not eliminate the subject in order to overcome the Cartesian mind/body duality. The person, the subject, only exists as embodied. Furthermore, the person—the embodied person—can only be fully understood in light of Revelation. Reflecting on the Genesis accounts of creation, John Paul II notes that in the first narrative man was created in the image of God as male and female. John Paul II extends the meaning of the *imago Dei* found in the first narrative to the Yahwist narrative and sees the second narrative as being a "preparation for the understanding of the Trinitarian concept of the 'image of God'." For, it is in the communion of persons— male and female—that the image of God is most clearly expressed.

In the mystery of creation—on the basis of the original and constituent "solitude" of his being—man was endowed with a deep unity between what is, equally humanly body, male in him and what is, equally humanly and through the body, female in him.[31]

---

[27] John Grabowski, "Theological Anthropology and Gender Since Vatican II: A Critical Appraisal of Recent Trends in Catholic Theology," Ph.D. diss., Marquette University, 1991. I am indebted to Dr. Grabowski for drawing my attention to this point.

[28] Karol Wojtyla, *The Acting Person*, trans. Andrzej Potocki (Boston: D. Reidel Publishing Co., 1979), 76-80.

[29] *Ibid.*, 84. It is impossible within the limits of this article to adequately treat Wojtyla's discussion of nature and person. However, a dialogue between Wojtyla and certain postmodernists on this point would prove interesting.

"The integration [of nature and person] could not consist solely in the individualization of nature by the person. The person is not merely an 'individualized humanness;; it actually consists rather in the mode of individual being that pertains (from among all the types of existing beings) to mankind alone. This mode of being stems from the fact that the peculiar type of being proper to mankind is personal." (83)

[30] John Paul II, *Original Unity of Man and Woman: Catechesis on the Book of Genesis*, comp. Daughters of St. Paul (Boston: St. Paul Books and Media, 1981), 57.

[31] *Ibid.*, 74.

According to John Paul II, the theology of the body, which from the beginning is bound up with the creation of human persons in the image of God, becomes at the same time a theology of sex, "of masculinity and feminity." Sexuality has a profound theological significance for, while each person is in made in the image and likeness of God, it is in the complementarity, the intimate communion of man and woman with one another that each best images the God who is Love, who is Trinity.

Gender/sexuality, far from being the source of domination, was meant from the beginning to be the occasion for the communion of persons, the way in which man and woman would best incarnate the image and likeness of God wherein they find their equality and dignity.[32] The sexualized body is not, as Judith Butler would have it, the effect of power relations by which the heterosexual culture has inscribed gender upon the surface of the body "for the regulation of sexuality within the obligatory frame of reproductive heterosexuality."[33] Rather, as Sara Butler points out, and as we have seen above, for John Paul II, "sex is integral to the identity of the body-person."[34]

To the degree that postmodern feminism seeks to eradicate male domination and the oppression and subordination of women, Pope John Paul II's synthesis of Thomist, personalist, and phenomenological philosophies can provide a firm theological/philosophical basis for the dignity and equality of man and woman as embodied, gendered persons. On the other hand, by supposing that the solution to male domination is to be found in the denial of "any ontological status to the gendered body;"[35] by supposing that modernist mind/matter, body/spirit, subject/object dichotomies can be overcome only by the elimination of one term or the other, postmodern feminism will necessarily fall prey to the desexualization of gender and the depersonalization of the body. In this case,

---

[32] Pope John Paul's reflections on the theology of the body provide a wealth of material to be further plumbed by Christian feminists. For an excellent essay on his theology of the body see Sara Butler, "Personhood, Sexuality and Complementarity in the Teaching of Pope John Paul II" *Chicago Studies* 32 (April 1993), 43-53.

In response to feminist concerns regarding a relationship of "complementarity" which, as she points out, has historically been one of domination rather than complementarity, Sara Butler refers her readers to John Paul II's teachings on the disorder which original sin has introduced into the relationship between man and woman — a disorder which has been healed through the redemption of Christ, so that "there is not male and female; for you are all one in Christ Jesus" (Gal. 3:28). (50-54)

[33] Judith Butler, *Gender Trouble: Feminism and the Subversion of Identity*, 136.

[34] Sara Butler, "Personhood, Sexuality and Complementarity in the Teaching of Pope John Paul II," 49.

[35] Judith Butler, *Gender Trouble: Feminism and the Subversion of Identity*, 140.

sad to say, for postmodern feminists, embodied persons become simply "passive bodies."[36]

Feminism will shape our future as a people—and whether it does so for good or ill entails a heavy responsibility.[37]

---

[36] See note 17 above, McNay, "The Foucauldian Body," 137.

McNay presents an interesting critique of the Foucauldian theory of the body (presented above in the context of Judith Butler's writing). "The paradox which Foucault's work presents for feminists is that by placing so much emphasis on the body as an historically specific entity, he bypasses any notion of individuality and experience. Thus, whereas feminists have recognized the need to show that women are more than passive victims of domination — through the rediscovery and re-valuation of their experiences and history — Foucault's understanding of individuals as passive bodies has the effect, albeit unintentional, of pushing women back into this position of passivity and silence."

[37] Fox-Genovese, *Feminism without Illusions: A Critique of Individualism*, 10.

The Revival of Prudence

Thomas S. Hibbs

In *The Setting of the Summa Theologiae of St. Thomas,*[1] Leonard Boyle, O.P., argues that Aquinas wrote the *Summa Theologiae* for the sake of the voluminous *secunda pars*. Boyle calls the *Summa* Thomas' sole Dominican work, a work intended to correct certain tendentious features in the most influential Dominican manuals for the care of souls. What Thomas found objectionable in the manuals was the haphazard collation and schematic consideration of moral topics. Thomas' corrective consists in placing moral matters within the context of Christian anthropology, indeed within the whole of speculative theology. A study of the manuscripts of the *Summa Theologiae* in the century or so after Thomas' death indicates that Thomas' intention was systematically ignored. The *secunda pars* regularly circulated autonomously, and even that part was often not available in its entirety. Those interested in guidance for confessors found the *secunda secundae* to be by far the most useful section of the *Summa*.

A different sort of selectivity and distortion in the reading of Aquinas' ethics occurs in early modern scholasticism, where the focus shifts and narrows to the topic of law. The emphasis upon moral rules led to a neglect of the virtues, especially prudence. That neglect lasted well into the present century. In 1925, Garrigou-Lagrange accuses moral theologians of a "quasi-suppression du traité de la prudence."[2] Joseph Pieper would echo these sentiments more than thirty years later.[3] Disregard for prudence, as Joseph Pieper argues, is likely to make Christian ethics a "'science of sins' instead of a doctrine of virtue or a theory of the Christian idea of man."[4] The retrieval of prudence, conversely, is likely

---

[1] Toronto: Pontifical Institute of Medieval Studies, 1981.

[2] "Du caractère métaphysique de la théologie morale de Saint Thomas," *Revue Thomiste* 8 (1925), 345.

[3] *Prudence*, trans. Richard and Clara Winston (London: Faber and Faber, 1959).

[4] *Ibid.*, 49.

to recover something of the integrity of Thomas' original project, since prudence both applies principles to concrete circumstances and is reciprocally related to all the moral virtues.

The integrity is lost in crude formulations of natural law ethics, which assume that the appraisal of particulars, their classification and their subsumption under rules is not problematic. Yet Thomas makes no such assumption. In the questions on law, he repeatedly refers to concrete circumstances of actions as "variable and uncertain." He simultaneously asserts the immutability of the most common precepts, which can be altered only by addition (*Summa Theologiae*, I-II, 84F 4). Yet the proximate, detailed principles can be changed by subtraction, as they may fail in certain circumstances (I-II, 94, 5). Thomas does compare practical reasoning to the deductive character of speculative reason. He states, for instance, that human laws can be derived as conclusions from premises of the natural law; for example, the prohibition against killing can be directly derived from the general precept against harming. Yet the relation between human and natural law is not always a matter of deduction. Thomas speaks of an alternative way of moving from one to the other, by means of *determinatio*, which is more like an artist's realization of a general pattern in concrete reality than it is like deduction (I-II, 95, 20). Even where practical reason operates deductively, it remains at the level of proximate precepts. Thus, Thomas underscores the disparity between the practical and the theoretical orders. While the conclusions of demonstrative syllogisms reach necessary, universal truths, those of practical reason issue in conclusions having to do with particulars, which are true always or for the most part (*ut in pluribus*): the more we descend to particulars the more defects we find (94, 4). Thomas cites the precept that goods entrusted to another should be returned to their owner. Yet, in certain cases, returning the goods may "be injurious." It might seem that we could solve the difficulty by adding a list of qualifications to the original precept, but, as Thomas puts it, the more conditions we add the more ways there are for the principle to fail (I-II, 94, 4). Facility of moral reasoning cannot occur apart from prudence. Its restoration, then, would have the advantage of helping to specify the scope and limits of natural law.

A second advantage of focusing on prudence is evident in situations where principles appear to conflict. Indeed, a crude natural law view must resort to preposterous measures in order to salvage the coherence of the system of precepts. Indeed, without some basic capacity of discerning what rules are relevant and in what respect, the problem of an infinite regress of rules seems unavoidable. Following Aristotle, Thomas lists *synesis* and *gnome* as capacities for recognizing and applying universal and common principles to concrete circumstances, in ordinary situations and in cases where proximate principles fail (II-II, 52, 3 and 4). Moreover, to state which principles apply and which do not presupposes an appraisal of the circumstances that rules themselves cannot provide. This is the realm of the *visio* of prudence that operates through a certain collation (*per quandam collationem agitur*, II-II, 47, 1). Prudence requires experience, memory, and practice in perception (*experimentum prudentiae non acquiritur ex sola memoria sed ex exercitio recte percipiendi*, IIII, 47, 16, ad 2).

The retrieval of prudence might also help to correct a misunderstanding of the notion of the mean as primarily quantitative. Virtue is indeed a mean between excess and deficiency, but such a description remains at a certain level of generality. According to Thomas, prudence is the capacity for finding the mean in moral virtues (II-II, 47, 7). In particular actions, the mean operates as a sort of metaphor for an action that is correct in every way. As Thomas puts it, virtuous action must take into account the various circumstances of human acts (III, 18, 3). An action observes the mean when it is in accord with the rule of reason, that is, when the action is performed when and where it should be, for the right end and so forth (I-II, 64, 1 ad 2). Thus, the centrality of prudence is not for Thomas a way of weakening obligations; instead, the standard of virtuous action is more rigorous than that of a narrow legalism.

A third advantage of the retrieval of prudence is that it restores the harmony of reason and inclination to its proper place in ethics. The *recta ratio agibilium* of prudence cannot operate without rectified appetite: "the things to which the moral virtues incline are as the principles of prudence" (I-II, 65, 1-4). To be well-disposed with respect to ends, Thomas writes, "depends on the rectitude of appetite" (I-II, 57, 4). Unlike other intellectual virtues, which are lost primarily through forgetfulness, prudence is destroyed through "vicious passions" (II-II, 47, 16). There is a parallel to the precepts of the natural law which can also be abolished through corrupt customs and bad habits. The proximate ground of the precepts of the natural law is the order of natural inclinations. Thomas sees problems arising primarily at the level of particulars. But problems at the level of the concrete have of way of obstructing our apprehension of prior, more general precepts. The repetitious performance of vicious actions has consequences not only at the level of application but also at the level of proximate principles, since it can undermine principles as fundamental as the one against theft (I-II, 92, 4-6). As Aristotle puts it, to apprehend the starting points in ethics, one must have been well brought up. Of course, Thomas allows that individuals and groups have access to the most general precepts even in the midst of corrupt practices and this helps to explain how it is that individuals and groups can desire, recognize, and implement visions of the good that run counter to that of a corrupt, dominant culture. But it is unlikely that individuals or groups will make much progress in living in accordance with natural law or the life of virtue without implementing practices to succor the virtues. Practices inculcate habits that rectify the appetitive part of the soul with respect to appropriate ends. The correct ordering of inclination, its harmony with reason, is important not just as a prerequisite to the operation of prudence, but also as a mark of true virtue. On behalf of the thesis that moral virtue cannot exist without passion, Thomas quotes Aristotle: no one is "just who does not rejoice in just deeds" (I-II, 59, 5).

Thomas' emphasis on the indispensable need for experience and training in the moral life has led some recent commentators to shift entirely the balance from natural law to virtue. In a book entitled *The Priority of Prudence: Virtue and Natural Law in Thomas Aquinas and the Implications for Modern Ethics*, Daniel Mark Nelson goes further than any recent author in repudiating the view that Thomas is a proponent of natural law ethics.[5] From a reading of various sections of the second part of the *Summa Theologiae*, Nelson makes a cogent case for seeing virtue rather than law as the fundamental moral category. But his position cuts deeper than this. He relegates natural law to a negligible status in moral deliberation. What does Nelson have to say about the articles on natural law? "Such knowledge serves the explanatory function of accounting for how it happens that we came to reason practically and for the origin of the virtues. Thomas's general point is that we have a created, natural ability to act for the good appropriate to our nature and to develop the habits that perfect that capacity."[6] Clearly Nelson is right to think that the function of natural law is explanatory; the question is whether it does not have other functions. On his view, it is difficult to see what, if anything, natural law adds to Aristotle's comment that virtue is natural in the sense that we have the capacity to acquire it. But why call that "natural law"? The notion of law in "natural law," which is admittedly not obvious in Aquinas, would be reduced to mere metaphor. The problem with Nelson's account is that he has allowed polemics against his opponents, especially against those who see natural law as a sufficient guide for the determination of action, to set the terms of the debate. Nelson is right to note that in concrete circumstances natural law cannot "guide action" or "provide a formula" for correct choice.[7] But to deny these simplistic renderings of natural law does not entail the repudiation of natural law as an important part of moral reasoning.

Alasdair MacIntyre, perhaps the most influential moral philosopher writing on Aquinas today, has also been accused of neglecting the role of natural law

---

[5] University Park, Pennsylvania: The Pennsylvania State University Press, 1992.
[6] *Ibid.*, 103.   [7] *Ibid.*, 114 and 119.

in Aquinas. He argues that moral reasoning cannot take place apart from a tradition of inquiry and practice. But MacIntyre's opponent is not primarily Thomistic natural law but the modern, liberal view of individualism. Indeed, MacIntyre's current view seems to me not to be identical with the position of *After Virtue*, in which he rejected altogether the possibility of grounding ethics in nature. In his latest book, he writes that "evaluative judgments are a species of factual judgment concerning final and formal causes of the activity of members of a particular species."[8] The "Thomist," he writes, sees "evidence of the work of synderesis" in the "continuous reappropriation" of certain rules and in the recurring resistance to discarding them." These precepts, "to which cultural degeneration can partially or temporally blind us," can "never be obliterated."[9] Still, MacIntyre rightly insists that in order for the primary precepts of the natural law to have any efficacious influence on action, we must "engage with others" in such a way that we can become "teachable learners."[10] The pedagogy of virtue, which enables us to act rightly in concrete circumstances, requires a social setting, tradition, and authority.

The account of prudence provides the beginning of a response to certain criticisms of virtue ethics. In his book *Character*, Joel Kupperman argues that virtue ethics is akin to "genre criticism" in literature, which allows for the classification and appraisal of actions in terms of the standards appropriate to particular virtues.[11] The deficiencies of virtue ethics, Kupperman insists, surface when an action "spills out" of a particular category or when "two or more categories arguably are involved in what we are attempting to judge." Character ethics, Kupperman insists, is superior to virtue ethics precisely because it focuses on "what people are like when decisions are called for that involve factors of more than one kind." In his consideration of the resources of virtue ethics in such cases, Kupperman focuses upon justice as the principal and unifying virtue. He fails, however, to consider the role of prudence, which is precisely to appraise all the germane circumstances and determine what ought be done. Once prudence is introduced, the difference between virtue theory and character ethics may well be only verbal. Indeed, the centrality of prudence entails an emphasis upon character in moral education. Thomas embraces Aristotle's statement that as a man is so does the good appear to him.

Virtue theory is sometimes accused of being conservative, of lacking the resources for social critique; according to Habermas, it is susceptible to the

---

[8] *Three Rival Versions of Moral Enquiry* (Notre Dame, Indiana: University of Notre Dame Press, 1990), 134.

[9] *Ibid.*, 281.   [10] *Ibid.*, 136.

[11] Oxford: Oxford University Press, 1991, 106-08.

"dogmatism of life-practices."[12] Since prudence applies universals to particulars, it might seem that criticism could occur only at the level of general precepts. Prudence, on this view, would have the function of securing the goods already apprehended by reason. Thus, it would simply subserve, and not provide grounds for countering, goods already settled upon, for example, those of individual fulfillment or of the maximization of profit and pleasure. Thomas' coupling of natural law with prudence makes his position less vulnerable to such an objection. But it is important to see that prudence, understood Thomistically, is itself the basis of social criticism. Indeed, the parts of prudence and the list of vices opposed to prudence suggest a powerful critique of the practices to which so many American citizens are devoted. In his marvelous little book on prudence, Joseph Pieper begins by lamenting both the neglect of prudence by Catholic moralists and the contemporary misconstrual of prudence as "timorous, small-minded self-preservation." A prudent person is a "clever tactician," striving to "escape personal commitment."[13] Thomas' understanding of prudence is sufficiently determinant to put into question a social order that has given itself over to the pursuit of self-actualization, understood in terms of what Saul Bellow calls the quest for "creative, polymorphous pleasure."

Thomas begins his discussion of the parts of prudence by discussing memory. Indeed, Thomas regularly states that prudence arises from memory. As Pieper notes, memory means more than a capacity for recalling facts. Instead, Pieper calls it "true to being" memory, which can be succored only by "a rectitude of the whole human being."[15] The distinction between these two sorts of memory is a central motif in Saul Bellow's *Bellarosa Connection*, the narrator of which is a Jew who runs a financially successful Mnemosyne institute. He instructs corporate America on the pecuniary benefits to be derived from the resources of a capacious and well-organized memory. This sort of memory stands in contrast to the sort of memory his father attempts—with only moderate success—to inculcate in him. His Father likes to tell the story of Harry Fonstein, a relative who spent time in the concentration camps and who was freed through the assistance of Billy Rose, who arranged for his escape and transport to America. Billy Rose, also a Jew, is a huge success in America, with underworld connections and a flair for the theatrical. For example, Billy stages a Hollywood style celebration of Jewish history at Madison Square Garden. After his arrival in America, Harry Fonstein persistently tries to arrange a meeting with Billy to thank him for his assistance. Saying he wants to avoid "entanglements,"[16] Billy

---

[12] "A Review of Gadamer's Truth and method," in *Understanding and Social Inquiry* (Notre Dame, Indiana: University of Notre Dame Press, 1977). 357.

[13] Josef Pieper, *Prudence*, 11.   [14] *Ibid.*, 27.

[15] Saul Bellow, *Bellarosa Connection* (New York: Penguin, 1989).   [16] *Ibid.*, 50.

resists any meeting with those who wish to thank him. Billy and his intermediaries insist that he did what he could for Jews like Harry, but that he has no further obligations to them. What Billy seems to resist is the continuity and determination of the self that another's gratitude presupposes and evokes. Harry, on the other hand, has an abiding desire to meet with Billy and express his gratitude; he wants, as his wife expresses it, to bring his emotions to completion, to round them off. Harry's memory, the narrator notes, is not merely a catalogue of experiences or facts; instead, he was "doing something with his past."

The narrator stands between these two views of memory. While he thinks Harry's preoccupation with his past and his unrelenting desire to express his gratitude border on the obsessive, he finds Billy Rose to be a gaudy and truncated personality. Memory chains, he writes, are connected thematically. Where "themes are lacking there can be little or no recall." Billy Rose has "an unfortunate thinness for purely human themes—as contrasted with business, publicity, or sexual themes."[17] The reference to the themes that displace the purely human themes and hence undermine the kind of memory constitutive of prudence is instructive. The philosophic correlate to Bellow's narrative can be found in Aquinas' assertions that the vices opposed to prudence arise from *luxuria* and *avaritia*.

Among the set of vices that derail the process of deliberation, are *praecipitatio, inconsideratio*, and *inconstantia*. These correspond, respectively, to the three stages of practical reasoning: counsel, judgment, and command. Neglect of taking counsel arises from a lack of docility and in its extreme form from pride which opposes submission to the authority of another. Inconsideration condemns or neglects those things from which right judgment proceeds. Inconstancy, finally, signifies an incapacity to hold oneself firmly to a course of action that one judges to be good. Thomas traces these vices of omission to *luxuria*, which fosters division of the soul and duplicity of consciousness. Luxury is evident in the avoidance of making decisions, or more violently, in the frenetic process of making, unmaking, and remaking decisions, especially in circumstances that involve a commitment and definition of the self. This is precisely the sort of character that Bellow's Billy Rose embodies, a character that flourishes in contemporary America.

A second set of vices, opposed to prudence but allied to it by similitude, are the ones we have substituted for prudence. The cunning deployment of false means in the pursuit of real or apparent goods engenders lying and dissimulation. Thomas states that all these vices are rooted in avarice, the vice

[17] *Ibid.*, 67.

most damaging to justice. The same sorts of vices, then, are capable of undermining both prudence and justice. The daughters of avarice include not only fraud and illiberality, but also restlessness of soul (*inquietudo*), for the affections of the grasping are anxious about superfluous matters. Such restlessness was even in Tocqueville's time characteristic of the American soul. Like Tocqueville, Bellow detects in the isolationism characteristic of American individualism the motives for assimilation to the project of self-interest narrowly construed. The result of individualism, of the severing of ties to tradition, history, and local communities, is not a society of Nietzschean supermen. Instead, individuals become absorbed in the pursuit of petty pleasure and the endless accumulation of external goods. Modern America, states the narrator of the *Bellarosa Connection*, enables Jews to assimilate painlessly without converting: "Your history, too, became one of your options. The very notion of having a history was a 'consideration' totally up to you."[18] In such a social context, the memory that nourishes prudence would be eviscerated and the vices opposed to prudence, fostered. As Harry Fonstein's wife puts it at one point: "The Jews could survive Hitler but "then comes the next test—America. Can they hold their ground or will the USA be too much for them?"[19] The narrator comments that America is "so absorbing that one existence was too little for it."[20] Again, Bellow's narrative revives Thomistic themes. Thomas speaks of both luxury and avarice as absorbing the soul (II-II, 43, 6). Avarice incites restlessness of soul and thus impedes the contemplative moment that is the necessary prelude to prudent action, a moment involving both self-possession and an apprehension of the way things are in a concrete setting. Thomas speaks of *inconsideratio* as impeding the "act of understanding the truth of something" (II-II, 53, 4).

The alignment of prudence with liberalism and pluralism—in the writings of Martha Nussbaum, for instance—is problematic. I am not arguing that prudence cannot exist in a pluralistic society, but rather that the pedagogical dominance of notions like tolerance and equal regard tends to flatten the contours of our moral experience. Prudence presupposes moral education in specific practices as well as a fairly determinate conception of the human good. An impediment to the liberal appropriation of prudence is Aristotle's emphasis on the role of law in inculcating prudence. As he puts it at the end of the *Ethics (X,ix):*

> We must . . . by some means secure that the character shall have at the outset a natural affinity for virtue, loving what is noble and hating what is base. It is difficult to obtain a right education in virtue from youth up with being brought up under right laws. . . . But doubtless it is not enough for

[18] *Ibid.*, 72.   [19] *Ibid.*, 58.   [20] *Ibid.*, 87.

people to receive the right nurture . . . they must also practice the lessons
they have learnt, and confirm them by habit, when they are grown up.
Accordingly, we shall need laws to regulate the discipline of adults as
well, and in fact the whole life of the people generally.

The passage does not shift the emphasis from virtue to law; for, law is
pedagogically ordered to the inculcation of virtue. As Thomas puts it, laws
must be tailored to the customs of a people, ought not to be onerous, and
should lead from the imperfect to the perfect. Often cited in discussion of the
law's need for prudential application is Aristotle's discussion of equity. The
claim needs to be balanced by passages where Aristotle argues that changes in
laws are for the most part imprudent, since they erode customs that give rise to
the habits that make virtue possible.

Aquinas likewise underscores the pedagogical notion of law. He cites
Aristotle's statement that law is for the sake of virtue. The term *praeceptum*
means both command and lesson or instruction. Still, Aquinas goes further
than a pragmatic, pedagogical notion of law. In so doing, his view runs counter
to certain postmodern revivals of prudence. Martha Nussbaum argues that
irreducible particulars have greater "ethical value" than universals because
mutability, indeterminacy, and particularity characterize the realm of practical,
"non-scientific deliberation."[21]

While conceding the importance of "ongoing commitments and values,"
she insists that this "general background" of action is "not immune to revision
even at the highest level."[22] Aquinas would certainly concur that experience
and education enable us to understand better the import and scope of general
principles; he would even embrace that statement that "excellent choice cannot
be captured in universal rules."[23] Much more is required of us than mere
conformity to the rule. But, according to Thomas, conformity to certain rules
is required of us. At issue here is the relationship of principles to circumstances
and the mediating role of prudence. As we have already noted, Thomas holds
that principles are known through experience and that even basic principles
apply only for the most part. Some want to reason from this that Thomas
supposes the basic principles to be revisable. Does he?

The principle that borrowed goods should be returned is one that should
not be followed when doing so would be "injurious." The principle is itself a
specific rule following from more general principles of justice. In the case in
question, the ultimate purpose of the rule would be undermined by following

---

[21] *The Fragility of Goodness: Luck and Ethics in Greek Tragedy and Philosophy* (Cambridge:
Cambridge University Press, 1986), 301-02.

[22] *Ibid.*, 306.   [23] *Ibid.*, 303.

it. Thomas' remarks about the necessity of keeping promises is germane. The evil involved in not fulfilling a promise has to do with altering one's explicitly stated intentions (*animum mutat*). But Thomas allows that there are cases where promises need not be kept, for instance, when what one has promised is something evil. One is also excused from keeping the promise if "*sunt mutatae conditiones personarum.*" Thomas thinks that the stability of relevant circumstances is inherent within the practice of promising (II-II, CX, 3, ad 5).

In the discussion of the prohibition against theft, Thomas argues that, in cases of necessity, it is not a sin to take what one needs. One objection to the thesis is taken from Aristotle's statement in *Ethics, II,* 6. that certain names denote acts that are *secundum se malum*, and that theft is among these. Thomas responds that in the case of extreme necessity, taking what one needs does not have the *rationem furti*, properly speaking (II-II, 56, 7, ad 2). In a case of evident and urgent need (*evidens et urgens necessitas*), all things are common. Hence, Thomas does not regard the act of theft in cases of need as exceptions to the prohibition; rather, the conditions constitutive of the prohibition are no longer present. A similar strategy is operative in Thomas' discussion of whether it is permissible to kill sinners. The just and the innocent may never be killed, but those who sin heinously against the community may be slain: "*Homo peccando ab ordine rationis recedit; et ideo decedit a dignitate humana*" (II-II, LXIV, 2 ad 3).

Of course, Thomas' argument on behalf of the inviolability of certain precepts does nothing to minimize the role of prudence. In cases of uncertainty about the applicability of a principle, prudence must intervene. In the appraisal of circumstances, prudence is at work. Nussbaum seems to think that the presence of any non-gainsayable principles reduces ethics to *techne* and makes the idiosyncratic irrelevant. But, given what we have seen of Thomas' position, it is hard to see the merit of this objection. Indeed, Nussbaum's use of the language of irreducible particulars trades upon an ambiguity. Particulars, admittedly, are not universals and the sensation of a particular can never be reduced to a knowledge of universals. But in order to bring general principles into relationship with particulars there must be something about the particulars that makes them more than mere particulars. The merely particular would not be intelligible to us. Thomas states that the *intellectus* of prudence, which involves the apprehension of a particular, does not reside in a power of the external senses, but in the interior sense, which operates through a certain collation and judges of particulars (II-II, 47, 1 and 47, 2 ad 3).

Given that a virtue cannot be undermined by a particular vicious act, it seems that the emphasis on absolute rules is misplaced, unwarranted. Indeed, it is not the case that the rules are absolute, if one means by "absolute" equally applicable always and everywhere. Thomas does not hold that one can never act against any of the precepts; for, in some cases, lower precepts give way to higher ones. What one ought never to do is act against a relevant precept, that is, against the command of prudence. To do so would be to court imprudence and other vices. Thomas' account of the principles that cannot be abrogated is not grounded in a view of others' rights, nor is it grounded exclusively in the goods of others. For Thomas, it is equally a matter of who we are and what we become as moral agents that is involved in fundamental prohibitions. Without adherence to the basic precepts of the natural law, we cannot be virtuous persons. Of course, one vicious act here or there need not erode a virtuous character. But this seems a consideration more appropriate to one who lacks virtue, not to one who possesses, or longs for, virtue and understands with what cost and care virtues are cultivated. Each vicious act is a violation of the very perfection that the virtuous character naturally desires. Thomas' account of prudence. then, does not countenance a merely provisional or solely pedagogical view of moral precepts. On the contrary, it brings out what was missing in the neo-scholastic and Kantian emphasis on rules, namely, how these are inextricably bound up with the moral agent's view of his or her good.

All sorts of things put prudence and the other virtues at risk. One of them, as Saul Bellow indicates, is a failure to understand what binds one human being to another. For Thomas we need not start with complete agreement about the highest good but we should at least begin with the view of human life as a quest for the good. In his discussion of the prohibition of lying, Thomas states that "one man owes to another that without which human society is not able to be preserved" (II-II, CIX, 3, ad 1). Clearly, human society can survive without uniform adherence to the precepts of the natural law; indeed, we are tempted to think that it flourishes in contexts where moral rules are subordinate to Machiavellian *virtù* or prudence. But what Aquinas' account of the virtues, especially prudence, helps us to see is that it is not the mere survival of a group or its material pulchritude that is at issue, but rather the fragile existence of a community committed to a view of human life as a quest for the good. In so far as this is how we understand ourselves and our relationship to others, we will find that the cultivation of certain virtues presupposes and can never do without conformity to certain precepts.

Deconstruction and Artistic Creation: "Maritain and the Bad Boys of Philosophy"

Gregory Kerr

I know the errors that lay waste the modern world, and the fact that it has nothing great but its suffering; but this suffering I respect. Everywhere I see truths made captive. . . . Our business is to find the positive in all things; to use what is true less to strike than to cure.

Jacques Maritain[1]

I

Primarily, it was Friederich Nietzsche who made the twentieth century aware that there's more to reality than meets the logician's eye. In a brilliant passage in the *Birth of Tragedy* he writes of the last days of Socrates that:

> The voice of the Socratic dream vision is the only sign of any misgivings about the limits of logic: Perhaps — thus he [Socrates] must have asked himself — what is not intelligible to me is not necessarily unintelligent? Perhaps there is a realm of wisdom from which the logician is exiled? Perhaps art is even a necessary correlative of, and supplement for science?[2]

Nietzsche wanted to go beyond a logical discussion of good and evil, of an objective text, of a conceptually organized knowledge of things. This paper

---

[1] Maritain, *Art and Faith: Letters Between Jacques Maritain and Jean Cocteau*, trans. John Coleman (New York: Philosophical Library, 1948). This contains a translation of *Réponse à Jean Cocteau* (Paris: Librairie Stock, 1926).

[2] Friederich Nietzsche, *The Birth of Tragedy and the Case of Wagner*, trans. Walter Kaufmann (New York: Vintage Books, 1967), 93.

will reveal a certain Maritainian sympathy with this position of Nietzsche's and of the postmodern philosophers that follow him, by giving an analysis of comments made by Maritain concerning man *as artist*.

To do this we will examine the following Maritainian claims: a) that humans have a legitimate and autonomous transcendental drive for creating in and searching for beauty, along with, and distinct from, the other human drives to understand the truth, and to work towards the "good," b) that this drive is often in conflict with these other drives, and c) that it is only by, what may be legitimately called, the "deconstruction" of concepts and logical systems of thought that the great artist could truly satisfy this drive and create a work of art. Something like deconstruction, therefore, becomes a necessary condition of all great art; and, indeed, if the search for beauty is a legitimate aspiration of all human beings, of human growth as well.

While a Maritainian will oppose much of Nietzsche's and postmodern philosophy, *as philosophy*,[3] nevertheless, some of their "central" ideas about there being no objective truth and that language and concepts deflect meaning, are critical for the precarious aesthetic *moment*. It is within this context that a Maritainian can identify and open dialogue with Nietzsche and his progeny.

The creative drive is a legitimate one, and it should not be side-tracked by concerns for truth and moral goodness. In Maritain's classic, *Approaches to God*, where he treats of the many ways to God, he makes a separate claim for creation in beauty. He writes that the practical intellect has its ways of approach towards God—which are not theoretical demonstrations but belong to an existential and *pre*philosophic order. One of these ways is found in the poet's experience. Maritain's argument runs as follows: since beauty is a transcendental and since God is Subsistent Beauty, it is impossible for the artist, as he/she is devoted to created things, *not* to tend—however unconsciously—toward the principle of beauty."[4] Maritain tells us that this is not a rational knowledge, but a knowledge by connaturality which advances, and is, a spiritual inclination towards God, Himself.[5] Furthermore, this inclination is transcendental in nature. Maritain confirms this in his essay "Concerning Poetic

---

[3] A Maritainian would oppose the taking of the aesthetic viewpoint as a metaphysical view of the whole of reality. Specifically he or she would reject such statements as, "It is only as an aesthetic phenomenon that existence and the world are eternally justified (Nietzsche, *The Birth of Tragedy*, 52).

[4] Jacques Maritain, *Approaches to God*, World Perspectives, trans. Peter O'Reilly (London: George Allen & Unwin, 1955), 69ff.

[5] Knowledge, not rational and conceptual, but affective and nostalgic, the knowledge through connaturality which the artist has of beauty in his creative experience, is *in itself* (I do not say for him or for his own consciousness) an advance toward God, a spiritual inclination in the direction of God (Maritain, *Approaches to God*, 69-70).

Knowledge" where he specifically says that poetry is "an energy of [the] transcendental order like that of metaphysics." [6]

II

But while the drive for Beauty is legitimate and transcendental, it must be noted that it is often in conflict with the other aspirations of the human being; for as the whole human being operates concretely, the aspects of the world that he/she grasps are different. Only in God are the transcendentals united, for humans what is true may not be necessarily good and vice-versa.[7] Thus, the corresponding faculties of the human being grasp being differently. Maritain claims that our "will . . . does not of itself tend to the true, but solely and jealously to the good of man;"[8] and that the intellect by itself desires the truth, which of itself does not inspire but "only illumines."[9] In fact, Maritain would

[6] Jacques Maritain, "Concerning Poetic Knowledge" in Jacques and Raïssa Maritain, *The Situation of Poetry: Four Essays on the Relations Between Poetry, Mysticism, Magic, and Knowledge*, trans. Marshall Suther, (New York: Philosophical Library, 1955; reprint, New York: Kraus Reprint, 1968), 69-70. This work is a translation of *Situation de la poésie* (Paris: Desclée de Brouwer, 1938). Also he writes, "The fact is that all these energies, insofar as they pertain to the transcendental universe, aspire like poetry to surpass their nature and to infinitise themselves. . . . Art, poetry, metaphysics, prayer. . . (*Ibid.*, 56).

[7] In God alone are all these perfections identified according to their formal reason: in Him Truth is Beauty, is Goodness, is Unity, and they are He. In the things of this world, on the other hand, truth, beauty, goodness, etc., are aspects of being *distinct according to their formal reason*, and what is *true simpliciter* (absolutely speaking) may be good or beautiful only *secundum quid* (in a certain relation), what is *beautiful simpliciter* may be *good* or *true* only *secundum quid*. . . Wherefore beauty, truth, goodness (especially when it is no longer a question of metaphysical or transcendental good itself, but of moral good) command distinct spheres of human activity (Maritain, *Art and Scholasticism and the Frontiers of Poetry*, trans. Joseph W. Evans [Notre Dame, Indiana: University of Notre Dame Press, 1974], 174, no. 68.) This work contains translations of both *Art et scolastique*: troisième édition revue et corrigée (Paris: Louis Rouart et Fils, 1935); and *Frontières de la poésie et autres essais* (Paris: Louis Rouart et Fils, 1935); "C'est en Dieu seul que toutes ces perfections s'identifient selon leur raison formelle; en lui la Vérité est la Beauté, est la Bonté, est l'Unité, et elles sont Lui-même. Au contraire dans les choses d'ici-bas la vérité, la beauté, la bonté, etc., sont des aspects de l'être *distincts selon leur raison formelle*, et ce qui est *vrai simpliciter* (absolument parlant) peut n'être *bon* on *beau* que *secundum quid* (sous un certain rapport), ce qui est *beau simpliciter* peut n'être *bon* ou *vrai* que *secundum quid*. . . . C'est pourquoi la beauté, la vérité, la bonté (surtout quand il ne s'agit plus du bien métaphysique ou transcendantal lui-même, mais du bien moral) commandent des spheres distinctes de l'activité humaine" (*Art et scolastique*, 277, n. 68).

[8] Jacques Maritain, *Art and Scholasticism*, 7; "Volonté, qui de soi ne tend pas au vrai, mais uniquement et jalousement au bien de l'homme" (*Art et scolastique*, 8).

[9] Jacques Maritain, *Art and Scholasticism*, 26; "le vrai comme tel ne fait qu'illuminer" (*Art et scolastique*, 42).

continue, nothing with a drive toward the infinite—as is the human aspiration for truth or for goodness—is in accord with any other similar drive.[10] Maritain even tells us that they can be enemies:

> It is only in this conflict that they can exist and grow. Art, poetry, metaphysics, prayer, contemplation, each one is wounded, struck traitorously in the best of itself, and that is the very condition of its living. *Man* unites them by force, weeping all his tears, dying every day, and thus he wins his peace and their peace.[11]

We see the resulting conflict being played out in those who, according to Maritain, in the "spirit of Luther, Rousseau, or Tolstoy defend the order of the moral good,"[12] while others like Aristotle[13] and Aquinas defend the order of truth. "Here are two families which hardly understand each other, here as elsewhere, the prudent one dreads the contemplative and distrusts him."[14] However irresolvable the situation seems, Maritain still insists on the importance of the autonomy of the creative drive. He writes that "the spirit of Luther, Rousseau or Tolstoy has no place among us: if we defend the rights of God in the order of the moral good, we defend them also in the order of intelligence and beauty, and nothing obliges us to walk on all fours for the love of virtue."[15]

---

[10] "The fact is that all these energies, insofar as they pertain to the transcendental universe, aspire like poetry to surpass their nature and to infinitise themselves. . . . Art, poetry, metaphysics, prayer, contemplation, each one is wounded, struck traitorously in the best of itself, and that is the very condition of its living. Man unites them by force" (Maritain, "Concerning Poetic Knowledge" in *The Situation of Poetry,* 56); "A vrai dire toutes ces énergies, en tant qu'appartenant à l'univers transcendantal, aspirent comme la poésie à sortir de leur nature et à s'infinitiser. . . . Art, poésie, métaphysique, prière et contemplation, tout le monde est blessé, atteint traîteusement au meilleur de soi, et c'est la condition même de vivre. L'homme les unit de force" (*Situation de la poésie,* 113-114).

[11] Jacques Maritain, "Concerning Poetic Knowledge" in *The Situation of Poetry,* 56; "C'est dans ce conflit seulement qu'elles peuvent exister et grandir. Art, poésie, métaphysique, prière et contemplation, tout le monde est blessé, atteint traîtreusement même de vivre. *L'homme* les unit de force, en y pleurant toutes ses larmes, en y mourant chaque jour, et gange ainsi sa paix et leur paix" ("De la connaissance poétique" in *Situation de la poésie,* 113-4).

[12] Jacques Maritain, "An Essay on Art" in *Art and Scholasticism,* 98; "Discours sur l'art" in *Art et scolastique,* 167.

[13] Jacques Maritain, *Art and Scholasticism,* 33; "Mais touche-to-on au bien et à l'Amour, comme les saints, au vrai, comme un Aristote" (*Art et scolastique,* 74).

[14] Jacques Maritain, "The Freedom of Song" in *Art and Poetry,* trans. E. de P. Matthews, (New York: Philosophical Library, 1943), 103. This work contains translations of "Dialogues" ("Dialogues"), "Trois Peintres: Georges Rouault, Gino Severini, Marc Chagall" ("Three Painters"), and "La clef des chants" ("The Freedom of Song"), in *Frontieres de la poesie et autres essais*; "Voilà deux familles qui ne s'entendent guère, ici comme ailleurs le prudent redoute le contemplatif et se méfie de lui" (*Ibid.,* 220).

[15] Jacques Maritain, *Art and Scholasticism,* 220, n. 163 (added in 1927). We might remark

The creative drive follows none of the other drive's rules of fair play. This one is completely different. In Maritain's mature aesthetic work, *Creative Intuition*, he tells us in a note that, "We must thus admit, if we get rid of our 'scientist' modern prejudices, the existence of a poetic science [understand knowledge] which differs *toto coelo* from the theoretical (discursive) sciences."[16] While the opposition is firm throughout Maritain's aesthetic works, perhaps no passage is more vivid than the one in his *magnum opus*, *The Degrees of Knowledge*:

> The metaphysician breathes an atmosphere of abstraction which is death for the artist. Imagination, the discontinuous, the unverifiable, in which the metaphysician perishes, is life itself to the artist.[17]

III

Our discussion is now brought to the point where we might see the value of deconstuction in the creative act itself. While aesthetically, Maritain and Nietzsche and the Postmodernists, like Derrida, are worlds apart, nevertheless, Maritain does agree with them on three things at least within the creative realm: a) there are no objective (apart from the subject) conceptual realities or truths, b) the artist in the line of art is, in a sense, beyond good and evil, and c) there is at the *heart* of the creative domain no logo-centrality or conceptual organization.

First, following St. Thomas, Maritain holds that poetry and art have a *defect in truth*[18] so that works of art are neither intended to nor actually do address conceptual reason. On the contrary, the way in which art operates is by *seducing* the reason so that the viewer's understanding will be thwarted and his emotion and sympathy might grasp the significance of the work. Furthermore, Maritain

---

here, *contra* Maritain, that perhaps those who follow Luther pay as much or *even more* attention to beauty especially with regards to music in the liturgy than the followers of Aquinas.

[16] Jacques Maritain, *Creative Intuition in Art and Poetry*, Bollingen Series XXXV.1 (Princeton: Princeton University Press, 1977), 50 n. 4.

[17] Jacques Maritain, *Distinguish To Unite or the Degrees of Knowledge*, trans. Gerald B. Phelan (New York: Charles Scribner's Sons, 1959), 2; "A la naissance du métaphysicien comme à celle du poète, il y a comme une grâce d'ordre naturel. L'un, qui jette son coeur dans les choses comme un dard ou une fusée, voit par divination,—dans le sensible même, impossible à en séparer, l'éclat d'une lumière spirituelle où un regard de Dieu brille pour lui. L'autre, se détournant du sensible, voit par science, dans l'intelligible et détachée des choses périssables, cette lumière spirituelle elle-même captée en quelque idée. L'abstraction, qui est la mort de l'un, l'autre y respire; imagination, le discontinu, l'invérifiable, où l'autre périt, fair la vie de l'un: (*Distinguer Pour unir ou les degrés du savoir* [Paris: Desclée De Brouwer, 1932], 5).

holds that imitation, classically understood, is an impossible notion. The work of art does not represent anything objective, rather, says Maritain, the artist transfigures, transforms reality so that our normal conceptual grasp of the work of art is halted and we see something new. Imitation exists, for Maritain, but in a very unique way.

Second, no moral lesson should be preached by the artist, and he is responsible *as artist* for no moral values. According to Maritain, even evil people can be great artists. He writes in his last aesthetic work *The Responsibility of the Artist* that, "Oscar Wilde was but a good Thomist when he wrote: 'The fact of a man being a poisoner is nothing against his prose.'"[19] Here in this work Maritain quotes St. Thomas as saying, "The kind of good which art pursues is not the good of the human will or appetite [or the good of man], but the good of the very works done or artifacts (*Sum. Theol.* I-II, 57, 4.)."[20] Summing up our discussion thus far, Maritain writes,

> In this sense every thesis [an intention extrinsic to the work itself] whether it claims to demonstrate some truth or to touch the heart, is for art a foreign importation, hence an impurity. It imposes on art, in art's own sphere, that is to say in the very production of the work, a rule and an end which is not the end or rule of the production.[21]

If one sees in both Nietzsche and Derrida a resistance to a logically conceived and organized world, one sees it also in Maritain's aesthetics. According to Maritain's own aesthetic principles, it is by the deconstruction of concepts and metaphors that every genuine artist creates a great work of art. Not only is a theoretical and discursive grasp of the world different from the artist's, but Maritain finds that, as the artist creates, the resources of discursive reason are a positive hindrance to him. Perhaps this is particularly evident in the activity of the poet. Words, the obvious product of discursive reason, are the enemy. The poet must at some point disengage and loosen himself from language. Maritain is so strongly insistent upon this point and speaks of language with such abuse that one almost wonders whether Maritain even secretly wanted to be a poet rather than a philosopher.[22]

[18] Jacques Maritain, "Concerning Poetic Knowledge," in *The Situation of Poetry,* 67 n. 16.

[19] Jacques Maritain, *The Responsibility of the Artist* (New York: Charles Scribner's Sons, 1960), 24.

[20] *Ibid.,* 24.

[21] Jacques Maritain, *Art and Scholasticism* 62-3; "En ce sens-là toute thèse, qu'elle prétende démontrer ou qu'elle prétende émouvoir, est pour l'art un apport étranger, donc une impureté. Elle impose à l'art, dans sa sphère propre, c'est-à-dire dans la production même de l'oeuvre, une règle et une fin qui n'est pas la sienne." (*Art et scolastique,* 109).

[22] "There are never words for what it would be most important to say. Isn't it because of that we need poets and musicians?" See *The Peasant of the Garonne: An Old Layman Questions*

In his discussion of poetry, Maritain continually insists that language deflects the meanings of the poet. He writes: "Rational language is not cut out to express the singular . . . it does not only interfere with poetry, it perpetually sidetracks it."[23] One might speculate on what this might mean if one were to take this aesthetic and poetic view of the world as one's whole metaphysical perspective. Maritain continues by noting that poetry causes art to "long to be freed from reason."[24] While there are concepts in poetry, to be sure, they have been dethroned.[25] Ultimately, the poems want to take the viewer beyond words and concepts, for they simply get in the way.[26]

While the intellect of the artist does, of course, play a dominant role, for Maritain, its discursive and logical abilities play but a small part in the creative act. While there are many issues involved here, let us examine two in particular: the magical sign and the heart of the creative intuition.

It was a stroke of genius for Maritain to develop the notion of the "magical sign." He classically defines any sign as something that "makes manifest, makes known . . . something distinct from itself, of which it takes the place and with regard to which it exercises a ministerial function, and on which it depends as on its measure."[27] However, he is very unclassical, and perhaps even radical when he describes the "magical sign" and how it differs from the logical sign. The magical sign, the one used by the artist, is a "sign in the sphere of the dream."[28] It is a sign for the imagination that has dethroned the logos-dominated intelligence and has begun to rule the activities of the

---

Himself About the Present Time, trans. Michael Cuddihy and Elizabeth Hughes (New York: Holt, Rinehart and Winston, 1968) ,14; Also see Wallace Fowlie, "Maritain the Writer" in *Jacques Maritain: The Man and His Achievement*, ed. Joseph W. Evans (New York: Sheed and Ward, 1963), 46-57.

[23] Jacques Maritain, *Creative Intuition in Art and Poetry,* 74.

[24] *Ibid.*, 74.   [25] *Ibid.*, 323.

[26] Quoting Baudelaire favorably, he writes, "Great poetry is essentially *stupid*, it *believes*, and that's what makes its glory and force. Do not ever confuse the phantoms of reason with the phantoms of imagination: the former are equations, the latter are beings and memories" (*Ibid.*, 249; Also, Maritain writes, "In brief, it could happen . . . that a neo-classical reaction would ask poetry to *exhibit ideas and sentiments*, to charge itself with the rubbish of human notions in their verbosity and their natural meanness, and to fabricate *versified discourses* for the delectation of the formal intelligence. We should then see born a poetics "of abundance," of verbal abundance and of intellectual reduplication. And the word would again become master, the glory of the word, the endless and buzzing heroism of language—and all the stupidity of man" (*Situation of Poetry,* 60).

[27] Jacques Maritain, "Sign and Symbol" in *Ransoming the Time*, trans. Harry Lorin Binsse (New York: Charles Scribner's Sons, 1941), 218. This is a translation of "Sign et symbole," *Revue Thomiste*, XLIV (April, 1938) 299-300.

[28] Jacques Maritain, *Ransoming the Time,* 227; "Sign et symbole," 311.

soul.[29] Here consciousness is "immersed in the living ocean of the imagination."[30] Here the consciousness is at play, for as Maritain wrote on the "Experience of the Poet:"

> [The poet] is rather a child who tames things by calling them affectionate names, and who makes a paradise with them. They tell him their names only in an enigma, he enters into their games, blindfolded, he plays with them at life and death.[31]

This is not irrationalism or emotivism; the intelligence is present, but it is bound. Truth here is felt, lived, participated in, but not winnowed out for its own sake. The magical sign represents reality by asserting the living union of man with nature whereof the various primitive myths are symbols. To experience these magical signs is like believing in a story like a child does, but not being able to "wake up." Above all, and perhaps most amenable to Deconstructive sympathies, is the fact that in the case of the magical sign, various distinctions between things break down. The distinction between sign and signified disappears. For the viewer receiving the magical sign, there seems to be a physical interpenetration and fusion of the sign and the signified. In addition, according to Maritain, "the principle of identity does not exist," here and the "identity of things is constantly unmade and made again."[32] All of this becomes extremely interesting if viewed in the light of Nietzsche's existentialism and Derrida's dislike for both binary oppositions and logocentrism. According to Maritain, this magical sign constitutes a key feature to art at its best.

If the magical sign resists logic, so too does the artist's creative intuition in its beginning moments. We will argue here that, in the heart of the creative intuition, as explored in Maritain's discussion of it in the work of the same name, there is a subrational and musical beginning not a conceptual or logical one.

Maritain claims that the mind works in the three spiritual spheres of the soul: the preconscious, the imagination, and the region of conceptual reason,[33] and he relates these to three epiphanies or stages of the creative intuition: the flash of insight, the intuition as intellectually conceived, and the intuition as worked out into a concrete work of art.[34]

---

[29] The comparison between the magical sign, and its function in art, cannot but suggest certain doctrines of the Deconstructionists.

[30] Jacques Maritain, *Ransoming the Time,* 227; "Sign et symbole," 311.

[31] Jacques Maritain, "The Experience of the Poet" in *The Situation of Poetry,* 79. For further discussion see "Sign and Symbol" in *Ransoming the Time* 233ff.

[32] Jacques Maritain, *Ransoming the Time* 235-6; "Sign et symbole," 317.

[33] Jacques Maritain, *Creative Intuition in Art and Poetry,* 319.

[34] *Ibid.,* 365-370.

An image that might be helpful in describing the creative process, is that of a deep-sea diver coming up for air. In the beginning, the first phase of creative intuition, the first "epiphany," as Maritain calls it, the intuition begins in the preconscious of the soul where all of the powers are conjoined at the root—a place where intellect, will and emotion are one. This is place within the poet where she sees with her mind, will and emotion all synchronized together. This is a vantage point where she sees with her dreams and longings and perceives with her love. Here she sees into reality and has a flash of knowledge and a kind of music begins to stir within her soul. One may notice that at the origin the creative intuition is music. May one think of Dionysius?

The musical stir increases as the creative intuition seeks for expression in signs and makes its first attempt at it deep within the imagination with imaginal-emotional complexes known as musical pulsions.[35] These are rhythmically presented sets of images that bring together the flux of reality into a relatively depersonalized unity. One can think of them as intelligence trying to read or scan reality in its spatio-temporal environment.[36] Through these musical pulsions, through imagination and through emotion, the intelligence is trying to read a reality in process, a reality in Bergsonian duration or Heraclitean flux, and ultimately a reality that the mind's finished product, the *judged concept*, will—out of necessity—banish to irrelevance.[37]

The soul for Maritain is like a laboratory.[38] Everything that transpires in the pre-conscious and in the imagination is ultimately in the service of fashioning an end-product which is either a concept, an action, or a work made. Here, in what we shall term the primary area of the imagination, occurs the formation of images from the musical pulsions. Here at the frontiers of intelligence, the pulsions frame and put into cognitive and emotional perspective the reality to be grasped. Some newly born images will serve to illuminate for

[35] *Ibid.*, 302-4. According to one who knew Maritain, he was questioned by his colleagues at Princeton for his choice of the word. But, according to Maritain, while not commonly used in English or in French, it "is listed in the *Shorter Oxford Dictionary*" and it is the best word for describing the "kind of mental wave or vibration, charged with dynamic unity" (*Ibid.*, 302 n. 3) that he had in mind.

[36] Probably not unlike my eighteen-month old son, Theodore, who imitates the rhythms of what he hears, in order to better absorb the reality. Also, I have been amazed at some mentally "handicapped" people who, while unable to speak a sentence, nevertheless, can sing whole songs. These signs—these pulsions—are what allow what is outside of us inside.

[37] This is another reason why an artwork must be and present itself as "defect in truth." Concepts will only inhibit the flow of the concrete world. Maritain's philosophical mentor, Henri Bergson saw this well and is, no doubt, in Maritain's consciousness as he philosophizes here. For further discussion, see Bergson, *The Creative Mind: An Introduction to Metaphysics*, trans. Mabelle L. Andison (New York: Philosophical Library, reprinted by Citadel Press, 1946).

[38] Jacques Maritain, *Creative Intuition in Art and Poetry,* 106-111.

the intellect some obscure and pressing intelligibility that *discursive reason is incapable* of processing. These images, called by Maritain "immediately illuminating images,"[39] present to the viewer under the guise of one set of appearances a reality that is present but far away from the understanding. A brilliant example of this, according to Maritain, can be seen in this poem by John Berryman:

> Movements of stone within a woman's heart, abrupt and dominant. They gesture how fings really are. Rarely a child sings now.[40]

Here the image of large stones reveal a characteristic about the poet's experience of a woman's heart and about how we often find it, at least from a man's point of view, moving back and forth and feeling helpless, like a child, in our inability to stop it. The poet is not simply comparing a woman's heart to an already prefabricated, logically determined, and/or well-worn image of spring, flowers, roses, or warmth, but is using a rather unexpected and unforeseeable image that could reveal nothing to the discursive intellect to warn it ahead of time of the comparison. Rather, it is as if the image grew up with, was formed in secret for, the creating of the experience of a woman's character. Examples of immediately illuminating images can be seen in painting no less than in poetry. One might consider Chagall here.[41]

With our discussion of the magical sign and the beginning and heart of the creative moment, we can see that creating great works of art is not a matter of telling the truth about things, and if it were, one would have to be a liar who told it.[42] It is not a matter edifying the reader with sound moral values and it isn't a matter of argumentation. Ultimately, art is not motivated and guided by discursive reason either theoretically or practically, it is motivated by something far beyond and behind, something necessary but possibly dangerous. This is something that challenges the rational order of things. In conclusion, let us play with the following quote from Maritain:

> As in each case in which thought attacks a difficult task, it begins, in the conquering of new domains, and especially the interior domains of its own spiritual universe, by bringing on troubles, disasters. The human being seems to disorganize itself, and it happens in fact sometimes that these crises of growth end badly. They are nevertheless crises of growth.[43]

---

[39] *Ibid.*, 325-333.

[40] John Berryman, *The Dispossessed* (New York: William Sloane, 1948) quoted in Maritain, *Creative Intuition in Art and Poetry*, 293.

[41] For example, see the circle in Chagall's *Around Her*, plate 60 in Maritain, *Creative Intuition in Art and Poetry.*

[42] "The poet is a liar who always speaks the truth," Jean Cocteau.

[43] Jacques Maritain, "Concerning Poetic Knowledge," in *The Situation of Poetry,* 38.

A Heideggerian Critique of Aquinas and a Gilsonian Reply

John F. X. Knasas

I

In his book, *Heidegger and Aquinas: An Essay on Overcoming Metaphysics*, John Caputo investigates among other points a claim of Étienne Gilson's followers. Their claim is that Heidegger's charge of an oblivion or forgetfulness of being cannot be pinned on Aquinas.[1] Aquinas escapes the charge because he alone in the history of Western philosophy deepens the understanding of being to the level of *esse*. How could someone who has seized upon the fundamental principle of being be guilty of a forgetfulness of being? Caputo begs to differ. A Heideggerian would find the Gilsonian thesis unimpressive. What Aquinas has done remains too ontical, for it still deals with things and the principles of things. Something else escapes Aquinas' eye, and Caputo variously expresses the Heideggerian dissatisfaction:

> *esse* for Aquinas means that act by which a thing comes to be "real" rather than "present" in the original Greek sense of shining and appearing, revealing and concealing. . . . In St. Thomas the original Greek notion of presencing as the shining in which all appearances shine, as a rising up into appearance, into manifestness, has declined into an understanding of Being as "objective presence," the presence of what is mutely there, as a sound in an empty room is thought to be "there" in naive realism and common sense.[2]

Also:

> Hence, St. Thomas takes the being, not in its very Being—that is, in its quiet emergence into manifestness—but in its character as something *created*.[3]

---

[1] John Caputo, *Heidegger and Aquinas: An Essay on Overcoming Metaphysics* (New York: Fordham University Press, 1982), 100-1, 117-21.

[2] *Ibid.*, 199. [3] *Ibid.*, 200.

Then:

> The metaphysics of *actualitas* is basically at odds with the meditative savoring of the original sense of Being as presencing.[4]

Finally,

> The early Greek experience of *Anwesen*, of the simple emergence of things into the light, differs fundamentally from St. Thomas' metaphysics of actuality and science of first causes.[5]

Caputo's conclusion is that one cannot accept Heidegger's criteria of *Seindenken* and think that Aquinas meets them.[6]

But a Gilsonian might humbly take Caputo's correction and still feel constrained to note that if the issue is being in the sense of presencing, then another portion of Aquinas' philosophical doctrine becomes relevant, viz., Aquinas' elaboration of the mechanics of cognition. In sum, things are present to us insofar as our form has been informed by their forms. Formal reception of form allows us to become the really other without loss to ourselves. We are then sufficiently actuated to cause the presence of the real as the term of our cognitional activity.[7]

Once more, however, I believe that we have philosophers speaking past each other. For Heidegger believes that presencing requires an understanding of being as an *a priori* condition. Many texts to this effect exist. One of the most striking is from Heidegger's, *The Basic Problems of Phenomenology* (1927). In detailing what he means by "being" in the ontological difference between being and beings, Heidegger says,

> We are able to grasp beings as such, as beings, only if we understand something like being. If we did not understand, even though at first roughly and without conceptual comprehension, what actuality signifies, then the actual would remain hidden from us. If we did not understand what reality means, then the real would remain inaccessible. . . . We must understand being so that we may be able to be given over to a world that is, so that we can exist in it and be our own Dasein itself as a being. We must be able to understand actuality before

---

[4] *Ibid.*, 201.   [5] *Ibid.*, 209.   [6] *Loc. cit.*

[7] "knowing beings are distinguished from non-knowing beings in that the latter possess only their own form; whereas the knowing being is naturally adapted to have also the form of some other thing, for the species of the thing known is in the knower. Hence, it is manifest that the nature of a non-knowing being is more contracted and limited; whereas the nature of a knowing being has a greater amplitude and extension. That is why the Philosopher says that the soul is in a sense all things." Thomas Aquinas, *S.T.* I, 14, 2c; as edited by Anton Pegis in *The Basic Writings of St. Thomas Aquinas* (New York: Random House, 1945), Vol. I, 136. On the Aristotelian background, see Joseph Owens, "Aristotelian Soul as Cognitive of Sensibles, Intelligibles and Self," *Aristotle: The Collected Papers of Joseph Owens*, ed. John R. Catan (Albany: State University of New York Press, 1981), 81-98.

all experience of actual beings. This understanding of actuality or of being in the widest sense as over against the experience of beings is in a certain sense earlier than the experience of beings. To say that the understanding of being precedes all factual experience of beings does not mean that we would first need to have an explicit concept of being in order to experience beings theoretically or practically. We must understand being—being, which may no longer itself be called a being, being, which does not occur as a being among other beings but which nevertheless must be given and in fact is given in the understanding of being.[8]

What is Heidegger saying about being? As I understand him, he is saying that being is the expanse up and against which realities are seen as realities. The driving idea is that the individual is only known in the light of the universal. Undergirding this driving thought is Heidegger's description of what we experience. Does not saying that we experience beings, mean that the beings are appreciated as instances of something larger, viz., being? Similarly, to

---

[8] Martin Heidegger, *The Basic Problems of Phenomenology*, trans. Albert Hofstadter (Bloomington, Indiana: Indiana University Press, 1988), 10-11. Also, from *Being and Time*, trans. John Macquarrie and Edward Robinson (New York: Harper & Row, 1962): "Inquiry, as a kind of seeking, must be guided beforehand by what is sought. So the meaning of Being must already be available to us in some way" (25); "what is asked about is Being - that which determines entities as entities, that on the basis of which entities are already understood" (25-6); "But as an investigation of Being, [phenomenological interpretation] brings to completion, autonomously and explicitly, that understanding of Being which belongs already to Dasein and which `comes alive' in any of its dealings with entities" (96); "understanding of Being has already been taken for granted in projecting upon possibilities. In projection, Being is understood, though not ontologically conceived. An entity whose kind of Being is the essential projection of Being-in-the-world has understanding of Being, and has this as constitutive of its Being" (188-7); "If what the term 'idealism' says, amounts to the understanding that Being can never be explained by entities but is already that which is 'transcendental' for every entity, then idealism affords the only correct possibility for a philosophical problematic" (251); "At the bottom, however, the whole correlation necessarily gets thought of as somehow being, and must therefore be thought of with regard to some definite idea of Being" (252); "only if the understanding of Being is, do entities as entities become accessible" (255); "[Common sense] fails to recognize that entities can be experienced 'factually' only when Being is already understood, even if it has not been conceptualized" (363); "All ontical experience of entities - both circumspective calculation of the ready-to-hand, and positive scientific cognition of the present-at-hand - is based upon projections of the Being of the corresponding entities" (371); "[the paradigmatic character of mathematical natural science] consists rather in the fact that the entities which it takes as its theme are discovered in it in the only way in which entities can be discovered - by the prior projection of their state of Being" (414). In sum, Caputo, *op. cit.*, 53, remarks: "[In Being and Time] Being is the meaning or horizon of understanding within which beings are manifest. Thus instead of being an abstract concept, a vacuous abstraction when separated from concrete beings, . . . , Being for Heidegger becomes the meaning-giving horizon, the transcendental a priori, which precedes beings and renders them possible in their Being. It is not an abstraction drawn from beings, but an a priori which precedes them."

experience Fido as a dog means to experience Fido as an instance of dog. But unlike dog, being is underived from the beings that we experience. How could it be derived? Being sets up experienced beings in the first place. Whenever we have beings, we already have being. Hence, in the previous quote, Heidegger says that being is "before" all experience of actual beings and that the understanding of being is ". . . in a sense earlier than the experience of beings." Continuing this *a priori* construal of being, *Basic Problems* says that "the understanding of being has itself the mode of being of the human *Dasein*."[9] Elsewhere, Heidegger says that being is what is closest to us.[10] His science of being is also called a transcendental science for it adopts the original sense and true tendency of the Kantian transcendental. As such, transcendental science is uninvolved with the task of popular metaphysics that deals with some one being behind the known beings.[11] Finally, in the following chapter of *Basic Problems*, Heidegger analyzes perceptual intentionality and stresses that the uncoveredness of a being in perception means that the being of the being has already been disclosed.[12]

What would a Gilsonian Thomist say to all of this? What comes most readily to mind is that the datum, viz., a consciousness of something as a being, fails to indicate necessarily an *a priori* notion of being. For it may well be that the notion of being is immediately abstracted from things and subsequently employed to appreciate them as beings. Being is always found with beings because it is simultaneously derived from them.

Why does this alternative view apparently not even occur to Heidegger? The answer seems to be that the notion of being used to grasp a thing as a being Heidegger considers to be applicable to immaterial beings, including God. In lines just previous to the above quote from *Basic Problems*, God, too, is described as *a* being and so is apprehended through being: "What can there be apart from nature, history, God, space, number? We say of each of these, even though in a different sense, that it *is*. We call it a being." Likewise, Heidegger says elsewhere, "[Being] is not God, nor [some] ground of the world. Being is broader than all beings - and yet is nearer to man than all beings, whether they be rocks, animals, works of art, machines, angels, or God."[13] But how does a notion of being wide enough to include God come out of sensible things alone? The abstractive account of being chokes on this point. Better to say that being is not abstractive, or *a posteriori*, but is *a priori*. In short, because being is wide enough to include God, then it is underived from sensible things.

[9] *Ibid.*, 16.

[10] From Martin Heidegger's "Letter on Humanism," quoted by William J. Richardson, *Heidegger—Through Phenomenology to Thought* (The Hague: Martinus Nijhoff, 1974), 6.

[11] Martin Heidegger, *Basic Problems*, 17.   [12] *Ibid.*, 67.   [13] See *supra*, n. 10

At this time it is noteworthy that Caputo mentions two sources for Heidegger's thinking on being: Heidegger's university professor, Carl Braig,[14] and the sixteenth century Jesuit, Francisco Suarez.[15] For both thinkers being is amply wide to include God. This point is so true for Suarez that he regards the philosophical treatment of God as subdivision of ontology, or general metaphysics. On the notion of being, neither of these men were *apriorists*. Both were abstractionists. But in light of the incongruity between the notion of being that is "abstracted" and the sensible data, is not an *apriorism* for being an implication just waiting to be drawn? I believe so. And such an observation, in my opinion, goes a long way to explain why Heidegger took the *a priori* route.

II

If the mentioned incongruity constrains Heidegger to understand being as an *a priori*, then the Gilsonian need simply say that it is by no means obvious that things are originally known as beings in the light of such a grandiose notion of being. For starters a much less ample notion of being will suffice, and as less ample, the incongruity of its immediate abstract derivation from sensible experience disappears.

Moreover, in Aquinas the notion of being that runs through creatures fails to carry over to God, as Heidegger seems to think. Aquinas variously expresses the notion of being common to creatures as *ens commune* and as *ens inquantum ens*. I will elaborate upon this point later. Now let it suffice to say that Aquinas relates God to *ens commune* not as an instance thereof but as the transcending cause of *ens commune*.[16] God is not under *ens commune* but above it. It is true that Aquinas sees *esse* as analogically common to God and creatures. But again one must be careful to conceive this position correctly. The analogon of *esse* is not even intelligibly prior to God. Rather, the divine analogate instantiates the analogon.[17] God is *esse subsistens*. All other *esse* is *esse accidentale*. Aquinas traces *esse accidentale* to God not only causally but also intelligibly. In sum, for Aquinas unlike for Heidegger, even intelligibly speaking, nothing exists prior to God.

Heidegger has a much better case for the *a priori* status of being in respect to what Aquinas calls the subject of metaphysics. Aquinas' terminology of *ens*

---

[14] John Caputo, *Heidegger and Aquinas: An Essay on Overcoming Metaphysics*, 45-55.
[15] *Ibid.*, 69-70.   [16] *In de Trin.* V, 4c.
[17] Thomas Aquinas, *In I Sent.*, prol. q. 1, ad 2m. For a note on whether the analogy between God and creatures is basically one of proportion or proportionality, see John F. X. Knasas, "Aquinas, Analogy, and the Divine Infinity," *Doctor Communis*, 40 (1987), 79, n. 32.

commune and *ens inquantum ens* labels the subject of metaphysics. The terminology designates an intelligibility or commonality that one appreciates as having a capacity of realization in non-bodies.[18] The intelligibility is separate from matter both in being and in notion. As such *ens* is unlike the commonalities of man, horse, or ass. These are natures admitting realization only in matter. Aquinas also conveys this point by calling *ens commune* a transphysical commonality.[19] In this sense neo-Scholastics have used the term "transcendental."[20] But besides harboring the possibility of realization apart from matter, *ens commune* encompasses a composition. It is a composite transphysical commonality. Two parts, substance as potency and *esse* as act, comprise the composition.[21]

But various well-known attempts to formulate an *a posteriori* source for the subject of metaphysics have both philosophical and Thomistic problems. Both in whole and in part, I have told this story before.[22] For present purposes I must at least in succinct fashion repeat it.

III

Throughout many works, but especially in *Existence and the Existent* (1947) and *Approches sans entrave* (1973), Maritain presents as the entry to metaphysics a heightened judgmental appreciation of the *esse* of sensible things. Something about such *esse* so known informs us that to be a being is not necessarily to be a body.

The philosophical problem here is that Maritain abstracts a notion too great for the data to bear. From a number of judgments I can see that *esse* is an act

---

[18] "We say that being [*ens*] and substance are separate from matter and motion not because it is of their nature to be without them, as it is of the nature of ass to be without reason, but because it is not of their nature to be in matter and motion, as animal abstracts from reason, although some animals are rational." Aquinas, *In de Trin.* V, 4, ad 5m; trans. by Armand Maurer, *The Division and Methods of the Sciences* (Toronto: Pontifical Institute of Mediaeval Studies, 1963), 48-9. Also, "In this [second] way being [*ens*], substance, potency, and act are separate from matter and motion, because they do not depend upon them for their existence . . . Thus philosophical theology [also called metaphysics] investigates beings separate in the second sense as its subject, . . ." *In de Trin.* V, 4c; Maurer, trans., 45. See also Aquinas, *In Meta.*, proem.

[19] "Haec enim transphysica inveniuntur in via resolutionis, sicut magis communia post minus communia." *In Meta.*, proem.

[20] Jacques Maritain, *The Degrees of Knowledge*, trans. Gerald B. Phelan (New York: Charles Scribner's Sons, 1959), 210-18.

[21] "potency and act divide common being." Previous lines identify potency and act as substance and being [*esse*]. For a sketch of the subject of Thomistic metaphysics, see John F. X. Knasas, *The Preface to Thomistic Metaphysics* (New York: Peter Lang Publishing, 1990), 4-7.

that need not actuate this body or that body. Nevertheless, in every case of judgment so far, *esse* is still presented as the act of *some* body. From the data no indication yet exist that *esse* possesses an ability to actuate more than bodies. Texts from the *De Ente et Essentia* and *In de Trinitate* indicate that for Aquinas also abstraction is controlled by the data. Only if we increased the data to include existing non-bodies as well as existing bodies could we know that being need not mean a body.

Other *a posteriori* Thomists who criticize Maritain along the mentioned lines claim that the entry into metaphysics follows upon natural philosophy's demonstration of the immaterial. From Aristotle's *Physics*, one demonstrates separate substance as a required immaterial and immovable mover. From the *De Anima*, one proves the human soul to be immaterial. Such conclusions add to our data and enable us to stretch our original notion of being so that it is seen to apply analogically both to the material and immaterial orders.

But this approach fares no better than Maritain's. First, a proof for the immaterial on matter/form principles runs into a genuine Aristotelian problem. The proof appears to posit an efficient cause whose nature is form alone. But a case can be made, as Joseph Owens has, that in an Aristotelian context in which act is identified with form no pure form can be an efficient cause.

The natural philosophy approach is also at odds with the Thomistic texts. At *S.T.* I, 44, 2c, Aquinas has reasoning based on matter/form principles taking the philosopher to a universal cause that is still bodily, a celestial sphere. If philosophers reason further, the text continues, it is on the basis of *ens inquantum ens*. This basis is the metaphysical viewpoint. At *In de Trin.* V, 4c, Aquinas restricts philosophical knowledge of God and angels to metaphysics: "Philosophers, then, study these divine beings only insofar as they are the principles of . . . being as being." Finally, at *In II Phys.* lect. IV, n. 175, Aquinas assigns the study of the rational soul insofar as it is separable from matter to first philosophy, for natural philosophy considers any form only insofar as form has being in matter.

I find no texts that unequivocally give natural philosophy a demonstration of immaterial being. *In de Trin.* V, 2, ad 3m is often cited in behalf of the natural philosophy approach. Aquinas is replying to the objection that natural philosophy does treat what exists apart from matter and motion because it considers the First Mover that is free from all matter. In reply, Aquinas admits that natural philosophy treats the First Mover which is "of a different nature from natural things" but as the terminus of its subject that is about things in matter and motion. This seems to catch Aquinas giving natural philsophy proof of an immaterial being. Not necessarily, however. Bearing in mind, Aquinas' distinction between terrestrial and celestial matter (I, 66, 2c) and his references to the celestial bodies as first mover (*Primum movens, C.G.* I, 13), it is not too far out of line to say that the immaterial first mover about which Aquinas is speaking is a celestial mover free from *terrestrial matter*. This rendering would also prevent the text from contradicting Aquinas' mentioned claim a scant two articles later that philosophers know God and the angels only in metaphysics.

Hence, as I see it, the flashpoint between Aquinas and Heidegger is the subject of Thomistic metaphysics and the inability to ground that subject *a posteriori*. In Heidegger's eyes, Aquinas should frankly confess that *ens commune* is an *a priori*. Furthermore, Aquinas should see that his account of cognitional presence in terms of formal reception of form is lacking, for it makes no acknowledgment of the *a priori* factor of being. Going this route also means giving up traditional ontology understood as a search for the ultimate causes of things. In its wake follows a phenomenological ontology that uncovers ourselves as projectors of the being in the light of which we are conscious of beings. This is just what Heidegger wants.[23]

IV

I wish to defend Aquinas by upholding an *a posteriori* origin for Thomistic metaphysics. Yet, I will not be returning to Maritain or the natural philosophy Thomists. Instead I pivot to Gilson and his trumpeting of Aquinas as a discoverer of the existential dimension of being. In an essay criticizing Maritain's intuition of being position, Gilson speaks of metaphysicians who lack Maritain's intuition of being at the third abstractive degree but nevertheless possess an intuition of being simply in the sense of a grasp of the *esse* of sensible things.[24] Among

---

[22] "Immateriality and Metaphysics," *Angelicum*, 65 (1988), 44-76, and *Preface*, chs.1-3.

[23] "We are surmounting beings in order to reach being. Once having made the ascent we shall not again descend to a being, which, say, might lie like another world behind the familiar beings. The transcendental science of being has nothing to do with popular metaphysics, which deals with some being behind the known beings; rather, the scientific concept of metaphysics is identical with the concept of philosophy in general - critically transcendental science of being, ontology." Heidegger, *Basic Problems*, 17. Also, "If we are to understand the problem of Being, our first philosophical step consists . . . in not 'telling a story' - that is to say, in not defining entities as entities by tracing them back in their origin to some other entities, as if Being had the character of some possible entity." *Being and Time*, 26. Hence, Caputo, *op. cit.*, 98, remarks, "The Scholastic who wishes to respond to Heidegger's critique has to come to grips with the whole premise of transcendental philosophy." This is the challenge that I accept in this paper. Caputo also says, however, (94 and 239) that in his *Discourse on Thinking* (1959) Heidegger gave up transcendental critique.

[24] "There comes a point where certain thinkers refuse to push beyond the existent as existent (*l'étant comme étant*); they refuse precisely because they do not recognize the intuition of

these metaphysicians Gilson includes Avicenna, Aquinas, and Banez. Does this not imply that for Gilson the transphysicality of *ens* is a non-essential for starting metaphysics? I repeat, Gilson claims that Aquinas and others are metaphysicians and yet they lack what Gilson calls Maritain's intellectual intuition of being. What made them metaphysicians? Simply their grasp of *esse* as the most profound principle in the sensible existents before us. It appears to me that Gilson is saying that a grasp of Aquinas' essence/existence sense of *ens commune* sufficiently distinguishes the beginning of the metaphysical enterprise. The inception of the enterprise has no need of the other transphysical sense of Aquinas' notion of *ens commune*.

The consideration of sensible beings in the light of their *actus essendi* seems sufficiently distinctive for a speculative science. Natural philosophy can be left to consider real bodies as *habens forma*, and the empirical sciences can take them up as various *habens accidentia*. Both approaches leave room for a consideration of sensible existents as *habens esse*. Though both presume *esse*, neither focus upon it. What about transphysical *ens* as the subject of metaphysics? In the Gilsonian approach, *ens commune* would describe the subject of metaphysics at a later and mature stage. Metaphysical reflection upon *actus essendi* leads the thinker to possible immaterial beings. This conclusion is the rational basis for expanding the essence/existence distinction beyond the material order.

I find Gilson's position apt for stymying the Heideggerain reduction of Thomism to an *a priorism*. If we can initiate metaphysics by a notion of being that highlights the existential dimension of sensible beings, we protect ourselves from being forced onto an *a priorist* road. Contrary to Caputo's opinion, Gilson's thesis in *Being and Some Philosophers* that Aquinas alone was sufficiently attentive to the existential side of being is relevant for answering Heidegger's charge of the oblivion of being among Western philosophers. Aquinas does not forget what Heidegger calls Being in the ontological difference. Aquinas just moves it to a latter stage of *a posteriori* metaphysical reflection. If anyone has an oblivion of being, it is Heidegger. Heidegger seems to be unaware of the merely existential notion of being by which Aquinas initiates metaphysics.

---

being (*l'intuition de l'être*) as the ultimate and root of the existent (*l'étant*); such is for example the case of Duns Scotus. Others, quite rare indeed, but Avicenna, Thomas Aquinas, Banez and their successors, attest their existence, dare to affirm as the supreme act, the *esse* in virtue of which the existent exists." (my trans.) Étienne Gilson, "Propos sur l'être et sa notion," *San Tommaso e il pensiero moderno*, ed. Antonio Piolanti (Città Nuova: Pontificia Academia Romana de S. Tommaso d'Aquino, 1974), 16. For an extended analysis of Gilson's criticism of Maritain, see John F. X. Knasas, "Gilson vs. Maritain: The Start of Thomistic Metaphysics," *Doctor Communis*, 43 (1990), 250-265.

V

Before concluding, I must address two of a number of issues raised by Gilson's position on the initiation of Thomistic metaphysics.

First, does not Gilson locate in divine revelation the Thomistic basis for conceiving the thing's existence as *actus essendi* in divine revelation? In his *The Elements of Christian Philosophy*, Gilson does say that disputes among Thomists on whether to conceive existence as an act of the thing or simply as the fact of the thing are an invitation for us to give up the philosophical way and to try the theological way.[25] According to Gilson, Aquinas' *actus essendi* interpretation of existence was inspired by God's *ego sum qui sum* revelation to Moses. Aquinas took God to be saying that God is pure existence. God's creation should reflect the divine nature in a distinct existential act.

The theologizing charge against Gilson also suggests Heidegger's opinion from *The Basic Problems of Phenomenology*. Heidegger appears to regard the essence/existence distinction among the Scholastics as simply an *ad hoc* device fashioned to distinguish creatures from God.[26] The philosophical basis of the distinction is nugatory.

The above theologizing reading of Gilson fails to take account of Gilson's assertions, even in *The Elements*, that for Aquinas the thing's *esse* is apprehended by the intellect's second operation, also called judgment.[27] Also, Gilson is on record as saying that "what we call Thomistic philosophy is a body of rigorously demonstrable truths and is justifiable precisely as philosophy by reason alone."[28]

---

[25] Étienne Gilson, *The Elements of Christian Philosophy* (Garden City, New York: Doubleday & Company, Inc., 1960), 131.

[26] The *traditional discussion* of the second thesis, that essentia and existentia, or possible existence, belong to each being, lacks a solid foundation and a sure clue." *Basic Problems*, 78. "The problem [of the relation between essentia and existentia] must be understood in the philosophical context of the distinction between the concepts of the infinite being and the finite being." *Ibid.*, 81. John Caputo, *Heidegger and Aquinas: An Essay on Overcoming Metaphysics*, 67-8, correctly notes that Heidegger's subsequent Suarezian critique of the Thomistic distinction between essence and existence is insufficiently attentive to *esse* as a prior principle within the concrete being.

[27] The second operation, which is the composition or division of concepts—that is, the judgment—attains the thing in its very act of being . . . This conclusion, so firmly asserted by Thomas Aquinas, has often been overlooked or intentionally rejected by many among his successors. And no wonder, since it is tied up with the Thomistic notion of the composition of essence and the act of being in created substances." *Elements*, 232. See also Gilson, *Le Thomisme: Introduction a la Philosophie de Saint Thomas D'Aquin* (Paris: Librairie Philosophique J. Vrin, 1972), 184-5 and 188.

[28] Étienne Gilson, *The Christian Philosophy of St. Thomas Aquinas* (New York: Random House, 1956), 22. John Caputo, *Heidegger and Aquinas: An Essay on Overcoming*

In my opinion,[29] Gilson's talk about a turn to theology is merely his invitation for us to consider the hints, or suggestions, from revelation as to where the philosophical truth of the matter may lie.

Nevertheless, some characterizations that Gilson makes of judgment might cause the theologizing charge to arise once again. Gilson at least gives the impression of equating the judgment with the proposition. For example, "Existential judgments are meaningless unless they are meant to be true. If the proposition 'Peter is' means anything, it means that a certain man, Peter by name, actually is, or exists."[30] Also, "The formula in which this composition is expressed is precisely the proposition or judgment."[31] Such an equation is unfortunate because judgment is supposed to be the intellectual act that *grasps* the *esse rei*, while the proposition at best only *expresses esse*. As Aquinas himself points out, the enunciation, or proposition, signifies the *esse rei* that the *secunda operatio intellectus* grasps (*respicit*).[32] Gilson's equating of the judgment with the proposition results in the appearance of an undeveloped notion of the intellectual act of judgment itself that "*respicit esse rei.*"

The undevelopment might incline some to think that Gilson needs to theologize to obtain what he wants. But this shortcoming can be handled by two remarks. First, Aquinas generally describes the cognitional act of judgment this way: "Our intellect composes or divides by applying previously abstracted intelligibles to the thing."[33] This text, plus others,[34] enables the reader to understand that the intellect's second act of composition and division is what Aquinas elsewhere describes as the intellect's knowledge of singular existents. Such knowledge is attained by a certain reflection, *per quandam reflexionem*, back from the universal to the phantasm from which the universal had been abstracted and in which the individual is represented.

Metaphysics, 9, holds that Aquinas' metaphysics was the "concealed, discursive, representational—one is tempted to say 'alienated'—way" of expressing Aquinas' animating mystical experience. But Aquinas' metaphysics can be surmised within his earliest works, e.g., the commentary on the *Sentences* and his *De Ente et Essentia*. Both were written long before any evidence of Aquinas suffering mystical experience.

[29] See also Joseph Owens, *An Interpretation of Existence* (Houston: Center for Thomistic Studies, 1985), 132.

[30] Étienne Gilson, *Being and Some Philosophers* (Toronto: Pontifical Institute of Mediaeval Studies, 1952), 201. Also, 196 and 202.

[31] Étienne Gilson, *Christian Philosophy of Aquinas*, 41

[32] . . . prima operatio respicit quidditatem rei; secunda respicit esse ipsius. Et quia ratio veritatis fundatur in esse et non in quidditate, ut dictum est, ideo veritas et falsitas proprie invenitur in secunda operatione, et in signo ejus quod est ennutiatio, . . ." *In I Sent.* de. 19, q. 5, a. 1, ad 7m; Mandonnet ed., I, 489.

[33] Thomas Aquinas, *Summa Contra Gentiles* II, 96, *Palam.*

[34] See John F. X. Knasas, *Preface*, 131-4.

Second, the task remains of explaining how judgment in the just described cognitional operation sense is a *respicit esse rei* rather than simply the recomposition of an intelligible with some designated matter. As far as I know, Gilson nowhere performs this task. The task, however, can be accomplished and the Thomistic texts themselves provide the help. In sum,[35] they describe a consideration of the individual material thing itself as *possibile esse et non esse*. Such a consideration appears to be generated from data composed of the thing really existing, on the one hand, and the real thing cognitionally existing, on the other.[36] The consideration of the individual body as possible permits judgment to recombine the abstracted intelligible with the individual in a fashion that leaves the recomposition of the the individual with its *esse* as a further distinct and crowning moment in judgment.

The above sketch of judgment as the access to *esse* raises a a second problem to which I want to respond. The multiplicity that presents the existentially neutral individual has as one instance the thing really existing. I believe that a Heideggerian would want to object to the naiveté with which Aquinas accepts this instance. To the contrary, a Heideggerian would insist that a really existing thing is just a case of what *Being and Time* calls the present at hand, and such a case comes before us in consciousness only because of our antecedent projection of being as presence at hand. In short, the theoretical attitude characteristic of so much of Western philosophy is no exception to Heidegger's thesis that *Dasein* is in the world as care.[37] So, a Heideggerian would subvert Aquinas' judgment approach to *esse* by giving a phenomenological account of one of the key instances necessary for the judgment approach.

In reply, I am not sure why one must adopt the Heideggerian attitude towards what is present at hand. The best reason that I surmise is Heidegger's noted insistence than beings, in whatever sense, are seen only in the light of being.[38] In sum, we return to the argument for the *apriority* of being, quoted at length in *Basic Problems*. But then my previous replies again become relevant. Why cannot a notion of being as "present at hand" be understood as immediately abstracted from various things present at hand rather than projected upon them?

---

[35] Aquinas speaks of individual generable and corruptible things as *possibilia esse et non esse* at *Summa Contra Gentiles* I, 15, *Amplius* and II, 15, *Praeterea*.

[36] For an elaboration of this point, see John F. X. Knasas, *Preface*, 83-5.

[37] "This transcendence [of entities thematized] in turn provides the support for concernful Being alongside entities within-the-world, whether this Being is theoretical or practical." *Being and Time*, 415.

[38] Hence, Heidegger remarks of the theoretical science of mathematics, "it consists rather in the fact that the entities which it takes as its theme are discovered in it in the only way in which entities can be discovered – by the prior projection of their state of Being." *Ibid.*, 414.

In other words, it is encumbent upon the Heideggerian to show here some incongruity between the instances and the notion that would make the abstractive account of the notion questionable. Success in that task would swing the account of the notion into the *a priori* domain. But I fail to see Heideggerians performing this task for the notion of being as present at hand. Nor do I see how the task could be performed. Being as present at hand is not yet Aquinas' *ens commune* and as such it has no features that prohibit its abstractive derivation from real sensible existents.

In conclusion, Heidegger's *a priori* thinking about being can make its best case against Aquinas *vis-a-vis* what Aquinas calls the subject of metaphysics, *ens commune*. That argument is what I have tried to anticipate and to defend Aquinas from.

Unreliable Tools

Joseph Koterski, S.J.

Postmodernism can apparently mean a number of quite different things. Its practitioners seem to lose not a wink of sleep over the mutual incompatibility of certain projects that take shelter under its roof. Deconstruction, for example, has as its bedfellow the revisionism or constructive postmodernism that often appears in the SUNY series edited by D. R. Griffin. This is possible because its unity seems founded on one basic rejection rather than on a common constituent —rejection of the Enlightenment conception of reason—if not completely, at least in some significant part. In this respect it is a movement like existentialism. Few among those who claimed that mantle agreed on much by way of common doctrines. It was rather a fundamental rejection, the repudiation of essence as a mere instrument of the will to power, that proved enough to galvanize an entire generation of thinkers, and to reach for roots in Kierkegaard.

But there certainly were Christian existentialists—Marcel, of course, and perhaps Berdyaev and Dostoevsky. Can there not be Christian postmodernists? I suspect that there can. My worry is that their thinking will almost necessarily fade off into fideism, and thereby they hazard the same risks fideists always face, not only for themselves but culturally for the Christian body of which they are members. The historical reality of Christianity in culture is the reality of a religion that is logocentric at its very heart. I do not mean that by some accident of its early history it became inextricably entwined with Hellenism, but that Logos is the very name for the second person of the Trinity, and that this has implications for the nature of human thinking.[1] It was Word who became flesh and proclaimed a unique saving truth. Over on the far flank there is the opposite danger of making this religion, in the witness that it bears

---

[1] Joseph Cardinal Ratzinger has a fine meditation on this point in *A Turning Point for Europe? The Church in the Modern World - Assessment and Forecast* [1991], trans. Brian McNeil, C.R.V. (San Francisco: Ignatius Press, 1994), esp. 130-150.

to this Word and in its participation in this saving truth, ultimately to be a form of gnosticism. For the gnostic of any generation, it is mere knowledge of this secret truth that saves. But, on the contrary, orthodox Christian belief has always been that salvation comes not merely from knowledge but from faith in the Word who became flesh and transforms human life through and through. So, although it is not knowledge that saves, the Christian religion is marked by a truth-claim in the strongest possible sense, and this facet of the historical reality of Christianity inescapably entails doing theology.

With theology comes all the rationality and logic that any "-ology" implies. Can't we construct an apologetics specially geared for postmodern times that would escape logocentrism? One that would use distinctively postmodern tools against the powerful cultural forces that presently claim them exclusively?[2] As precedent for trying to use some new movement for religious ends, there is certainly the venerable tradition of adopting certain aspects of Hellenism for the purposes of evangelization, and, later, of appropriating the pagan Aristotle, correcting him at a few crucial junctures, and then building with his help a theological explanation of the universe comparable to the cathedrals being erected by the same age. If Rome could employ Athens in the service of Jerusalem, why not attempt a postmodern religious apologetics for a postmodern world? Why not? Need we stay silent, or as good as silent, by insisting on logocentrism, when nobody today is willing to listen to that anymore?

What might it mean? To adopt as our own the recent critiques of Enlightenment rationality does make some sense and might be an attractive strategy. There is no shortage of motives to be suspicious of in our opponents, so our own hermeneutics of suspicion could easily be a sharp sword in our own hands. In fact, there have been attempts to see philosophy not as a body of positive knowledge but as simply a study of the ideologies of an age. One Jesuit philosophy center in Europe took as its plan a concentration on the three masters of suspicion: Nietzsche, Marx and Freud, in the hope that thorough acquaintance with these figures would give the seminarians the edge they needed for critical analysis as they engaged in works of social concern out of their religious faith. The experiment has been a sad failure. Most lost their faith and were swallowed up by the culture they set out to critique. Well-intentioned as were the instructors, administrators and students, their faith was outflanked by forces too powerful for the tools they had been given.

In a sphere closer to home, we have the problem of finding methods for

---

[2] Merold Westphal has had tremendous success with this strategy in various works, including his book *Suspicion and Faith: the Religious Uses of Modern Atheism* (Grand Rapids, Michigan: W. B. Eerdmans, 1993).

religious catechesis currently prevalent in America. Frequently there is much well-intentioned emphasis on personal experience, chaperoned by such fine postmodern values as the sincerity of one's motives and channelled into the pedagogy of story-telling. This is not as contentiously postmodern as the cultivation of a hermeneutics of suspicion, but it seems to me to be the practical pedagogical application of the salient point of postmodernism—the rejection of reason and proof—and it generally works in practice by casting suspicion on doctrine and Church teaching as old-fashioned and dull, cold and insincere, without raising for reasonable consideration the historical matrix in which these theological solutions were worked out, or the importance of the philosophical distinctions needed to preserve biblical faith when biblical words were being twisted by opposing parties for their own ends, even at the risk of losing some crucial aspect of Christian faith. The doctrine of the two natures in Christ, for instance, was articulated in philosophical and not biblical categories so as to preserve biblical faith: we need to hold both the equality of the second member of the Trinity with the first (He couldn't save us unless He truly is God), and at the same time Christ's full humanity and our need deliberately and vigorously to imitate Him (He is the model and pattern for our lives; what He did not assume about our nature He did not heal).[3]

The desirability of having a postmodern strategy in apologetics is clear, and surely sincerity will be more attractive than suspicion. Perhaps we could just trust more to approaches we once scorned as fideist so as to give the young true opinions, letting the confidence and sincerity of believers' testimonies suffice. The telling of stories, after all, does tend to bring people to let their defenses down, and thus give room for the story to break in upon the mind: to challenge, to console, to convict, to convince.

I remain unconvinced that the tools of postmodern thought are sufficiently reliable for the project at hand. Any of these options might be tactically useful on some occasion, but good tactics do not yet a strategy make. The intellectual component of a religious renewal of culture needs a strategy, I contend, that is twofold: it must cultivate reverence for the Transcendent by articulate praise and by prayerful silence; but it must also educate, it must provide an enculturation into the faith by reasonable words. The cacophony of postmodern noise seems to me to miss the mark on both counts.

Wouldn't a strategy that insists on argumentation be saying, in effect, "put up your dukes"? Yes, it would. But in order to let in the light of contemplation,

---

[3] This is, of course, the project of St. Irenaeus of Lyons. A contemporary attempt to work this out for personal and cultural development according to the pattern of Christ is that offered by Paul M. Quay, S.J. in *The Mystery Hidden for Ages in God* (New York: Peter Lang, 1995).

it may first be necessary to knock down some of the most cherished defenses on the other side. Even if you cannot at first persuade, you may need the force of sheer reason to dis-convince, and that not by dirty tricks which only bring resentment. All the better if classical metaphysics can serve its traditional function of enculturating the young into the foundations for the values of genuine humanism. But at the very least we need to expose the debased forms of reasoning popular today, as for instance found in the claim that everyone is entitled to his or her own opinion, when this claim is really but a way to outlaw the holding of any opinion as cogent and compelling to the intellect. Or, to consider one of the preferred postmodern tools, the admission that our truths are tribal. The claim that some culturally relative tradition is legitimate for us because it is one of our tribe's truths is to go back to using the proverbial caveman's club—powerful at short range, but not very subtle.

My thesis is that espousal of postmodernism will make for bad strategy at any level of our religious enterprise. Its protest against Enlightenment reason does strike a chord in us because it is protesting something worth protesting, the aridity of rationalism. But for believers to embrace its repudiation of reason gone stale will only deepen the crisis, for the problem is not with reason, but with the Enlightenment's desiccated understanding of reason. The natural religion of Archdeacon Paley and the theodicy of Leibniz left no place for faith as a form of knowledge, so the successors to the Enlightenment concluded that faith must mean a leap into the dark. In fact, I suspect that that is precisely the fallacy of the Enlightenment's attempts at natural theology. As Christopher Dawson diagnosed the problem, those thinkers did not grasp that the difference between the discursive reason and the intuition of the contemplative is not the same as the difference between the natural and the supernatural, between reason and faith. These are simply different levels of consciousness, but are equally parts of human nature.[4] Or, as John Smith puts it in "Prospects for Natural Theology,"[5] there is a genuine function for reason within the ambit of faith: the contribution it makes is to help show religious beliefs to be intelligible and coherent even where it cannot demonstrate them the way a science would attempt to do so. By contrast, the Enlightenment identification of human nature exclusively with its discursive rational aspects confuses and prejudices the whole approach to religion as simply irrational.

Religion begins in the depths of the soul—not by the mere vitality of our psychic projections, but contemplatively, by our awe at the intuition of being. So far as I can tell, this is really the forcefulness of what are called the arguments

[4] Christopher Dawson, *Religion and Culture* (London: Sheed & Ward, 1949), 33-34.

[5] John Smith, "Prospects for Natural Theology" in *The Monist* 75/3 (1992), 406-420.

from design. They do not ever amount to a proof of the existence of God the way deists would like, for they never get us to an objective knowledge of the designer— God always exceeds our categories. But they stir in the soul a sense of the direction in which the designer must be.

Rightly to appreciate the relation of religion and reason, we actually need a stronger and richer sense of the levels of reason than the Enlightenment avers, and *a fortiori* than postmodernism commands. The conception of reason we need will be one far more alert both to intuition and to demonstration. Here I need to depart from Smith, who curiously seems to think that Aquinas drew a razor-sharp line between the spheres of faith and reason and then set out on the project of an elaborate natural theology. Rather than such a demarcation-line, what Aquinas offers is better seen as a pair of overlapping circles (the *preambula fidei*) where the overlap names a limited group of truth-claims demonstrable by reason but equally well accessible by faith. The sphere of claims where truth is known only on the basis of faith still involves reason in the sense Smith urges: reason is at work there to reflect on the meaning of the claim and to bring out the intelligibility and coherence, but trust and belief in the revealer and in the content of the faith is authoritative here. Human reason, however, does have a sphere where it can operate independently by its own lights. Aquinas' picture is not the Augustinian map Smith seems to approve.[6] Rather, the powers of cognition present in the human knower, when developed and trained in themselves and alerted to the cognitive traditions of human experience passed from one generation to the next, can know all sorts of things (e.g., reasoning from effect to cause) without recourse to divine illumination.[7] The Thomistic picture seems to me to try to avoid both the extremes of fideism and rationalism by carrying a place for reason within faith and for reason operating under its own God-given natural powers. To do so requires a stronger theory of knowledge than Augustinian illumination but not the hubristic elimination of faith as a genuine source of some knowledge.

This return to the Thomistic vision of overlapping spheres is not, I maintain, to hide our heads in the sands of the past. In fact, in the ages of faith a purely natural theology had no separate existence in the sociology of knowledge.[8] Except to professional theologians, it had no independent significance but was simply a part of the common Christian theology—witness the way in which

---

[6] E.g., He makes the rather strong claim: "'in Thy light shall we see light'—all understanding requires this light," 414.

[7] W. Norris Clarke, S.J., provides an excellent example of how to do this in "Is a Natural Theology Still Viable Today?" in *Prospects for Natural Theology*, ed. E. Long (Washington D.C.: The Catholic University of America Press, 1992), 151-182.

[8] Christopher Dawson, *Religion and Culture*, 7.

one of the high points of philosophical autonomy, Anselm's ontological argument, is simply part of the movement of faith seeking understanding. Bonaventure uses the same type of argument, but he cannot even imagine philosophy without Christ at the center. While the highly intellectualist thought of Aquinas puts the proofs at the very start of the *Summa*, it would be a fundamental misunderstanding to take them as the heart of his theological program, a misunderstanding often reflected today in the utter mystification of students presented with only this snippet of Aquinas. They generally do not find it compelling, and it only leaves a distaste, while students given a far larger portion of Thomas and a more integrated picture of reason and faith as complementary sources of knowledge find far more satisfaction in the experience and can better discern the different types of challenge to their religion from the secular world, having been practiced in the discernment of various sources of truth-claims and various patterns of explanation and defense.

The point is that such rudimentary knowledge of God as natural theology can give assumes far more importance in an era like ours not possessed of religious unity and not as culturally soaked in the living habits of religion as the ages of faith were. Historically, natural theology went hand in hand with Western humanism, the humanism of Erasmus and More and the Christian Platonists, as a way to appreciate the good of nature and human dignity. The basically rational order of the world was justified for them only by being seen as the work of divine reason, as the product of divine artistry. It persevered in importance during the age of religious division as "a certain and universal foundation of religious truth in a world where everything was disputed,"[9] for the more completely new science took hold, the more its adherents needed the idea of God as the source and principle of intelligibility.

If pre-moderns held that without God, there would be no knowledge, the postmoderns seem to say that we have no God and no knowledge. In resisting the epistemological despair of postmodernity, what we need is not so much to defend modernity—whose chief *animus*, after all, was attack upon religion as irrational—but a defense of reason as larger than the limits within which modernity set to confine it. This, I think, was Maritain's point in *Antimoderne*, when he wrote:

> Reason is the faculty of the real, or more correctly, the faculty by which our spirit becomes adequate to the real, and by which our spirit knows, no doubt analogically and very distantly but truthfully, the reality of realities, God. Reason is made for truth, made to possess it.[10]

[9] *Ibid.*
[10] My translation of Jacques Maritain, *Antimoderne*, Nouvelle edition revue et augmentée

The distinction he proceeds to make between reason and intellect, not as two different faculties, but two different aspects or modes of operation of one and the same faculty, is intended to contrast with the general tendency in modern philosophy from Descartes forward to treat reason as purely discursive and thus doomed to the critical project whose emptiness will bring epistemological despair.[11] By contrast, he offers a picture of faith as able to complete and perfect reason, much as grace completes and perfects nature. Faith, he explains, is a full and voluntary adhesion of intelligence to the truths revealed by God.[12] What faith provides has intelligibility to our minds by reason of its author, the source of all intelligibility, even if it goes beyond what a given person could figure out by using unaided rational powers at the disposal of nature. To make such a distinction between reason and intellect is to avoid the Cartesian reduction of all cognitive activity to the domain of a pure, impersonal, autonomous and self-sufficient reason able unaided to grasp with perfect transparency all that is real and worth knowing.

Not all postmodern thinkers seek to make the same radical denial of the possibility of objective truth, but the apparently tempered claims of the more moderate voices risk the same fate as the radical fringe to the extent that they abandon the claim of human reason to gain some real purchase on the causal structures of reality. If they claim that all access to objective truth is blocked in principle, their argument will be self-destructive by being internally contradictory, and little more will need to be said beyond reminding them of the performative self-contradiction involved in their claim to inform us of that truth.[13] But the voices which only claim that we have no rational access to significant truths about the divine and insist that all religious truths are entirely the product of faith risk missing what we can know, given our natural drive to know and our innate cognitive structures. To correct the rationalist thesis that only what we humans ourselves can analyze and synthesize is real and knowable does not require abandoning the legitimate claims of reason to know some things beyond the immediately visible or sensible through the principle of causality. What it does require is a chastened habit of reasonable affirmations made by responsible thinking about the meaning latent in the data we receive and responsible

---

(Paris: Desclée de Brower, 1922), 29: "La Raison est la faculté par laquelle notre esprit devient adéquat au réel, et par laquelle nous connaissons, d'une manière analogique sans doute et très lointaine, mais vérridique, la réalité des réalités, Dieu. La Raison est faite pour la vérité, pour posséder l'être."

[11] Jacques Maritain, *Antimoderne*, 56.

[12] *Ibid.*, 38.

[13] This point has been well-worked out by James Marsh in "Postmodernism: A Lonerganian Retrieval and Critique" in *The International Philosophical Quarterly* 35/2 (1995), 159-173.

judgment grounded on the evidence available to the inquirer. However limited or incomplete our cognitive claims have to remain, there is no reason to suppose that they open on to nothing or are directed only inwardly toward the knower rather than outwardly toward reality. Preserving this confidence will not be helped by unreliable tools.

Postmodernism: A Lonerganian Retrieval and Critique*

James L. Marsh

A Lonerganian critique of postmodernism might seem appropriate now, since Lonergan certainly is an example of a kind of enthusiastic modernist who draws the critical fire of postmodernism. The methodical, systematic character of his work, its grounding in the knowing, choosing self, its orientation to universality and to metaphysics, and its unabashed commitment to modern, western rationality make Lonergan an apt target of postmodern critique. Indeed such critiques have already begun.[1]

A natural question that arises in this context, therefore, is whether Lonergan has any kind of response. It is my conviction that he does and, moreover, that on a Lonerganian basis one can construct a critique of postmodernism that is compelling, that, while incorporating valid aspects of its project, brings it into question.

My stance in this essay, therefore, is sympathetic and critical towards postmodernism. I believe Lonergan is basically correct on the fundamental issues that divide him from postmodernism and in relation to which there is a judgmental and volitional "either/or." But I think that postmodernism raises questions that deserve consideration, comes to insights that Lonergan and other modernists can employ and incorporate, and interprets the pathology of the modern in a way that has to be taken seriously. The Lonergan, then, that emerges from the encounter with postmodernism is different, chastened, broader, deeper, more conscious of the limits of rationality, more fallibilistic,

* Reprinted with permission of the *International Philosophical Quarterly* v. 35 (1995), 159-173.
[1] See, for example, Ronald McKinney, "Deconstructing Lonergan," *International Philosophical Quarterly* 31 (March 1991): 81-93, and my "Reply to McKinney on Lonergan: A Deconstruction," *International Philosophical Quarterly* 31 (March 1991): 95-104.

more aware of the ways in which human reason and history can go wrong, more committed to a progressive social agenda.

THE POSTMODERNIST CRITIQUE OF RATIONALITY

Modernism is committed to the project of self-reflective, critical rationality and freedom. From Kant's concept of the Enlightenment as the emergence from self-incurred tutelage to Husserl's return to the things themselves, modernism at its best is characterized by this orientation to reflexive, self-conscious understanding and critique. Postmodernism is a challenging, insightful, profound attempt to undermine that project. In the grip of such a *Ratio* being tends to be covered over and difference and individuality tend to be submerged. Western *Ratio*, in the eyes of postmodernists such as late Heidegger, Derrida, Adorno, and Foucault, is oriented toward an identity that excludes difference and an active, conceptualizing stance that inhibits receptivity to being.[2]

The motivation for such a critique of reason is, second, that modern reason itself, as defined and described by the postmoderns, is oriented to totalizing, alienating objectification. The description of rationality as such a closed, objectifying system rests upon three models or descriptions that interact and complement one another. First, rationality is equated with science and technology, either in the sense of explicit identification, generalizing the traits of dominance, prediction, objectification, and control to the whole domain of rationality, or emphasizing and thematizing scientific rationality as the dominant form of rationality and leaving other forms unthematized. Second is the model of the logical system, which Derrida criticizes in

---

[2] For representative examples of the critique of Western *Ratio*, see Martin Heidegger, *The Question Concerning Technology and Other Essays*, trans. William Lovitt (New York: Harper Colophon, 1977), 3-35; Michel Foucault, *Discipline and Punish* (New York: Vintage Books, 1979); Theodore Adorno and Max Horkheimer, *The Dialectic of Enlightenment*, trans. John Cumming (New York: The Seabury Press, 1972); Jacques Derrida, *Of Grammatology*, trans. Gayatri Chakravorty Spivak (Baltimore: Johns Hopkins University Press, 1975-76), 3-93.

[3] For examples of the equating of rationality and science and technology, see Heidegger, *The Question Concerning Technology*, 3-35; and Adorno and Horkheimer, *The Dialectic of Enlightenment*, 4-14. For Derrida's critique of structuralism see *Of Grammatology*, 27-73. For their critiques of Husserl and Hegel, see Adorno, *Against Epistemology*, trans. Willis Domingo (Cambridge: Massachusetts Institute of Technology Press, 1982); *Negative Dialectics*, trans. E. B. Ashton (New York: The Seabury Press, 1973), 300-60; *Drei Studien zu Hegel* (Frankfurt: Suhrkamp verlag, 1971); and Derrida, *Speech and Phenomena*, trans. D. Allison (Evanston: Northwestern University Press, 1973); and *Glas*, trans. John Leavey and Richard Rand (Lincoln, Nebraska: University of Nebraska Press, 1986).

structuralism. Third is the metaphysical or ontological system or systematic approaches, which Adorno and Derrida criticize in their treatments of Husserl and Hegel.[3]

These three models interact within and between each postmodernist thinker in various ways. For example, if metaphysics for Heidegger has a long history of the forgetfulness of being, science and technology are the final, most recent flowering of such a forgetfulness. If for Adorno an illegitimate identitarian thinking is present in such thinkers as Hegel and Husserl, science and technology linked to and in the service of late capitalism become the most important contemporary versions of such thinking, reducing all persons and things to versions of the same quantified, commodified logic. We could say in general that operating in all of these thinkers is a disillusioned scientism, a cynical logicism, and a metaphysics ill at ease with itself. These different models come together in each thinker to form a concept of rationality as repressively totalizing: "instrumental reason" in Adorno, "logocentrism" in Derrida, "calculative thinking" in Heidegger, "discipline" in Foucault.[4]

Because of such an equation of rationality with totalizing objectification and because such an equation, according to the postmodernists, necessarily covers up or obscures reality, the only alternative is an overcoming of metaphysics, a transcendence of evidential reality, a movement beyond conceptual objectification. Again, these thinkers describe this alternative differently: "negative dialectic" in Adorno, "deconstruction" in the case of Derrida, "Denken" in the thought of Heidegger, "genealogy" in the project of Foucault. This alternative is not irrationalism, but rather a form of reflection claiming to go beyond traditional western concerns with method, evidence, argument, and definition.[5]

We note here a similarity and difference from positivism, scientism, logicism, and technocracy, in general, with those who equate rationality with

---

[4] Heidegger, *The Question Concerning Technology*, 116- 20. Adorno and Horkheimer, *Dialectic of Enlightenment*, 4-14. For representative quotations, consider Heidegger: "Machine technology remains up to now the most visible outgrowth of the essence of modern technology, which is identical with the essence of modern metaphysics," 4; and Adorno and Horkheimer: "Knowledge, which is power, knows no obstacles: neither in the enslavement of men nor in compliance with the world's rules . . . Technology is the essence of this knowledge. It does not work by concepts and images, by the fortunate insight, but refers to the method, the exploitation of others' work, and capital," 4.

[5] Adorno, *Negative Dialectics*, 3-57; Jacques Derrida, *Margins of Philosophy*, trans. Alan Bass (Chicago: The University of Chicago Press, 1982), 329; Martin Heidegger, *What Is Called Thinking*, trans. Fred D. Wieck and J. Glenn Gray (New York: Harper & Row, 1968); Michel Foucault, *The Archeology of Knowledge & The Discourse on Language*, trans. A. M. Sheridan Smith (New York: Harper & Row, 1972), 3-17.

describing or affirming an actual or possible state of affairs. If we recall the positivists' triumphalistic equation of reason with science, technology, and formal logic, and come to a negative rather than a positive evaluation of the equation, then we have an essential element of the postmodern stance. In many respects the postmodernist reflects a disillusionment with positivism and technocracy; "reason" in these senses has not worked and needs to be transcended. For this reason we have the strong emphasis on negativity in most of these thinkers, strongest in Adorno and Derrida, but present in Foucault and Heidegger as well. Negative is to positive, in their eyes, as postmodern is to modern.

On another more concrete, hermeneutical level there is a similar disenchantment. If we recall Comte's triumphalistic account of the progress from religion to metaphysics to science as defining the modern and add a sign of negation, we have essentially the postmodernist hermeneutics of modernity. Modernity is essentially a development and consolidation of scientific and technological control. Development is essentially progress in domination, whether that is defined as increase in the reign of "instrumental reason," "logocentrism," "calculative thinking," or "discipline." Such movement, postmodernists powerfully argue, covers up, dominates and alienates nature, human beings and being. The final form of modernity is an iron cage, from which there is little or no exit.[6]

Finally at the most concrete level, the political implications that flow from such a stance are dire and pessimistic. If reason equals science and if modernity is essentially growth in the dominance of instrumental reason, then, even though in postmodernism an ethical-political will to transcendence of modernity exists, there would seem to be little possibility of transcendence, few counter-tendencies contesting the reign of one-dimensionality. The historical dominance of instrumental reason leads to a one-dimensional society in which all or most traces of transcendence are rubbed out. Again we can contrast the negative reading of this situation in such works as *Dialectic of Enlightenment* with the positive reading present in such works as Luhmann's *The Differentiation of Society* or Skinner's *Beyond Freedom and Dignity*. Depending on whether one is a technocrat or postmodernist, being a mere

---

[6] Adorno and Horkheimer, *The Dialectic of Enlightenment*, 3-42; Derrida, *Of Grammatology*, 6-26; Heidegger, *Discourse on Thinking*, trans. John Anderson and E. Hans Freund (New York: Harper & Row, 1966), 43-57.

[7] Herbert Marcuse, *One-dimensional Man* (Boston: Beacon Press, 1964), 1-120; Foucault, *Discipline and Punish*; Adorno and Horkheimer, *Dialectic of Enlightenment*, 120-67; B. F. Skinner, *Beyond Freedom and Dignity* (New York: Vintage, 1971); Niklaus Luhmann, *The Differentiation of Society* (New York: Columbia University Press, 1982).

object for political, economic, and social technique can be either good or bad.[7]

I need to qualify this characterization in the following way. Any attempt to catch a group of thinkers under a conceptual rubric, here that of postmodernism, runs risks and has inevitable limits. First of all, there are real differences among these thinkers; Foucault, for example, is politically leftist in a way that Heidegger is not. Second, I do not think that all of them are consistently postmodernist. In Adorno, for example, there are strong modernist elements co-existing with postmodernism. Third, I do not mean to suggest or imply that the pessimistic political implications of postmodernist thought necessarily are manifest in the lives of those thinkers. Foucault and Derrida, for example, have been politically active in a way that may not square with their own thought. These, then, are the traits of postmodernism as I am characterizing it here: a questioning of modern, western evidential rationality, a definition of such rationality as a closed, totalizing, objectivizing system, a negative hermeneutics of history, and a generalizing of the thesis of one-dimensionality as it applies to politics and economics. Because this definition of postmodernism moves from abstract to concrete, from rationality to ethics and politics, my critique will similarly move from abstract to concrete in four different interrelated stages: logical (in a self-referential sense),descriptive, hermeneutical, and ethical-political.

A LONERGANIAN CRITIQUE:
THE ISSUE OF SELF-REFERENTIALITY

Lonergan, along with Habermas, is perhaps the most adept contemporary practitioner of the self-referential argument, that is, the argument that anyone in attempting to deny or reject rationality inevitably ends up contradicting herself or being arbitrary. Either the critique of rationality is made rationally with evidence or it is not. If it is made rationally, then the critique of rationality is self-contradictory. If it is made without evidence, what is arbitrarily asserted can be rationally questioned or denied.[8]

One important place where such an argument occurs in Lonergan is in the chapter in *Insight* on the self-affirmation of the knower. Let us recall that argument briefly as Lonergan sets it up in syllogistic form. If I am an experiencing, understanding, judging subject characterized as a unity-identity whole and characterized by acts of seeing, perceiving, imagining, inquiring,

[8] See Jurgen Habermas, *The Philosophical Discourse of Modernity*, trans. Frederick Lawrence (Cambridge: Massachusetts Institute of Technology Press, 1987), 119, 136, 185-86, 277-86, 336-37, 294-95.

understanding, formulating, reflecting, and grasping the unconditioned, then I am a knower.

The unconditioned is a combination of a conditioned, a link between the conditions and the conditioned, and the fulfillment of the conditions. The conditioned is the claim, "I am a knower." The link between the conditions and the conditioned is given in the major premise. The fulfillment is given in consciousness.

The conditioned is clear and offers no difficulty. The link between conditioned and conditions offers no difficulty because it is just a statement of meaning, a definition of what it means to be a knower. The problematic aspect is the fulfillment of the conditions in consciousness as stated in the minor premise. Consciousness for Lonergan is not an immanent look at oneself but an awareness accompanying cognitional acts. Whether I am seeing a color, hearing a symphony, understanding a proposition, or judging a truth claim, I am aware not only of the contents of these acts, but of these acts themselves and of myself as a unified subject performing these acts. One indication of this point is that I can recall later what I was thinking about or doing at a certain time when I was not explicitly adverting to my acts at the time I was performing them: "What were you thinking about when you were driving home?" Recall of what I was thinking would be impossible if I were not implicitly aware of my acts and of myself performing the acts at the time I was performing them. Explicit remembering is founded on implicit awareness of myself as a knower.[9]

Consciousness is, then, an awareness immanent in cognitional acts. Since such acts differ in kind, the awareness differs in kind. An empirical awareness is present in seeing or hearing, an intelligent awareness in understanding, in activities of inquiry, insight, and conceptualization asking and answering the questions "what is it?," "why is it?," and "how is it?;" and reflective or rational consciousness in acts of reflection and judgment asking and answering the questions "is it so?" or "is it true?"[10]

Not only is consciousness diverse, but it is also unified. Contents culminate in unities; what is perceived is what is inquired about; what is inquired about is what is understood; what is understood is what is formulated; what is formulated is what is reflected upon as possibly true or false; what is reflected upon is grasped as unconditioned, as having the conditions for its truth fulfilled; what is grasped as unconditioned is affirmed. Similarly we note a unity on the side of the subject who moves from experiencing to understanding

---

[9] Bernard J. Lonergan, *Insight: A Study of Human Understanding* (New York: Longmans, Green, and Co. 1957), 319-21.

[10] *Ibid.,* 322-24.

to judging. I see the body fall, I formulate the law of falling bodies, and I judge that as true after I have performed certain verifying experiments. Lonergan argues that were the unity of consciousness not given, it would have to be deduced in a Kantian sense; otherwise the diverse contents could not coalesce into one known. Since such a unity is given, however, we have the basic evidence for affirming the subject as a unity-identity-whole.[11]

Now that we have indicated what we mean and do not mean by consciousness and the fulfillment of conditions in consciousness, we can turn to the question, "Am I knower?" Here each one has to ask the question for himself or herself, and there are two possibilities. Either I affirm that I am knower, or I do not. If I affirm that I am, the answer is coherent, for, if I am a knower, I can know that fact by having recourse to conditions present in consciousness. Do I see or not? Do I understand or not? Do I judge or not? But the answer "no" is either arbitrary or incoherent, inconsistent, self-contradictory. For the judgment that I am not a knower is either arbitrary or it is not. If it is arbitrary, what is arbitrarily asserted can be rationally questioned or denied. If the claim is made with evidence, then I have experienced the evidence, understood the proposition, "I am not a knower," and have made the judgment. I truly know that I do not know is a self-contradiction.[12]

How does this line of argument apply to postmodernism? The Lonerganian move here is to treat postmodernism as a self-referentially inconsistent kind of skepticism that is incoherent because of its total negation of modern, Western reason. Postmodernism falls into a contradiction between the present transcendental condition for knowing and the negative content that denies such knowing. If I criticize rationality, either I do that rationally or not. If I do it rationally, then I experience, understand, define, reflect, and judge. I am in fact affirming *in actu* what I explicitly deny. If I do not make the critique rationally, what is arbitrarily asserted can be rationally questioned or denied.

The dilemma works itself out differently in each postmodernist. If rationality is described in Adornian terms as instrumental rationality, science and technology oriented to class or group domination, then a rational critique of instrumental rationality becomes impossible. Adorno and Horkheimer posit a *mimesis*, a dialogical, reciprocal relationship with nature, as a way out of the iron cage of modernity, but they can argue this point only with a theory of *mimesis*, which they are incapable of providing because such a theory would presuppose the possibility of a non-instrumental conception of rationality. They are caught in the trap of setting instrumental reason on the path of truth and yet contesting the idea of truth itself. In Habermas' words the "critique of

---

[11] *Ibid.,* 324-28.   [12] *Ibid.,* 328-32.

instrumental reason conceptualized as negative dialectics renounces the theoretical claim while operating with the means of theory."[13]

If with Heidegger we say that the kind of reason to be transcended is calculative, science-technology that eclipses being, the question arises about why we are to do that. Either such transcendence is arbitrarily asserted or it is not. If it is arbitrarily asserted, it can be rationally questioned or denied. If the claim is argued, then from Heidegger's perspective I am using a form of metaphysics, calculative thinking, to transcend calculative thinking.

One further aspect or implication of this argument for the self-affirmation of the knower is the reality and necessity of the self as subject. If Lonergan is correct, the judgment that I am a knower implies the subject: "I am a self" or "I am a subject." Such an implication renders problematic postmodern minimizing or denying of selfhood, the "end of man" as Foucault put it. One cannot, without self-referential inconsistency, deny knowing, the value of rationality, and the reality of the self.[14]

DESCRIPTIVE ADEQUACY

From a Lonerganian perspective, the descriptive question that arises about postmodernism is whether it is too one-dimensional. Are there not different forms of the experience of reason, some pathological, some not. Lonergan, I argue, has in *Insight* and *Method in Theology* a phenomenology of the different forms of rational activity that allow him to claim against postmodernism that he is the true or truer friend of difference.

Let us briefly recall some of these different forms. a) First of all, already noted, is the distinction among experience, understanding, and judgment. When we add to these the fourth level of freedom, of choosing, committing myself, loving, then we have a four-level transcendental structure of the self as experiencing, understanding, judging, and choosing. Such transcendental structure functions as a genuine Lonerganian *a priori* which the human subject brings to different forms of activity.[15]

b) Lonergan distinguishes between science as a form of empirical method oriented to external data of sense, quantitative formulation of hypotheses and experimental verification; and philosophy as a form of generalized empirical

---

[13] Jurgen Habermas, *The Theory of Communicative Action, II: Reason and the Rationalization of Society*, trans. Thomas McCarthy (Boston: Beacon Press, 1984), 387, 389-90.

[14] Michel Foucault, *The Order of Things: An Archeology of the Human Sciences*, trans. unidentified (New York: Vintage Books, 1973), 386-87.

[15] Bernard J. Lonergan, *Method in Theology* (New York: Herder & Herder, 1972), 3-25.

method reflecting on data of consciousness, qualitative definition and self-affirmation. Both are expressions of cognitive structure, but each is different in having a different kind of data to reflect upon, different goals, different criteria of certainty.[16]

c) Lonergan affirms different patterns of experience of which each is an expression of cognitional-volitional structure, but each of which is essentially different from the others in aim, criteria, and object reflected upon. Common sense is pragmatically oriented toward short range results whereas the intellectual pattern of experience is oriented to rigorous knowledge for its own sake. The aesthetic pattern of experience is oriented to perceptible patterns of experience in a way that the religious pattern is not. The religious pattern of experience, falling in love with God, has a transcendent object in a way that common sense or science or art do not.[17]

d) Lonergan distinguishes among different aspects or stages on different levels of cognition; for example, the movement from question to insight to definition on the level of understanding or the movement from evidence to reflective grasp of the unconditioned to assertion on the level of judgment. e) Lonergan distinguishes among different kinds of bias, egoistic, group, dramatic, and general oriented to the short range and empirical and indifferent to the long range and speculative solution, on the one hand, and the immanent, norm-guided dynamism of inquiring intelligence and reasonableness, on the other hand.[18] f) There is a distinction between authentic subjectivity, in which the self's thought and behavior correspond to the transcendental structure of experience, understanding, judgment, and decision and inauthentic subjectivity, in which there is contradiction between one's behavior and the structure. g) Finally, we note the difference between a just society, that institutionalizes the imperatives of inquiring intelligence and reasonableness and one that does not, that engages in domination and exploitation. I will develop this distinction further in the last section, in which I show how instrumental rationality illegitimately dominates practical, lived moral intersubjectivity.[19]

The relevance of these distinctions to the postmodernist problematic is salient. In general, the tendency to identify reason with science, technology, or domination is simplistic, in that it misses the experienced, lived difference in forms of rationality. More specifically, we can say, first, that science-technology is just one form of rationality, legitimate when in its own sphere,

---

[16] Bernard J. Lonergan, *Insight: A Study of Human Understanding*, 243-44, 271-73.

[17] *Ibid.*, 181-89, 251, 268, 385.   [18] *Ibid.*, 3-13, 271-304.

[19] Bernard J. Lonergan, *Method in Theology*, 20, 104, 265, 291.

but not equal to reason as such. Second, one reason that such an equation is invalid is that philosophy as a form of generalized empirical method is distinct from science. Third, because of the interplay between conceptual and pre-conceptual on the levels of understanding and judgment, any rejection of reason as simply logical or conceptual is invalid. Logicism and conceptualism are one-sided accounts of rationality that ignore its pre-conceptual aspects. Fourth, because of Lonergan's broad conception of reason and of rational method, he can incorporate valid postmodern insights. Heidegger's claim, for example, that questioning is the piety of thinking can enrich and be enriched by Lonergan's account, which already gives a high priority to questioning.

Derrida's critique of immediate presence and his emphasis on the structural dimensions of language can enrich Lonergan's critique of immediate realism by adding insights into language not developed by Lonergan. The insistence that one meaning or thing is not simply itself but is mediated by a play of difference is a further basis for rejecting the claim that knowing is merely immediate looking. Lonergan already has a critique of presence that can enrich and be enriched by Derrida's critique of presence. If one conceives rationality and philosophy in a sufficiently broad and deep way, the question oriented to being and the linguistic play of difference are within rationality and philosophy, not outside of them. All that the postmodern prodigal thinks he has to leave home to find is already present in modernist rationality as he is welcomed home, penitent and forgiven by his modernist father.[20]

Fifth, because of the distinctions between authentic and inauthentic subjectivity, just and unjust societies, reason does not equal domination, injustice, exploitation. Rather these can be criticized in the light of rationality as irrational, as at best incomplete, truncated manifestations of a deformed rationality. Finally, Lonergan recognizes a legitimacy in the desire present in postmodernism to transcend rationality, but Lonergan locates this transcendence in a movement to the fourth level of freedom, of commitment, of falling in love with persons or with God. Such transcendence does not reject rationality but rather builds on and presupposes it. Transcendence of rationality is not rejection of it but completion. As he puts it, the fourth level necessarily sublates the first three cognitional levels. The desire to know naturally completes itself in the desire to love. All that glitters, therefore, in postmodern transcendence is not gold. Such legitimate transcendence also allows Lonergan to make a critique of presence: mystery is rooted in the desire to know's

---

[20] Martin Heidegger, *The Question of Technology*, 35; Derrida, *Of Grammatology*, 27-73. *Cf.* 250-54.

anticipation of a totality of correct answers contrasting with the finite set that we do have and the mystical experience proper to falling in love with God.[21]

HERMENEUTICAL ADEQUACY

Lonergan's challenge to postmodernism on the level of a hermeneutics of history is similar to his challenge on the level of phenomenological description. Has the postmodernist given an account of history, modernity, and the development and/or devolution of modernist rationality that is too undifferentiated or dedifferentiated and thus does violence to these realities? Has the postmodernist, contrary to his stated intentions to respect difference, obliterated or minimized it? Is the postmodern account of modernity, rather than being that of a dialectical interplay between positive and negative, progress and decline, forward moves and regressive moves, one-sidedly bleak and negative? The Lonerganian answer to all of these questions is a resounding "yes."

As is well known, Lonergan's account of human cultural history presents it as moving through three stages of meaning. These stages progressively differentiate the patterns of experience, common sense, science, philosophy, and religious interiority, discussed in the previous section. The first stage is, in the language of *Insight*, mythic and, therefore relatively undifferentiated. Common sense, science, philosophy, and religious interiority intermingle in a confused fashion. The second stage is the discovery of mind by the Greeks, in which theory is rigorously distinguished from common sense. To adequately define something, Socrates tells Meno, is not just to give particular examples of that reality in the manner of common sense, but to understand and formulate the essence of something as universal, the essence of justice or piety or courage. Philosophical enlightenment for Plato is moving out of the undifferentiated-mythic reality of the Cave and into the sunlight of the Forms illumined by the Good.

The third stage of meaning characterizing modernity involves and implies a further distinguishing among science, philosophy as reflection on cognitive and volitional interiority, and religious interiority. Philosophy's proper function is to promote the self-appropriation that cuts to the root of and can resolve philosophical difference, and has the further function of distinguishing among the patterns of experience, grounding methods of science, and promoting their unification.[22]

---

[21] Bernard J. Lonergan, *Insight: A Study of Human Understanding*, 348-50, 530-49; *Method in Theology*, 104-107, 120-21.

[22] Bernard J. Lonergan, *Method in Theology*, 85-99. *Insight: A Study of Human Understanding*, 385-430.

To the extent that differentiation and integration have occurred in history, progress has occurred. But in addition to progress, there is also decline. In addition to genetic method allowing us to account for forward moves in history, there is also dialectical method that allows one to account for decline and to criticize it. Criteria for progress and decline are in the normative exigencies of the subject giving rise to four transcendental precepts: "be attentive," "be intelligent," "be reasonable," and "be responsible" corresponding to the levels of experience, understanding, judgment, and decision respectively.[23]

Next, criteria for interpretation lie in the exigencies of the intelligent, rational, free subject, giving rise to the canons of hermeneutics: relevance, complete explanation, successive approximations, parsimony, and residues. Relevance is oriented to the universal viewpoint of a totality of possible interpretations potentially and/or actually manifest in a series of genetically and dialectically related texts. Complete explanation demands that we achieve as complete and nuanced an interpretation of the text as possible. Successive approximations is an ideal of ever more closely approaching an adequate account of the text. Parsimony negatively excludes the unverified and unverifiable and positively invokes critical reflection verifying or invalidating claims by having recourse to passages in the text. Residues alerts us to the possibility and actuality of contradictions and anomalies in the text. Here Derrida's practice of "deconstruction" can be taken as a version of the canon of residues; in Lonergan, however, the canon of residues is linked to the other four canons in a way that it is not in Derrida.[24]

Finally, Lonergan can sharply distinguish between positions and counter-positions as they manifest themselves in the history of culture and philosophy. A philosophical claim will be a position if the real is being and not the immediate "already out there now," if the subject is known through intelligent and reasonable affirmation and not through some prior existential state or inward look, and if objectivity is the fruit of authentic subjectivity expressed in intelligent inquiry and reasonable reflection and not a property of vital anticipation, extroversion, and satisfaction. On the other hand, a claim will be a counter-position if it contradicts one or more of the above positions.[25]

All of the preceding relates to the postmodern critique of modernity in the following ways. a) Lonergan has the advantage over postmodernism in that he can articulate precise criteria for progress and decline, whereas postmodernism's rejection of modernist normativity is so thoroughgoing that it has trouble

---

[23] Bernard J. Lonergan, *Insight: A Study of Human Understanding*, 458-87, 484-85.

[24] *Ibid.*, 586-94. Derrida, *Grammatology*, xliii-1.

[25] Bernard J. Lonergan, *Insight: A Study of Human Understanding*, 386-87.

specifying such criteria. It does often validly indicate and criticize decline, but, because postmodernism lacks criteria, its critique at a certain point becomes arbitrary. b) If Lonergan is correct, differentiation is preferable to lack of differentiation and mediation to immediacy. To wish to move back in a Heideggerian manner to a pre-Socratic stage of unity and immediacy is to be fundamentally mistaken. Such a move confuses legitimate objectification with alienation, and the real with the immediate. Such orientation to a pre-critical immediacy has to be rejected in whole or in part as a counter-position.[26]

c) Lonergan disagrees with the postmodernists over the interpretation of modern philosophy. Is it mostly or all a negative story, a gradual and progressive forgetfulness of being in favor of the calculable, a mostly triumphalistic story, or a dialectical story, a unity of truth and error, position and counter-position, light and darkness? Lonergan's argument with postmodernism is that the third alternative is the best and that his account of method can spell out why his method is preferable, whereas the postmodern critique of modern philosophy is negatively one-sided and cannot spell out criteria for its critique.

By Lonergan's criterion of complete explanation, an account must be as comprehensive and as nuanced as possible. Thus Descartes' turn to the subject is valid, but he sinks into dualism and overemphasizes apodicticity. Kant's discovery of the transcendental was valid, but in his doctrine of things in themselves he unwittingly falls prey to a pre-critical realism, claiming that knowing of the real world should be immediate. Hegel's notion of dialectic contains some acceptable insights but is overly conceptual, too much on the level of understanding and not enough on the level of judgment and of freedom.[27]

d) Like Heidegger in his account of the gradual eclipse of being in modern history and philosophy, Lonergan discusses a longer cycle of decline rooted in the general bias of common sense toward practical, short-range solutions linked to group domination, manifested in ever more restricted viewpoints, and culminating in totalitarianism. Unlike Heidegger, however, Lonergan does not see such decline as testifying to the bankruptcy of metaphysics, but to its necessity. One feature of the longer cycle is its rejecting of detached, disinterested intelligence and subordinating it to solutions that are ever more short-sighted. If the pathology of the longer cycle is the gradual subordination of theory to common sense, then such pathology can be overcome only by a restoration of such detached, disinterested intelligence.[28]

---

[26] Martin Heidegger, *Introduction to Metaphysics*, trans. Ralph Manheim (Garden City, New York: Anchor Books, 1961), 79-172.

[27] Bernard J. Lonergan, *Insight: A Study of Human Understanding*, 339-42, 385-430.

[28] *Ibid.*, 226-38.

To put the point in Heidegger's terms, metaphysics does not need to be overcome but to be restored, chastened and fallibilistic through its encounter with postmodernism. To put the point in Lonergan's terms, Heidegger's overcoming of metaphysics is part of the problem, not part of the solution: it is a cultural product of the longer cycle and mistakes rationality with one of its pathological, positivistic forms.

If rationality, however, is critical and dialectical, then the longer cycle which is the product of a contradictory relationship between narrow, commonsensical intersubjectivity and inquiring, disinterested intelligence can be reversed.

The genuine modern discoveries about the subject, critique, and dialogue can be brought to bear on the concrete social order, which itself has progressed, in spite of the longer cycle, toward greater insight into human dignity, individual rights, democracy, and welfare. Modernity and human history show themselves to be genuinely dialectical, an interplay between truth and falsity, light and darkness, progress and decline, not simply or primarily negative as postmodernists are wont to say.[29]

Nonetheless, from a postmodern perspective, one can question whether Lonergan has done full justice to the pathology of the modern; his own politics seems to lead to a liberalism too comfortable with and uncritical of the capitalist status quo currently taking the form of the New World Order. One of the genuine contributions of postmodernism is here, whether one talks about Heidegger's account of *Gestell* or "enframing," Adorno's instrumental reason functioning as a lackey of late capitalist domination, Derrida's critique of logocentrism, and Foucault's critique of capitalism as a disciplinary society oriented to domination, exploitation, and normalization. My own sympathies lie with the proponents of a left-wing Lonerganianism such as Lamb and Doran who argue for full democracy transcending the injustice both of late capitalism and state socialism. Only such a radical political solution does justice both to the exigencies of intellectual, moral, and religious conversion and the depths of modernist pathology. I will develop the implications of such conversion in the next section.[30]

---

[29] See Bob Doran, *Theology and the Dialectics of History* (Toronto: The University of Toronto Press, 1990), especially 355-470, for an insightful unfolding of the social-political implications of Lonergan's thought.

[30] See my "Praxis and Ultimate Reality: Intellectual, Moral, and Religious Conversion as Radical Political Conversion," *Ultimate Reality and Meaning* 13, No. 3 (September 1990): 222-40, for a further development of radical political conversion and its links to Lonergan's thought; Matthew Lamb, *Solidarity With Victims, Toward A Theology of Social Transformation* (New York: Crossroads, 1982).

ETHICAL-POLITICAL COGENCY

When one reads *Insight* and *Method in Theology* together, it becomes apparent that Lonergan is more than just a cognitional theorist and metaphysician. What emerges in *Method in Theology* is the importance of the fourth level of freedom, commitment, and love as sublating the three cognitional levels, ethical value as a product of experience-feeling, understanding, judging, and choosing, the importance of intellectual, moral, and religious conversion, and objectivity as a fruit of authentic subjectivity. Objectivity, whether on the level of knowing or of ethical choice, is not a matter of taking a value-free look at something, but is itself a result of subjectivity functioning authentically in conformity with the four transcendental precepts and as a product of the three conversions.[31]

Lonergan up to this point can admit to some of the claims made by Foucault about the necessary link between truth and power: all truth claims are made as a result of my own will to power and are imbedded in discursive power-knowledge regimes such as science and technology serving late capitalism. Foucault thus denies that knowledge is a value-free look at data divorced from relations of power: interest, influence, domination, and submission between groups and individuals. Truth and power, he argues, are intrinsically related. Individuals and groups tend to interpret the world from the perspective of their own will to power: their will to dominate, to control, to direct the wills of other men. Women will thus have a different "take" on the world from men, labor from capital, black from white.[32]

One issue that arises here is that of relativism. If the world is interpreted according to my own particular will to power, then how are objective truth claims possible? How can Foucault's own claims, putatively true and universal, about modern disciplinary societies and the reign of bio-power, his preference for the oppressed, or his claim about truth and power be justified?[33]

Lonergan can respond to this *aporia* in the following ways. a) He makes the distinction between authentic and inauthentic subjectivity. Thus the rejection of a naive notion of objectivity and value, which rejection he shares with Foucault, does not entail relativism: "objectivity is the fruit of authentic subjectivity." b) Lonergan makes the distinction between cognitional structure and patterns of experience. Cognitional structure operates in each pattern of

---

[31] Bernard J. Lonergan, *Method in Theology*, 27-55, 165.

[32] Michel Foucault, *Power/Knowledge*, ed. Colin Gordon, trans. Colin Gordon, Leo Marshall, John Mepham, Kate Soper (NewYork: Pantheon Books, 1980), 78-133.

[33] See Jurgen Habermas' critique of Foucault's "crypto-normativism" in *The Philosophical Discourse of Modernity*, 279-86.

experience, but it operates according to different interests. The interest of the scientist in prediction and control is not the same as the aesthete's interest in beautiful works of art; the interest of common sense in a rough, pragmatic truth is not the same as the religious interest expressed in "falling in love with God." Yet these interests internal to the domains in question do not compromise their truth, objectivity, or normative rightness; they help constitute it. In a way analogous to Habermas, Lonergan can affirm knowledge-constitutive interests.[34]

c) Such knowledge-constitutive interests are different from externally imposed claims rooted in power or domination. Thus, a scientific claim asserted because it is a more comprehensive account of the data is internal to the domain of scientific knowledge and legitimate; a claim made or rejected because it satisfies or fails to satisfy a certain group funding the project is external and illegitimate.

Lonergan, then, can make the distinction between legitimate and illegitimate forms of power in a way that Foucault cannot. He can also make the distinction between just and unjust forms of social interaction. Foucault here remains curiously decisionistic or self-contradictory. Either the decision to resist modern forms of power is morally justified or it is not. If it is morally justified, then there seems to be tacit appeal to a moral humanism and sense of right that Foucault has already rejected. If such a decision is not justified, what is arbitrarily asserted can be rationally questioned or denied. It is hard not to agree with Habermas when he asks, quoting Nancy Fraser,

> Why is struggle preferable to submission? Why ought domination to be resisted? Only with the introduction of normative notions could he begin to tell us what is wrong with the modern power/knowledge regime and why he ought to oppose it.[35]

A possible way out for Foucault is his preference for the marginalized and subjugated forms of knowledge and groups. Indeed there is something analogous to a "preferential option for the poor" or oppressed in his work that is exemplary and deserves attention. But here again the question arises, "Why should one prefer the oppressed?" and "Which groups of marginalized should one prefer?" An account of justice is lacking here that would allow Foucault to justify such preferences. Such an account is present in Lonergan; justice emerges when the dictates of authentic subjectivity and intersubjectivity take precedence over bias, the transcendental precepts are respected, the ethical

---

[34] Bernard J. Lonergan, *Insight: A Study of Human Understanding*, 181-89. Jurgen Habermas, *Knowledge and Human Interests,* trans. Jeremy Shapiro (Boston: Beacon Press, 1971), 301-17.

[35] Jurgen Habermas, *The Philosophical Discourse of Modernity*, 284.

demand for consistency between knowing and doing is fulfilled, and a society emerges that satisfies the legitimate demands of its citizens for human rights, participation, and human welfare; arbitrary exclusion for reasons of racial, sexual or class bias, different kinds of group bias, is to be rejected. A just economy will be one that interacts fruitfully in a non-reductionistic way with culture and the polity and that satisfies the material needs of all citizens, not simply or primarily the few at the top. It will ensure a fruitful dialectic between instrumental practicality and moral intersubjectivity. Foucault, however, has no way of distinguishing between the legitimately marginalized, racists, sexists, and classists whose values no longer obtain in a just society, and the illegitimately marginalized who are victims of racism, sexism and classism. Why could not Donald Trump, Hugh Hefner, and George Wallace use *Discipline and Punish* or *The Order of Things* to make a comeback? In the hell of the marginalized there are many shacks or mansions, not all of which deserve our compassion or sympathy.[36]

All of which is not to deny that on a concrete sociological and historical level there is much that is true and insightful in Foucault. His account of the disciplinary society as the growth of modern power/knowledge regimes that oppress and tame and normalize subjects in such a way that they become "good students," good academics," or "good workers" in thrall to an unjust New World Order needs to be incorporated into Lonergan's account of the long cycle. In this way not only is Lonergan's thought enriched but it becomes one that is more explicitly aligned with the oppressed. A marriage between Foucault and Lonergan on this level leads to a more radical Lonergan. The following seems plausible, although not fully proven in this essay: if one is genuinely and fully intellectually, morally, and religiously converted, then a radical political conversion emerges that is on the side of the oppressed. Elsewhere I have developed this line of thought more fully. If I am committed to justice and to the critique of institutions that cause injustice, then I must side with the oppressed. The proposition is analytic, an analytic principle in Lonergan's terms.[37]

CONCLUSION

On the basic questions dividing Lonergan and postmodernism, self-referential consistency, descriptive adequacy, hermeneutical comprehen-

---

[36] Michel Foucault, *Power/Knowledge*, 81-82; Bernard J. Lonergan, *Insight: A Study of Human Understanding*, 207-44; Doran, *Theology and the Dialectics of History*, 387-417.

[37] See the whole of *Discipline and Punish*, especially 135-94, and my "Praxis and Ultimate Reality."

siveness, and normative cogency, I have given the nod to Lonergan. Postmodernism, however, raises certain questions, comes to certain insights, questions forms of modernist, capitalist, and state socialist pathology, and takes certain political stances that can be incorporated into a Lonerganian perspective. Heideggerian questioning as the piety of thinking, for example, can be incorporated into a philosophy of the subject that is metaphysically oriented. One does not need to go beyond metaphysics to do justice to such questioning, provided that one's conception of knowing is broad enough and nuance enough. Again I have argued that Derrida's practice of deconstruction can enrich a Lonerganian use of the canon of residues, but now such practice is given a broader hermeneutical context and is linked to the other canons of interpretation.

Here I think that it is important to do full justice to the critique of presence offered by Derrida and others. Western metaphysics has certainly been guilty at times of trying to achieve illegitimate closure, excessive certainty and repression of difference. Postmodernist insights can enrich and enhance a critique of presence already going on in Lonergan: his distinction between immediate knowing as looking and knowing as mediated experiencing, understanding, and judgment, the distinction between the finite set of judgments that we have made and the totality of correct judgments anticipated by the desire to know, and the distinction between an inauthentic mythic consciousness and an authentic orientation to mystery rooted in the desire to know, anticipation of a totality of correct answers that it does not have, and the mystical experience of falling in love with God. Here postmodernism helps philosophy realize its own deepest *telos*; illegitimate presence is a betrayal of philosophy. Philosophy can, but does not necessarily have to fall into such presence.

I have also argued that postmodern accounts of the pathology of modernity can enrich Lonergan's account of the longer cycle of modern history while being incorporated into a broader, deeper, more differentiated interpretation of modernity stressing its positive as well as its negative aspects. At the same time it seems to me that the political radicalism of the French, Foucault, Derrida, Deleuze-Guattari, Lyotard, and Baudrillard, brings into question a bourgeois, liberal or conservative Lonerganian reading of ethics and politics, in Lonergan himself and in some of his disciples. The question of the French to Lonergan himself is this: to the extent that rationality becomes merely bourgeois mirroring and justifying an oppressive capitalist status quo, does not rationality compromise itself and mutilate itself? Does not rationality in its full cognitive, ethical, and religious range point toward liberation from all injustice: racist, sexist, classist? The question of Lonergan to the postmodernists is this: do you not cut the links between evidential reflective rationality and critique at your peril? Does not such critique negate itself as critique, becoming arbitrary, inconsistent, violent?

Continuing this mutual questioning, Lonergan could ask whether there is not at the root of a postmodern questioning of modern reason a hankering after an immediacy that a rigorous account of objectivity and knowledge shows that we cannot have. One thinks here of Heidegger's return to Pre-Socratic immediacy and lack of differentiation as well as Adorno's and Horkheimer's positing of *mimesis*, an immediate oneness with a reconciled nature. Similarly does not Derrida's post-structuralism betray one-sided idealistic tendencies present in a post-structural play of difference on the level of understanding and ignoring too much the complementary levels of experience and judgment? To what extent is Foucault's impatience with modern normativity and his problematizing of all mediated truth claims the result of one-sided hankering, coming to full expression in his late work, after an aesthetic immediacy and a one-sided voluntarism not doing justice to the three cognitive levels and turning reason into an instrument of the will to power? To such tendencies, Lonerganians would reply with the following dictum: positions tend to develop, counter-positions tend to reverse themselves.[38]

---

[38] Bernard J. Lonergan, *Insight: A Study of Human Understanding*, 388. Michel Foucault, *A Foucault Reader*, ed. Paul Rabinow (New York: Pantheon Books, 1984), 76-97, 292-389. Lonergan correlates empiricism, idealism, and critical realism with the three regions of experience, understanding, and judgement respectively. Critical realism embraces all three levels in proper proportion and relation; see *Insight: A Study of Human Understanding*, 414-23. Idealism and empiricism represent a one-sided emphasizing of either understanding or experience, and a tendency to reduce knowing to one of those levels.

When one considers transcendental method as a conscious experiencing, understanding, judging, and choosing of myself as an experiencing, understanding, judging, and choosing subject in relation to being, then a fourth possibility arises, a reduction of the levels of knowing to that of freedom, which is Foucault's tendency. Such a tendency is to be contrasted to an authentic sublating of cognition by the fourth level of freedom while maintaining cognition's distinctiveness and validity, which is Lonergan's option (see *Method in Theology*, 120-22). The differences may seem slight, but they are enormous.

For a critique of Derrida's idealism using Ricoeur's notion of discourse, see my "Ambiguity, Language, and Communicative Praxis," in *Modernity and Its Discontents*, eds. and co-authors, James L. Marsh, John Caputo, and Merold Westphal (New York: Fordham University Press, 1992), 105-06.

Maritain and Postmodern Science

Matthew S. Pugh

All Thomists must by now realize that postmodern science poses a real challenge to Thomism, for the most serious philosophical implication of postmodern science strikes at the very heart of Thomist epistemology. That implication has been described by physicist and philosopher P. W. Bridgman in the following way: "[T]he structure of nature may eventually be such that our processes of thought do not correspond to it sufficiently to permit us to think about it at all. . . . The world fades out and eludes us, . . . we are confronted with something truly ineffable. . . . We have reached the limit of the vision of the great pioneers of science, the vision, namely, that we live in a sympathetic world in that it is comprehensible to our minds."[1]

Now given its obvious seriousness, every Thomist, then, must face the challenge of postmodern science, because no Thomist can in good conscience ignore science and its findings, or fail to take seriously the philosophical concerns of its most knowledgeable practioners. Nor can Thomists simply pretend that empirical science has no bearing on Thomistic metaphysics, for as St. Thomas and his most profound twentieth century interpreter saw, the knowledge disciplines, though apparently autonomous, in fact exist as interdependent members of a true hierarchy. This hierarchy includes the empirical sciences, mathematics, and mathematical physics, as well as the philosophy of nature, metaphysics, and natural and revealed theology. When working together and properly ordered, they make cosmology possible. But as *human* disciplines, each must ultimately be grounded in what is given to the intellect in sense knowledge. Consequently, any viable cosmology must also be grounded in the empirical sciences, since these are the disciplines which deal directly with the material world. If, however, the very sciences which supposedly ground the hierarchy of knowledge reveal to the intellect a

---

[1] Quoted in *Beyond the Postmodern Mind,* Huston Smith, (Wheaton, Illinois: Theosophical Publishing House, 1982), 8.

fundamentally incomprehensible world, then the entire knowledge superstructure is threatened with collapse.

Jacques Maritain understood this, and that is why he devoted so much of his intellectual energy to working out an epistemology that would be not only true to St. Thomas and the notion of the degrees of knowledge, but also to the spirit of contemporary science. For Maritain, any epistemology that claims to be inclusive must be able to accomodate science even in its most contemporary forms.[2] But he also knew that the empirical sciences necessarily seek completion in a higher wisdom, the philosophy of nature, which justifies and defends the principles of empirical science, without absorbing those principles into itself. Barring that completion, science is cut off from a higher intellectual light, while the hierarchy of knowledge is dispossessed of its empirical grounding. Thus, establishing the true relationship between the empirical sciences and the philosophy of nature is a most important, though most difficult one.

It is my belief that Maritain's philosophy of science provides the most successful account of that all-important relationship, and that when properly understood, is well able to overcome the epistemic conundrum in which postmodern science finds itself. What follows, then, is an attempt to show how Maritain's philosophy of science achieves this by laying out some of its most important themes, then defending it against some basic and fundamental criticisms.

MARITAIN'S PHILOSOPHY OF SCIENCE

According to Maritain, science, taken generally, is a perfect knowledge in which the intellect, under the compulsion of evidence, points out in things their reasons for being.[3] Hence it is a knowledge properly explanatory, and because perfect in mode, of that which is necessarily true. Science has, therefore, for its formal object intelligible necessities. Yet, because science bears on the material real, it also bears on the contingent, the singular. Consequently, science distinguishes between "thing" or material object, and intelligible formality, or proper "object," disengaged from the former through abstraction. Science, in effect, makes known essences and the necessary properties of essences realized in sensible singulars.

Essences, however, and the intelligible necessities immanent in them,

---

[2] Maritain's most important works along these lines are, *The Degrees of Knowledge* (New York: Charles Scribner's Sons, 1959); *Philosophy of Nature* (New York: Philosophical Library, 1951); *Science and Wisdom*, trans. Bernard Wall (New York: Charles Scribner's Sons, 1940); *Reflections Sur Intelligence* (Paris: Desclee de Brower, 1924).

[3] Jacques Maritain, *The Degrees of Knowledge*, 23.

manifest themselves concretely in terms of experimental constancies—the outward signs of those necessities. Indeed, experimental constancies provide the basis for the laws which science formulates, for scientific law captures the necessity inhering in such relations. But necessary relations derive their necessity from the fact that they have their locus in intelligibles, in essences. Science, then, in studying the essences of concrete existents, is bound to study not only the necessities immanent in natures, but also the concrete manifestations of these necessities inhering in experimental constancies.

It is for this reason that Maritain divides science into two kinds: sciences of explanation and sciences of observation. The sciences of explanation, like mathematics and philosophy, are purely deductive in nature, and make known in themselves the intelligible necessities immanent in their objects. Because they make known effects by principles or reasons for being, these sciences are explanatory in the proper sense of the term. The sciences of explanation, then, deal with essences as known, and the mode of intellection proper to them is called dianoetic intellection.

Sciences of observation, on the other hand, deal with essences as hidden, that is, as hidden in the experimental constancies manifest among concrete effects. In the sciences of observation, essences are known only in sign and symbol substitutes; they never uncover in themselves the intelligible necessities immanent in their objects. As such, they are strictly inductive in nature, being grounded in sense experience, and so are not explanatory in the proper sense of the term. Properly speaking, the sciences of induction are not real sciences, or are only imperfect sciences, and the mode of intellection proper to them is called perinoetic intellection.

Now, according to Maritain, the distinction between these two kinds of science is absolutely sharp; they cannot be reduced to each other.[4] Certainly the sciences of observation *tend* toward the sciences of explanation, for the former seek completion in the latter; that is, they seek completion in a properly explanatory science. The intellect obviously cannot remain content with a knowledge that does not penetrate to the essence, that does not apprehend real causes for being. Thus the sciences of observation and that science of explanation operative at the first degree of abstraction, namely the philosophy of nature, together constitute the realm of what the ancients called *physica*.

Nevertheless, though both sciences share the same material object (sensible being), they do not share the same formal object, for these sciences study sensible being from two entirely different standpoints. In other words, there is a real distinction between them. The inductive sciences focus on the sensible

---

[4] *Ibid.*, 34.

dimension of sensible/mobile being, while the philosophy of nature focuses on the being of sensible/mobile beings. For example, the scientist attempts to understand the behavior of matter through the formulation of laws derived from experimentation, while the philosopher of nature attempts to know *what* matter is.[5] In effect, the scientist proceeds from the visible to the visible, while the philosopher of nature proceeds from the visible to the invisible.[6]

Given, then, that the empirical sciences and the philosophy of nature, though interrelated, do not overlap in any fundamental way, the inductive sciences are free to operate unrestricted in their respective realms. It is the function of the philosophy of nature to explain and justify the principles of science, but science does not depend on the philosophy of nature for either knowing or using its own principles. Most importantly, however, this means that empirical science is relinquished from having to determine what is real, for its proper mode of intellection cannot tell us what is real, or how things really are, and cannot tell us what something is, or ultimately even resolve conflicts between equally viable but contradictory explanatory hypotheses.

Of course at this point one might be tempted to say that the history of science proclaims just the opposite, namely, that empirical science and the deductive sciences do overlap in a fundamental way, for is not the development of mathematical physics precisely the story of the joining of physics, which has for its object sensible/mobile being, and mathematics, which has for its object mathematical being? Certainly, but as a *scientia media* mathematical physics constitutes a special case which by its very nature cannot resolve the problem. Mathematical physics is very relevant to that problem, however, which is clearly revealed when considering the nature of that science.

As all Thomists know, physics and mathematics belong to two entirely different orders of being, for their formal objects have different degrees of remotion from matter. Physics retains common sensible matter in the definition of its proper object, and so studies beings which depend both for their being and their being known on sensibles. Mathematics, however, retains only common intelligible matter in the definition of its proper object, and so studies beings which depend for their being, but not their being known, on sensibles. Initially, mathematical abstraction abstracts its objects from concrete existents, but it reconstructs them formally and ideally in imaginative intuition. Through abstraction these objects of thought then become independent of their material matrix. Absolutely speaking, mathematical entities can exist only in the mind.[7] Once mathematics has established the ideal existence of its object, truths concerning it are deductively established through their formal intelligible

[5] *Ibid.*, 46.   [6] *Ibid.*, 38.   [7] *Ibid.*, 54.

relations. Consequently, mathematical judgments are verified either directly or indirectly in imaginative intuition, for the ideal existence of mathematical entities can be either of the nature of a possible existent like "square" or "line," or of the nature of a being of reason, like irrational number, imaginary number, or transfinite number.[8]

Now in mathematical physics, the physics is properly subalternated to mathematics. This means that though its material object is sensible being, its formal object and principles of explanation are taken from the higher science of mathematics.[9] It is mathematics which provides mathematical physics with its method of conceptualization.[10] Hence because physico-mathematics studies

---

[8] *Ibid.*, 140-144. The latter, of course, are based upon the former, and are constructed deductively therefrom, but remain unfigurable in imaginative intuition. All mathematical beings, however, are at least indirectly grounded in the imaginative intuition, because all are derived from the mathematician's special consideration of the accident quantity. The philosopher of nature, of course, considers quantity from the standpoint of the extension of concrete bodies; from the standpoint of actual divisibility. The philosopher of nature thus treats quantity as a real property of bodies. (It is in fact the first accident in bodies; all the others emanate through it.) The mathematician, however, disengages quantity from its material matrix by formal abstraction, and then treats what has been separated in the mind as something separate in reality. Being is, in effect, reconceived by the mathematician in terms of relations of order and measurement. Given, then, their very nature, these mathematical objects must, of course, be apprehended by an intuition, but an intuition which is neither purely sensory nor purely metaphysical. They must, rather, be apprehended by an imaginative intuition, an internal sense only indirectly dependent upon sensory intuition. Thus even though imagination presupposes sensory intuition, and even though quantity precedes quality in proper ontological order, imaginative intuition is able to penetrate to quantity precisely because imagination is free from the contingency of sensory experience. Mathematical beings are therefore free to manifest themselves in symbol substitutes independent of the contingency of sensibles. Some, such as the objects of Euclidean geometry and basic number theory, are directly figurable in imaginative intuition. Others, such as non-Euclidean geometries and imaginary and transfinite numbers, are not. In effect, mathematical quantity must be grounded in quantity as conceived by the philosopher of nature.

[9] The empirical sciences, as seeking completion in a science of explanation, must be subalternated to that science. Thus, empirical science is subalternated to either mathematics or philosophy. But a science is either properly or improperly subalternated to another science. A science is subalternated to another when it derives its principles from the other, the subalternant science. The subalternant science resolves its conclusions into first principles, which in turn become the principles of the subalternate science. The subalternate science then adds to the subalternant science an accidental difference, as in optics, where ther formal object is *visual* line. In proper subalternation (again, as in optics), there is subalternation both with regard to principles and object, but there can also be proper subalternation in regard to principles alone. (This is the case, says Maritain, with theology and the knowledge of the blessed; they share the same object, but theology borrows its principles from the latter.) In improper subalternation, which is best called subordination, the sciences share the same object, but view it under completely different lights. (This is the case with the non-empiriometric sciences—the

sensible being by transposing it mathematically, that is, by treating it mathematically and not as physically real (it reduces all of its concepts to the measurable, since only the measurable behavior of nature revealed by instruments of measurement is real for it), mathematical physics gives up the search for real causes, for the kind of causes which the philosophy of nature seeks.

This is certainly apparent in the ever more frequent use which physico-mathematical science makes of mathematical beings of reason. Given that mathematical beings of reason are unfigurable in imaginative intuition, the universe that mathematical physics constructs using these beings of reason in its explanations becomes as unfigurable, as unimaginable, as those beings themselves.

Indeed, the history of mathematical physics is the history of an ever increasing move away from ontology, away from the philosophy of nature, and toward the mathematical world of the preter-real. This is most important, for mathematical physics' hypothetical reconstruction of the physical real, based as it is on a network of mathematical relations which attempt to "explain" the measurements of experiment by utilizing beings of reason, leads to a divorce in science between the true and the real. As Maritain says (and here it is best to quote him in full):

> Physico-mathematical theory will be called true when a coherent and fullest possible system of mathematical symbols and the explanatory entities it organizes coincides, throughout all its numerical conclusions, with measurements we have made upon the real; but it is in no wise necessary that any ontological law in the world of bodies correspond determinately to each of the symbols and mathematical entities in question. The need for causal physical explanation still immanent to the mind of the physicist, finally issues (in the highest synthesis) in the construction of a certain number of beings of reason based on the real and providing an image of the world (or a shadow of an image) apt to support his mathematical deduction.[11]

In light of this definition of truth, there can obviously be many true or viable physico-mathematical theories, as long as these are mathematically coherent and do not violate the measurements and data taken from experimentation. Thus, it is conceivable that there be a number of conflicting physico-mathematical models of the physical real, each true because each coherent and consistent with the data, i.e., able to "save the phenomena."

---

empirioschematic sciences—and the philosophy of nature.) Improperly subalternated, or subordinated sciences need the subordinant science as provider, not of its own principles, but of regulative principles. Improperly subalternated sciences do *not* form a *scientia media*. (*Philosophy of Nature*, 102-113.)

[10] Jacques Maritain, *Degrees of Knowledge*, 41-42.   [11] *Ibid.*, 62-63.

Certainly, the physico-mathematical scientist does not intend to forsake causal explanations, nor to completely sever his connection to the real (and for this reason causality enters obliquely into his science, as when a physically conceivable entity is used at the start of a new theory), but he is entirely indifferent to the distinction between real being and the being of reason, and so holds that as long as his explanatory entities are defined by theoretically realizable operations of measurement they are real, because they really describe the behavior of physical matter; measurements, of course, are taken from the real.[12] Indeed, that connection of measurment with the real is what enables mathematical physics to remain a physical science, for ultimately its judgments must be verified in the sensible.

There is, then, in physico-mathematics a kind of double movement of the intellect. Because its material object is the sensible singular, and because it is a physical science, mathematical physics attains the essence only obliquely and in its effects. However, because it is formally mathematical, what it attains of the essence is attained in mathematical sign substitutes, by reconstructing the ontological essence in terms of mathematical being; either a possible being or *ens rationis*. As such, physico-mathematics is never able to transcend the mode of perinoetic intellection.[13]

The development of relativity theory and quantum mechanics support Maritain's analysis of the nature of mathematical physics. For example, relativity theory has done away with absolute space and absolute time, absolute mass, and absolute systems of reference, by applying a non-Euclidean geometry to nature in such a way as to make a reconstruction or reconception of space and time in terms of that mathematical being of reason not only possible, but more satisfying for explaining the data in question. In effect, relativity theory substitutes a mathematical absolute for a real absolute. Indeed, special relativity theory says that nothing can travel faster than light. Here the numerical value of the speed of light has itself become an absolute, for light's velocity remains the same regardless of the systems of reference of its observers. In fact, the whole of relativity physics proceeds from a concern to make its *laws* absolute by making them independent of observers and their systems of reference. Thus in relativity theory the course of events in nature becomes relative, but its laws obtain absolutely.[14]

When considering quantum theory we find that the nature and behavior of subatomic particles have been completely reconceived in terms of mathematical

[12] *Ibid.*, 140.

[13] "Thus in a general fashion, within the whole empiriological register, the resolution of concepts is made in an infra-philosophical direction." *Ibid.*, 141.

[14] *Ibid.*, 156.

beings of reason, as attested by the general reconstruction of de Broglie's "matter waves" into "probability waves."[15] Though electrons were initially thought to have real wave properties, these properties were subsequently reconceived by Schroedinger and others strictly in terms of mathematical probabilities. Indeed, in the wave mechanics developed by Schroedinger, the energy of a system is related to a wave function in such a way that that system can have only certain allowed values—the four absolute quantum number limits. But the wave function itself merely represents the probability that a particle will be found within a certain volume. In fact, much of quantum physics has to do with the imposition of numerical limits on various subatomic energy systems. Nevertheless, because the electron does exhibit real wave-like properties, one outcome of quantum mechanics (Bohr's complementarity principle[16]) leads to the understanding that the behavior of such a particle is unfigurable in imaginative intuition—how can one imagine and/or think an entity that is both particle and wave at the same time? Yet, such a particle *is* entirely conceivable in terms of *ens rationis.* Thus seemingly contradictory explanatory hypotheses can account for the behavior of the same entity.[17] Of course, many other examples from physics could be brought forth to demonstrate the same thing.[18]

Postmodern physics, then, displays the contrary motion of an ever greater immersion in the physical real considered as quantity, and an ever greater absorption in non-real mathematical beings of reason. Both movements tend to sever empiriological science from the philosophy of nature, from any ontological concern. As Maritain says, at the same time that mathematical physics reconceives the real in terms of measurements and pointer readings, it

---

[15] Cf. Heisenberg's *Physics and Philosophy*, (New York: Harper and Row, 1958.)

[16] Bohr's principle of complementarity simply states that an electron may be described either in terms of particles or wave motion, and that these views are somehow complementary.

[17] According to E. Picard, "[S]ome wonder whether or not the electron does not have purely analytical existence, since it is only a center of vibration in a wave system to which reality really belongs. For others only the waves have an analytical existence; a fictitious continuous field has been substituted mathematically for a discontinuous surrounding field" (Quoted in *Degrees of Knowledge*, 62, footnote 1). But whether these competing views represent real causal entities or are mere mathematical reconstructions of the real is of no importance to the physicist, as long as they account for the data.

[18] For example, related to Schroedinger's probability mechanics is Heisenberg's uncertainty principle, which states that if both the position and the momentum of an electron cannot be established (since one must invariably disturb a system in the very act of observing it) then the physicist cannot be sure that the consecutive observations of what he takes to be the same electron do not in fact belong to two distinct electrons. Individual electrons, therefore, cannot be identified, and there is only a mathematical probability that a particle will be found within a given volume.

turns "[a]side from the ontological by declining to integrate into the scientific tableau of nature the absolute elements that philosophy and common sense recognize in the real and by replacing those elements with beings of reason elaborated according to the exigencies of the deductive system to be constructed."[19] And I dare say that in severing science from the imagery of common sense and its grounding in the real, as well as from the philosophy of nature which provides the ontology for the world of common sense,[20] postmodern physics, *regarded in isolation from philosophy*, truly places man in the epistemic situation lamented by P. W. Bridgman.

Yet, when considered from the standpoint of its being a *scientia media,* the history of mathematical physics has been nothing less than inevitable, for the rise of mathematical physics could only have led to the conflict between science and the philosophy of nature which in fact ensued upon its discovery.[21] There were two movements to this drama; the first resulting in the collapse of the philosophy of nature into physico-mathematics; the second resulting in the complete expulsion of the philosophy of nature and ontology from mathematical physics. The first movement culminated in the creation of the great system of Newtonian mechanics, which sought to use mathematical physics to give ontological explanations of the phenomena of nature. The second movement culminated in the overcoming of classical mechanics, science's recognition of its own nature, and its subsequent understanding that science cannot penetrate to the real as it is in itself.

But the expulsion of ontology and the philosophy of nature from empiriological science, when seen from the perspective of science, is not to be regretted, for it was precisely the development of mathematical physics and its post-Newtonian separation from the philosophy of nature that made science's great advances possible. Therefore, scientists need not regret the fact that science has become divorced from imaginative intuition, or that it presents to the intellect a welter of conflicting hypotheses each true (because each "saves the phenomena"), but none of which, or only some of which, or all of which indifferently represents the real, for science has finally recognized that its concern is not with the real, or at least not with the real as it is in itself.

However, when seen from the standpoint of wisdom and the philosophy of nature, from the standpoint of the intellect's desire to know, to be left with nothing but sign or symbol substitutes in place of real causes—to be left with nothing but contemporary science—is a catastrophe, for only a wisdom which

---

[19] Jacques Maritain, *Degrees of Knowledge*, 157.

[20] *Ibid.*, 159. Also, "The New Physics dissolves the imagination into a world of symbols . . ." Cf. *Degrees of Knowledge,* 159-160, quote from Eddington.

[21] Jacques Maritain, *Science and Wisdom*, 40-41.

penetrates to the very nature of the sensible real can satisfy the intellect's desire to know the reasons for being of the sensible real. Only a true wisdom, a philosophy of nature operative at the first degree of abstraction, can make such a knowing possible. Only a philosophy of nature which views the sensible from the ontological standpoint can decide among science's conflicting hypotheses, can determine which of its "true" theories correspond to the real, or best represents the real.[22] It is the philosophy of nature, not mathematical physics, that is capable of deciding, for example, if space is ultimately Euclidean or non-Euclidean;[23] if atoms are real; if there is a *telos* in nature; if there is vital principle in living beings which cannot be reduced to the physico-chemical constituents of their bodies; and what must be the true meaning of determinism in science. It is also, therefore, the philosophy of nature, and not contemporary science, which must choose among the images of science those which will best suit its proper cosmology; for that a cosmology must be grounded in some image or set of images is inevitable.[24]

[22] Jacques Maritain, *Degrees of Knowledge, 50.*

[23] Maritain's reflections on the relationship between Euclidean and non-Euclidean geometries are particularly interesting. From the geometer's standpoint all mathematically possible spaces are real; that is, all spaces are real as long as they are consistent and derivable from their basic axioms. The mathematical physicist builds on this notion and holds any space to be real which is mathematically possible and explains the phenomena at hand in a coherent and comprehensive way. The philosopher of nature, however, defines a space as real, when, as a mathematical being, its characteristics pertain to quantity as actually existing in the world of bodies. Thus, while all mathematically possible spaces are true, only a few, or one, will be real. Now, it is possible to tell if a mathematical being is real in two ways. First, the genesis of the notion must be analized to see if it is incompossible with extra-mental existence. Secondly, to be real the being must be able to be constructed in imaginative intuition. Imaginative intuition, of course, presupposses sense experience, for mathematical beings are real only because they are ultimately grounded in sense existence. Hence, only Euclidean space is real from a philosophical standpoint, since only Euclidean geometry can satisfy these conditions. As Maritain says, "It is only by the intermediary of this space that others can satisfy the conditions posited" (*Degrees of Knowledge,* 168, footnote 1). Einstein's space, therefore, saves the phenomenon of gravity by embodying peculiar geometric properties, which nevertheless lack reality. Real space and geometric space are irreducible. Euclidean space is the best geometric representation of real space.

[24] "For the philosophy of nature cannot do without a scientific imagery. It needs the image . . . or the symbol that the science of its day fashions of the world" (*Degrees of Knowledge,* 182). The image that physico-mathematics provides the philosophy of nature with is of a universe whose ultimate entities can only be reductively based in the figurable. Thus, though these sciences lead the imagination into a realm of shadow and confusion, they also remind the physicist that the elements which make up the concrete existents of nature need not be directly representable to our senses. In this way empiriometric science is then free to formulate hypotheses based on models contradictory from an imaginative standpoint. Nevertheless, mathematical physics remains grounded in the figurable, and so the cosmological image which the philosophy of nature chooses must remain true to that grounding.

MARITAIN'S CRITICS

Now as we have seen, Maritain believes that the philosophy of nature can achieve these goals only by rising above empiriological science, taken both in its pure sense and in the sense of mathematical physics. This is why he insists so strongly on the need to recognize that empiriological science and the philosophy of nature work with two distinct formal objects. Maritain's critics, however, maintain that he has made too hard and fast a distinction between the sciences of explanation and the sciences of observation,[25] and that furthermore, such a distinction, *as he makes it,* is impossible from a Thomistic standpoint. Maritain's philosophy of science, they say, hinges on there being a plurality of specifically distinct sciences *within* the same degree of abstraction, namely, the first degree of abstraction.[26] These critics claim that there can only be one science within the first degree of abstraction, the philosophy of nature, and that what Maritain calls the empirical sciences are nothing more than a dialectical extension of the real science that is the philosophy of nature. The only way to create specifically distinct sciences, they say, is to identify specifically distinct principles, but since the science which deals with the genus also deals with the species that fall under it,[27] the only way to formulate specifically distinct sciences *within the same degree of abstraction* is to bring in principles *ab extrinsico.* This is in fact what happens in physico-mathematics, but there we have a *scientia media* straddling two distinct degrees of abstraction, not a specifically distinct science within the first degree of abstraction.

In addition, complain the critics, Maritain's conception of the philosophy of nature incorrectly leads the intellect toward ever greater potentiality instead of actuality, by forcing the intellect of the philosopher of nature up the Porphyrian tree of generalities. The correct notion of the philosophy of nature, on the other hand, indicates that the intellect of the philosopher of nature must descend toward ever greater actuality. Thus for these critics the true philosophy of nature begins with generalities and ends in concretion; that is, ends in empirical or dialectical science, which, because immersed in the sensible singular, can at best give us only probable knowledge. Taken by itself, such dialectical science cannot be called true science.

Finally, the critics of Maritain maintain that by mistaking a difference in

---

[25] Benedict M. Ashley, "Thomism and the Transition from the Classical World View to Historical Mindedness," in *The Future of Thomism,* ed. Deal W. Hudson and Dennis W. Moran, (Notre Dame, Indiana: University of Notre Dame Press, 1992), 113.

[26] Bernard I. Mullahy, "Thomism and Mathematical Physics," Dissertation (Gregorian University, Rome, 1946, 105-120).

[27] *Ibid.,* 109.

degrees of generality for a real difference marking specifically distinct sciences, he has inappropriately applied what the Commentators call total abstraction, *abstractio totalis*, to the philosophy of nature. In light of this misapplication, Maritain's ontological analysis of the sensible real can end only in the being of reason, not real being.

Taking these criticisms in reverse order, however, one finds that Maritain's critics are wrong on all counts, and that Maritain has not made the mistakes his detractors accuse him of having made. First of all, the philosophy of nature, being at the first degree of formal abstraction, does not, obviously, operate via total abstraction, *abstractio totalis*. True, total abstraction leads to ever greater potentiality, since it identifies the universal precisely from the standpoint of the logical relations which it bears to its inferiors. But the type of abstraction operative at the first degree of abstraction, as Aquinas says, is *abstractio totius*, which abstracts the essential *ratio* of an individualized nature; abstracts, that is, the intelligible essence, the whole (a form/prime matter composite) of the concrete existent, from the individual matter (the particulars or parts) that shroud its intelligibility. Since *abstractio totius* does grasp the essential *ratio* of as concrete existent — which as a form/matter composite separated from signate matter may be likened to a form disengaged from matter *per se* — *abstractio totius* is nothing more than a special instance of *abstractio formalis*.

Of course, the function of this type of abstraction (formal abstraction) is to grasp precisely the actuality, the real essence of the existent, not from the standpoint of the logical relations which such an essence bears to its inferiors, but from the standpoint of intelligibility. The function of *abstractio totius* is, then, to abstract from matter as the principle of unintelligibility, not from matter as the principle of individuality. Thus the philosophy of nature, in using *abstractio totius*, does identify and deal with actualities; namely the real essences of concrete singulars. If it did not do this, it would not be a wisdom in the proper sense.[28]

Furthermore, it *is* possible to have specifically distinct sciences within the same degree of abstraction. Generically, sciences are specified by the way in which the abstractive operation withdraws from matter. For Maritain, there are three ways in which abstraction withdraws from matter, specifying the three great general degrees of abstraction. Non-generically, however, sciences are specified according to the way in which the abstractive operation constitutes the object at a determined degree of immateriality.[29] Hence the degree of

---

[28] Cf. Edward D. Simmons, "In Defense of Total and Formal Abstraction," *The New Scholasticism.* XXIX (1955): 427-440.

[29] Jacques Maritain, *Philosophy of Nature,* 89.

immateriality of the formal object founds the specific diversities between the sciences. There can be, then, specific differences between sciences which belong to the same generic degree of abstraction; geometry and arithematic in mathematics being the prime examples. In effect, the ultimate principle for the specification of the sciences is the mode of defining, the way of conceptualizing a science's proper object and of constructing its notion and definitions.[30]

It is true, of course, as Maritain admits,[31] that Aquinas and the Commentators saw the empirical sciences and the philosophy of nature as belonging to the same specific class wherein the differences have to do with greater or lesser degrees of concretion, not a difference between distinct formal objects. But, as Maritain says (and this seems to be fully born out by the history of science, which has witnessed science's unsuccessful attempts to both appropriate ontology and to exclude ontology), when comparing and contrasting the empiriological sciences with the philosophy of nature, it is not just a matter of seeing the same formal object under greater or lesser degres of concretion; it is a matter, rather, of conceiving the same material object in entirely different ways. The philosophy of nature studies that object from the standpoint of its being, while empiriology studies the relations between the material notes of such beings, as these signify intelligible necessities, and as those in turn signify essential connections, essences, and their properties. The first concentrates on the concrete existent as an intelligible being; the second focusses on the material effects which the concrete existent presents to the senses. Both disciplines withdraw from matter in the same way, but constitute their formal objects through entirely distinct conceptualizations. Empiriology thinks its object in terms of being *as* sensible. But being — even the being of the concrete existent — is not to be identified with matter. As he does in *Approches Sans Entraves,* Maritain would say that the philosophy of nature studies being from the standpoint of a being's being present-in-the-world, not from the standpoint of being *qua* being. Nevertheless, what is grasped in the philosophy of nature and in the basic existential judgment of existence operative at the first degree of abstraction is not merely the sensible, but being *as* sensible.

CONCLUSION

In conclusion, we find that not only can Maritain's philosophy of science meet the criticisms of its challengers, it can, more importantly, resolve the epistemic dilemma raised at the beginning of this paper. The empirical sciences

---

[30] *Ibid.,* 98.   [31] *Ibid.,* 91.

do not penetrate to the essence of the sensible real, they impinge on it only obliquely and in terms of the mathematical reconstruction of sensible effects and experimental constancies whose epistemological status is at best that of probability. Mathematical physics, in particular, has replaced the ontological real cause with mathematical preter-real causes, and so has inevitably led the intellect away from mathematical physics' initial grounding in the concrete and the imaginative intuition's reconfiguration of the concrete, toward an ever greater dependence on ultra-abstract *ens rationis*. Mathematical physics, then, has led the way in expelling the philosophy of nature from science. Given the latter's immersion in the world of symbols and its distance from the real, it should surprise no one that postmodern physics finds itself in a state of epistemic chaos, for its ultimate concern is no longer with what is real, but what works in terms of coherence, consistency, and "saving the phenomena." If this means that the world presented by science is unthinkable because literally unimaginable, so be it. It cannot be otherwise, given the very nature of empirical science. Thus empirical science, when taken in isolation from the hierarchy of knowledge grounded in it, is clearly insufficient from a higher philosophical perspective.

But empirical science is not the end of the story, for though autonomous in terms of its principles, empirical science does not exist in isolation from the degrees of knowledge resting upon it. As we have seen, empirical science seeks completion in a higher wisdom that is the philosophy of nature (not metaphysics).[32] That wisdom, centered as it is in intelligible being and so in certainty, is the final arbiter when it comes to the great themes of nature. It tells us that there is absolute space and absolute time; that space is ultimately Euclidean; that all concrete beings are really divisible into matter and form; that living sensible beings are really divisible into body and soul; that there is a *telos* in nature. Yet, as a higher wisdom, the philosophy of nature is a science specifically distinct from the empirical sciences, and that is how it is able to accommodate the findings of science, and to allow them their freedom while at the same time justifying and defending their very principles. Only a philosophy of science which understands the special relationship between empirical science and the philosophy of nature can show how, *together*, these knowledge disciplines (with, of course, mathematics, metaphysics, and theology) make a true cosmology possible—a cosmology able to accommodate

---

[32] Nevertheless, for Maritain the philosophy of nature is a participation of metaphysics, for the first degree of abstraction participates the third (*Degrees of Knowledge*, 40, 178-179). Yet metaphysics studies being as being, while the philosophy of nature studies being as mobile, as sensible (Cf. *Philosophy of Nature*, 118-120).

change[33] and the most contemporary forms of science, but grounded in the imaginative intuition and common sense. Maritain's is that philosophy of science, and Thomists would do well to pay it more attention.

[33] Maritain's philosophy of science fully recognizes the contingent and the changeable, and makes a prominent place for these in its conception, for the world of concrete existents that empirical science comes in contact with is "[n]ot the world of pure intelligible necessities. Essences and natures exist within existing reality; from it they (or their substitutes) are drawn by our mind, but they do not exist there in a pure state. Every existing thing has its own nature, and amongst them there are encounters which are themselves not natures, the necessity for which is not prescribed in any nature. Existing reality is therefore composed of nature and adventure. That is why it has a direction in time and by its duration an irreversible history— these two elements are demanded for history, for a world of pure natures would not exist in time, there is no history for a world of Platonic archetypes" (*Degrees of Knowledge,* 26). This is also why probability plays an ever greater part in physics. As it does so, it thrusts the notion of causality into the background, particularly in the subatomic world where classical mechanics cannot account for the behavior of particles in such a way as to enable the physicist to say that they are completely determined at each instant. Hence Heisenberg's indeterminacy principle. Of course, as science divorces itself more and more from the philosophy of nature, it comes to rely more and more on probability.

Contextualizing Theoretical Reason: Thomas Aquinas and Postmodernity

Gregory M. Reichberg

The fundamental negations of postmodern thought are well known and have occasioned much controversy: claims to universal truth are a hidden mask for the will to power; reason has no stable unity across the deep ruptures and fragmentations of history; radical contingency undermines the search for necessities in thought; reason is never just reason, but reason contextualized in this individual, this group, this time or this place. At first sight the main theses of Thomistic noetics appear at odds with their postmodern counterparts; for theoretical reason, according to Aquinas, is fully at home only in the grasp of atemporal, universal necessities. *Scientia*, the perfect work of reason, consists in just such a grasp, while the inferior intelligibility of the contingent is left to the imperfect habitus of opinion. To contextualize reason is thus to abandon the stance of *scientia* for the fluctuations of opinion, or worse, to reduce thought to the level of the imagination, whose objects *phantasms* are always particularized and never self-identical.

Within the great diversity of things known by the theoretical or speculative sciences, the Aristotelian-Thomistic tradition has constantly emphasized those common characteristics that render these things *objects* of scientific knowing. Necessity, timelessness, and universality are accordingly posited as formal properties attaching to all objects of theoretical *scientia*. Postmodern thinkers have sharply criticized this emphasis, identifying it as "the specific form of the will to knowledge that is Plato's legacy to western thought. . . . a love of an ideal intelligibility that can be separated from appearance, of a sameness that seeks to institute an identity amid multiplicity." [1] To counter this legacy, they have sought to place a wedge into our philosophical self-understanding,

---

[1] James W. Bernauer, *Michel Foucault's Force of Flight: Toward an Ethics for Thought* (Atlantic Highlands, New Jersey: Humanities Press, 1990), 93.

"permitting the introduction into the very roots of thought, of notions of *chance, discontinuity,* and *materiality.*" [2]

The classical ideal of *scientia* and the postmodern search for a narrative of reason's contingency thus face off as two competing and mutually exclusive paradigms of reason. But Thomists true to their Common Doctor cannot settle comfortably into this status quo. Questionable as postmodern claims may be, we must nevertheless seek to uncover whether they do indeed have some foundation in truth. With this in mind I propose the following thesis.

Thomists should continue affirming the necessity, timelessness, and universality of the proper objects of theoretical *scientia*. In this respect the gulf which separates us from postmodern philosophy is not easily crossed, and is perhaps unbridgeable. Yet we should not infer that these predicates of speculative *objects* extend to the cognitive *acts* by which such objects are known. On the contrary, these acts are not exempt from the conditions of contingency and temporality that so deeply affect our lives as individual and social beings. On this level there is, I think, much that the Thomist may learn from postmodern explorations into human thinking. By the same token we must affirm that a recognition of contingency within human cognitive acts need not entail the rejection of necessity, timelessness, and universality, in respect to the *objects* known by those acts. In other words, the contextualization of human cognitive acts in the lives of individual agents, lives which are situated within a complex interplay of social, political, and historical determinations, need not militate against the objectivity of those acts.

The argument will proceed on three levels. First, we shall consider the respect in which the speculative intellectual act, despite the universality of its object, is nevertheless individualized in individual knowers, a point emphasized by Aquinas in his debate with the Latin Averroists. Next, we shall investigate how theoretical cognitions are temporally situated in human lives. Lastly, in order to integrate postmodern reflections on "the power effects of knowledge," we shall consider the manner in which theoretical knowing enters the field of voluntary, human action. In each case I wish to indicate how Aquinas's approach to theoretical knowing, at first sight so antithetical to postmodern concerns, does, in fact, create an opening through which those concerns may pass. My hope is that a keener awareness of Aquinas's teaching on the individuality, temporality, and voluntariness of theoretical cognitions may serve as a springboard for dialogue between Thomists and postmodern thinkers.

---

[2] Michel Foucault, "The Discourse on Language," trans. Robert Swyer and published as appendix to *The Archaeology of Knowledge* (New York: Harper Colophon, 1971), 231. Cited by Bernauer, *Michel Foucault's Force of Flight: Towards an Ethics for Thought.*, 92.

AFFIRMING THE INDIVIDUALITY OF COGNITIVE ACTS "AGAINST THE AVERROISTS"

The Averroists held that the possible intellect, source of intellectual knowledge in humans, is a power existing in separation from those individual subjects who come to know by its mediation. On this view the agency responsible for acts of intellectual cognition does not belong to individual humans but rather to a separate substance. If a multitude of humans are together capable of knowing a thing numerically one, this can only be possible, they argued, because human beings all participate in a unitary intellectual act, an act that is one in number and not just one in kind. Aquinas summarizes this position in the polemical treatise *De unitate intellectus contra Averroistas*: "Therefore, it is impossible that there be numerically two things understood in me and in you. There is, one alone, then, and numerically only one intellect in all."[3] The same point is made even more succinctly in the early work *De ente et essentia* where the author writes that "the Commentator . . . wanted to conclude that the intellect is one in all men from the universality of the apprehended form."[4]

Aquinas could neither embrace this position nor reject it outright. An unqualified embrace was impossible, since both moral responsibility and man's participation in the Beatific Vision require the personal possession of mind. An outright rejection was impossible, due to his unwavering commitment to the objectivity and intersubjectivity of knowledge. "Therefore it must simply be conceded," he writes, "that the understanding of one thing, say a stone, is one alone, not only in all men but also in all intelligences."[5] Moreover, Aquinas clearly perceived the difficulty that his own position regarding the individuality of the act of knowing raises in relation to the equally important exigency of universality among knowers. He does not hesitate to state this difficulty boldly, as two objections to his own theory:

> If my intellect is distinct from your intellect, my intellect is individual (quodam individuum), and so is yours. . . . Now whatever is received into anything must be received according to the condition of the receiver. Therefore the species of things would be received individually into my intellect, and also into yours: which is contrary to the nature of the intellect which knows universals.
>
> Further, the thing understood is in the intellect which understands. If,

---

[3] *De unitate*, chap. 5 (43:311/128-31). Unless otherwise indicated, in referring to Aquinas' works I shall use the Leonine edition, *Sancti Thomae de Aquino opera omnia* (Rome, 1982-), citing volume, page, and line number (when available). Translations of the *De unitate* are taken from *Aquinas against the Averroists: on there being only one intellect*, Ralph McInerny, trans. (West Lafayette, Indiana: Purdue University Press, 1993).

[4] *De ente*, chap. 3 (43:375/107-10).   [5] *De unitate*, chap. 5 (43:312/159-63).

therefore, my intellect is distinct from yours, what is understood by me must be distinct from what is understood by you. . . . But this is contrary to the nature of the intellect; for then the intellect would seem not to be distinct from the imagination. It seems, therefore, to follow that there is one intellect in all men.[6]

In order to respond to this challenge Aquinas found himself drawn into a seeming paradox. On the one hand, his metaphysics will not permit any exception to the ontological law that only particulars can be said to exist. True especially of primary substance, this principle applies without exception to the operations of substance, cognitive acts included. To emphasize this point Aquinas restates the phrase "hic homo singularis intelligit" throughout the *De unitate intellectus*, using it as a kind of *leitmotif.*

On the other hand, whenever Aquinas speaks about human thinking, he stresses the properties of universality and receptivity, which characterize this activity. To know is to engage in an operation which directs the cognitive agent to the unlimited field of being outside of itself. The possible intellect is thus defined as a radical openness to being, an internal capacity to receive the forms of external things and behold them within the immanence of the self: "The intellect is a receptive power (*vis passiva*) in regard to the whole of universal being."[7]

This, then, is the paradox. The faculty of knowing is particularized in each individual. This includes both the agent and the possible intellects, which together concur to produce concrete acts of intellection in cognitive agents. Yet these same acts are ordered beyond the limited bounds of each individual knower to a grasp of the universal. Aquinas speaks of this duality in his *Quodlibet 7*, where he notes that knowledge (*notitia*) may be considered from two different sides: "either according as it is compared to the one knowing, in which case it inheres in the knower as an accident in a subject. . . . Or according as it is compared to what is known, and in this way it does not inhere in something, but rather is ordered to something else (*ad aliud sit*)."[8]

The object which specifies the acts of theoretical knowing is therefore not the soul itself or the cognitive faculty, but rather the quiddity of sensible things, grasped in the light of universal principles: "the intellect cannot know the singular in material things directly and primarily. . . . Hence our intellect knows directly the universal only."[9] We thus encounter the paradox of an intellectual

---

[6] *Summa theologiae* [ST] I, qu. 76, art. 2, objections 3 and 4 (5:216). Translations of the ST are from the 1947 Benzinger edition, with occasional alterations.

[7] *ST* I, qu. 79, art. 2, ad 3 (5:260).

[8] *Questiones quodlibetales* 7, qu.1, art. 4 (R. Spiazzi, ed. [Turin: Marietti, 1956], 138).

[9] *ST* I, qu. 86, art. 1, c. (5:347).

activity which is fully individualized and unique to each person, but which at the same time is formally specified by a knowledge of the universal.

This paradox is related to what has often been described as a tension in the heart of Aristotle's philosophy. Commentators have frequently noted that the Aristotelian metaphysics is centered on the primacy of individual substances, while his rational psychology is centered on the intelligibility of the universal. The impression of a fundamental dualism is thereby created.[10] Aquinas takes this a step further by transporting the apparent dilemma into the heart of the intellect itself. Hence, this tension arises in a more acute way for Aquinas than it did for the Stagirite, since the former holds explicitly that the agent and possible intellects are proper to each individual human being, thereby committing himself to the position that the intellect is both a particular power in each person and a faculty for apprehending the universal. Aquinas is fully aware of the tension in his account of knowledge. His approach here, as in other areas, is to embrace the difficulty in order to show how the terms of the dilemma, which at first sight seemed mutually exclusive, are compatible aspects of a unified whole.

He begins the task of unraveling the philosophical knot wherein singular subjects are opposed to the intelligibility of the universal by casting a critical eye on the terms of the dilemma. Is it true that the individual *as such* stands in opposition to the universal? Or is it the case that only individuals of a certain kind necessarily exclude such a reference? A brief response to this query is offered in the final chapter of the *De unitate intellectus*:

> Therefore, there is one thing that is understood by me and you, but it is understood by means of one thing by me and by means of another by you, that is, by different intelligible species, and my understanding differs from yours and my intellect differs from yours. Hence Aristotle in the *Categories* [chap.2, 1a25-27] says that knowledge is singular with respect to its subject. . . . Hence when my intellect understands itself to understand (*intelligit se intelligere*), it understands some singular activity; when, however, it understands understanding simply (*intelligit intelligere simpliciter*), it understands something universal. It is not singularity that is repugnant to intelligibility, but materiality. . . .[11]

The basic thrust of this passage can be summarized as follows. First of all, as social beings we are conscious of sharing common objects of perception. On

---

[10] In *Aristotle and the Problem of Value* (Princeton: Princeton University Press, 1963), Whitney J. Oates voices this reading of Aristotle: "The dilemma may be stated in this way: On the one hand, Aristotle holds that the individual particular is that which is ultimately real; yet, on the other hand, we can never know this real individual particular, for the general, the universal, is the genuine object of our knowledge, something we abstract from particulars" (74).

[11] *De unitate*, chap. 5 (43:312/226-38).

a tennis court the two players are attentive to the very same tennis ball. They share a common cognitive focus on a unique thing, "one thing that is understood by me and you." But at the same time, although the ball is one, the actual perceptions are multiplied according to the diversity of knowers; for this reason one player can strike the ball while the other can miss: "it is understood by means of one thing by me and by means of another by you." Paradoxically, while an object may be shared by several knowers it still remains proper to each one of them: "and my understanding differs from yours."

This in turn leads to a second common perception about knowing. When I engage in the act of knowing I am aware that this act is outwardly directed; it aims at an objective content. I don't just know indeterminately, I know this or that. Cognitive acts always have intentional objects. In addition, such intentional objects are never completely immersed in a *hic et nunc* singularity, since they always include a relation to many other things of like kind, a relation that is part and parcel of the perception itself. True, I am now playing with this singular tennis ball. But it is not the fact that it is an absolutely unique something that directs my attention when I use it to play tennis, but rather those common properties it shares with all other tennis balls. It is because this particular ball is like all other balls that it is a suitable instrument for playing tennis, not because it is exclusively different and unique. All objects of human perception (as opposed to purely animal sensing and imagining) include the awareness of common properties which extend over particulars and which unite those particulars into classes of different kinds. This is presumably what Aquinas means when he states that "when it [my intellect] understands understanding simply, it understands something universal."

Finally, although I perceive the act of understanding to be outwardly directed to what is universal, it remains true that I also perceive my particular self as the possessor of that cognitive intentionality. I am never so absorbed in an object of cognition that my individual identity completely disappears from view. Hence, at the same time that I perceive the object of cognition to be directed to the universal, I implicitly perceive my act of knowing to be a particular act originating from my individual being: "when my intellect understands itself to understand, it understands some singular activity." Aquinas holds that these two poles *universal object/singular act* are indissolubly united in all acts of intellectual cognition; the ordinary human experience of knowing necessarily includes both sides of the equation. Since singularity and universality are thus present within the "given" of the human experience of knowing, it would be erroneous to posit them as mutually exclusive properties: "it is not singularity that is repugnant to intelligibility, but materiality." By this last qualification Aquinas indicates that what inhibits certain subjects from enjoying an apprehension of the universal is not their individuality but their existence in matter.

On the basis of this distinction between the two poles present in all human knowing *individuality of the act/universality of the object* Aquinas subsequently notes that the study of mind may proceed along two distinct but complementary paths: "one way, according as the intellect is apprehensive of being and universal truth; the other way, according as the intellect is a certain thing (*quaedam res*), a particular power having a determinate act."[12]

The first of these approaches is metaphysical in nature, an *ontology of knowing*, while the second pertains to the sphere of moral psychology and may be termed an *ethics of knowing*.[13] Intellectual knowing is clearly an object for metaphysical discourse, for it is an activity requiring immateriality both on the part of the subject exercising the activity and on the part of the mode in which intentional objects are united to the subject. The metaphysician accordingly studies cognitive being insofar as it transcends the conditions proper to matter, motion, time, and the individuality of epistemic agents. This consideration does not entail the thesis that human knowing bears no relation to such conditions, but only that it does not pertain to the science of being qua being to describe them in detail.

The metaphysical nature of Aquinas's approach to the study of knowledge can easily mislead his readers into concluding that he altogether neglects the temporal and social dimensions of human knowing that are emphasized in postmodern treatments. Yet this criticism would be founded on a misunderstanding and a neglect of the full scope of his teaching on knowledge, which is not limited to the abstract and universal perspective of metaphysics. He also studies knowledge from within the vantage point of what he terms "moral science" (*scientia moralis*) or "operative science" (*scientia operativa*). The groundwork for this approach is laid out in the *prima secundae* of the *Summa theologiae* and in the disputed question *De virtutibus*, where he argues that since theoretical cognitive acts are exercised by free choice of the will,

---

[12] *ST* I, qu. 82, art. 4, ad 1 (5:303).

[13] Joseph Maréchal is one of the few Thomists to explicitly recognize a distinction between two approaches to knowledge, although he calls the metaphysical treatment of reason "logical" and the ethical treatment "psychological:" "La manière dont, en fait, nous abordons les données nouvelles qui pénètrent dans notre conscience, dépend donc de dispositions complèxe, spéculatives, affectives et volontaires, renforcées ou modifiées au fil de l'expérience 'écoulée.' Une théorie logique de l'opération intellectuelle comme telle peut faire abstraction de ces facteurs contingents; une théorie psychologique des opérations intellectuelles qui s'enracînent effectivement en nous, devrait, au contraire, tenir compte des 'habitus' spéculatifs et pratiques." *Le point de départ de la métaphysique,* cahier V (Paris: Desclée de Brouwer, 1950), 405.

they require guidance from practical reason, as do all freely chosen acts.[14] To an objection which states that speculative reason is entirely detached from the will, the principle of human acts (and thus morality), Aquinas replies that the faculty of will applies even the speculative reason to its operation of understanding and judging.[15] He subsequently notes that these willed acts of theoretical cognition are preceded by the *imperium*, a practical judgment ordaining the accomplishment of a determinate operation, thus grounding the assertion that practical reason can ordain the performance of even theoretical cognitive acts.[16]

Unlike metaphysics, moral science does not approach the individual entity in order to discern how it exemplifies a universal principle of explanation. On the contrary, as a practical science, ethics considers universal principles only insofar as they contribute to a comprehension of the persons to be guided in their actions. And as Aquinas never tires of repeating, actions are as fully singular as the persons whence they derive and the unique conjunction of circumstances in which they occur, *actus sunt circa singularia*.[17] Moral science accordingly achieves completion when it discerns the concrete, existential conditions specific to human acts.[18] As a result, those features of reality which a metaphysical analysis would regard as merely contingent and outside the scope of its consideration, become essential to the perspective of moral science.

More specifically, those features of human knowing that metaphysics or logic leave aside as accidental properties, become crucial when ethics addresses how human beings make use of their cognitive powers to moral ends. In this manner the ethicist seeks to determine how individuals appropriate their own cognitive teleology, taking into account the context of their choices, affective inclinations, character, historical and social context, and the like. Accordingly

---

[14] See especially *ST* I-II, qu. 17, art. 6, sed contra: "Actus rationis exercentur per liberum arbitrium" (6:122); cf. De virtutibus, qu. unicius, art. 7: ". . . verum possit esse volitum, prout homo vult intelligere verum" (E. Odetto, ed. *in Questiones disputatae* [Turin: Marietti, 1965], 724).

[15] *ST* I-II, qu. 16, art. 1, ad 3: ". . . etiam ipsa ratio speculativa applicatur ad opus intelligendi vel iudicandi, a voluntate" (6:114).

[16] See *ST* I-II, qu. 17, art. 6, c. (6:122). For a treatment of Aquinas's views on the possibility and nature of moral responsibility within the activity of speculative thought, see Gregory Martin Reichberg, "Aquinas on Moral Responsibility in the Pursuit of Knowledge," in David Gallagher, ed., *Thomas Aquinas and His Legacy* (Washington, D.C.: The Catholic University of America Press, 1994), 61-82.

[17] See for instance, *Sententia Libri Ethicorum 3*, 1 (47.1:119/143-45): ". . . quia vero actus sunt singularia, magis est iudicanda condicio actus secundum considerationes singularium quam secundum considerationem universalem."

[18] *ST* I-II, qu. 6, prologue: "Quia operationes et actus circa singularia sunt, ideo omnis operativa scientia in particulari consideratione perficitur."

the virtue of prudence can, and should, give direction to even speculative cognitive acts,[19] insofar as the intellect is actualized according to determinate circumstances, as are the other powers of the soul.[20]

For instance, it is from within the perspective of the ethical employment of human cognition that Aquinas takes up a discussion of the intellectual virtues.[21] These habitus are rooted in the concrete historicity of the individual; they express the manner in which a person's past activity influences his or her cognitive action in the present.[22] Similarly, he discusses how a catastrophe of historical and social dimensions—the sin of our first parents—has affected our intellectual operations and must be taken into account in order to understand why truth is so difficult to attain in our present circumstances.[23]

Further examples of Aquinas's attention to the temporal and social dimension of human knowing could be multiplied, and would surely merit more extensive treatment. Yet in view of our present purpose we must advert to an even more fundamental issue, which is presupposed in any such investigation. If intellectual cognition in humans is indeed an immaterial operation, as Aquinas clearly maintains, how can this operation possibly be in any way affected by temporal context, if, as he also maintains, time is the measure of corporeal beings subject to motion? Are immateriality and temporality mutually exclusive properties of mind?

---

[19] The role of prudence in directing the concrete exercise of the speculative acts is explicitly affirmed in *ST* II-II, qu. 47, art. 2, ad 2: ". . . ipse actus speculativae rationis, secundum quod est voluntarius, cadit sub electione et consilio quantum ad suum exercitium, et per consequens cadit sub ordinatione prudentiae" (8:349). Aquinas is quick to add, however, that the influence of prudence does not extend into the very relation between the speculative act and its object, for here the speculative intellect is alone sufficient to determine itself to the object: "Sed quantum ad suam speciem, prout comparatur ad obiectum, quod est verum necessarium, [actus speculativae rationis] non cadit sub consilio nec sub prudentia" (*ibid.*).

[20] This is an extension of the general principle that active or passive powers cannot act or be acted upon at any time whatsoever, but only in a determinate way and in some definite time. On this point see *In duodecem libros Metaphysicorum Aristotelis expositio 9,* lect. 4, no. 1816 (R.M. Spiazzi, ed. [Turin: Marietti, 1950], pp. 434-35)

[21] The primary loci of such discussion are *ST* I-II, qq. 56-58, and *Sententia Libri Ethicorum 6.*

[22] The relation between habitus and the concrete historicity of the individual person has been well noted by Maréchal: "l' 'habitus' est, pour ainsi dire, une second nature, interposée entre l'acte premier et les actes secondes: c'est la pesée sourde du passé sur l'activité du présente. L' 'habitus' s'ajoute à la forme naturelle de chaque puissance, pour influencer à l'avance tout exercice de celle-ci" (*Le point de départ,* cahier V, 405).

[23] As a representative statement of this position, see *ST* I-II, qu. 85, art. 3. For a systematic, contemporary treatment of this theme, see Jacques Maritain, "Réflexions sur la nature blessée," *Oeuvres complètes,* vol. 13 (Fribourg, Switzerland; Paris: Éditions St. Paul, 1993), 768-822.

THE TEMPORALITY OF THINKING

Clearly many *objects* of human cognition include direct reference to temporal context. This holds especially for the objects of practical cognition, human actions, which are always situated within a temporal and historical continuum. So moral science and prudence can discharge their respective functions only by conscientiously weighing the temporal context of the acts they must guide. Notwithstanding the temporal and historical character of many cognitional objects, particularly those pertaining to the sphere of action, to assert that *all* intellectual objects are temporally referenced would surely miss the mark. Aquinas is quick to point out that neither mathematics nor metaphysics include matter or motion within their formal objects. And the exclusion of matter and motion, whether by abstraction or separation, necessarily entails the exclusion of temporal considerations, since time is the measure of change.[24]

Aquinas does soften this exclusion by noting that although mathematics and metaphysics prescind from treating motion and time *per se*, nevertheless their respective principles may be applied *per accidens* to things that change and are in time. This is the work of the natural and intermediate sciences.[25] Moreover, he does acknowledge that all intellectual *judgments*, including the purely theoretical judgments of mathematics and metaphysics, involve an indirect reference to temporal determinations, owing to the "return to phantasms" necessary for all completed cognitions. In reply to an objection stating that "the intellect abstracts from time, as also from other individual conditions," Aquinas writes that "for as much as the intellect turns to the phantasms (*ad phantasmata convertit*), composition and division of the intellect involve time."[26] In another, earlier text, he establishes this same point in greater detail, noting that time enters into the intellectual operation of the human being for two reasons: (i) this knowledge *originates* from phantasms, which always have a determinate temporal reference, and (ii) this knowledge comes to completion in the judicative act, composition and division, whereby our intellect uses phantasms *to apply* previously abstracted intelligibles to the sensible things of our experience.[27]

Despite there qualifications, he still contends that this temporal horizon does not characterize metaphysical or mathematical objects directly and of themselves.

---

[24] This is discussed in *Super Boetium De Trinitate*, qu. 5, aa. 3-4.

[25] *Ibid.*, art. 3, ad 5.

[24] *ST* I, qu. 85, art. 5, ad 2 (5:341).

[27] *Summa contra gentiles* 2, chap. 96, Item: ". . . operationi autem intellectuali nostrae adiacet tempus, quod a phantasmatibus cognitionem accipimus, quae determinatum respiciunt tempus. . . . Componit autem aut dividit applicando intelligibilia prius abstracta ad res: et in hac applicatione necesse est cointelligi tempus" (13:572).

The principle of non-contradiction or the Pythagorean theorem are as true for us today as they were for Aristotle or Euclid; in this sense they are timeless truths. The reason: the human intellect grasps the essential properties of things by abstracting intelligibles from sensible conditions, "so that in this operation it comprehends the intelligible apart from time and the condition proper to sensible things."[28] In this manner Aquinas carefully delineates the extent to which temporal duration can shape our thinking: The apprehension of indivisibles – the mind's first operation – enjoys greater freedom from time than composition and division – the mind's second operation. So the human intellect's relationship to time is complex: "in composition and division our intellect always links up with time, past or future, but not in understanding what a thing is."[29]

In any event, regardless of the a-temporality of such theoretical objects, Aquinas does not hesitate to affirm the temporality of human cognitive acts, even those of the metaphysician and mathematician. Again he discerns an ontological duality between the cognitive act and its corresponding object, a duality that nevertheless co-exists with the intellect's natural or acquired proportion to its object, requisite for all truthful cognition.

Let us begin with a possible objection to the thesis that *all* cognitive acts are bounded by time. If the act of knowing is indeed an instance of immanent activity, then it is difficult to conceive how it may be measured by a temporal duration; for any operation *per se* involves time if it stands in need of something future to attain its proper completion. Yet intellection (*intelligere*) is not a motion, a way to completion; rather it is an *actus perfectus,* possessing its complete form at the very instant of its enactment.[30] In this sense it is true to say with Thomas that intellection is above time, *intellectus est supra tempus.*[31]

Still, while transcending time in its formality as intellection, human thinking is nonetheless measured by temporal duration, in three ways: (i) *per accidens*, by reason of its union with the body; (ii) *per se*, insofar as it is an operation which includes reasoning or inquiry; and (iii) *by participation,* because it is intellection only imperfectly and not by its very essence.

---

[28] *Ibid.*

[29] *Ibid.*; cf. *Quodl.* 4, qu. 9, art. 2, c.: ". . . [tempus] per se commiscetur operationi intellectus humani componentis et dividentis . . ." (Marietti, p.82).

[30] *De veritate*, qu. 8, art. 14, ad 12: ". . . illa operatio per se cadit sub tempore quae exspectat aliquid in futurum ad hoc quod eius species compleatur, sicut patet de motu qui non habet speciem completam quousque ad terminum perducatur: non est enim idem specie motus ad medium et ad terminum; operationes vero quae staim habent suam speciem completam, non mesurantur tempore nisi per accidens, sicut intelligere, sentire et huiusmodi . . ." (22.2:266/302-311).

[31] *ST* I, qu. 85, art. 4, ad 1 (5:339); I-II, qu. 113, art. 7, ad 5 (7:339): "Mens autem humana quae iustificatur, secundum se quidem est supra tempus, sed per accidens subditur tempori."

In the first way (i), Aquinas notes that *per accidens* cognitive acts are immersed in time insofar as they are operationally joined to corporeal sensory organs subject to motion. Dependency on the sense powers, external and internal, affects human thinking with an inevitable temporal dispersion. The phantasms produced by our internal senses play an especially important role in this regard: as images of individual sensible things immersed in time, they too are intrinsically measured by time. Consequently, since there is no actual thinking without them, there can be no thinking without succession and time: *nihil potest homo intelligere sine continuo et tempore.*[32]

In the second way (ii), Aquinas writes that "since the intellect passes from potentiality to act, it has a likeness to things which are generated, which do not attain to perfection all at once but acquire it progressively,"[33] because "everything which is moved [from potency to actuality] acquires something by its movement, and attains to what it had not had previously."[34] This is the act of reasoning, whereby we think with succession: from one thing understood something else is subsequently inferred; the mind is thus led from knowledge in potency to knowledge in act. Hence, insofar as human knowledge is inherently progressive, it is a *discursus*; as a *discursus* it is a motion, and as a motion it is in time. Accordingly, to the extent that human knowing is a *ratio*, it is measured *per se* by time.[35]

At this juncture one might justifiably reply that not all acts of human knowing are ratiocinations, while conceding that most are. Acts of intuitive awareness (*intellectus*) do occur and in such moments our thoughts seem measured by a

---

[32] Aristotle, *De memoria et reminiscentia*, 450a7-10, cited approvingly by Aquinas in *Sentencia Libri De sensu et sensato* 1, 2, with the following explanation added: "Quod quidem accidit in quantum nichil potest homo intelligere sine fantasmate: fantasma enim oportet quod sit cum continuo et tempore, eo quod est similitudo rei singularis que est hic et nunc" (45.2:108/51-57).

[33] *ST* I, qu. 85, art. 5, c. (5:341); cf. qu. 58, art. 3, ad 1: ". . . discursus quendam motum nominat. Omnis autem motus est de uno priori in aliud posterius" (5:83).

[34] *ST* I, qu. 9, art. 1, c. (4:90).

[35] Aquinas never states outright that the operation of reasoning is measured *per se* by time. In a famous passage from the commentary on *De anima* 1,10 he appears to state the contrary, arguing that the operations of the intellect are called motions in a metaphorical sense only, *operationes autem intellectus non dicuntur motus nisi metaphorice* (45.1: 51/ 12-13). Yet here he clearly has in mind *intellectus*, the act from which the intellect takes its name, which, being an *actus perfecti*, transcends motion and time. In another context (ST I, qu. 64, art. 2, c.), where he takes care to distinguish intellectus from ratio, the mutability of the latter is contrasted to the immobility of the former: "Angelus apprehendit immobiliter per intellectum, sicut et nos immobiliter apprehendimus prima principia, quorum est intellectus: homo vero per rationem apprehendit mobiliter, discurrendo de uno ad aliquid, habens viam procedendi ad utramque oppositorum" (5:141).

duration other than time. Jacques Maritain refers to the super-temporality of thought in his *Approaches to God*:[36]

> The operations of the human intellect are in time, and indeed, subject to time, but in an extrinsic manner and only by reason of the materiality of the senses and the imagination to whose exercise they are bound. In themselves they are not subject to the flux of impermanence. They emerge above time. They exist in a duration which is a deficient imitation of eternity, a succession of fragments of eternity, for it is the perseverance in being of spiritual acts of intellection or of contemplative gaze. Thus this duration is composed of instances superior to time, each of which may correspond to a lapse of time more or less long, but is in itself without flow or movement or succession a flash of permanent or non successive existence. Such is the duration proper to thought.

Should we conclude that Aquinas's comments regarding the temporality of human thinking thus apply to *some* acts of thinking but not unqualifiedly to them all? In other words, do acts of *intellectus* escape the temporal condition? Does the Thomistic teaching on intuitive insight decisively set itself apart from the postmodern emphasis on temporality in human thinking?

This question may be answered both affirmatively and negatively. Yes, some intellectual acts are non-discursive. No, even these intuitive acts are never wholly independent of time; they too involve succession, albeit of a very special kind. True enough, the act of intuitive awareness is not a *kinesis*, but an *energia,* wholly complete at the very instant of its enactment, thus standing outside the order of motion and time. Nevertheless, in created or participated knowers such acts are necessarily multiple. No one act of human or angelic cognition can grasp the whole of what is, otherwise we would be God, who utters Himself and the universe in one Word only.

Our intuitive insights, when we have them, are fragmentary; so too are the intellections of the angels, who can know the cosmos only through a multitude of ideas (*species intelligibilis*). No two intelligible *species* may be considered simultaneously, or to put it more simply, it is impossible for the human or angelic intellect to actually think of two things, formally distinct, at once.[37] Thus, when engaging in acts of intuitive insight we (angels and humans) pass from one actual consideration to another, from one focus to another, and here there is a real succession. It is not that we think of one thing *from* another, as in reasoning, but merely that we think of one thing *after* another (discontinuous succession of intuitive insights). Consequently, while there is no before and after in the act

---

[36] Jacques Maritain, *Approaches to God*, trans. Peter O'Reilly (New York: Harper & Brothers, 1954), 77.

[37] For example, see *De veritate*, qu. 8, art. 14; *Contra gentiles* 2, chap. 101; *ST* I, qu. 58, art. 2.

by which an angel (or human having an intuitive insight) understands a single intelligible form, there is nothing to prevent a number of such operations from being ordered according to before and after.[38] Due to the creaturely condition of intellectus, by its very nature a *participated* intellectus, acts of intuitive insight are never perfectly continuous; thought must pass from one thing to another, never resting immobile in the self-same intelligible word. The succession of intuitive insights thus affords us a third way (iii) in which thinking is measured by time, for here there is a real distinction of prior and posterior instants.

Yet Aquinas adds an important caveat to this claim. This succession of immobile operations is of a quite different order from the succession of corporeal substances: it is a passage from one complete act to another complete act, rather than a passage from potency to act (as occurs in reasoning); and it is non-continuous. Thus Aquinas concludes that the measure of this discontinuous succession is "not the same as the time which measures the movements of the heavens, and whereby all corporeal things are measured, which have their changeableness from the movement of the heavens."[39] By this caveat he thus shows how our inner psychic life possesses its own distinctive temporal measure, rejoining Husserl, Heidegger and others, who argue that the temporality of thinking is irreducible to the worldly time measuring bodies in motion. And lest

---

[38] See *De veritate*, qu. 8, art. 15, c., where Aquinas distinguishes between knowing one thing *in* another, and knowing one thing, *from* another: "Differt autem cognoscere aliquid in aliquo et aliquid ex aliquid" (22.2:268/89-90). The first type of mediation in knowing is compatible with the intuitive insight of the angels, while the second is excluded. In the previous article (14, ad 12), however, Aquinas notes how angelic cognition is not altogether exempt from succession: "Unde patet quod ipsum intelligere angeli neque per se neque per accidens cadit sub tempore; unde in una eius operatione qua intelligit una intelligibile, non est prius et posterius; sed hoc non prohibet quin plures operationes possint esse ordinatae secundum prius et posterius" (22.2:266/319-23). Cf. *Contra gentiles* 2, chap. 101: "Est igitur in intellectu substantiae separatae quaedam intelligentiarum successio. Non tamen motus, proprie loquendo: cum non succedat actus potentiae, sed actus actui" (13:600). Aquinas adds, however, that this succession of discontinuous instants does not characterize all acts of angelic thinking, but only those acts by which the angel knows things other than itself through its infused species. By contrast, the angel's self-knowledge includes no succession whatsoever; it is thus measured by aevum, and not by time (continuous or discreet). On this last point see *De potentia*, qu. 4, art. 2, ad 19.

[39] ST I, qu. 53, art. 3, c. (5:35). In the reply to the first objection (ad 1), Aquinas further clarifies the nature of this angelic succession, speculating that if this succesion is indeed non-continuous (as he does in fact maintain), then "non habebit proportionem ad tempus quod mesurat motum corporalium, quod est continuum: cum non sit eiusdem rationis" (Ibid). Cf. qu. 85, art. 4, ad 1: "intellectus est supra tempus quod est numerus motus corporalium rerum" (5:339); also I-II, qu. 113, art. 7, ad 5: "Sed in his quae sunt supra tempus, aliter se habet. Si qua enim successio sit ibi affectuum vel intellectualium conceptionum, puta in angelis, talis sucessio non mesuratur tempore continuo, sed tempore discreto . . . (7:339).

one suppose that this pertains only to rare moments of intuitive insight, and not to the daily fabric of human life, Aquinas reminds us that all completed intellectual cognitions, including those reached by reasoning, include some share of intuition: "for the discourse of reason always begins from simple understanding (*ab intellectu*) and concludes with simple understanding (*ad intellectum*): for we reason by proceeding from principles simply understood, and the discourse of reason is perfected when we grasp with simple insight what hitherto was unknown."[40]

DESIRE FOR TRUTH AND THE POWER EFFECTS OF KNOWLEDGE

Thus no created intelligence can attain to the timeless immobility of divine intellection: since no created intelligence is perfectly exempt from succession, and all succession is measured by time (continuous or discrete), we may conclude that no such intelligence is entirely exempt from temporal duration. At this juncture Aquinas raises a question: If created intelligences cannot think about all that they can know with perfect simultaneity, what enables them to *shift their attention* from one object of thought to another? The intellectual faculty is itself unable to effect this shift, because while it actually thinks about one intelligible, it remains in potency to all other intelligibles. Insofar, however, as it is in potency, it cannot function as the efficient cause of its own passage to actuality: Things are drawn from potency to act by an agent already in act, and the same thing cannot be both mover and moved at the same time and in the same respect. Yet we do move ourselves from one act of thinking to another; without a doubt this is one of the most conspicuous features of our cognitive life. Hence we cannot elude the question: What agency is the cause of this vicissitude in our mental operations?

Aquinas's reply to this query should be of little surprise, for it dovetails with the reflective awareness of our cognitive activity that is part and parcel of our daily lives: cognitive agents are impelled by *desire* to seek out objects for reflection. This voluntary employment of the mind is most manifest in those instances when we advert to knowledge already in our habitual possession,

---

[40] *ST* II-II, qu. 8, art. 1, ad 2 (8:66-67). For a discussion of intuitivity in reasoning, see Jacques Maritain, "Pas de savoir sans intuitivité," *Oeuvres complètes*, vol. 13, op. cit., especially 937-47. For further elucidations on Aquinas's understanding of temporality in human and angelic knowing, the reader may profitably consult J. Peghaire, *Intellectus et Ratio selon S. Thomas d'Aquin* (Paris: Vrin; Ottawa: Inst. d'Études Médiévales, 1936); and Carl J. Peter, *The Doctrine of Thomas Aquinas Regarding Eviternity in the Rational Soul and Separated Substances* (Rome: The Pontifical Gregorian University, 1964).

bringing into conscious awareness an insight preserved in the intellectual memory:

> The angelic intellect is not identically related to all the [cognitional] forms it has within itself, because sometimes it is in perfect act in regard to one form but not with regard to others. The will reduces the intellect from potency to act. Consequently, Augustine says that an angel understands when it wills (*cum voluerit intelligit*).[41]

This claim arises within Aquinas' discussion of succession in angelic thinking, but its application is not restricted to the sphere of the separate intelligences; similar remarks about the role of the will in cognition appear in the context of his discussions about human thinking. Particularly telling is *Summa theologiae* I-II, qu. 9, art. 1, where he points to a twofold potency of the human mind, a twofold indetermination that must be overcome if concrete acts of intellection are to occur: first, with respect to its actuation by the intelligible object, originally open to all intelligible objects, the intellect must be *specified* by one of them in order to be knowing in act; second, with respect to the very *exercise* of the intellectual act, originally open to the option of either thinking or not thinking about any particular object, the epistemic agent must effect a choice in order to be actually knowing. The first potency pertains to the register of formal causality (order of specification) and is overcome by the reception of an intelligible form; the second potency pertains to the register of efficient and final causality (order of exercise) and is overcome by an impulsion that springs from the will of the epistemic agent, directing the intellectual faculty to actually consider a determinate intelligible form, for the sake of a desired good.

Crucial, then, to Aquinas' account of created thinking is the role ascribed to the will, the primary source of efficient causality within the rational agent. Using a formula attributed to St. Anselm, he calls the will "the motor of the soul's powers" (*motor omnium virium*), explicitly indicating that the intellect too is comprised under its governance.[42] In modern parlance we would say that persons know determinate objects only under condition that they *attend* to them. Attending is voluntary (especially in the realm of intellectual cognitions, while sensory cognitions, in contrast, frequently escape our voluntary control) in at least this minimal sense: objects of intellectual cognition never compel our consideration to such a degree that we are unable to avert our gaze from them. Thinking can never be inwardly or outwardly coerced: "no matter what an object

---

[41] *De veritate*, qu. 8, art. 14, ad 17 (22.2:266/345-49); cf. *Contra gentiles* 2, chap. 101.

[42] For a representative passage, see *De veritate*, qu. 10, art. 2, ad 4: ". . . et de hoc modo [habitualiter] cognitionis [intellectus possibilis] reducitur in actum perfectum per voluntatem quae, secundum Anselmum, est motum omnium virium" (22.2:302/203-206).

might be, Aquinas observes, it is in a man's power not to think of it."[43] Moreover, many of our cognitions are voluntary in a stronger, more positive sense, by virtue of their inception in desire: for we frequently engage in inquiry as a consciously willed project, setting out by choice to reflect along determinate lines, in view of a desired end. "There is as much movement, as much controlled, directed, purposive, goal-directed movement, as much desire, force, vigor, energy, drive, urge, and urgency in intellectual action as in physical action."[44]

Verum est bonum intellectus.[45] By this formula Aquinas succinctly summarizes his understanding of the relation between thinking and voluntary desire. *Verum* refers to the mind's conformity with reality in the act of judgment. *Bonum* refers to the perfection that accrues to the mind by virtue of that conformity. Since each existing thing desires its own completion, the human intellect too, as an inherent form, is inclined to truth as to its connatural good. This inclination the intellect knows when it spontaneously reflects on its own act, apprehending its apprehension of being as perfective for itself, thus awakening the soul's power of conscious appetition – the will. Desired when lacking and enjoyed when possessed, speculative truth thus enters the field of the will's dynamic attraction to the good.[46]

To say that truth is a good is not equivalent to affirming the *moral* goodness of all truth seeking. Aquinas is quick to point out that the knowledge of truth, although good in itself, may *per accidens* become morally bad, by reason of some disorder arising in its pursuit.[47] Perfective of the human mind, truth invariably has the *ratio boni*; nonetheless, desire for the truth and satisfaction in its attainment may stray from the bounds of legitimate moral rectitude[48] This

---

[43] *ST* I-II, qu. 10, art. 2, c. (6:86).

[44] Michael Stocker, "Intellectual Desire, Emotion, and Action," *Explaining Emotions,* A.O. Rorty, ed. (Berkeley: University of California Press, 1980), 328.

[45] Aquinas makes abundant use of this formula, e.g. in *De veritate*, qu. 1, art. 8, c. (22.1:28/ 140-41); *ST* I, qu. 94, art. 4, c. (5:418); I-II, qu. 57, art. 2, ad 3 (6:336); II-II, qu. 1, art 3, ad 1 (8:12).

[46] In *ST* I, qu. 82, art. 4, ad 1, Aquinas explains how the intellect's operation is encompassed within the will's motion to the good: "Si vero consideretur voluntas secundum communem rationem sui obiecti, quod est bonum, intellectus autem secundum quod est quaedam res et potentia specialis; sic sub communi ratione boni continetur, velut quoddam speciale, et intellectus ipse, et ipsum intelligere, et obiectum eius, quod est verum, quorum quodlibet est quoddam speciale bonum. Et secundum hoc voluntas est altior intellectu, et potest ipsum movere" (5:303).

[47] *ST* II-II, qu. 167, art. 1, c.: "Sed ipsa enim veritatis cognitio, per se loquendo, bona est. Potest autem per accidens esse mala, ratione scilicet aliquius consequentis: vel inquantum scilicet aliquis de cognitione veritatis superbit . . . vel inquantum homo utitur cognitione veritatis ad peccandum" (10:345).

[48] *Ibid.*: ". . . appetititus vel studium cognoscendae veritatis potest habere rectitudinem vel perversitatem."

is an application of the principle that deliberately willed acts are never morally indifferent when exercised *in concreto.*

Considered as a free operation of an individual agent, occurring at a definite time, aiming at a end, and using determinate means, engagement in theoretical inquiry never is morally neutral. Like all other human acts, the actual exercise of theoretical knowledge receives its moral quality by virtue of its specific object, end, and circumstances. In this vein, Aquinas comments that making "use of an acquired science is due to a motion of the will," and concludes that "a virtue which perfects the will, as charity or justice, confers the right use of these speculative habitus [the theoretical intellectual virtues]."[49] Inversely, vices such as pride and injustice can vitiate the appetite for knowledge, breeding a *"curiositas* about intellective sciences," destructive of human fulfillment.[50] Aquinas explicitly discusses the moral use of knowledge under the heading of "studiositas," which designates a moral virtue whose office consists in rectifying the will to knowledge.[51] "The virtue of attentiveness" would, I think, be a suitable translation for this Latin term, in the new moral sense given it by Aquinas.

Aquinas' analysis of the will's role in theoretical thinking can afford the Thomist a vantage from which to integrate postmodern reflections on the relation between knowledge and power. To speak of "integration" may surprise those who, in the wake of Habermas, view postmodernity (especially in Foucault's formulation) as a recrudescence of medieval nominalist voluntarism (in Nietzschean garb), standing in perfect antithesis to the primacy of theoria over praxis championed by the classical tradition.[52]

Yet a case may be made that this reading of Foucault suffers from the misguided assumption that the French post-structuralist does in fact intend to (i) equate "relationships of power" with domination or repression and (ii) collapse knowledge into power, whereby claims to truth are purely and simply reducible to the power effects they have.[53] Addressing the first assumption, a recent commentator explains that by "power" Foucault understands "particular

[49] *ST* I-II, qu. 57, art. 1, c. (6:364).

[50] *ST* II-II, qu. 167, art. 1, sed contra: "Ergo circa intellectivas scientias potest esse curiositas vitiosa" (6:345).

[51] *ST* II-II, qu. 166: "De studiositate."

[52] Louis Dupré, for instance, in "Postmodernity or Late Modernity? Ambiguities in Richard Rorty's Thought" (*The Review of Metaphysics* 47 [1993]: 277-295) traces Foucault's genealogies of power structures to Ockham's nominalist theology; see, in particular, 284-85.

[53] For instance, in *The Philosophical Discourse of Modernity,* Jürgen Habermas writes that "Foucault abruptly reverses power's truth-dependency into the power dependency of truth" (274) adding that for Foucault "validity claims are functionistically reduced to the effects of power" (F. Lawrence, trans. [Cambridge, Massachusetts: The Massachusetts Institute of Technology Press, 1987], 276).

exercises of control over one's actions and those of others; not just dominations or repressions, negative control, but the positive control of reasonings and creatings as well," adding that "Foucault is bent on cooly describing how the modern subject constitutes itself a governor of its own and others actions."[54] As to the second assumption, the same commentator underscores Foucault's own distinction between power relations on the one hand and relationships of communication on the other, citing his explicit denial that the latter are simply "reducible" to the former.[55] Even more pointedly, Foucault cautions his readers that "those who say that for me *savoir* is a mask for *pouvoir* do not seem to me to have the capacity to understand."[56]

While Foucault recognizes a distinction between truth and its power effects, he plainly takes the latter as his primary concern, suggesting that his own project consists largely (although not exclusively) in disclosing the structures operative in the "political, economic, institutional regime of the production of truth."[57] Thus each society has its regime of truth, its 'general politics' of truth: that is, the types of discourse which it accepts and makes function as true; the mechanisms and instances and which enable one to distinguish true and false statements, the means by which each is sanctioned; the techniques and procedures accorded value in the acquisition of truth; the status of those who are charged with saying what counts as true.[58]

Situating this project within the Thomistic architecture of human knowing presents a number of serious difficulties, two of which merit special mention.

First, Aquinas' various discussions of the appetite for knowledge elucidate how *individual subjects* make moral use of their cognitive faculties; this remains true even when he examines whether or not the ordering of theoretical disciplines falls within the legitimate province of political authority, for the holder of such authority is always an individual person (or persons), who may or may not

---

[54] Thomas R. Flynn, "Foucault and the Politics of Postmodernity," *Nous* 23 (1989): 188.

[55] "No doubt communicating is always a certain way of acting upon another person or persons. But the production and circulation of elements of meaning can have as their objective or as their consequence certain results in the realm of power; the latter [relationships of communication] are not simply the result of the former [relations of power]." "Afterword" to Dreyfus and Rabinow, Michel Foucault, *Beyond Structuralism and Hermeneutics*, 2nd edition, rev. (Chicago: University of Chicago Press, 1983), 239; cited by Flynn, 191.

[56] Interview with François Eweld, "Le souci de la vérité," *Magazine Littéraire* 207 (May, 1984), 22; cited by Flynn, 191.

[57] Michel Foucault, "Truth and Power" (from an interview conducted by A. Fontana and P. Pasquino), in Paul Rabinow, ed., *The Foucault Reader* (New York: Pantheon Books, 1984), 74.

[58] *Ibid.*, 73.

exhibit good qualities of personal political judgment (*prudentia politica*).[59] Foucault, by contrast, is less interested in studying individual exercises of power than in describing how determinate relations of power are embedded within each discursive formation. Individual epistemic agents do not establish these relations; rather it is the relations themselves that constitute these agents in their very subjectivation. From this standpoint it becomes altogether plausible to speak of "strategies without a strategist" and "exercises of control without a controller."[60] Political power is thus no longer conceived solely (or even primarily) as the personal attribute of an individual agent acting through intellect and will.

A second difficulty arises from Foucault's contention that *desire* (comprising power relations and power effects) is constitutive of discursive practice, intrinsic to its very nature.[61] This appears to fly in the teeth of Aquinas' repeated assertions that the will's action, although necessary for the occurrence of concrete acts of intellection, nevertheless remains extrinsic to the very relation of the mind to its speculative object: "the consideration of truth is not science insofar as it is an object of volition, but according as it tends directly to its object."[62] Ordained by the will in the line of their actual *exercise*, theoretical cognitions are nevertheless elicited directly by the intellect in the line of their objective *specification*.

Despite the seeming incompatibility, and even because of it, Foucauldian explorations into the politics of truth merit close examination by the Thomist, for at least two reasons. First of all, such an engagement can heighten our awareness of what Maritain called *l'esprit dans sa condition charnelle*. As social

---

[59] In his *Commentary on Aristotle's Ethics* (*Sententia libri Ethicorum* 1,1), Aquinas asks whether the political ruler, as possessor of the "architectonic science," may regulate not just practical but even speculative science. His reply is instructive: "Sed scientiae speculativae praecipit civilis solum quantum ad usum, non autem quantum ad determinationem operis; ordinat enim politica quod aliqui doceant vel addiscant geometriam, huiusmodi enim actus in quantum sunt voluntarii pertinent ad materiam moralem et sunt ordinabiles ad finem humanae vitae; non autem praecipit politicus geometrae quid de triangulo concludat, hoc enim non subiacet humanae voluntati nec est ordinabile humanae vitae, sed dependet ex ipsa rerum ratione. Et ideo dicit quod politica praeordinat quas disciplinarum debitum est esse in civitatibus, scilicet tam praticarum quam speculativarum, et quis quam debeat addiscere et usque ad quod tempus" (47.1:9/134-48).

[60] Thomas R. Flynn, "Foucault and the Politics of Postmodernity," 192.

[61] ". . . neither the relation of discourse to desire, nor the processes of its appropriation, nor its role among non-discursive practices is extrinsic to its unity, its characterization and the laws of its formation" (*The Archaeology of Knowledge*, 68).

[62] ". . . veri consideratio non est scientia in quantum est volita, sed secundum quod directe tendit in obiectum." De virtutibus in communi, qu. un., a. 7 (Marietti, 724).

beings we are also social knowers; attention to this dimension of human knowing can supplement Aquinas' very formal treatment of knowledge, furnishing a better understanding of the human intellect in the various modalities of its concrete employment. Secondly, the sharp line drawn by Aquinas between the exercise and the specification of knowledge, and the exclusion of voluntary appetition from the latter, holds true only for those cognitions which terminate in the grasp of an intelligible necessity, viz., judgments of the type *scientia*. In all other judgments, whether of prudence, belief, opinion, and even error, the will must intervene to fix the mind's assent.[63] When one considers that most judgments of everyday life are of this second kind, even many that we are accustomed to call *scientific*,[64] then the exigency of grasping *"the possible positions of desire in relation to discourse"*[65] is incumbent on any Thomist seeking to articulate a theory of knowledge adequate to real cognitive practice.

[63] For a representative statement of this position, see *ST* II-II, qu. 1, art. 4; cf. *De veritate*, qu. 14, art. 1.

[64] Yves R. Simon aptly describes this aspect of scientific knowing: "What goes on . . . under the name of science is to a very large extent made up of factual information, educated opinion, and probability; yet this aggregate owes its existence to a nucleus of hard objective necessity, to which it is connected by the scientific habitus" (*Work, Society, and Culture* [New York: Fordham University Press, 1971], 166). In *A General Theory of Authority* (Notre Dame, Indiana: University of Notre Dame Press, 1962), he likewise mentions how the will may intervene in such judgments: "Objectivity is held in check by obscurity. An assent which is firm without being necessary cannot be anything else than voluntary (92).

[65] Michel Foucault, *The Archaeology of Knowledge*, 68.

The Forgetfulness of Beings

Robert Royal

I am not a professional philosopher, but a writer on public policy for much of the time and on comparative literature for the rest. I cannot settle with authority questions about whether Heidegger's Ontological Difference was already present in Aquinas or other philosophical technicalities that shape postmodernism. In fact, a few years ago when I left the Georgetown Library after a day reading *Being and Time*, I couldn't remember where I'd parked the car. In overcoming the forgetfulness of Being, I'd become even more than usually forgetful of beings (something both my wife and assistant previously thought impossible).

But perhaps Heidegger's effect on my memory is not so merely a biographical accident. Except for some exceptionally hardy intellects, reading Heidegger has meant for many people in many fields precisely not being able to remember where the car is parked. As someone who splits his time between postmodern theory and postmodern Washington—the differences are not as great as might first appear—perhaps I might best contribute to an analysis of Thomism and postmodernism by looking at some of the already clear consequences, and likely future effects of the forgetfulness of beings in postmodernism.

Let us begin, like Plato, with a homely example:

> An Englishman, a Frenchman, and a German each undertook a study of the camel. The Englishman, taking his tea basket and a good deal of camping equipment, went to set up camp in the Orient, returning after a sojourn of two or three years with a fat volume, full of raw, disorganized, and inconclusive facts which, nevertheless, had real documentary value. The Frenchman went to the Jardin des Plantes, spent half an hour there, questioned the guard, threw bread to the camel, poked it with the point of his umbrella, and, returning home, wrote an article for his paper full of sharp and witty observations. As for the German, filled with disdain for the Frenchman's frivolity and the Englishman's lack of general ideas, he locked himself into his room, and there he drafted a multiple-volume work entitled: *The Idea of the Camel Derived from the Concept of the Ego*.[1]

The story used to end here, but I'd like to add a coda:

> An American postmodernist became acquainted with the camel problematic in a graduate seminar on "Speciesism in the Bible." She did not feel comfortable with the Englishman's acquiescence in established social hierarchies, the Frenchman's obviously phallic probing with his umbrella, and the German's attachment to metaphysics, and started a series of self-help workshops (soon to be the subject of a PBS special hosted by Bill Moyers) entitled "Beyond the Eye of the Needle, or Getting Through the Eurocentric Reduction of Non-Western Signs and Species to Patriarchal, Phallocentric, and Onto-theo-logic Hegemonies."

That we can now easily identify and even parody the rhetoric and aims of much postmodern discourse suggests to me that we are really at a point that I would call post-postmodern. The owl of Minerva, as we know, flies only at dusk. And in the better perspective we have gained from no little acquaintance with postmodern theory, I would like to explore a set of postmodern problems that I hope Thomism and postmodern Thomists may help answer for those of us who are not professional philosophers.

I

There is a great deal that is both good and powerful in postmodernism and poststructuralism. It is important, in my view to keep these two terms distinct, even though they are related. Poststructuralism, as I would use the term, refers to a family of theories about language, truth, identity, and organizing "master narratives" of various kinds. For the most part, these theories basically take their origins from a group of French Heideggerians. Luc Ferry and Alain Renaut have formulated this neatly: Foucault = Heidegger + Nietzsche; Lacan = Heidegger + Freud; the French political theorist Pierre Bourdieu = Heidegger + Marx; and Derrida = Heidegger + the style of Derrida. Whatever the justice of this formula, it shows how the old modern binary cleavages such as rational and irrational in Nietzsche, unconscious and ego in Freud, bourgeoisie and proletariat in Marx—which were all once thought to explain one known identity by reference to a slightly more obscure identity—have all been undermined and rendered problematic by French Heideggerians.

Postmodernism as I use the term is broader than these specific changes both in its conceptualization and, I believe, in staying power. Outside of formal

---

[1] Quoted as the frontispiece to Luc Ferry and Alain Renaut, *French Philosophy of the Sixties: An Essay on Antihumanism*, trans. Mary H.S. Cattani (Amherst, Massachusetts: University of Massachusetts Press, 1990). The story originally appeared in *Le Pèlerin*, 1 September 1929, 13. I have rearranged the story slightly to make its connections with the text more orderly.

philosophy, postmodernism reflects a curious large-scale perception already present in the nineteenth century. There is no better formulation than Matthew Arnold's in "Stanzas from the Grande Chartreuse," where he speaks of our age as "Wandering between two worlds, one dead/ The other powerless to be born." The dead world was the old modern world including, we can now see, its Christian vestiges. The world powerless to be born is partly modern and partly something hard to specify. It's very essence is to remain in a zone of unresolvable ambivalence: hence the name, postmodern.

Clearly, such an epochal shift is a serious affair. Nietzsche and Heidegger recognize as much, Derrida too, to a less serious extent. And this makes the often silly politicization of postmodern and poststructuralist thought (as in our camel parable) all the more distressing. Arnold's notion of powerlessness, of impotence and incapacity to issue in a live birth, is something I want to dwell on for a few minutes, because I have the impression that the silliness results precisely from something that postmodern philosophy either cannot or has not done in its emphasis on the difficult task of remembering Being.

Let me start with Jean-François Lyotard, the most influential French theorist of postmodernism. Lyotard in a typically combative formula called philosophy "the mental illness of the West."[2] Many people who come upon phrases like that in postmodern theory understandably get the impression that postmodernism is itself a mental illness and that it portends the decline of the West. In fairness to what is good in postmodernism, I'd like to draw a distinction that may prevent unnecessary conflict. During the existence of the late, unlamented Soviet Union, sophisticated Marxists, mostly in the West, defended themselves by denouncing "vulgar Marxists." I would argue that there is a fairly large cadre of vulgar postmodernists, mostly situated on campuses and in editorial offices and in television and film studios, who know little of Heidegger or Nietzsche, and operate in a spirit far different from theirs. And they give ample reason to fear that we are in the throes of a barbarian invasion in which all human structures and civilization shall be undermined and "problematized" in the name of we know not what.

Yet knowing a bit about Lyotard's work, when I first read the statement about philosophy as mental illness, it reminded me not of Oswald Spengler, but of G. K. Chesterton, who titled a famous chapter in his *Autobiography* "How to Be a Lunatic." Chesterton recounts how as a young man the passion to be absolutely rational, in the modern sense of rational, drove him back to thinking about the very wellsprings of thought—and also almost drove him

<hr>

[2] Thomas Pangle, *The Ennobling of Democracy: The Challenge of the Postmodern Age*, (Baltimore: Johns Hopkins University Press, 1991), 31.

mad. In *Heretics* and *Orthodoxy* he describes the narrow infinity of a certain kind of reason that presumes it can specify all of reality as the maddest use of mind. It takes an effort of imagination to break out of this iron circle—something I want to come back to later. Imagination in these conditions is not mere fantasy or poetry, in the bad sense of the term.

I don't invoke Chesterton here for mere nostalgia's sake. In Chesterton, several things are present that, in spite of his non-philosophical method, put into question whether postmodernism is quite as unprecedented as we suppose. Chesterton and some other pre-modern figures, I would place Maritain's friend Charles Péguy among them, were pre-moderns who nevertheless anticipated both where modernism was headed and some of the postmodern reactions to that course. Paradox plays a large role in Chesterton, for example, precisely because he knows that any simple discursive use of language at the end of the modern age must appear either as a reductivist objectivity bordering on scientism, or as impressionist subjectivism. I do not know whether the ontological difference may already be found in Saint Thomas, but I am sure that Chesterton, who was no mystic, intuited it, or something very like it, on the basis of orthodox Christianity and Western sanity. If you doubt this, re-read the failures of explanation and the failure of an entire menagerie of animals to suggest the identity of Sunday, who is God or something like Being, at the conclusion of *The Man Who Was Thursday*.

Chesterton, who I'm sure never even heard of Heidegger, often sounds like him. For example, who wrote this?

> There is at the back of all our lives an abyss of light, more blinding and unfathomable than any abyss of darkness; and it is the abyss of actuality, of existence, of the fact that things truly are incredibly and sometimes almost incredulously real. It is the fundamental fact of being, as against not being; it is unthinkable, yet we cannot unthink it, though we may sometimes be unthinking about it; unthinking and especially unthanking. For he who has realized this reality knows that it does outweigh, literally to infinity, all lesser regrets or arguments for negation, and that under all our grumblings there is a substance of gratitude.[3]

Or this? "All our heart's courage is the/echoing response to the/first call of Being which/ gathers our thinking into the/play of the world."[4] The first was Chesterton, the second, Heidegger.

The literary critic George Steiner emphasizes a dimension of Heidegger,

---

[3] G. K. Chesterton, *Chaucer* (New York: Sheed and Ward, 1956), 26. Though a late text in the original edition (1932), this passage echoes a sentiment that may be found in varying forms throughout Chesterton's whole *oeuvre*.

[4] From Martin Heidegger, "The Thinker as Poet," in *Poetry, Language, Thought* (New York: Harper and Row, 1971), 9.

little-noticed among the fruitier postmodern literary theorists but not lost on pure philosophers and theologians: "I have come to believe that Heidegger's use and exploration of the seventeenth-century Pietist tag *Denken ist Danken*, 'To think is to thank,' may well be indispensable if we are to carry on as articulate and moral beings."[5] That basic gratitude and piety, "a piety of thinking" toward Being as Heidegger always insisted, is lacking in many of what I have called the vulgar postmodernists. And it is no wonder that many people therefore think that postmodernism makes it, in Steiner's words, impossible to carry on as articulate and moral beings.

Following Steiner's lead, we might look at how the postmodern might be made to confront some older concepts. And as a comprehensive set of pegs on which to hang some reflections I thought I might use the three transcendentals: the good, the true, and the beautiful.

II

Let's begin with the good. I find postmodernism most vulnerable in its apparent inability to state an ethic. And by an ethic I mean something more than the mere deconstruction of "master narratives," the reversals of margin and center, and the questioning of identities that make up the moral appeal of postmodernism to those so inclined. To put this very simply, we may undermine existing religion, metaphysics, politics, and domestic life because we think their foundations are insubstantial and their traditional conceptualization oppressive— or even terroristic. But that does not guarantee that the result will be more free and just. Most American inner cities today contain large numbers of young people who have been freed from the old Western master narratives of patriarchy, religion, and enlightenment democracy, and in light of the result of that liberation it would seem, to borrow a well-known formula of Heidegger's, that "only a god can save us now." Also, in a world where ethnic cleansing, political uses of famine, and totalitarian regimes still exist, ironic undermining is a very weak weapon with which to pursue justice. At the absurd limit, we find figures like Richard Rorty saying that because liberal societies lack universal foundations the "liberal ironist," like himself, faced with an Adolf Hitler could only try to "josh him out of" his anti-Semitic obsessions.[6]

In addition, I think we have to say the real-life histories of the central postmodern figures present us with a cautionary tale. Nietzsche and Heidegger

---

[5] George Steiner, *Martin Heidegger* (Chicago: The University of Chicago Press, 1978), 15, 131, and 146.

[6] See, for example Rorty's *Contingency, Irony, and Solidarity* (New York: Cambridge University Press, 1989).

both display strong signs of what Philippa Foot has recently called simple "immoralism."[7] The Nazi appropriation of Nietzsche of course falsified his work somewhat. And Heidegger's adherence to nazism—an adherence he never entirely renounced—must be thought through in non-Heiddeggerian terms. The famous sentence from the *Der Spiegel* interview in which he describes the inner greatness of Nazism as its participation in the global struggle with technology puts the case in a nutshell. All that may very well be. But with all due respect to Martin Heidegger, who is beyond doubt one of the great philosophical figures of this century, if you get the proportions of actual existing nazism wrong on such a scale, you might do better to sit down and figure out where the car is parked before you say any more about history and technology.

I cannot go here into the intricacies of the argument, but let me state baldly that both Nietzsche and Heidegger fail—and cannot help but fail—as moral thinkers because, whatever their other accomplishments, they have no place for absolute moral truths or universal principles of justice. Maritain discerned a similar problem in the "ontological gap" of Bergson: "The most captivating thing about Bergsonian ethics is precisely that morality, in the strictest sense of the word, has been eliminated from it. In it, man is caught between something *social*, infra-rational, and something *mystical*, supra-rational."[8] *Mutatis mutandis* the same might be said of Nietzsche and Heidegger.

To put an end to slavery, for instance, as happened primarily through the agency of British Christianity in the nineteenth century, requires a deep belief in and willingness to sacrifice for the truth that slavery is wrong. Would Nietzsche, looking at the pitiful condition of the so-called "last men" ravaged by Christian "slave morality" and the modern world feel such a burning need? Nietzscheans will no doubt object that his revolt against that decadence was spurred precisely by the will to free those poor creatures. But in the meantime, it is clear, he feels—and shows—a good deal of contempt for the slaves.

A related set of problems persists in Jacques Derrida in spite of his own worries about Nietzsche and Heidegger's connections to Nazism. In particular, Derrida worries that any "proper of man," as Heidegger put it in his "Letter on Humanism," is the root of all Nazisms.[9] Astonishingly, however, Derrida says in his latest book *The Other Heading* (*L'autre cap*) that universal principles of justice must be maintained in human societies, or disasters will follow.[10] As

[7] See Phillippa Foot, "Nietzsche's Immoralism," *New York Review of Books*, 13 June 1991, 18-22.

[8] Cf. Jacques Maritain, "Bergson's Morality and Religion," in *Redeeming the Time* (London: Geoffrey Bles, The Centenary Press, 1944), 82.

[9] See my "Human Nature and Unnatural Humanisms" in *From Twilight to Dawn*, ed. Peter Redpath, (Notre Dame, Indiana: University of Notre Dame Press, 1990).

Europe goes about unifying itself, he continues, it must also deconstruct the old hegemonic view of itself as the exemplary culture. Europe must see itself as defined both by its past and by its openness and recognition of the Other.

I agree with all of this, after a fashion. But I don't understand where in Derrida's thought these universals could possibly find a place, let alone a grounding. Deconstruction is almost by definition the enemy of identity, "henophobic." For the vulgar postmodernists, at least, there is no self who could be the subject of rights or universal principles. Paradoxically, for the same vulgar postmodernists along with many other people, this insubstantial self still has an ever expanding set of desires conceived of as rights.

I would propose Thomists try a different starting point to address this question of universal principles. In writing my book *1492 and All That*,[11] I ran across the central ethical question of the European expansion throughout the world: by what principles do we judge good and bad behavior in Western and non-Western societies? I am prepared to say that we do so on the basis of Western notions that emerged in the reflection of a group of scholastic theologians at Salamanca in Spain, Francisco de Vitoria, most prominently among them.[12] These theologians had to decide how Christians should treat the newly discovered peoples in the Americas—peoples who clearly had had no significant previous contact with Europe, could not have known the Old or New Testaments, and lived in societies that partly observed, and also grossly violated the natural law.

The answers of Vitoria, Cano, and—later—Suarez set us on the road toward Locke, the U.S. Constitution, the Declaration of the Rights of Man, modern international law, and the U.N. Universal Declaration of Human Rights, which reads in many places as if it had been lifted from Vitoria. I am well aware that these later developments are not without their own philosophical difficulties. To go back to Vitoria, however, might enable us to make a fresh start at thinking about rights again, but at a point before some of the later difficulties in rights theories appear. If we all value, at least to some extent, modern rights and liberties, we might do well to recall from what soil they sprang. It was not from the soil of sentimental bows to the Other, or from the undermining and

---

[10] Cf. Jacques Derrida, *The Other Heading: Reflections on Today's Europe (L'autre cap)* Pascale-Anne Brault and Michael B. Nass, trans., (Bloomington, Indiana: Indiana University Press, 1992.

[11] Robert Royal, *1492 and All That: Political Manipulations of History* (Washington, D.C.: Ethics and Public Policy Center, 1992).

[12] On this point, see James Brown Scott, *The Spanish Origins of International Law* (Washington, D.C.: Georgetown University Press, 1928).

unmasking of our own discourses of power, but from a scholasticism confronting a wholly new human condition.

We may see the importance of universal principles in a recent and notorious case. Salman Rushdie has written what I consider to be one of the most remarkable postmodern fictions, I mean *The Satanic Verses.* Despite his quarrels with Islam and his often silly denigration of Margaret Thatcher and the United States, Rushdie paints a remarkably funny, rich, and imaginative portrait of the strange disorientations of self, society, and reality currently under way in the entire world as various cultures meet and mingle. That said, though, Rushdie's real-life adventures do not lead us to put much confidence in Rushdie-the-novelist's postmodern discourse on multiculturalism and non-Eurocentric categories.

Margaret Thatcher used to be called the Iron Lady. But had she been a postmodern Ironist Lady and not been supremely confident in the justice of using the British Special Forces to protect Rushdie from the Other, namely the Ayatollah Khomeini, Rushdie's doubts about the truth of Islam and the existence of the world to come would have been settled, one way or another, long ago. No amount of talk about multiculturalism, anti-colonialism, perspectivism, relativism, or antifoundationalism can get around disputes of this kind. We have to decide what we think good and right here, and be able to give reasons that can have cash value, as William James used to say, in the world.

For me, the best place to begin thinking about that ethical question is in late scholasticism, not Heidegger.

III

What about the second transcendental, the true? In spite of vulgar postmodernism's posturings and play with the abyss, one of the strongest claims of postmodernism, it seems to me, is its greater truth compared with the old modernism, even if postmodernists would probably not put the relationship quite that way. The reductive visions of modernism and technological scientism are so obviously false that almost any movement that reopens forgotten regions of Being cannot help but appeal to anyone sensitive to the riches and mysteries of the world. When all is said and done, Heidegger simply has a vision of the world that is a recognizably more human place than the old modernity. Death means something there besides extinction. Things are both themselves and part of something larger and more significant.

Postmodern literature has been the locus for some of the most lush effects of those insights. On the whole, I prefer the Latin American and Central European postmodernists rather than the North Americans. North American postmodernist writers, like North American postmodernist theorists, tend to run riot with subvertings and decenterings of hegemonies that, compared to their counterparts at most times and places in human history, are not very powerful or oppressive in the first place. Some postmodern critics have argued that the first-world postmodern fiction is really hypermodern fiction and therefore not a contribution to solving the old modern aporiai.[13] There is unfortunately no terminological police force or justice system to which we can appeal on these issues. So it is useful to keep in mind that there are several forms of sensibility that have been given the name postmodern.

The Czech Milan Kundera, for example, exhibits something that rises beyond the mere destruction, *mise en abîme*, and shaking of foundations that characterizes much American and French postmodernism. At the end of the *Book of Laughter and Forgetting*, we find this remarkable scene at—of all places—a Czechoslovakian nude beach:

> a man with an extraordinary paunch began developing the theory that Western civilization was on its way out and we would soon be freed once and for all from the bonds of Judeo-Christian thought—statements Jan had heard ten, twenty, thirty, a hundred, five hundred, a thousand times before—and for the time being those few feet of beach felt like a university auditorium. On and on the man talked. The others listened with interest, their naked genitals staring dully, sadly, listlessly at the yellow sand.

Could any American, with the exception perhaps of the late Walker Percy, have written that moving statement of the potency of postmodern sexual aspirations and, at the same time, the clear postmodern or post-postmodern insight that all this points only to dust and death?

Kundera has quarrelled with another Czech postmodernist, the current president of the Czech Republic, Václav Havel in ways we should look at briefly. Tomás, a character in *The Unbearable Lightness of Being,* chooses to make his wife happy by staying with her instead of participating in a public protest on the grounds that the resistance to a totalitarian regime "can't do any good anyway." Havel, of course, has spent much of his life trying to live out what had become a slogan among the Eastern European thinkers influenced by Husserl and Heidegger. They speak of "living in Truth." Living in truth meant not compromising with the system and accepting that seemingly hopeless acts of resistance would be useless only if you yourself decided to lose hope.

Havel and Kundera have each had their solid successes, but in light of the second transcendental, the True, I think we can begin to see the problem with

---

[13] See, for example, the terminological distinctions drawn by Albert Borgmann, *Crossing the Postmodern Divide* (Chicago: The University of Chicago Press, 1992).

some of the postmodern attempts to subvert all large-scale theories of meaning, whether pre-modern or modern. The postmodern strategy usually denies those "master narratives" in favor of the *petites histoires*, that is, personal stories as the only locus of rich meaning open to us. In this view, all the old *grands récits*—Christianity, Hegelianism, Marxism, even Liberalism—are dangerous totalizing and terroristic illusions.

We should probably not identify Kundera's character Tomás, with Kundera himself. But can Havel's "living in truth" be accommodated in postmodernism? Perhaps the most powerful attempt to derive that sort of commitment from postmodernism is Edith Wyschogrod's *Saints and Postmodernism*.[14] For Wyschogrod, saints are a non-originating, non-foundational stimulus to act selflessly, but not in imitation or repetition of them. Perhaps someone may be so moved. I think it much more likely, however, that "living in truth" is both a better account and a better model for the work of the world. Havel even speaks in his book entitled *Living in Truth* of the virtue of Hope, a strange virtue based not on any immediate earthly prospect of success that yet carries on for a worldly purpose.

The contemporary Thomist, faced with continuing political and spiritual struggles, way wish to consider how hope and living in truth may be justified in spite of all postmodern challenges. After all, if the *petites histoires* were everything, much of the world might still be enslaved, and more would be threatened. Alexander Solzhenitsyn prophetically concluded his Nobel Prize lecture with the old Russian aphorism: "One word of truth outweighs the whole world." If we admire the results of such heroism, we must find better ways to account for it.

IV

This brings us to our third transcendental, the beautiful, and the question of aesthetics. Art has become more important in the postmodern world, it seems to me, because the truth claims of philosophy, theology, ethics, and even nature seem weak. The argument on many campuses over the canon has taken on added heat precisely because, where truth is assumed a priori not to exist, images and atmosphere will shape how most people think.

Literature in particular is one of the few remaining loci where we come upon whispers of transcendence. Sensing that postmodern theory and practice threaten to close off even that escape hatch, George Steiner has defended some older views of works of art under the intentionally religious title *Real*

---

[14] *Saints and Postmodernism: Revisioning Moral Philosophy* (Chicago: The University of Chicago Press, 1990).

Presences.[15] At the outset, he disputes all the current postmodern theories claiming that languages can refer only to other uses of language. Instead, he argues that the "capacity of human speech to communicate meaning and feeling is underwritten by the assumption of God's presence."[16]

In the inquiring spirit of Maritain's *Creative Intuition in Art and Poetry*, however, we have to approach the multiple, polylectic, at times self-contradictory forms of postmodern art and aesthetics for what they tell us about current notions of the world. Lyotard has formulated the task of postmodern art as "presenting the unpresentable in presentation itself" an almost religious aspiration. And under postmodern conditions this means denying ourselves what Lyotard calls the "consolation of beautiful forms." At the other extreme, Susan Shell has explained the difference between existential and postmodern art as follows:

> The dizzying horror of the abyss is replaced by the virtuosity of performance—a kind of perpetual mid-air tap dance, in which the ground isn't needed—not as in the land of [car]toons, because its absence isn't noticed, but because the ground itself is no longer sought.[17]

These two formulations show the ambivalent—even contradictory— aspirations of postmodern aesthetics. In part, with Heidegger, it points toward what exceeds the concept in the direction of Being and of the Kantian sublime. For the much larger part, however, it looks to performance art, because performance "artists" are always still available to us when all that is solid melts into air.

Sometimes the two tendencies appear in the same work. For example, the American Paul Auster's anti-detective novel, *City of Glass*. An anti-detective novel, if you have not read Auster or Robbes-Grillet's *Les Gommes*, turns the usual story line upside down. The detective starts out with the familiar investigation, but then identities, meanings, characters start to slip into an abyss of mysteries. Sometimes the real-life author shows up by name as a troubled and troubling character. It's as if Kafka were called in to do a re-write of Raymond Chandler. There is both a destruction of the usual frameworks of life on the way toward a transcendence that never comes and a tapdancing in mid air. I confess to a soft spot for this kind of stuff. (Chesterton curiously anticipated this, too, in *The Man Who Was Thursday*).

The two different postmodern aesthetics, the sublime and the performative

---

[15] George Steiner, *Real Presences*, (Chicago: The University of Chicago Press, 1989).

[16] *Ibid.*, 3.

[17] Susan Shell, "Preserving the Humanities," Address to the Madison Center Conference on the Humanities, Washington, D.C., 1989.

seem opposed but stem, I think, from a common source, a turning away from existing beings. For example, there is little discussion of natural beauty in postmodern theory largely because postmodern belief in the constructedness of all reality has occluded nature itself, even though nature is talked about a great deal. This does not bode well, by the way, for those trying to think through the question of technology and, more broadly, questions about the environment.

When pre-modern people looked at nature they saw both change and, more rarely, permanence. Whatever order and reason could be introduced into the environment by pre-modern man was seen as an achievement that perfected untutored and often threatening nature. At the same time, attempts to reproduce the cosmological order in political systems and even within the human spirit (microcosm answering to macrocosm) sought to rise above the inevitable processes of generation and corruption. In his poem "Sailing to Byzantium," W. B. Yeats shows a similar impulse in protesting against his own old age:

> O sages dancing in God's Holy fire
> As in the gold mosaic of a wall
> Come from the fire, perne in a gyre
> And be the dancing masters of my soul.
> Sick with desire and fastened to a dying animal
> It knows not what it is. And gather me
> Into the artifice of eternity.

Note the connection here: eternity is, for man, the product of a wisdom, almost a craft, that enables him to step outside even his own most intense desires. Yeats is a modernist, but his existential situation, his realization of being-toward-death, leads him back to an old solution for old mortality.

A much different mood emerged as modern technologies began their dominance over the world. Since at least the eighteenth century, for most artists regular mechanism and artifice have become "mechanical and artificial." The romantic revolt against artificiality and dead social and moral forms is more than an emotional outburst. Mechanism, more than at any time in human history, is perceived as threatening human particularity and spontaneity. In a world of mechanism, all that seems left for the authentically human is the uncanny, the inassimilable, perhaps even the teratological. Much of the postmodern talk about transgressing boundaries, open or fragmentary art forms, draws on this sentiment.

Those postmodern currents that took their start from a one-sided desire to free the human person from all mechanism and "closed" social systems have now worked out their own logic. They wind up denying the existence of the person, the intelligibility of world, and the possibility of a just order. Given the vacuum they have created it is no wonder that nature has rushed in to fill the void and we find quite authoritarian forms of feminism, gay rights, and anti-

European ideologies speaking, quite incongruously, a uniform language of deconstruction in several diverse fields. Iris Murdoch has recently explained why:

> Philosophy, anthropology, history, literature have different procedures and methods of verification. It is only when the idea of truth as relation to separate reality is removed that they can seem in this odd hallucinatory light to be similar. With the idea of truth, the idea of value also vanishes. Here the deep affinity, the holding hands under the table, between structuralism and Marxism, becomes intelligible.[18]

Philosophy must be philosophy, not poetry, but in spite of imagination's dangers, which Plato already warned about, I would still like to point out that imagination, even postmodern imagination, may be a powerful tool for the philosopher. While no one with any sense expects a novelist or poet, painter or composer, to render the philosophical truth about the human condition, forms of the imagination, as Maritain shows clearly in *Creative Intuition in Art and Poetry*, are an important testimony of the modes of being and truth in any period.

But I think we need to go even a step further. There are some forms of art that do not seem to me to be merely fantasies, but point toward transcendent truths and realities. Some art is only amusing or decorative, and has its own reason for being in that. However I agree with Simone Weil that art may also be a form of attention, or the first faint flickering of a light that can lead us out of the Platonic cave.

The particular difficulty in dealing with postmodern art forms is that they combine the potentially transcendent and the trivial in ways that leave you dissatisfied with both, as in Auster. Thus the power of true imagination, which Coleridge was the first to distinguish from mere fantasy, is darkened. Postmodern philosophy has allowed various forms of fantasy, not imagination, to present themselves as profoundly philosophical art works. Any image that can claim vague relationship with the subverting of identities in Heidegger or Derrida is automatically granted a certain profundity before we have even looked at the real aesthetic value of the product; hence the crucifixes in the jars of urine and the performance artists smearing their bodies in chocolate who receive financial support from the U.S. government itself and claim they are penetrating commentators on postmodern reality.

True imagination will emerge where and in whatever forms it wishes. But in the spirit of Maritain I think some counter-theorizing now has to be undertaken to show first, that many postmodern themes were not entirely

---

[18] Iris Murdoch, *Metaphysics as a Guide to Morals* (New York: Allen Lane, The Penguin Press, 1993), 202.

unknown to pre-modern thinkers and artists. But second, we also need a philosophical border patrol that will undertake to show, without a clumsy crushing of exploratory imagination, that some postmodern situations may bear quite different artistic registrations and resolutions than currently thought.

V

Let me conclude with a plea that Thomists in particular, like Thomas, begin to reconstruct a language that is philosophically potent enough to allow the new, powerless world, first discerned by Matthew Arnold, finally to be born. That language must not talk solely of difference and absence, it must be able to affirm in some fashion, especially for non-philosophers, identity and presence. At the limit it must of course be able to defend not only presences, but — for some of us — the Real Presence. To do so does not require, I think, a school of vulgar Thomists to meet the vulgar postmodernists point for point. Rather, we need a whole generation of philosophers who better understand their obligations not only to Being, but to beings — including human beings.

The conclusion of Chesterton's *Heretics* sounds the battle charge for the kind of struggle I envision. I regard this passage as a kind of post-postmodern ideal that both tap dances over the void as lightly as any postmodern Fred Astaire, yet never forgets where the car is parked:

> Truths turn into dogmas the instant they are disputed. Thus every man who utters a doubt defines a religion. And the skepticism of our time does not really destroy the beliefs, rather it creates them; gives them their limits and their plain and defiant shape. We who are Liberals once held Liberalism lightly as a truism. Now it has been disputed, and we hold it fiercely as a faith. We who believe in patriotism once thought patriotism to be reasonable, and thought little more about it. Now we know it to be unreasonable, and know it to be right. We who are Christians never knew the great philosophic common sense which inheres in that mystery until the anti-Christian writers pointed it out to us. The great march of mental destruction will go on. Everything will be denied. Everything will become a creed. It is a reasonable position to deny the stones in the street; fires will be a kindled to testify that two and two make four. Swords will be drawn to prove that leaves are green in summer. We shall be left defending, not only the incredible virtues and sanities of human life, but something more incredible still, this huge impossible universe which stares us in the face. We shall fight for visible prodigies as if they were invisible. We shall look on the impossible grass and the skies with a strange courage. We shall be of those who have seen and yet have believed.[19]

---

[19] G. K. Chesterton, *Heretics*, (New York: John Lane Company, 1909), 304-5.

On Postmodernism and
the "Silence" of St. Thomas

James V. Schall, S.J.

Oh my soul, I gave you back the freedom over the created and uncreated; and who knows, as you know, the voluptuous delight of what is yet to come?

Nietzsche, *Thus Spake Zarathustra*, III.[1]

There is the *extraordinary regime* of intelligent creatures insofar as they are *free agents*: *to receive without having asked.*

Jacques Maritain, *Notebooks.*[2]

I have begun these reflections on the "silence" of St. Thomas and postmodernity with two very curious, very contrasting remarks, each in its own way, I think, pertinent to the subject at hand. One citation is from Nietzsche, who more than any one else, sensed the death of modernity and defined the nihilist attractions of postmodernity. The other passage is from Jacques Maritain, who saw in St. Thomas that human liberty would be most free precisely when it received into itself, not exclusively itself, but rather *all that is.*

Nietzsche accused classical metaphysics and Christianity of a kind of weakness or even cowardliness. Nietzsche would not allow the suspicion, contained both in classical metaphysics and Christianity, that what is to be given to man is more than man can ever imagine by himself. That is, all humanly constructed utopias are insufficient precisely as utopias. This is the most telling judgment of revelation on all rationalism. Indeed, when spelled out, what man would be given would be precisely what he would want if he could have it. This perception that we do not even realize what it is we are to

---

[1] Nietzsche, *Thus Spake Zarathustra*, iii.
[2] Jacques Maritain, *Notebooks* (Albany, New York: Magi Books, 1984), 280.

ask for, of course, is the sense of Maritain's remark that free agents are to receive what is properly theirs "without having asked."

The struggle between these two positions, the one that creates its own world, its own pleasure, and the one that receives what in fact *is*, is, in a way, a struggle over utopias. But it is over advanced utopias that have themselves previously rejected the utopias of the philosophers (Plato) and of those utopian thinkers who wish to establish the kingdom of God on earth (the Enlightenment) because, it is thought, the religious location (i.e., eternal life) has failed or is impossible. The issue in this sense is not primarily an intellectual one but a spiritual one, one that sees within itself the possibility of receiving or rejecting a love that is genuine and best for the receiver, but one not intrinsically formulated by the receiver.

David Walsh's remark about Nietzschean tradition is to the point:

> The analysis (of modernity) must recognize that the closure (the refusal to accept a natural or supernatural order) is motivated at root by the revolt against God, and that it is only the grace of divine reconciliation that can finally overcome it. If the problem could be resolved through the discovery of an acceptable intellectual formulation, then it would have been remedied long ago; it would not have been a spiritual crisis, in which the refusal to acknowledge what we know we should acknowledge constitutes the crux of the issue.[3]

Walsh was here developing a theme familiar in Voegelin, namely, that the denial of God is not primarily an intellectual problem about proving God's existence but a spiritual problem, a murder in fact. There are basic questions that we refuse to ask so that our problem is not really intellectual but spiritual, a problem of will and not of intellect.[4]

To bring up the question of the silence of St. Thomas in the context of postmodernism hints, I presume, at a common, but dubious, suspicion that the configurations and gyrations of the contemporary mind are so unique and so original that they cannot possibly find response in the perennial philosophy of St. Thomas. Modernity, for its part, which we perceive to be largely over, was indeed confronted by the efforts of the sundry famous and not so famous neo-Thomists, even by those neo-Thomists who identified themselves as Thomists and not neo-Thomists, as most did. And the specter of Nietzsche has always stood for a kind of mocking challenge to modernity, prodding its adherents to have the faith of their convictions. Since God is dead, these superior men can

---

[3] David Walsh, "The Crisis of the Modern World: Nietzsche and Nihilism," *World & I*, ii (May, 1987), 564.

[4] See Eric Voegelin, *Science, Politics, and Gnosticism* (Chicago: Regnery, 1968), 83-84.

inaugurate their own rights and their own delights, free from both the "created" and the "uncreated," as Nietzsche put it.

The modern project, to use Leo Strauss' term, conceived itself to be erected over the tomb of St. Thomas. Strauss himself knew of this tomb but did not think it pertinent except as a marker on the road to Aristotle. The modern project is also that against which postmodernity claims to rebel. The modern project consisted in the effort to use human intelligence for the charitable benefit of man. It based intellect on nothing but itself as the only criterion for valid knowledge of reality. This project seems to have run full course in the failure of Marxism and the growing statism of liberalism.

What has appeared among us instead of the perfect society, much to our surprise, has been pure thought with an unexpectedly inhuman face. Paradoxically, this face was most distorted when modernity sought to put into being its highest longings with the best of intentions. We have denied the possibility and necessity either of defining or of practicing virtues as the classics understood them, only to be rather astonished at the sorts of conduct, based on the premises of this very denial, that have appeared among us. The denial of original sin and the declarations of the goodness of man only seemed to make matters worse.

The effort to exclude systematically from modern life anything that could claim human attention from revelation was proposed to be the essence of humanism and the core of the project for human improvement. Religion, subsequently, has come to be identified as the only vice that remains recognized among us, that is, "fanaticism." The only acceptable world was the self-made world of pure reason. The only true evil is "intolerance;" that is, the claim that some truth demanding attention and obedience exists and can be discovered by the human mind.

This theoretic analysis of modernity led to a brave project, to be sure, one reminiscent of the account in *Genesis* of the Tree of Knowledge of Good and Evil, of the claim of man to decide for himself the distinctions between good and evil. Interestingly enough, this claim of autonomy has been fought out largely in the name of "human rights," in perhaps one of the most ironic twists of intellectual record ever witnessed by the philosophic historian. If we pay careful attention to their intellectual origins and justifications, human rights in

---

[5] See Henry Veatch, *Human Rights: Fact or Fancy?* (Baton Rouge, Louisiana: Louisiana State University Press, 1985); James V. Schall, "Human Rights as an Ideological Project," *The American Journal of Jurisprudence*, 32 (1987), 47–61; "On Being Dissatisfied with Compromises: Natural Law and Human Rights," *Loyola Law Review* (New Orleans), XXXVIII (#2, 1992), 289–309.

modernity are not equivalent to the classical "natural law."[5] It is especially dangerous to make them so.

Human rights find their origins in Hobbes' notion of will presupposed to nothing but itself. This will, in itself, has an absolute right to everything. The "war of all against all" is natural right in its purest form. With considerable irony, human rights have come to function as the replacement for and, as to their content, the contradiction of what was considered to be the content of natural law. Natural law, for its part, did not depend on the human will or intellect for its content or for the fact that this content constituted the human good itself if freely understood and chosen. The natural law corresponded to the true human good.

Strauss' exact words about the modern project need to be repeatedly pondered:

> The modern project was originated (by philosophers) as required by nature (natural right) . . . to satisfy . . . the most powerful natural needs of men: nature was to be conquered for the sake of man who himself was supposed to possess a nature, an unchangeable nature; the originators of the project took it for granted that philosophy and science are identical. . . . The conquest of nature requires the conquest of human nature and hence . . . the questioning of the unchangeability of human nature: an unchangeable human nature might set absolute limits to progress. . . . The natural needs of men could no longer direct the conquest of nature; the direction had to come from reason as distinguished from nature, from the rational Ought as distinguished from the neutral Is.[6]

This remarkable passage underscores better than any other I can think of the reason why theories of human autonomy and human right have turned against human nature.

Ideologies, that is, world views whose content depend on nothing but will, seem to be the logical political alternatives to substitute for classical philosophy and revelation as a guide for human action. Ideology is formulated by a "rational Ought" that does not derive its content from any given nature, natural, human, or divine. The mind is free to speculate independently and with presumably exhilarating liberty about what it wants. It is thus free to establish an "Ought" independently of an "Is," since no "Is" by itself supposedly engages human intellect. As a result, the reason why an "Ought" might be limited by or, better, fulfilled by a given nature or "Is" has been theoretically eliminated by a science that can find no "reasons" or secondary causes in nature.[7]

---

[6] Leo Strauss, *The City and Man* (Chicago: The University of Chicago Press, 1964), 7.

[7] The manner in which this relationship works itself out is best traced in Charles N. R. McCoy, *The Structure of Political Thought* (New York: McGraw–Hill, 1963).

The postmodern project appears at first sight, as it were, to be more humble. Nevertheless, it takes off from the unexpected and dire results of the modern project as Strauss understood it. Postmodernism doubts not only these grandiose rationalist schemes to transform the world in the name of autonomous man, but also the very notions of universal good, knowledge, and prosperity, on whose majestic premises the modern project was, in its own view, initially based.

Chesterton remarked in *Orthodoxy* that the problem of the modern mind is that it has mislocated the virtue of humility by putting it in the human intellect. Thereby, this pseudo–humility makes the intellect incapable of affirming the truth of anything. The proper place of humility is rather in the human will. Postmodernity, in an odd fashion, agrees that will not intellect is the crucial power. For the classical and medieval thinkers, however, will was to follow intellect, whereas for the postmoderns it was to be independent of it.

The problem with modernity, then, was not that it did not discover vast reaches of the human mind and hand. Rather it was that it did not want to see these reaches to be anything but products of the human intellect presupposed to no criterion but what it imposed on itself. Modernity was still under the assumption that the conquest of nature was guided by mind. But this guidance was not through reference to a divine mind that might lie at the origin of the distinction in things, including the distinction between human, non-human, and divine things.

Reacting to this anthropocentric view, the postmodern mind suspected in fact that one of the directions that we could and perhaps should take, once modernity reached its own impasse, something made most vivid by the fate of Marxism, was towards a revival of virtue, classical metaphysics, and revelation. The historic and philosophic reasons why these classic ideas were rejected by modernity did not in retrospect hold. Realizing that the ideologies that took the place of religion could also themselves turn out to be the opium of the people, postmodernity took steps to protect itself from any implication that classical metaphysics and revelation might still be valid and true alternatives to the impasse of modernity.

This postmodernist defense of itself was by way of defining all knowledge, including religious and especially moral knowledge, as simply power. As McCoy pointed out, prudence was replaced by art as a guide to reality.[8] What caused the intellect to move was not, as Aristotle had held, wonder, but rather self-interest and control. In a move of what can only be called desperation, rather than admitting some normative value to truth and being, postmodernism doubted the very capacity of intellect itself to know anything at all.

---

[8] *Ibid.*, 31–36.

Solzhenitsyn recently described the situation quite accurately:

> For a postmodernist, the world does not possess values that have reality. He even has an expression for this, "the world as text," as something secondary, as the text of an author's work, wherein the primary object of interest is the author himself in his relationship to the work, his own introspection. Culture, in this view, ought to be directed inward at itself; it alone is valuable and real. For this reason the concept of play acquires a heightened importance – not the Mozartian playfulness of a universe overflowing with joy, but a forced playing upon the strings of emptiness, where an author need have no responsibility to anyone. A denial of any and all ideas is considered courageous. And in this voluntary self-delusion, "postmodernism" sees itself as a crowning achievement of all previous culture, the final link in its chain. We can have sympathy for this constant searching, but only as we have sympathy for the suffering of a sick man.[9]

Solzhenitsyn, be it noted, here stresses the same point of "a universe overflowing with joy" over against "the strings of emptiness . . . with no responsibility to anyone" that I tried to emphasize earlier in my remarks on Nietzsche and Maritain.

Postmodernism allows no apparent opening to anything that might suggest that there was in fact an objective truth to which the mind was naturally oriented. The given world for the mind to know, a given world that was, to recall Aristotle's definition of knowledge, "to become" his after the mind's own manner of being, could not be reached. However "courageous" it might be to live with the denial of everything, that empty world was in fact most dangerous since everything was now permitted.[10]

"In literature, postmodernism amounts to a denial of the fixity of any 'text,' of the authority of the author over the interpreter, of any 'canon' that 'privileges' great books over comic books," Gertrude Himmelfarb has perceptively summarized this position's central theses.

> In philosophy, it is a denial of the fixity of language, of any correspondence between language and reality, indeed of any "essential" reality and thus of any proximate truth about reality. In law (in America, at any rate), it is a denial of the fixity of the constitution, of the authority of the founders of the constitution, and of the legitimacy of law itself, which is regarded as nothing more than an instrument of power. In history, it is a denial of the fixity of the past, of the reality of the past apart from what the historian chooses to make of it, and thus of any objective truth about the past.[11]

[9] Alexander Solzhenitsyn, "How the Cult of Novelty Wrecked the 20th Century," *American Arts Quarterly*, 10 (Spring, 1993), 18–19.

[10] See Peter Shaw, "The Rise and Fall of Deconstruction," *Commentary*, 97 (December, 1991), 50–53.

[11] Gertrude Himmelfarb, "Telling It As You Like It: Postmodernist History and the Flight from Fact," *Times Literary Supplement* (London, October 16, 1992), 12.

Fact and truth are thus looked upon as tyrannical in postmodernity because they prevent the free human intellect from creating what it wants, what it could do if it would.

While modernity was willing to consider that truth could be found if thought were left free to be thought, which is what science originally meant, postmodernity argued that an objective world to which the intellect was open and from which it could learn something would necessarily restrict that same intellect from doing what it wanted if the world was not the way it would like it to be. If human nature is changeable, and thus open to scientific manipulation since *what is* need not be what it is, only the boldest souls will be able to choose that into which it ought to change.

In Milan Kundera's novel, *Immortality*, we read the following extraordinary passage:

> Because people in the West are not threatened by concentration camps, and are free to say and write what they want, the more the fight for human rights gains in popularity, the more it loses any concrete content, becoming a kind of universal stance of everyone toward everything, a kind of energy that turns human desires into rights. . . . The desire for love the right to love, the desire for rest the right to rest, the desire for friendship the right to friendship . . . the desire to shout in the street in the middle of the night the right to shout in the street.[12]

Kundera has sensed here what I have suggested earlier, that there is a specific relation between the rise of human rights, as they are most commonly understood, and the loss of any sense that might imply an "unchangeable human nature," to use Strauss' words.

Desires thus become rights without the benefit either of clergy or even of nature. And desires, by themselves, are strictly speaking unlimited, as Plato already understood. Human rights, when based solely on desires, mean ultimately nothing other than what we want them to mean. In this context, moreover, "we" is usually a political we, since individual rights have no grounding against collective ones. In other words, we have the strange phenomenon of human rights with no standard of what it is to be human other than what we might want. No transcendent or natural notion of the human good is either possible or wanted.

In Josef Pieper's wonderful opusculum, *The Silence of St. Thomas*, we read these words:

> The last word of St. Thomas is not communication but silence. And it is not death which takes the pen out of his hand. His tongue is stilled by the

---

[12] Milan Kundera, *Immortality*, Grove/Weidenfeld, in *The Wall Street Journal*, July, 16, 1991

superabundance of life in the mystery of God. He is silent, not because he has nothing further to say; he is silent because he has been allowed a glimpse into the inexpressible depths of the mystery which is not reached by any human thought or speech.[13]

Pieper in context, of course, is referring to the fact that St. Thomas, who wrote an incredible amount of the profoundest of things before he died at fifty, did not finish his great *Summa Theologiae*.

St. Thomas did not finish his great work, Pieper emphasized, because he suddenly died or because he was prevented to finish it by some natural or political reason. He did not finish it because of a vision he had in which he realized, as he said, in a remarkable phrase, that all he had written, compared to the depths of God, was "but straw." For Pieper this event signified that it was part of the essential nature of St. Thomas' work that it was "unfinished," as if to imply that human knowledge could not by itself ever penetrate to all the things that were to be known, especially the highest things.

Let us ask, then, what might be St. Thomas' position were he to have encountered "postmodernism," always a dangerous supposition, I know. What happens, we might ask, when this postmodernist "right" to "shout in the streets," to take up Kundera's remark, meets the silence of St. Thomas? In the first place, we know that the proper Thomist approach to a thing like postmodernism would be initially the effort to formulate accurately what it is, to formulate it perhaps better than postmodernist writers themselves could formulate their own position. Even in this most skeptical postmodernist position, there is some truth or point that can be distinguished, some truth that can be accepted.

I want to suggest that the effort to escape from reality that Gertrude Himmelfarb rightly saw in the postmoderns is, in a way, the logical antithesis of St. Thomas' mysterious silence. But to establish this point, or at least to clarify its possibility, I want to cite a passage from a lecture of Professor Richard Kennington about the strange position of charity in modernist thought, a point that Leo Strauss had also emphasized. In his *Thoughts on Machiavelli*, Strauss had remarked that modernity had rejected the means that were implicit in medieval (that is revelational) theories about the grace needed to achieve many of the elevated positions of charity and mercy that were introduced into the world by revelation.[14] Even though modernity rejected these means, it did not reject the goals to which they pointed. Hence the characteristics of the city in

---

[13] Josef Pieper, *The Silence of St. Thomas* (Chicago: Regnery, 1957), 38. See also, James V. Schall, "The Law of Superabundance" (Maritain), *Gregorianum*, Rome, 73 (#3, 1991), 515–42.

[14] Leo Strauss, *Thoughts on Machiavelli* (Chicago: The Free Press, 1958), 85, 231–33.

speech or the city on the hill were thought now to be feasible in a way that neither the classics nor revelation itself warranted.

Kennington wrote, in this regard,

> The secularization of charity is . . . a constituent element of the founding of modern philosophy. For the fruits of this charity both motivate the philosopher, guaranteeing him the love and gratitude of all mankind, and supply those benefits that anchor this love and gratitude in the self-interest, "rightly understood," of the rest of the human race. The right of mankind "to be satisfied," in Hegel's phrase, . . . has been placed on a solid footing. But humanity needs desperately . . . some standard of the good and evil of life, by which to choose among satisfactions, if only because universal satisfaction is not available for all individuals, races or peoples. The very goal of mastery of nature, that appeared to put us on the road to universal satisfaction, is the reason why nature, the standard of the good and right, of natural right and natural law, can no longer have for us that function. The secularization of charity is held hostage by the secularization of nature.[15]

Bacon's goal of the mastery of nature to result in universal satisfaction through material goods has eliminated as a criterion of good and evil nature and especially human nature.

This project was what was meant by the famous "lowering of the sights" so that questions of the higher things would not be elements of the public order because they were seen as interfering with material progress. Human nature, as Strauss remarked, came to be seen as a dangerous limit on the progress of science. Without this unchangeable nature, however, the distinction of good and evil disappears. The secularization of nature prevents grace from working on nature to achieve the elevated goals that were introduced into the Enlightenment world as a secularization of the eschaton. This strain to achieve the unacknowledged higher means by science alone came to justify the significance of ideology in the public order in modernity

If we return to St. Thomas' silence, then, it is possible to suggest, at least, that the order of the world, which Thomas did so much to articulate, with its relation to revelation, which he integrated into a way of looking at both, of accounting for both, leaves us with the famous Socratic knowing that we know nothing, or with St. Thomas' negative theology, with the fact that what we do know about God is that we know nothing. Both Thomas and postmodernism do, in a strange manner, testify to the insufficiency of the actual world. St. Thomas testifies to it while granting its wonder and radiance and light. Postmodernism testifies to it while affirming that nothing in the world is at all

---

[15] Richard H. Kennington, "Theories of Secularization and Their Relation to Modern Legitimacy," Lecture, American Enterprise Institute, Washington, D. C., April 22, 1993, 13–14.

binding or true in comparison to imagined worlds presumably better than the one *that is* about which we can know nothing.

Gertrude Himmelfarb sought to take up a kind of Thomistic effort to suggest how bright young historians, tempted by the dead-end of postmodern theory, might think their way back into reality. Her way was, perhaps not too unremarkably, the very way of Aristotle and Thomas in their approaches to the existence of God through the reality of particular things.

> [The postmodernist argument in history] has meant abandoning not only the conventions regarding the presentation and documentation of evidence, but the very idea of historical reasoning, of coherence, consistency, factuality. The postmodernist argument is that these are the "totalizing," "terroristic" practices of an "authoritarian" discipline. But they are also the hard practices of a difficult discipline. Gresham's law applies in history as surely as in economics: bad habits drive out good, easy methods drive out hard ones. And there is no doubt that the old history, traditional history, is *hard*.
>
> Hard – but exciting precisely because it is hard. And that excitement may prove a challenge and inspiration for a new generation of historians. It is more exciting to write true history (or as true as we can make it) than fictional history, else historians would choose to be novelists rather than historians; more exciting to try to rise above our interests and prejudices than to indulge them; more exciting to try to enter the imagination of those remote from us in time and place than to impose our imagination upon them. . . .[16]

This excitement has, as its grounding, not the discovery of some imagined history, of some imagined account of how things might have been were we gods to recount them, but the humble respect for what we can know and for what did happen.

The epistemological skepticism about either our knowing faculties or the moral skepticism about our ability to see beyond your own self-interest can both be faced head on. We can show that skepticism is itself theoretically contradictory. We can experience our ability to subject self-interest to common good and objective reality. We can also follow the path of what happens when we deny in theory either of these bases of thought and morality.

The "silence" of St. Thomas, I think, is of a very different nature from that which professes to be able to account for nothing except what it freely chooses because nothing to contradict our own thoughts can, presumably, affect us. Pieper has stated the alternative well:

> Man, in his philosophical inquiry, is faced again and again with the experience that reality is unfathomable, and Being is mystery – an experience, it is true, which urges him not so much to a communication as to silence. But

---

[16] Gertrude Himmelfarb, "Telling It As You Like It: Postmodernist History and the Flight from Fact," 15.

it would not be the silence of resignation and still less of despair. It would be the silence of reverence.[17]

The "silence of despair," it would seem, would characterize the postmodern enterprise, if by despair we mean that, in the end, what we encounter and can encounter in the world is only ourselves. The "silence of reverence," on the other hand, would grant how little we actually might know about things in their order, but it would recognize that since even the tiniest thing has its existence, its being outside of nothing, from the only source that can cause something to stand out of nothingness in the first place, that our not knowing is but an invitation to knowing, "to receive without having asked."

In his *Approaches to God*, Maritain remarked that "what we prove when we prove the existence of God is something which infinitely surpasses us – us and our ideas and our proofs."[18] What we should not conclude from this is that the effort to know as much as we can about God, the effort to state clearly and accurately what we know about Him and about *what is*, is either futile or contrary to our nature and faculties of knowledge. If we might agree with postmodernism about the vastness of what we do not know about ourselves and the world, we can still agree with the silence of St. Thomas in recognizing that the proper path to understanding what it is we do not know is only through what it is we do know.

"We can never properly grasp this correspondence between the original pattern in God and the created copy, in which formally and primarily the truth of things consists," Pieper wrote.

> It is quite impossible for us, as spectators, so to speak, to contemplate the emergence of things from "the eye of God." . . . The reason for is that things are *creaturae*, that the inner lucidity of Being has its ultimate and exemplary source in the boundless radiance of Divine Knowledge.[19]

The silence of reverence and the humility we need before *what is* are the true sources of excitement, of the real drama of our lot which knows that we did not create ourselves.

Voegelin's remark to a group of students in Montreal, in conclusion, is decisive here: "We all experience our own existence as not existing out of itself but as coming from somewhere even if we do not know from where."[20] This initial experience itself can be misunderstood, deliberately misunderstood, to mean that the source of our own radical experience that we "come from somewhere"

---

[17] Josef Pieper, *The Silence of St. Thomas*, 110.

[18] Jacques Maritain, *Approaches to God* (New York: Collier, 1962), 24.

[19] Josef Pieper, *The Silence of St. Thomas*, 63.

[20] *Conversations with Eric Voegelin*, ed. R. Eric O'Connor (Montreal: Thomas More Institute Papers, 1980), 9.

not ourselves is not primary. The silence of St. Thomas witnesses to the expectant awe of *what is*, of what we did not ask for in the presence of a postmodernism that can listen only to itself. The freedom over the created and the uncreated, the delight of what is yet to come, finds its proper context in St. Thomas rather than Nietzsche precisely because we do not experience our own existence nor that of anything else as coming from out of ourselves. That is, we are agents free enough even to receive a gift, even the gift of ourselves, without our having had to ask for it.

The Deconstruction of
Western Metaphysics:
Derrida and Maritain on Identity

Brendan Sweetman

Many have taken the work of Jacques Derrida to constitute a radical and powerful attack on the whole of the Western philosophical tradition. In a series of books since 1962, drawing on key themes in Ferdinand de Saussure, and in Sartrean existentialism, Derrida has suggested that the central concepts and categories of the Western tradition—substance, sameness, essence, identity, subject, object, inside/outside, etc.—must be *deconstructed*. This means that such notions draw on something outside themselves for their meaning, and this "something" has been overlooked, ignored, and even suppressed throughout the history of Western philosophy. As a result, the zealous desire of Western philosophers to develop a "metaphysics of presence"—a set of concepts which reflect, capture, or otherwise adequately represent reality in human knowledge (however this was conceived by individual thinkers)—has succeeded only in seriously *misrepresenting* it.

Yet despite Derrida's alleged radical attack on Western metaphysics, there has been little *genuine dialogue* between him and proponents of the view he is attacking. Indeed, at first sight it seems that Derrida and his followers, on the one hand, and those philosophers he is criticizing, along with his many detractors, on the other, are like ships passing in the night. Certainly their radically different approaches to philosophy—and especially to the questions of knowledge, language, and meaning—suggest that each side can have very little to say to the other. All of this has been reinforced by popular misconceptions as well as misapplications of Derrida's thought. The upshot of this wide divergence between the two sides is that those who take Derrida seriously are much more likely to be sympathetic to, and inspired by, his work than to approach it from a critical perspective, and those who do not take his work seriously tend to be openly dismissive of his ideas. This has led to an increasing isolation and polarization of both sides. This paper will be an attempt to bridge something of this gap which has opened up between the two camps.

However, I will not attempt to bridge the gap by suggesting that all of these philosophers are really advocating the same position, or that there is sufficient common ground between them from which one could form a consensus view. Rather, I will suggest that *there is enough common ground to enable us to understand both positions fairly clearly—that of Western metaphysics and that of Derrida—and to adjudicate between them.* This move would probably not be welcomed by Derrida, since he resists the view that his work is accessible to systematic presentation, and indeed it has obviously been carefully constructed to resist systematic examination. Nevertheless, I believe that one *can* clearly discern and present the main points of his position in a fairly systematic way, and I hope to illustrate this later. I will go about my task by comparing the general philosophical position of Derrida with that of Jacques Maritain, focusing especially on the notion of *identity*.

My main claim about Derrida's thought can be expressed as follows: he is advancing a thesis (or a view or a theory) about the nature of reality (although he denies this), the key notion of his thesis is the notion of *identity*, and his thesis, although interesting and often profoundly presented, is very implausible and not well supported by argument. My second claim is that Maritain (who I take as an eminent representative of the metaphysics of presence for the purpose of this discussion) advocates a view of identity which concurs with the dominant Western philosophical view attacked by Derrida, and that this traditional view of identity is essentially correct. In the first part, I shall lay out my own understanding of Maritain's metaphysical views on the nature of reality focusing in particular on his view of identity, and employing some of the terminology which will recur in the discussion on Derrida. In the second part, I shall attempt to present as clearly as possible what I understand to be Derrida's philosophical position on identity, and illustrate how this position motivates his attack on the metaphysics of presence. Derrida does not, so far as I know, directly attack Maritain, or Thomistic philosophy, but there can be no doubt that the metaphysics of presence developed by Maritain is a classic instance of the "error" Derrida wishes to expose (and correct) in Western philosophy. Finally, drawing on the analysis in the first two parts, I will present my critique of Derrida's attack on Western metaphysics.

Although I will outline Maritain's view of identity in the first part, I should emphasize at the outset that I believe that the "metaphysics of presence" in Western thought (of which Maritain's view is a particular instance) is correct. In my view, the onus of proof falls on those who would claim that the history of Western thought is fundamentally misguided. Derrida's position is one such position. Moreover, given the radical consequences of Derrida's position, it is of considerable philosophical interest to attempt an assessment of his alternative to the metaphysics of presence. Accordingly, the main objectives of my discussion throughout will be: i) to state clearly Derrida's position; ii) to examine how he supports his position; and iii) to investigate whether or not his position is true, or at least plausible.[1]

MARITAIN ON IDENTITY

Maritain's position on identity is developed in a short section in his main work on metaphysics, *A Preface to Metaphysics*.[2] I shall rely primarily on this work for an elucidation of his view, supplementing it and clarifying it where I think it is necessary, and occasionally expressing his view in language more typical of the language of deconstructionism. This will be helpful when we come to discuss Derrida's position.

Before I come directly to Maritain's position on identity, it will be necessary to sketch roughly the main lines of his metaphysics, for without this background understanding one cannot properly appreciate his view of identity. Maritain fits squarely into that tradition of Western philosophers who hold that being is

---

[1] Richard Rorty draws attention to two different ways in which Derrida has been read by his American admirers. On one side are those who read him as a "transcendental" philosopher, i.e., as a philosopher who is making substantive claims which are either true or false, and for which he offers arguments (and which, if true, could possibly motivate social and political agendas). On the other side are those who see him as having invented a splendidly ironic way of writing about the philosophical tradition in which the playful, distancing and ambiguous features of his texts are emphasized, and not the substance. Rorty prefers to read Derrida in the second way. As a philosopher, I see little value in reading Derrida in the second way. I think the most responsible option is to read him in the first way, especially since this is how he is most often read. Indeed, this is the way in which he *must* be read if his work is to provide philosophical support for social and political conclusions. I argue here that Derrida has little to offer when read as a transcendental philosopher. See Richard Rorty, "Is Derrida a Transcendental Philosopher?" in Gary B. Madison ed., *Working Through Derrida* (Evanston, Illinois: Northwestern University Press, 1993), 137-146.

[2] See Jacques Maritain, *A Preface to Metaphysics* (New York: Mentor, 1962), especially 90-96; see also *Distinguish to Unite or the Degrees of Knowledge*, trans. under the supervision of Gerald B. Phelan (New York: Charles Scribner's Sons, 1959), 82ff; see also *Existence and the Existent*, trans. Lewis Galantiere and Gerald B. Phelan (New York: Doubleday, 1956), 20-55. For an excellent overview of Maritain's metaphysics and epistemology, see Raymond Dennehy, "Maritain's 'Intellectual Existentialism:' An Introduction to His Metaphysics and Epistemology," in Deal W. Hudson and Matthew J. Mancini eds., *Understanding Maritain: Philosopher and Friend* (Macon, Georgia: Mercer University Press, 1987), 201-233.

real, that a large measure of reality is made up of particular beings, and that being can be known. It can be known because there is an essential conformity of the mind to being. Maritain describes being as the "intelligible mystery,"[3] a phrase with which he hopes to convey both the fact that being can be known in conceptual knowledge, and at the same time that being overflows conceptual knowledge. In this sense, being is both mysterious and intelligible. Being as a general term refers to that which exists, or can exist, i.e., to *being as such*; and, according to Maritain, it is this which is the subject of metaphysics.

According to Maritain, one initially comes to know being as such through intuition, a term which he inherited from Bergson, a philosopher who had a significant influence on Derrida. For Maritain, being presents itself as an object of knowledge initially in intuition.[4] Yet unlike Bergsonian intuition, which was non-conceptual, Maritain argues that the intuition of being produces an idea, which is the idea of being in general, or of being as such. This intuition of being as such reveals that being is *transcendental*, i.e., it reveals to the intellect the insight that being is real and is all there is. However, it also reveals to the intellect an insight into the *analogical* nature of being. This is the insight that although all existents have being in common, they also differ by means of their individual essences.

This fact is concretely grasped by abstraction in the act of judgment. In the act of judgment the mind asserts not simply *that* a thing is, but also *what* it is. It grasps a real distinction between the *essences* of things (what they are) and the *existence* of things (that they are). Maritain explains that the act of existing is limited by the essence of a being, which defines the nature of the being. Existence is never given by itself but always with an essence. Nevertheless, both aspects of being are essential features of the nature of reality. The act of existence brings into actuality, if we might put it like this, a potency, which then, because of its essential structure, takes on a certain definite nature, or identity. The essence constrains the act of existence to develop along a certain definite and specifiable path, and maintains the permanence, constancy or *identity* of the object over time, until its demise. This is the structure of reality, according to Maritain, and we get our initial insight into this structure by means of the *intuition* of being. Metaphysical reflection then makes explicit by abstraction and acts of judgment that which has been implicitly revealed in the intuitive grasp of being.

It is important to stress here that Maritain does not hold that *the mind* in the act of judgment divides reality up into that which it has in common (being as such, or existence), and that which gives it discreteness, or separateness

---

[3] See Jacques Maritain, *A Preface to Metaphysics*, 12.   [4] *Ibid.*, 48ff.

(particular beings, essences).[5] Rather, he is saying that *this is the way reality is*, and the mind grasps this fact and makes it explicit in the act of metaphysical reflection. In this way, for Maritain, the intellect knows the thing *as the thing really is*; more generally, the intellect knows reality as it really is. This is because of the essential conformity of the mind to the nature of reality. Maritain is definitely an epistemological realist. This brief sketch of Maritain's metaphysics leads us directly to his discussion of the principle of identity.

Maritain's general metaphysical position must be kept in mind before one turns to his view of identity, for otherwise it might appear as if identity for him is simply a principle of thought, or of the mind. This in turn may lead to the mistaken impression that while he can consistently hold that the world in some sense exists outside the mind, the *essences* or *identities* which the mind grasps might still be *mind-dependent*. If this were the case, Maritain might indeed be guilty of the general charge levelled against Western metaphysics by Derrida. However, it is not the case. For the principle of identity, according to Maritain, is not derived from the structure of the mind, but from the *structure of reality*.[6]

In order for the mind to grasp the identity of an object and to know the object fully as it is, according to Maritain, it is not necessary to appeal to anything *outside* the object. But this is not because the mind constructs the identity of an object, it is because the object really has an essence which is then grasped by the mind in an act of intuition, eventually leading to acts of abstraction and explicit metaphysical judgments. For Maritain, the identity of a thing, therefore, is fully presented in our knowledge of its essence, or nature, because this is the way it really is in the external world. It is the identity of the thing which makes it the kind of thing which it is, and which constitutes its permanence, independence, and constancy over time.

In the language of Derrida, we might say that, for Maritain, being appears to the mind as *presence* (i.e., as an extra-mental self-contained, self-identical reality), but it *also* appears to the mind in its real, particular concrete existences, as *presences*, or as identities. In this way, we capture the univocity as well as the diversity of being. Maritain is careful throughout to say that although the mind grasps the univocity of being, it does not grasp it in its fullness, for being always overflows the mind's grasp of it, overflows the categories of the intellect.[7] The mind in judgment asserts both that a thing is and what it is but only because of the extra-mental nature of being as *presence*, and of being as *presences*. The principle of identity emerges out of this insight, because as Maritain says, "No sooner do we possess the intuition of intelligible extra-

---

[5] *Ibid.*, 93.   [6] *Ibid.*, 94.   [7] *Ibid.*, 51.

mental being than it divides . . . into two conceptual objects."[8] He goes on to say that the mind affirms the following principle: each thing is what it is, where each being "is being given to the mind, and 'what it is' is its intelligible determination. . . ."[9] It is because being both *exists*, and exists *in a certain way*, that the mind grasps the identity of being. And to grasp the "what it is" (i.e., the essence) of a particular being, we do not need to grasp the "what it is" (i.e., the essence) of any other being, or of any feature of another being, or of *anything* outside the being in question.

Maritain, however, goes further. He holds that the principle of identity also means that being is not *non-being*. This means not only that being exists, and in so far as it exists, it cannot not exist, but—and this will be especially pertinent to our discussion of Derrida's position—it also means that being is *self-identical*. That is to say, we do not need to appeal to anything outside of a particular being in order to grasp its essence or nature. Each being is what it is and not another thing. Or to put it another way, each being contains the means of its identity within itself. In order for the mind to grasp this identity it does not need to appeal to anything else outside the object in question. The principle of identity is thus not, as Maritain puts it, "a law of thought but the first law of objects outside the mind. . . ."[10] It is in this sense and this sense only that the principle of identity can be said to be *self-evident*. It is a self-evident principle concerning how the mind grasps beings as presences only because of the actual nature of beings as presences outside the mind. Similarly, the claim that every being is what it is is not, therefore, tautologous because it expresses not only *that* a thing exists but also *what it exists as*. In short, for Maritain, *a thing cannot exist without having an essence, or an identity*.

So, for Maritain, things exist, they are real and mind independent, they have self-identity (presence), and this presence can be understood by the mind without recourse to anything outside the presence. For this is how the presence *is what it is*, and how it is known by us. It is clear, I think, even from these brief remarks that Maritain is an excellent representative of the metaphysics of presence. His notion of essence, or identity, of the individuality of things, of the discreteness and self-containedness of the various objects of our experiences as they present themselves to the mind, is broadly in agreement with that of Plato (forms), Aristotle (substances), Descartes (clear and distinct ideas) and Husserl (essences). However much these philosophers differ among themselves, their basic understanding of reality as presence is the same, and it is surely no coincidence that all of the major philosophers of the Western tradition each held some variant of the notion of *being as presence*. In the

---

[8] *Ibid.*, 91. [9] *Ibid.*, 92. [10] *Ibid.*, 94.

light of this, it is especially important to examine a theory which holds *not* that Maritain's view of identity is wrong in the details, but that, like every significant view of identity before it, it is fundamentally misguided, and completely off track in its very *foundations*. Hence, we turn to Derrida directly.

DERRIDA'S CRITIQUE OF THE MARITAINIAN VIEW OF IDENTITY

I am especially concerned to attempt to state Derrida's main thesis *clearly*, for it seems to me that this is one of the main difficulties with the philosophy of deconstructionism. Derrida and his disciples seldom provide a clear account of the main points of their philosophy. There are varying reasons for this, of course, not least their claim that they are not asserting a philosophical theory, or even a position, at all. This reluctance to state clearly what it is they wish us to take away from their thought has the effect of at once isolating deconstructionism from philosophical debate, while at the same time protecting it from critical examination.

I want to suggest that a main organizing idea, theme, or motif in Derrida's thought is that of *identity*. The main thesis in his thought can be stated in terms of this idea, and most of the central points he makes revolve around this one pivotal notion. The main thesis of Derrida's position can be stated as follows: *all identities, presences, predications, etc., depend for their existence on something outside themselves, something which is absent and different from themselves.* Or again: all identities involve their *differences* and *relations*; these differences and relations are aspects or features outside of the object— different from it, yet related to it—yet they *are never fully present*. Or again: reality itself is a kind of "free play" of *différance* (a new term coined by Derrida); no identities really exist (in Maritain's sense) at this level; identities are simply constructs of the mind, and essentially of language.

In the language of textual analysis, what Derrida is proposing is that there are no *fixed meanings* present in the text, despite any appearance to the contrary. Rather, the apparent identities (i.e., literal meanings) present in a text also depend for their existence on something outside themselves, something which is absent and different from themselves. As a result, the meanings in a text constantly shift both in relation to the subject who works with the text, and in relation to the cultural and social world in which the text is immersed. In this way, the literal readings of texts, along with the intentions of the author, are called into question by Derrida's view of identity. Derrida's thesis, however, is not restricted to books or art works, for texts may consist of any set of ever-changing meanings. Hence, the world, and almost any object or combination of objects in it, could be regarded as a "text."

This is the main thesis presented in Derrida's thought. Further, it is, in my view, one of the central themes of postmodernism. Derrida expresses this thesis every few pages in most of his main works, usually beneath layers of rapidly changing, and often barely penetrable, metaphors, double and triple meanings, multiple references, puns, imaginative and often shocking imagery, etc.[11] This philosophical/literary style may aid his point that an identity both is not what it is and is what it is not, but it also serves to "mask" this main point from the reader. A lot of excavating is required before one can begin the task of philosophical scrutiny. However, I submit that interwoven throughout Derrida's many readings of philosophical texts lurks mainly this one substantive claim repeated over and over again, and that once one discerns his philosophical style, one can read his work quite easily.[12] Moreover, this main thesis of Derrida's is essentially a very simple thesis, at least when considered mainly in the *abstract* (attempting to get more *concrete* about it will cause problems, as we will see later); it is, therefore, all the more easy to assess philosophically. However, before we can begin this task, it is necessary to elaborate further on Derrida's basic thesis.

Derrida's work, like the work of several philosophers before him from the same tradition, who had a considerable influence on him, including Bergson and Heidegger, is best understood or explained in terms of two main realms, or two main levels. In Derrida's case the realms are the realm of reality (or of

---

[8] *Ibid.*, 91.   [9] *Ibid.*, 92.   [10] *Ibid.*, 94.

[11] Derrida's main works include: *Speech and Phenomena and Other Essays in Husserl's Theory of Signs*, trans. D. B. Allison (Evanston, Illinois: Northwestern University Press, 1973); *Of Grammatology*, trans. G. Spivak (Baltimore, Maryland: Johns Hopkins, 1976); *Writing and Difference*, trans. A. Bass (Chicago: University of Chicago Press, 1978); *Dissemination*, trans. B. Johnson (Chicago: University of Chicago Press, 1981); *Margins of Philosophy*, trans. A. Bass (Chicago: University of Chicago Press, 1982); *Glas*, trans. J.P. Leavey, Jr. and R. Rand (Lincoln, Nebraska: University of Nebraska Press, 1986). For a brief but helpful synopsis of Derrida's major works by S. Critchley and T. Mooney, see Richard Kearney ed., *Twentieth Century Continental Philosophy* (London: Routledge, 1994), 460-467.

[12] Many people report (including many who are at home when dealing with complex philosophical issues) that they find Derrida's work unreadable. I believe that there is some justification for approaching much of his work already equipped with an understanding of his main themes. Indeed, some of Derrida's works seem intent on presenting no substantive points at all, and appear purely metaphorical, e.g., his later work *Glas*. It appears as if Derrida's rhetorical strategy in *Glas presupposes* and *depends upon* knowledge of his previous work (which would be all well and good if his general aim was not to deconstruct "knowledge" in the process!). One of the most helpful summaries of Derrida's central ideas that I have seen emerges in his interview with Richard Kearney, in Richard Kearney, *Dialogues with Contemporary Continental Thinkers* (Manchester: Manchester University Press, 1984), 105-126.

différance), and the realm of identities (or of predication and presence). The realm of reality (or *différance*) is the main realm, for him, and by "main realm" I mean that it is *ontologically prior* to the realm of presence. That is to say, the realm of presence, of identity, of predication, must ultimately be understood or explained in terms of the realm of *différance*. The realm of *différance*, however, is ontologically basic. In the realm of *différance*, there are no identities as we understand them, no self-contained presences, which do not depend for their essential being on anything outside themselves. Rather, this is a realm which is *non-cognitive*, which cannot be fully captured by means of any set of concepts, or logical system which makes things "present" to the mind. As Derrida puts it in *Margins of Philosophy*, "It is the domination of beings that *différance* everywhere comes to solicit . . . to shake . . . it is the determination of being as presence that is interrogated by the thought of *différance*. *Différance* is not. It is not a present being. It governs nothing, reigns over nothing, and nowhere exercises any authority. . . . There is no essence of *différance*."[13] So Maritain's view that each thing is what it is and not another thing overlooks completely the realm of *différance*. Maritain has made the mistake of thinking that being, and particular beings, are known by the mind because of the essential structure of reality, whereas it is actually the operating power of naming and predication that produce the "identities" everywhere to be found in his work.

Yet, according to Derrida, the realm of *différance* is also a realm which never occurs *without* cognitive knowledge because our contact with it in human experience always takes place by means of concepts, or predication.[14] It is, therefore, best described by metaphors like *différance* to convey the dual notions of differing and deferring, for *différance* is a realm where *identities are never complete* but are instead always differing and being deferred.[15] This is simply because, for him, the identity of an object *involves its relations*; however, the relations of an object in any system are always changing (differing), and hence meaning (i.e., identity) is forever postponed (i.e., deferred). This realm is also called a *trace*, by Derrida, because the objects of our experience—the identities and presences which constitute human history and human experience—emerge out of it, are somehow "touched" by it, "produced" by it, but are not themselves it. Also, because of their nature as self-identical they do not provide us with any insight (or "conceptual grasp") into this ineffable and inexpressible realm of *différance*. This realm is best hinted at by means of metaphor—because it is the nature of metaphor to

---

[13] Jacques Derrida, *Margins*, 21-25.
[14] See Jacques Derrida, *Writing and Difference*, 112-113.
[15] See Jacques Derrida, *Margins*, 7-8.

signify without signifying, to communicate without communicating, to refer to something without referring to it—and this conveys something of the Derridean notion of *différance*.[16] Derrida employs many different metaphors to make this same point over and over again: margins, trace, flow, archiwriting, tain of the mirror, alterity, supplement, etc. To get round the problem of giving *expression* to the notion of *différance*, Derrida, following Heidegger, sometimes resorts to the practice of *erasure* to indicate that the "object" (understood now in his special sense) is both present *and* not present, since part of its essence is what it is *not*.[17] This brings us to the realm of *presence* in Derrida, and to the *relationship* between this realm and the realm of *différance*.

According to Derrida, identities arise out of (in some way) the realm of *différance* by means of the violence of predication and conceptual knowledge. Since he holds that consciousness is essentially linguistic, we can say that language produces the identities and literal meanings which constitute our world. And it produces *all* of the identities including the identities of the self, of historical movements, of academic disciplines, of cultural and social meanings, even the identities which make logical thinking, and hence "rationality" itself, possible. It is in this sense that language can be said to do violence to *différance*, or that naming and predication are "violent".[18] Let us try to illustrate this point more concretely; in doing so, we can also bring out the remainder of Derrida's essential points.

The identities which human beings grasp in knowledge—of table, chair, desk, of historical events and movements, of the self, of numbers, of moral values, of any self-contained presence, of Maritain's essences—do not really exist. What exists is the realm of *différance* where there are no *presences* in our (human) sense. Rather, the identities which make up human life and experience emerge over time through the violence of naming and predication. It is this predication that makes identity possible at all in human experience. Language and naming make possible the establishment of identities but only because they "abstract from," or "pull out of," the realm of *différance* what is really there not simply, or singularly, as presence, but as (in some way) both presence and absence, in a realm where objects, in the words of one of Derrida's disciples, are "their own differences from themselves."[19]

[16] For a discussion of Derrida's thesis concerning the metaphorical features of philosophical discourse, see his essay "White Mythology: Metaphor in the Text of Philosophy," in *Margins*, 207-271.

[17] See Jacques Derrida, *Margins*, 6.

[18] See Derrida's essay "Violence and Metaphysics: An Essay on the Thought of Emmanuel Levinas," in *Writing and Difference*, 79-153, especially 133.

[19] Barbara Johnson in the Introduction to Derrida's *Dissemination*, xiii.

A further crucial point must now be made. Language and predication produce these identities over history; hence they are not, and are never, the product of any particular *individual* human being. Rather, a particular human being inherits a set of identities already present in the language and culture into which he or she is born, and on which he or she inevitably becomes linguistically dependent. Yet it is obvious that there would be no meanings, identities, presences, if no human beings existed at all. So it is not true to say for Derrida that meaning is *arbitrary*, that, if what he says is true, we are free to interpret any object, or create or produce any meaning, in whatever arbitrary way we wish. While it is true that any meaning (understood in terms of presence) could emerge from history and culture, and that no meaning is sacrosanct, in the sense of being a timeless, trans-historical, or extra-linguistic truth, it is also true that each human subject inherits a set of meanings currently operative in, and constitutive of, his or her cultural and social world. These meanings are operative in our culture, and we as individuals cannot change them by ourselves. Meanings emerge in a flow, a trace, a process of *différance*, but they are not the product of any one individual mind, nor can any one individual mind change them.

It must also be pointed out that Derrida does not claim that the objects of our experience do not exist. Clearly, in some sense they do exist, since the realm of *différance* exists. Yet, equally clearly, the objects or identities of our experience really exist but *not* as they are produced by, or presented to, the mind. For in the realm of *différance*, identities are *forever deferred*. Yet each person will always be born into and will develop into a set of identities and meanings and it is necessary to at least begin philosophical reflection with this set. In this sense, meaning is not locally arbitrary, although it may be ultimately arbitrary.

Maritain—and all of the leading figures of Western "logocentrism"[20]— have been seduced by the notion of being as presence. Maritain, in his desire to explain reality in terms of both the transcendentality and the analogical nature of being—which enabled him to safeguard the Western notions of existence and essence—fails to appreciate the reality of *différance* which is really there, and *which is operative in his work whether he acknowledges it or not.* How are we to handle philosophers who make this mistake? This brings me to the *method* of deconstruction as a way of reading texts.

The history of Western thought has been an attempt to render all of reality intelligible in terms of being as presence. If Derrida is right, this has

---

[20] See Jacques Derrida, *Of Grammatology*, 10-18, and 43, for a discussion of "logocentrism."

obviously been a mistaken approach. It is now necessary, he holds, not to give up on Western philosophers altogether, but to read their work in a different way.[21] In particular, we must attempt to show how their texts, which attempt to explain the nature of reality in terms of being as presence, actually continually presuppose absence, *différance*, relations, etc., at every turn. It is this task which Derrida is supposed to be carrying out, I take it, in his essays on Western thinkers.

I have presented what I believe to be a fair rendering of Derrida's alternative to the Western notion of identity, along with an exposition of his other main points, and radical it certainly is. I now want to move on in the final part of my discussion to consider Derrida's general philosophical *support* for this position, and assess his critique of the Western notion of identity. A main question which will concern me is: what *reasons* does Derrida offer for why we should accept the truth of his central thesis? What reasons does he offer to challenge Maritain's view, reasons which might cause us to suspect that the traditional view of identity might be widely wrong?

IS DERRIDA'S CRITIQUE SUCCESSFUL?

I wish, initially, to reflect on some straightforward logical difficulties facing Derrida's main thesis. Of course, the first point he might make in reply is that he is not offering a theory about the nature of reality. In no sense, he might claim, is he presenting a *thesis*. And in one sense this might be true, if it means that Derrida is trying to avoid advocating yet another theory which explains the nature of reality in terms of *presence* and *identity*. He is keen to avoid this mistake, a mistake he believes both Heidegger and Levinas made.[22] Derrida would add that since *différance* is ineffable and inexpressible one must to some extent use language and concepts, presences and identities, to hint at what is not present, non-identical, non-repeatable, different and absent. All of this I cheerfully grant.

However, despite these qualifications and disclaimers, Derrida does *not* avoid a straightforward *logical* problem which faces his position—that *any* theory, thesis, view, etc., whatever it is, and however it is conceived and presented—is telling us how things *really stand*, or *how things really are*.

---

[21] See Jacques Derrida, *Positions*, trans. A. Bass (Chicago: The University of Chicago Press, 1981), 42-43.

[22] See Jacques Derrida, "Violence and Metaphysics: An Essay on the Thought of Emmanuel Levinas" for a discussion of Levinas; and "The Ends of Man" in *Margins*, 109-136 for a discussion of Heidegger. See also Richard Kearney, *Dialogues with Contemporary Continental Thinkers*, 110.

Insofar as it does this, it is a substantive thesis, and must be firmly within the metaphysics of presence. So not only does Derrida not avoid the metaphysics of presence, but I would claim that it is logically impossible to avoid the metaphysics of presence due to the structure of reality and its relationship to thought. This is a point which Maritain has illustrated clearly in his epistemological realism.

Let me elaborate this point further. The two realms which I have described are part of Derrida's overall view of how things really are. They are supposed to reveal to us how things *really stand*. The realm of *différance*, in particular, tells us that things are never self-contained, never self-identical, never contain their essence simply within themselves, but are always essentially "touched" by those other "things" in the system (whatever this could possibly mean in practice). But since this "touching" is constantly changing and being deferred, meaning, and hence any identities or presences or literal meanings which emerge in and through meaning, are never the whole story. My point is that, if all this is the case, then, for Derrida, it is *true* to say that reality is *différance*, and not presence. This point is clearly supported by the fact that Derrida's works are littered with substantive (or metaphysical) claims *about the natures of language and meaning*, e.g., "The self identity of the signified conceals itself unceasingly and is always on the move."[23] Or: "There is not a single signified that escapes . . . the play of signifying references that constitute language."[24] Or: "Whether in the order of spoken or written discourse, no element can function as a sign without referring to another element which itself is not simply present."[25] These are the *literal meanings* which Derrida wishes us to take away from *his* texts.

Derrida's claim that we must use logic (i.e., identities) in order to hint at the realm of *différance* does not, it seems to me, diminish the force of this point one bit. According to him, reality is *this way* (*différance*) and not that way (presence), it has *this* essence and not *that* essence (however difficult it may be to *specify* the essence.) It is *this identity* which Derrida's work is attempting to convey to us. But if reality is this way, and not that way, then we are still clearly within the metaphysics of presence. Let us call *différance* Y, and Derrida's work X. My point is simply that what is going on in deconstructionism is that X purports to tell us about the nature of Y. One can now substitute whatever one prefers for X and Y (e.g., Maritain's work illustrates the nature of reality in terms of being).

What I am drawing attention to here is just a specific form of a general

---

[23] Jacques Derrida, *Of Grammatology*, 49.   [24] See *ibid.*, 7.
[25] Jacques Derrida, *Positions*, 26.

criticism that can be made of any theory which purports to be anti-metaphysical, in the sense that the theory attempts to rewrite the notion of *identity* in favor of some form of relativism. Derrida's philosophy, when systematically presented and understood, is, I believe, clearly vulnerable to this criticism. It does not seem possible to describe the nature of reality without thereby committing oneself to the metaphysics of presence. Despite the complexity of his exposition, Derrida doesn't seem to come close to developing a theory which avoids the metaphysics of presence. The reply that his theory is not vulnerable to logical difficulties because logic itself is precisely what is being called into question is not available to him either, at least at the beginning of the enquiry. For it is exactly this point about logic which he is supposed to be establishing. This conclusion can only come (if it comes at all) at the *end* of the enquiry. I am suggesting here that this logical problem is insurmountable.

Derrida is advancing what he takes to be the *true account* of the nature of reality, and in this sense he is clearly in the Western tradition. For, if his theory is known to be true, then we can say that his theory is known by the mind (however inadequately) as the kind of thing that it is (precisely as *this* kind of thing, and not *that* kind of thing), and that this "knowing" is dictated by the nature of the object, i.e., by *différance*. In other words, being as presence is still the object of knowledge, just as Maritain claimed. Except that in Derrida's case, it is *différance* which is the "presence" (or object of knowledge), not in the sense that it is present to the mind, of course, since Derrida holds that this is not possible, but in the crucial sense that it *exists objectively* outside the mind, just as being does for Maritain.

If Derrida should reply that he is not presenting a *truth* about the nature of reality, then it really is difficult to know what to make of his work. And he is surely not going to suggest that his theory is *false*. A rejection of this pair of categories altogether may be a good rhetorical device in the attempt to *convey* his account of how things essentially stand, but even here he is, as I have illustrated, firmly within the metaphysics of presence. He might reject the notions of the true and the false, understood as objects of consciousness (and hence as products of predication), and claim that he is simply concerned with a *description* of the nature of reality. However, this move will not succeed either in avoiding the metaphysics of presence, for a description is simply another way of illustrating his main thesis, which he is still putting forward as *true*, and hence as *present*. Derrida's claim that *his own work too can be deconstructed* must be seen in the context of this critical point. For this can only mean (a) that different concepts, metaphors, etc., could be employed to illustrate the reality of *différance*, but it cannot mean (b) that *différance might not be the way things really are*. For if it could mean *that*, then we are back in the metaphysics of presence once again, *and* in the traditional sense!

These are logical difficulties which, I believe, face any position—Derrida's no less than any other—which attempts to reject metaphysics altogether. And, of course, if reality *must* be ultimately understood in terms of presence then we must continue with the traditional debate over which metaphysical account of presence is most adequate. This brings me to consider Derrida's *positive* case or argument for *his* account. Laying aside for the moment the logical difficulties facing Derrida's position, what positive case does he offer for the truth of his views? Here I have to report that I have been unable to find *any* positive argument or supporting reasons advanced in his work in defence of his thesis. I do not think it is unfair to say that he has provided no argument. Rather, his style involves the employment of an abundance of metaphors and rhetorical devices, intermixed with detailed, exhaustive and much-labored readings of classical and contemporary texts, in an attempt to reveal his position. Now let us recall what he is supposed to be revealing. He is supposed to be revealing that reality is *différance*, and that all philosophers who attempt to capture or represent reality as presence, not only distort reality, but actually *presuppose* absence all along. Although *différance* is ineffable, it is, it seems, unavoidable. However, I think that it is clear from a careful reading of any of Derrida's so called "deconstructions" of the work of Western philosophers that rather than illustrate that the philosopher in question *is* using or presupposing *différance*, however unwittingly in his or her text, all Derrida really does is weave into his expository comment and metaphor-laden analysis of the text in question *repeated assertions and statements of his general thesis*. But reasons in favor of this thesis are very thin on the ground.[26]

[26] See, as examples, *Writing and Difference*, 178-181; 278-282; *Of Grammatology*, 6-15; 30-38; 44-50; *Margins*, 7-12; 95-108; 209-219. (Derrida's ambivalence between repetition/demonstration is interestingly alluded to in *Positions*, 52.) As good illustrations of the same tendency in some of the secondary literature on Derrida, see Christopher Norris, *Derrida* (Cambridge: Harvard University Press, 1987), especially Chapters Two and Three. These chapters illustrate two problems which appear frequently in the secondary literature on Derrida. Firstly, throughout Norris's commentary on Derrida's reading of the work of traditional philosophers, Norris offers frequent *statements*, but no *argument* or *reasons*, for his general conclusions. Secondly, he appears to be guilty of making the logically fallacious move from the fact that we *can* (with much inventiveness and energy) read texts in ways other than the literal one, to the fact that this is how we *ought* to read texts, or that there are no literal meanings, or that there is no truth present in a text. The first point may be of aesthetic significance (and it may not), but no *metaphysical conclusions* follow from it. Yet it is metaphysical conclusions which Norris (and Derrida), and others, are supposed to be establishing. See also Jonathan Culler's essay on Derrida in John Sturrock (ed.), *Structuralism and Since* (Oxford: Oxford University Press, 1979), 154-180, for a very readable and clear overview of Derrida's main claims, but one which

It is also interesting to speculate about whether or not a deconstructionist reading of a text could *fail*, or be wrong? If it could not fail, this seems to imply that *any* reading of a text *is* legitimate, and if it could fail, which is surely the right answer to our question, then yet again we are constrained by the metaphysics of presence. For a "correct" deconstructionist reading implies that there is a certain truth (*différance*) which it is our business to reveal in our reading of a text. We must reveal *this*, and not something else. But this pair of identities illustrates again that we are unable to avoid the metaphysics of presence. But it is fuzziness about just these kinds of issues which has rightly earned Derrida and his disciples the reputation for advocating the view that meaning, and standard logic and rationality, are arbitrary.

Not only does all of this mean that Derrida does not appear to give us any reason to accept his view, but it also leads us to ask *why* he does not provide an argument in support of his position. It seems to me that this is because the notion of *différance* is unintelligible in the sense that it seems impossible to give any *meaningful content* to the notion. It appears to be vacuous. *Différance* is not only indescribable, but it does not seem possible to conceive or grasp concretely what it means to say that reality is really *différance*, which, as I have pointed out above, is really to say that there are no identities. It is made impossible partly by the fact that, as Maritain rightly makes clear, the mind through intuition grasps the nature of reality, not only in its existence, but also in its essences, or identities. As Maritain pointed out, this is a self-evident truth. It appears to be simply nonsense to assert the opposite—that the mind (which, for Derrida, means language) "produces" the identities—especially in the absence of *any* clear demonstration of how this occurs.

A parallel case from traditional philosophy will help to illustrate this point. The nature of God, for Maritain, cannot be fully grasped by the human mind, and a certain negative theology is useful in our attempts to gain an insight into the essence of God. However, it is still possible for us to gain some insight into the nature of God; for example, that God is powerful, loving, merciful, etc. Even though our knowledge of God is limited, we can at least know that God exists, and something of the nature of God. But not even a limited knowledge of *différance* is possible. What can it possibly mean to say that the objects or

---

offers no arguments or reasons for why we should accept these claims as true or at least plausible. Dallas Willard argues forcefully in a recent essay that Derrida's view of intentionality is similarly afflicted by the absence of supporting reasons and argument. Willard illustrates that it is not so much that Derrida's account of intentionality is wrong as that it is really no account at all of intentionality. See Dallas Willard, "Predication as Originary Violence: A Phenomenological Critique of Derrida's View of Intentionality" in Gary B. Madison, *Working Through Derrida*, 120-136.

presences of our experience are "their own differences from themselves"[27] or that "*différance* is the systematic play of differences, of traces of differences, of the *spacing* by means of which elements are related to each other."[28] What can it possibly mean to say that the identity of an object is determined in part by its relations to other objects in the same system of meaning, and yet that this is true for all the objects in the system? When Maritain says that the principle of identity is self-evident, he means that we cannot logically conceive of how it could be otherwise. Derrida's notion of *différance* may be likened to the notion of time-travel: when considered in the abstract it is interesting and meaningful in the sense that one can talk about it, but when considered in the *concrete* it is unintelligible.

It is very difficult to find in postmodernist thought *any clear account* of how language in individual minds, and in history, produces the objects of consciousness. It is highly significant that Derrida never provides one concrete example of how this process works. How does language create, produce, modify the objects of consciousness, such as the self, chairs, tables, etc? It is not enough to suggest, with the structuralists, that *a* only derives its meaning in relation to *b*, *c*, *d*, etc; in short, in relation to the other elements of the system of which *a* is a part. While this might be at least *partly* true (and the "partly" here, of course, is crucial), it must be concretely demonstrated in a few cases in order for us to accept it. This is one of the central theses not only of Derrida's thought, but of the whole of postmodernism. Yet concrete illustrations of it are in extremely short supply. It is also crucial to point out that while (i) the meaning of *a* may be partly derived from its relation to the other elements in the system of which *a* is a part, it does not logically follow from this that (ii) the meaning of *a* is *constituted* by its relation to the other elements of the system. It is this second thesis which needs to be established by philosophical argument.

It is certainly *interesting* to suggest that Maritain's notion of identity— where the object is what it is and not another thing, and is known by the mind precisely because this is the ontological structure of reality—might be false. But it is not enough for a philosophical theory to be interesting (especially one with such far-reaching consequences as Derrida's), it must also be plausible. By giving no descriptions of concrete cases at all to support a positive account of intentionality, I cannot judge Derrida's position to be plausible.

By contrast, a detailed and very plausible account of intentionality—of the mind's relationship to being—is to be found in Maritain. One may disagree

---

[27] See note 19 above.
[28] Jacques Derrida, *Positions*, 27.

with some of the details of Maritain's account, but surely his basic insight that the objects of our experience really exist and can be known is not challenged by a philosophy so empty of philosophical content as Derrida's? Maritain, of course, was led to his account by reflection on the nature of reality and how it is known by the mind. Now, however much we may disagree over the details, isn't he right to assert that it is the object in the world which becomes the object of consciousness? Isn't it extraordinarily implausible to suggest—especially without any account of how this occurs—that it is in fact language and predication which somehow "produce" the object, the *identity*?

I have discussed Maritain's position on identity as an illustration of the metaphysics of presence, and Derrida's deconstructionist critique of this metaphysics. I have pointed out the specific logical problems associated with Derrida's position, and also suggested that, even if we leave these problems aside, Derrida seems to offer no *positive argument* in support of his thesis. I have argued that this is because the notion of *différance* is unintelligible. On these grounds, I conclude that Derrida does not pose a powerful challenge to Western metaphysics. Insofar as he has no arguments for his main thesis, he poses no challenge to it at all.[29]

[29] I wish to thank Edward Furton, Doug Geivett, and Curtis L. Hancock for helpful comments on an earlier version of this paper.

Thomism and Postmodernism

Joseph M. de Torre

THE ORIGINAL SYNTHESIS OF ST. THOMAS AQUINAS

From the nominalism and voluntarism of William of Ockham (1300-1350), already adumbrated by the formalism of Duns Scotus (1266-1308), to the skepticism of Montaigne (1533-1592) and Francisco Sanchez (1522-1623), there was a logical development, aided by the so-called religious wars occasioned by Protestantism and, in the previous century, by the Hussite revolt in Bohemia as well as the lingering conflict with the Moslem Turks. The attention of philosophers was diverted to politics, economics and experimental sciences with the consequent weakening in metaphysical insights.

For St. Thomas Aquinas (1225-1274), God is *Ipsum Esse Subsistens*, Subsistent To-Be Itself, while *being* (the object of metaphysics) is conceived as the subject or bearer of the *act* of being: all created beings participate or partake of the act of being according to the capacity of their respective essence (conceived as *potentiality* of being as opposed to *act* of being). Therefore the being of creatures is determined by their manner of being: things are unified in their being (*esse*), and diversified by their respective essences. This variety of participations is the *real* basis for the *logical* attribution of the term—being— to beings, which is an *analogical* attribution, i.e., partly in the same sense, partly in different senses. It is attributed primarily to God, who is the Fullness of Being, whose existence and *creative* activity explains the existence and *productive* activity of all other beings, which only participate being.

The existence of many beings-by-participation implies the existence of One who is by essence (I AM WHO AM) and causes all other beings to be. God is thus the First Efficient Cause. But, since there is no efficient causality without an end and design, God is also the Last End or Ultimate Final Cause, as well as the Exemplary Cause of all beings. Divine Omnipotence (efficient causality) is the result of divine Wisdom (final and exemplary causality). Divine Law is the design in the divine Intelligence (*ratio divinae sapientiae*), while divine Government and Providence are the action of the divine Will. To this deeply metaphysical view of reality there corresponds St. Thomas' classical definition of law as the ordering of reason for the common good, made by him who has charge of the community, and duly promulgated so that it can come to the *notice* (knowledge) of everyone. A community of wills can only exist on the basis of a community of minds and hearts—knowing and loving the same common good.

THE PROCESS OF DECADENCE

This doctrine was profoundly altered, first by Duns Scotus with his conception of being as univocal (as distinct from analogical), i.e., equally applying to all beings in their formality as beings, although, as he says, they are differentiated by their ultimate formality, which he calls thisness (*haecceitas*), which in the case of God consists in his infinity. In other words, what distinguishes God from all other beings is not his radically distinct manner of being (by essence, not by participation), but simply that his being is infinite.

This was joined to a theological voluntarism (things are right and wrong not in themselves, but because God has decided so: will is prior to reason) which became much more explicit in William of Ockham, for whom our ideas have absolutely no counterpart in reality (nominalism), and the only explanation for everything is the omnipotent divine will. Thus for example stealing is wrong because God has decided so, not because it is intrinsically wrong in itself.

These differences were bolstered by the revival of Latin Averroism in Italy in the 15th century. But they had been initiated already in the 13th century by the antagonism of the Augustinian tradition represented by Henry of Ghent, who had a great influence on Duns Scotus and many other Franciscans.

After the death of St. Thomas in 1274, his *Summa Theologiae* was beginning to be widely used as a textbook. But various opponents of Thomism began to write the so-called *correctoria*, i.e., additional commentaries correcting whatever statements in the *Summa* they disagreed with. The Thomists counteracted with what they called *correctoria* of the *corruptoria* and by the end of the 14th century the Dominican friars, who were the bulk of the Thomists, had been ousted from the center of Christian learning at that time, the University of Paris.

In these controversies, however, even though the Thomists put up a spirited defense of their master, in some metaphysical questions they fell into the trap of joining battle on their opponents' terms. This point deserves consideration.

ATTEMPTS AT RECOVERY

The core of St. Thomas Aquinas' synthesis of faith and reason, theology and philosophy, is that "sublime truth" that God is *Ipsum Esse Subsistens*, as Étienne Gilson has shown in many of his works. St. Thomas found this truth in Christian Revelation (a truth of faith: the I AM WHO AM of *Exodus* 3:13-14) and examined it rationally: God is (*esse* = to be). On the other hand, creatures are composed of essence and *esse*, not as of two beings or essences or forms, but of two metaphysical (i.e., purely intelligible, not sensible or imaginable) principles of their total being.

Esse (to be) or *actus essendi* (act of being) is not a thing or essence: it is rather the perfection of all the perfections of an actual being, what makes it both to be and to be known. "A being (*ens*) is that which has being (*esse*)."

What the mind grasps is being (*ens*, not *esse* alone) as composed of *actus essendi* (act of being) and *potentia essendi* (potency of being, i.e., essence or subject or bearer of the act of being). In that composition the *esse* is participated or partaken of by the essence, and related to it as act to potency; it is therefore really distinct from it (a conception far beyond Aristotle's metaphysical range). This marks, for St. Thomas, the infinite difference between the creature and the Creator, in whom *esse* is *really* identical with essence: His essence is to be. This is why St. Thomas never used the word "existence" for *esse*, but left this most luminous and mysterious notion in the infinitive mood of the verb to-be.

"Existence," on the other hand, which began to be used after him by all, including the Thomists themselves, is a noun, and therefore expresses an essence or manner of being, rather than the act of being. It seems as though they could not resign themselves to the fact that our concepts can only grasp at a time only one aspect of the mystery of reality, never all of it at once (let alone the supernatural mysteries revealed by God) that our minds have to learn how to swim, so to speak, in the vast ocean of *esse*, without trying to enclose that *natural* mystery of reality into a concept, even though it is the light in which we are able to form all concepts. Be it as it may, this was real mutation, however much St. Thomas might turn in the grave, seeing the fate of his precious insights at the hands of both his opponents and his followers.

As we mentioned above, still in the last third of the 13th century, just after St. Thomas' death, Henry of Ghent, who was also heavily influenced by the Arab philosopher Avicenna (950-1037), thought that Thomistic philosophy showed dangerous concessions to pagan Aristotelianism. He tried to avoid this danger by means of a Platonist essentialism whereby *esse* was conceived as form of things, which would be expressed by the noun *existentia*. This term, like "to exist," denoted a state rather than an act. That is why St. Thomas does not use it as synonymous with *esse*. For him *esse* is an inner act so to speak, not the accomplished fact of existing. With these premises, Henry of Ghent rejected the real distinction of existence and essence.

Allegedly defending St. Thomas, Giles of Rome (1247-1316) opposed Henry of Ghent by stating that essence and existence are really distinct in creatures, but at the same time accepting this new terminology which implied already the shift to formalism or essentialism. Meanwhile, Duns Scotus and his followers developed a downright formalist philosophy in opposition to St. Thomas.

By formalism here we mean the metaphysical doctrine which, forgetting that the radical act of things is their *esse* (to be), puts the center of reality in the *essence* or in the form. It is practically synonymous with *essentialism*.

This formalist tendency in the conception of being continued in the 11th century and infiltrated the Thomists, including John Capreolus (c. 1380-1444), who in almost all points was a faithful commentator of St. Thomas.

St. Thomas' doctrine had enjoyed the backing of the Popes ever since his canonization by John XXII in 1323. At the Council of Trent (1545-1563), that doctrine rendered great services to the exposition of revealed truth thanks to the work of outstanding Thomistic theologians. Among those who had greater influence at the Council are Francisco de Vitoria (1483-1546), the theologian of political morality, popular sovereignty, human rights and international law, and especially Melchor Cano and Domingo de Soto.

They all, however, continued to show an inclination to formalism, and concentrated on specific points of debate (the religious and political hot issues of the day) without trying to go back to the original insights of their master.

Among them, Domingo Baez (1528-1604) deserves particular attention for his attempt to somehow recover the original notion of *esse*. He did not, however succeed, as he understood it again in a formalistic way, namely as *entitas* or *esse* in *actu*. He continued to refer to the real distinction of essence and "existence," and spoke of the "existence" of the accident as distinct from the "existence" of the substance, whereas for St. Thomas himself the accidents have no *esse* of their own, but rather as *in-esse* (to-be-in): they are actually *in* the substance as participating in the being of the substance (which is the real being properly speaking, *ens cui competit esse per se-ens* is said to be *unum* on account of its *esse*, which is only one for each being). In other words, for St. Thomas accidents are not properly speaking *entia* (beings) but *entis* (of being).

One can see this only if this does not formalize or essentialize or substantialize the act of being by turning what can only be expressed by a verb (*esse*) into a noun (existence or subsistence). *Esse* is not any *thing*, but the *actus essendi*, the perfection of all perfections of any thing, the actuality of being. *Esse* is a *substance*, i.e., a being-by-itself, only when it actually *subsists*, i.e., is-by-itself (God) in all other beings, it is their actuality, which is limited by their potentiality, i.e., by what they can actually be (their essence).

THE TRANSITION INTO RATIONALISM

This inability to see the radical difference between the Creator and the creature as St. Thomas had seen it (the *esse* of creatures is a necessarily limited and therefore differentiated—participation in the unlimited *Esse* of God, who has therefore created them *from nothing*, and so they depend on Him in their *esse* and operations, but with a definite nature, which He, being its Creator, naturally respects), led Baez to affirm that there is not only a "physical pre-motion on the part of God for all operations of creatures, but a "pre-determination," thus coming very close to the Calvinist notion of predestination (which denies the freedom of man), for which he was opposed by Luis de Molina (d. 1600) and other Jesuits defending the freedom of man vis-a-vis divine causality, a controversy which would soon link up with the Jansenist crisis of the 17th century. The Society of Jesus produced a remarkable number of theologians at this time, characterized by both vast erudition and a polemical stand vis-a-vis Thomism. It is not surprising, however, that in view of the type of formalistic Thomism being taught, this new batch of thinkers should continue the trend towards a more and more essentialistic and thereby emasculated and man-centered metaphysics. Their most prominent figure was Francisco Suarez, who was to have a deep influence on future rationalism.

In the 17th century, many Scholastics wrote what they called "Philosophical Courses" in the style of Suarez' *Metaphysical Disputations*, namely, systematic courses tending to petrify a formalistic Scholastic philosophy into a static system of abstractions resembling more and more the ideological system of rationalism, and further and further removed from the original synthesis of St. Thomas Aquinas, although paying lip service to him. It was the age of the Baroque, of the cult of mathematics and of the Apollonian form patterned after the human mind, an age of anthropocentric rationalism coming after the intial onrush of Renaissance humanism, and of corresponding theological decline: a new age of State absolutism and victimization of the Church, with the perpetual danger for the latter to compromise with the earthly or secular city.

The trend continued during the 18th century with a wider infiltration of Cartesian, Leibnizian, Wolffian and even Lockian elements into Scholasticism. On the other hand, among the Protestant thinkers, Luther's original metaphysical phobia gave way to a more systematic and rationalistic approach on the part of Melancthon and Calvin, which led to a kind of Protestant Scholasticism, like that of Leibniz and Wolff, more open to Suarezian metaphysics.

Among the traits of a good number of Scholastics in those centuries, as far as the core of metaphysics is concerned, we can note the following:

> (i) It is considered by some that through *existence* the *essence* is placed "outside possibility and outside causes," with the implication that the essence has already a sort of ideal being of its own without actual existence. Thus, the root of the perfections of something is no longer the *esse* (reduced hereby to mere facticity), but the ideal or possible essence. Contact with concrete things is thus lost, and philosophy becomes more and more abstract, constructed mathematically, with definitions and theorems.

> (ii) They distinguish between essence and existence not as two constituent principles, but as two *states*: in one and the same reality. This foundation is their dependence on the Creator, which is merely extrinsic, since it does not form part of the structure itself of the concrete being. They rightly consider that the creature proceeds from God, but do not admit that created being as such has a real composition of *esse* and essence, thus losing this important criterion of distinction between God and finite things.

> (iii) Every creature is contingent, in the sense that the essence of the creature does not imply its existence necessarily, for God might not have created it. Aquinas' distinction between *esse per essentiam* and *ens per participationem* is replaced by the distinction between Necessary (God) and contingent (creature), a recurrence of Avicenna's distinction between necessary being and possible beings. It is thus overlooked that, as Aquinas explains, contingent creatures are properly the corruptible ones (corporeal), while the spiritual beings (angels and human souls) are necessary, as they cannot cease to be by their very nature (though their necessity is *ab alio*, from another, i.e., from God). What is proper to the creature as *such* is not to be contingent, but to possess *esse* by participation.

APPROACHING OUR TIMES

My purpose is not in any way to claim a monopoly of the truth for Thomism. St. Thomas himself would be the first to reject such a claim: he was always open to the truth as such, regardless of where it came from, and never hesitated to accept truths from non-Christian sources. The aim of what follows is properly historical, to report on the actual events regarding this philosophy, taking into account its objective importance, and its relevance to the humanism of modern philosophy.

Amidst the growing development of the various Cartesian branches of modern philosophy, Thomistic philosophy, anchored in being, went on its course throughout these centuries. Cultivated generally by Catholics, mainly in ecclesiastical environments, the encouragement of the Popes gave it an increasing relevance as a beacon-light in an age of philosophical subjectivism, and as a scientific instrument of reason in the latter's instrumental role with regard to theology. During the twentieth century it has spread to non-ecclesiastical environments, to universities and other teaching institutions, and made its presence felt in many international congresses.

To this has been added an almost total acceptance of the properly philosophical medieval European thinkers, already included in standard textbooks on history of philosophy which usually give prominence to Aquinas, in contrast to similar textbooks of the last century which used to by-pass the Christian centuries for their being rather under theology, thinking that a "Christian philosophy" is not possible.

It has happened sometimes, in the last century as well as in this, that some specific point of Aristotle's philosophy, partially recalled, has triggered a revolution in thought. Thus, for example, recalling that intentionality towards an object is an essential property of knowledge gave rise to the phenomenological method. Another example is the thesis of the substantial form as the soul of the living, which has led some authors to overcome their mechanistic views, toward an understanding of the totality, the configuration of things, the primacy of whole over parts.

There are some modern discoveries which were well-known in Aristotelian-Thomistic philosophy: the primacy of quality over quantity (Bergson), the real priority of the individual person (Kierkegaard), the unity of personality as against Cartesian dualism (personalist psychology), the close union of thought and sensible perception (*Gestalt* theory), the nuclear characteristics of the thinking about being (Heidegger), and the contingency of natural phenomena (modern physics).

DEVELOPMENTS AFTER LEO XIII

As a result of the labors of Leo XIII's pontificate, Thomism began to flourish in almost all theological and philosophical studies, although there was no lack of deviations.

One of these occurred precisely in the school of Louvain and originated with Cardinal Mercier himself; the so-called critical realism, the keynote of which is to admit the Cartesian critical doubt and the starting from consciousness, so as to reach a realism by way of conclusion: it is the so-called problem of the bridge from thought to things. In 1899 Mercier published his *Criériologie générale ou théorie générale de la certitude*, a significant title, as it highlights the extreme importance attached to the critique of knowledge and to the problem of the criteria of certainty. This line was followed by other authors like Descoqs, Rousselot, Picard and Noel. Gilson, in his celebrated *Methodical Realism*, has shown that realism is a primary datum, a starting point and a method, and cannot be the conclusion of a reasoning.

From this nucleus issued the transcendental neo-scholasticism advocated by Joseph Maréchal, S.J. (1787-1944). This author attempts an agreement of St. Thomas and Kant: the transcendental (in the Kantian sense) study of the human faculties and of their tendency to their formal object becomes the *a priori* basis for realism. This dynamism of the intellect towards Being or the Absolute, Maréchal maintains, contains the implicit affirmation of God, and justifies the objectivity of knowledge, thus responding to the Kantian "I think." On Maréchal depend other philosophers like Lonergan and Lotz, as well as theologians like Metz and Rahner. The latter has also attempted an agreement of St. Thomas and Heidegger.

In the last few years, in not a few scholastic authors one can detect a sort of dissolution of Thomism by dint of these attempts of adaptation which gradually recede from the sources, and make increasingly ambiguous and far-fetched interpretations of the texts of Aquinas. Thus there have been attempts to harmonize the philosophy of St. Thomas with Marx, Freud, Husserl, Hegel and so forth. This becomes possible, for example, if the *esse* is interpreted as existence in the existentialist sense, the *intellectus agens* in the constitutive sense (not merely active) of the spontaneity of the thinking act in modern philosophy; the doctrine of the proper object of faculties as the Kantian *a priori*; the *conversio ad phantasma* as the being-in-the-world of Heidegger, and so on and so forth. These are no doubt praiseworthy attempts, but hardly ever satisfactory.

On the other hand, true Thomism, which is not just simple neo-scholasticism, has effectively risen in the 20th century. From *Aeterni Patris* there has been a spread of Thomistic studies in various countries and circles. The thought of St. Thomas has been studied in its own source, clearly distinguishing it from other lines or interpretations within Scholasticism. Historical studies about the Middle Ages and their philosophies have multiplied (Grabmann, Mandonet, de Wolf, Gilson, Vansteenkiste, Walz). The study of the nuclear points of the philosophy of St. Thomas (Del Prado, Geiger, Fabro, Collins, Forest, Lakebrink, Verneaux, Gardeil, Sertillanges, Pieper, Manser and many more) has given rise to a more clear and profound response to the various immanentist philosophies. The Angelic Doctor's doctrine has shown its vitality not only in the abundant teachings of the Popes, but at the hands of various authors (Garrigou-Lagrange, Boyer, Cordovani, Journet and others) to refute Modernist errors and those of the neo-Modernism of the *Nouvelle Théologie*, greatly aided by Jacques Maritain (1882-1973). Under the interpretation of several commentators of later Scholasticism like Cajetan and John of St. Thomas, Maritain has attracted attention as a Thomist in wide intellectual circles and in relation to current cultural issues in education, the arts, sciences and political philosophy. Let it be pointed out, however, that his theses on "integral" humanism and on democratic secular faith, as well as his ideas on personalism, all of them very influential, could lend themselves to diverse interpretations, perhaps through not having been sufficiently worked out and refined. They have been, however, openly endorsed by both Paul VI and John Paul II.

Two authors of particular relevance in the renewal of contemporary Thomism are Étienne Gilson (1884-1979) and Cornelio Fabro (1911). Both have emphasized (the former in the Anglo-Saxon cultural area, and the latter in the Latin-German) that the keynote of Thomism is the notion of *esse* or *actus essendi*. Gilson has successfully popularized the bulk of Thomistic doctrine, while Farbo has delved more directly into its metaphysics (highlighting crucial points like participation, causality, intellectual knowledge of the singular, freedom) and has assessed modern thought in the light of Thomistic principles.

THOMISM TODAY

And finally, what about the so-called postmodernism? If what this term suggests is that modernism is passé, it is logical to look on modernism as ironically antiquated or left behind in the ever progressive march of history. I am aware of the chaotic gibberish of this statement—the type of gibberish so tragicomically dramatized by C.S. Lewis in *That Hideous Strength*.

Those who prided themselves on being modernists thought all the time that this distinguished label was synonymous with being progressive and up to date, having left behind ideas or institutions no longer applicable to modernity. This was their death sentence, as they in their turn would be surpassed by the irreversible march of time. The realization of this *aporia* has led to a deep crisis of the idea of progress and its gradual substitution by the idea of nihilism. Our crisis is similar to the pre-Socratic deadlock between Parmenides' permanency and monism, and Heraclitus' fluidity and pluralism, which led to the Sophists' relativism and the rise of the salvation philosophies and hedonistic ethics of Stoics and Epicureans. But in the midst of all this cultural and socio-political upheaval stood Socrates with his commitment to the truth and his fearless opposition to any form of relativism.

In our time, the idea of nihilism, of "faith in nothing," has crystallized in various forms of anarchism or absolute freedom, sometimes with a Spinozan, Hegelian and Marxian freedom as "acknowledgment of necessity," imposed by the notorious totalitarian regimes so well discussed by Henri Daniel-Rops and Paul Johnson.

The denial of individual freedom through Hume's psychologism, and Freud's pyschoanalysis, has finally led, through the nihilistic moralism of Nietzsche and the drifting existentialism of Sartre, to the more recent deconstructionism of Derrida, quite remarkably counteracted by Paul Ricouer, the most faithful disciple of Edmund Husserl.

After some attempts at constructionism in the Cartesian sense, such as those of Hegel, Dilthey, Nicolai Hartmann and John Dewey among others, the deconstructionists are now trying to devise ways and methods to unmask the secret intentions ("Hermeneutics of suspicion") of all the great thinkers, "determined" in a Marxian sense, by their so-called infrastructure, whatever it may be: language, accepted standards, ecology, traditions, ancestral consciousness, genes, or whatever. One gets an overwhelming impression of massive disintegration.

Heidegger was right in his diagnosis of the crisis of civilization as having lost the "sense of being," though his prognosis was too erratic and multifaceted to provide any sure guidance. The present Pope, on the other hand, pointed to the philosophy of St. Thomas Aquinas as "the proclamation of being," while accepting the positive gains of modern philosophy regarding the value of personal subjectivity.

This philosophy of being, also called *philosophia perennis,* has been "constructed" through the centuries, and St. Thomas would be the first to pay tribute to all those who have contributed to it in any way, regardless of race, religion or culture. But we have good grounds to maintain the unique force and depth of his original insight on the meaning of *esse* and how this is the answer to the crisis of postmodernism. After the dead-end of postmodernism and nihilism, where do we go? Where else can we go but back to the contradictory of non-being, namely *esse*? To be or not to be: that is the question. *Sum, ergo cogito.*

Onto-theo-logical Straw: Reflections on Presence and Absence

Merold Westphal

Reginald, I cannot [continue writing the *Summa*], because all that I have written seems like straw to me . . . compared to what has now been revealed to me.

St. Thomas Aquinas[1]

At the interior of thought, nothing could be accomplished that would prepare for or contribute to determining what happens in faith and in grace. If faith summoned me in this manner, I would close down shop.

Martin Heidegger[2]

What might lead one to abandon one's life work in metaphysical theology as worth no more than straw? One might be awakened from one's dogmatic slumbers by some kind of skepticism, Humean or Kantian, Pyrrhonian or postmodern. There is, of course, a very powerful skepticism at work in the thought of St. Thomas, rooted in his Aristotelian empiricism and expressed both in his deep dependence on Pseudo-Dionysius and in his consistent insistence that "in this life we cannot know God by means of that form which is identical with the divine essence." Although we can employ names that "signify the divine substance," if we take seriously the distinction between the *res significata* and the *modus significandi* we will see that this "does not imply

---

[1] As cited by James A. Weisheipl, O.P. in *Friar Thomas D'Aquino: His Life, Thought, and Work* (Garden City, New York: Doubleday & Co., 1974), 321-22.

[2] Quoted from *Heidegger et la question de Dieu*, trans. Jean Greisch (Paris: Grasset, 1980), 335 by Jacques Derrida in "How to Avoid Speaking: Denials," *Derrida and Negative Theology*, ed. Harold Coward and Toby Foshay (Albany, New York: SUNY Press, 1992), 130.

that we can therefore either define or comprehend God's quiddity."[3] The answer to the question, "Did Paul See God Through His Essence When He Was Enraptured?" may well be yes; but this only signifies that his rapture involved a temporary transcendence of human experience, even under the influence of grace, "in this life."[4]

The constantly recurring phrase, "in this life," in the Wippel essay I've been quoting, especially when juxtaposed to the discussion of Paul's rapture in *De Veritate* and other texts which discuss the beatific vision as the permanence of such rapture in the life to come, are a useful reminder that Thomists are Kantians and not Hegelians, that they do not identify human thought and experience as we now embody them with thought and experience as such. Just because the theology of St. Thomas offers us a knowledge of God that differs radically from divine self-knowledge since it is not a knowledge of God "through his essence," we can say that it is phenomenal and not noumenal knowledge. Thomistic theology is like Kantian physics, for while it claims to show us its proper object as it ought to appear to human knowers, it does not claim to reveal that object to us as it is in itself, as it truly is, as it is for God's own normative knowing. One might even take this to be a kind of Humean warning against extrapolating dogmatically on the basis of our experience to the present moment.

But this is not a very promising path for understanding the strawy silence of St. Thomas. For this skepticism is an integral part of his metaphysical writings, including both of his *Summas*. In the full awareness of this crucial limitation of human knowledge, nay, in vigorous insistence upon it, Aquinas produced a long shelf full of metaphysical theology in a relatively short period of time. Remembering the importance of this negative moment in his thought is a useful reminder both to Thomists and their critics that Thomism is not and cannot be a metaphysics of presence. But it does not throw much, if any, light on those strange words to Reginald.

The reference to St. Paul's rapture as recorded in 2 *Corinthians* 12 provides another approach. It is not skepticism but mysticism that turns metaphysics to straw. Anselm can help us here, I believe. Most discussions of his *Proslogium* do not get beyond the third chapter. (Indeed, some don't get past the second!) But in the twenty-fourth chapter, all congratulations and celebrations at having produced the ontological argument are replaced by an Anselm who seems to

---

[3] John F. Wippel, "Quidditative Knowledge of God," in *Metaphysical Themes in Thomas Aquinas* (Washington, D.C.: The Catholic University of America Press, 1984), 217, 235; cf. 239. My own sense is that to get St. Thomas right we must read his Aristotelianism as radically qualified both by the negativism of the Areopagite and the personalism of Augustine.

[4] *De Veritate*, Q. 13, A. 2.

have stepped forth from the chapter on Unhappy Consciousness in Hegel's *Phenomenology*. Speaking to his soul, he writes, "But if thou hast found him, why is it thou dost not feel thou hast found him? Why, O, Lord, our God, does not my soul feel thee, if it hath found thee? Or has it not found him whom it found to be light and truth?" A couple of chapters later he adds, "Truly, I see not [the unapproachable light in which thou dwellest], because it is too bright for me. And yet, whatsoever I see, I see through it, as the weak eye sees what it sees through the light of the sun, which in the sun itself it cannot look upon. My understanding cannot reach that light, for it shines too bright. It does not comprehend it . . . In thee I move, and in thee I have my being; and I cannot come to thee. Thou art within me, and about me, and I feel thee not."[5]

The verb here is *sentio*, to feel or to perceive. John Smith has put the point nicely by portraying Anselm as eager to exchange the rational necessity of his proof for experiential presence.[6] Anselm longs to see God face to face but knows, that like Moses in *Exodus* 33, he has only been permitted to see God from behind. He would have easily understood Thomas' "like straw," for he would have assumed immediately that to Thomas was granted what he longed for while he was writing chapters twenty-four and twenty-six.

A soldier, separated from her beloved during a tour of duty in Kuwait or Somalia, may carry his picture with her, looking at it repeatedly and even kissing it from time to time. The loss of the picture would be a source of great desolation. But when the two are reunited back at home, it is the beloved and not his picture that gets the kisses, and the loss of the picture would be no great catastrophe. It would be accompanied by no mourning. If it is retained, this would be for sentimental rather than for spiritual reasons. The picture fades into insignificance in the presence of the one pictured. Representation cannot rival its referent. It is in terms like these that Anselm would understand Thomas.

Something like this is, I suppose, the standard interpretation of the end of Aquinas' career as a theologian, and perhaps nothing more needs to be said about it. But the homely soldier simile leaves us a bit uneasy if we dwell on it. For unless we assume (on what evidence?) that St. Thomas remained in a state of ecstasy for the rest of his life, we are left with the question why the theological portrait did not regain its importance after the temporary experience of divine presence. Perhaps this question only shows the limitations of the simile, but we could also take it as an invitation to look beyond the traditional solution.

My years at Fordham University have been fulfilling and fruitful in many

---

[5] *St. Anselm: Basic Writings*, trans. S. N. Deane (LaSalle, Illinois: Open Court, 1962).

[6] This may be in print somewhere. I am drawing on a course he gave in the sixties on the ontological argument.

ways. But there is an element of disappointment, too. It stems from the fact that these years have not overlapped with those of Bill Richardson. I would love to have known him as a colleague. For like so many of you, I am indebted to him in so many ways, not the least of which is his ability to write about Lacan with greater clarity than anyone else I know. In his splendid contribution to a recent *Festschrift* for Adriaan Peperzak,[7] he examines Lacan's suggestion that there is a strong analogy between the "subjective destitution" in which psychotherapy culminates and the "theological" or "onto-theo-logical" destitution expressed in St. Thomas' famous phrase, "like straw" (93-94, 97-98).[8]

This suggestion surely points in a different direction from the one just sketched. In order to appreciate its force we need to notice the difference between Lacanian and Freudian psychoanalysis. Both are, to be sure, atheistic. But in Freud's case the atheism is external. This can be seen in several ways. 1) Insofar as he justifies his atheism, Freud does so by appeal to a generic scientism (nineteenth century positivism, if you like) that has nothing psychoanalytic about it. It neither entails nor is entailed by psychoanalysis. 2) Atheism is not an essential ingredient in the theory of the id and the unconscious, much of which constitutes a better analysis of original sin than most theologians are capable of.[9] 3) Nor is it an essential ingredient in the goals of therapy, whether these are expressed in the slogan, "Where id was, there ego shall be," or in the notion of "transforming [one's] hysterical misery into common unhappiness."[10] Ricoeur is quite right, I think, in saying that Freudian psychoanalysis as theory and practice is compatible with both faith and unbelief.[11]

Lacan, by contrast, seems to have more metaphysics built into the theory and practice of analysis. Theoretically, the real is defined as what "does not work" (98), which I take to be shorthand for the claim that the universe, apart from whatever meanings we may "secrete" (98) into it or try to impose on it, is

---

[7] William J. Richardson, "'Like Straw': Religion and Psychoanalysis," in *Eros and Eris: Contributions to a Hermeneutical Phenomenology/Liber Amicorum for Adriaan Peperzak*, ed. Paul Van Tongeren, *et al.* (Dordrecht: Kluwer, 1992).

[8] Page references given in the text are to the essay described in the previous note, including citations from Lacan.

[9] I have argued this in "The Atheist Dr. Freud as Theologian of Original Sin," Chapter 13 of *Suspicion and Faith: The Religious Uses of Modern Atheism* (Grand Rapids, Michigan: Eerdmans, 1993).

[10] These references are from *The Ego and the Id* and *Studies on Hysteria*, respectively. See *The Standard Edition of the Complete Psychological Works of Sigmund Freud*, ed. and trans. James Strachey (London: Hogarth, 1953-74), 22:80 and 2:351.

[11] Paul Ricoeur, *Freud and Philosophy*, trans. Denis Savage (New Haven, Connecticut: Yale University Press, 1970), 235.

hostile or indifferent to human aspirations. This means that our deepest loss and longing is for an object lost "forever" and "in some primordial way, never to be found again"(94). Successful therapy, therefore, has the character of "desolation" and "destitution" because it has the character of "castration" (94), the permanent loss of the profoundly desired. It is the definitive end to a longing whose futility one has seen through. Therapy finds its fulfillment in seeing that the real "does not work." The clear implication of this view is that religious meaning represents a "repression of the real" (93).

I agree with Richardson's claim that 1) there is a fundamental difference between the "subjective destitution" in which analysis culminates, according to Lacan, and the "theological" or "onto-theo-logical" destitution expressed in Thomas' famous phrase, "like straw" (97, 101); and that 2) for this reason religious meaning, as Thomas understands it, does not necessarily represent a repression of the real (98). Lacan's analogy between completed therapy and Thomas' termination of theology is a bad one, since the differences are more significant than the similarities. Lacanian analysis and Thomas' religion have diametrically different conceptions of the real. For Thomas, as for religious believers of many kinds, the real is neither what "does not work" nor what is lost "forever . . . never to be found again." Freudian therapy, in its theological neutrality, can offer the modest hope of lessened misery and greater freedom. But Lacanian therapy, it would seem, is pure despair. Stoic resignation is before a real conceived as Reason and Logos. But Lacanian destitution is before a real devoid of any saving graces. Whether Christian hope or Lacanian despair is a repression of the real depends on which of the two accounts of the real does a better job of pointing us toward it.

We must not confuse these conceptions of the real with the real itself. They belong to the symbolic and to the imaginary. But this, of course, does not keep them from being dramatically different. Of course, Christians, including Thomas, hold that evil is real in the Lacanian sense, that beyond our capacity to picture or to speak it, it is a mysterious power that cannot be wished away. But the Christian conception of evil differs from the Lacanian sense of the real in two ways. First, to describe it as what "does not work" would be horribly to understate the case. Second, this aspect of the real is not taken to be either original or ultimate. Only the God who is goodness itself is originally and ultimately real.

This discussion already suggests that the Lacanian distinction between human meaning on the one hand, whether in the symbolic or the imaginary order, and the real on the other hand, that always exceeds and escapes not only our pictures but our logos as well, is a distinction that works in the religious context quite well. Anselm and Aquinas are quite aware of the distinction between the conceptual systems they erect and the real they intend, and they are willing at a moment's notice to abandon the former for a direct encounter with the latter.

But this means, to repeat, that onto-theo-logy is not a metaphysics of presence, at least in the forms given us by Anselm and Aquinas. St. Paul says that as long as we are not "at home with the Lord . . . we walk by faith, not by sight" (2 *Cor.* 5:7-8). He says that though we have "the light of the knowledge of the glory of God . . . we have this treasure in earthen vessels" (2 *Cor.* 4:6-7). And he insists that "now we see in a mirror dimly," not yet "face to face" (1 *Cor.* 13:12). The eschatological hope of being one day "at home with the Lord" and seeing God "face to face" sharply distinguishes Christian faith from the Lacanian despair for which the deepest object of our desire is "lost in some primordial way, never to be found again" (1). But this presence is precisely what Christians, following Paul, have understood themselves not to have in this present life. Like Christian thinkers of every type, Thomists need to be reminded of this in order to avoid lapsing into the epistemological triumphalism that sometimes mars their work; and the opponents of Thomism or of Christian thought in all its forms need to be reminded of this in order to avoid the cheap victories that can be gained by refuting a straw man (or woman). No pun intended.

According to one account of the relation between faith and reason, this notion of distance, absence, unhappy consciousness, eschatological hope, etc., characterizes the faith of ordinary believers, the articulation of which is in a symbolical realm deeply enmeshed in the imaginary. Its favorite genre is narrative, the world of moving images. Reason is able to go beyond faith by freeing the symbolic (intelligible) from its ties to the imaginary (sensible), thereby rendering being fully present to the intellect.[12] The paradigm for this has always been Plato's picture of the "pure knowledge" we can have when we "contemplate things by themselves with the soul by itself" (*Phaedo* 66e).

But Plato speaks of this as occurring when we are "rid of the body," and while he sometimes seems to entertain the possibility of a kind of mystical foretaste of glory divine in this life, the notion is for him essentially an eschatological one. Similarly, the later Christian tradition has, if we may put it this way, postponed presence to the future. Mystical experience may provide a preview of pure presence for some individuals on certain occasions, but this will be the normal condition for all only in a hoped for life to come.

It is Hegel who decisively eliminates this element of epistemological hope

---

[12] In *Fear and Trembling*, Kierkegaard allows Johannes de Silentio to frame the entire meditation on the Abraham story between satires on this Hegelian notion of "going beyond" faith.

in a realized eschatology in which the conditions of this life constitute no essential barrier to sheer presence.

Nothing makes clearer, I think, the difference between Hegel and authentically Christian theology, which restricts pure presence to mystical experience and eschatological fulfillment, than the references to Anselm and Aquinas before us. Within the Christian tradition they are paradigms of onto-theo-logy, but their understanding of the difference between faith and reason is not the one sketched above. For them it is the task of faith to go beyond reason, whereas for Hegel is it the task of reason to go beyond faith.

But it is also true that for them, onto-theo-logy, like the narratives and images with which the prereflective believer is content, is one of the ways we walk by faith and not by sight. Or, to put it a bit differently, reason itself is not sight; it is re-presentation and does not preside over presence, and this is not true just of those portions of theology that depend on divine revelation. This, to repeat, is not what Heidegger and Derrida tell us about metaphysics; it is what Anselm and Aquinas tell us about their own theologies.

For both of these onto-theo-logians, metaphysics not only intends what it does not possess, but it knows that it is unable to capture its prey. Thus, if Lacan, in keeping with both structuralist and poststructuralist analyses of discourse points to "discontinuity," "split," "rupture," and "absence" (99); if he is right in seeing the bar between signifier and signified as a "barrier resisting signification" by virtue of "an incessant sliding of the signified under the signifier" (99); and if Richardson's formulation holds, that "meaning is never fixed or permanent" and that "conscious discourse is never without ambiguity" (99), this does not deny to onto-theo-logy a possibility of presence it had claimed for itself. Not only narrative theology but metaphysical theology as well can acknowledge and appropriate such analyses, whenever they are convincing (which I think is very often), as part of what it means that we see "in a mirror dimly."

To be sure, to affirm the existence of God is to point to a closure of "the signifying chain upon a center that would 'hold,' where the signifier and signified would be 'one' in a Supreme Subject-presumed-to-know . . . which would thus become the absolute foundation of meaning" (100). But whose meaning would thereby gain an absolute foundation and unity? Not yours and mine, but that of this Supreme Subject. In a slightly different vocabulary, Climacus says in Kierkegaard's *Postscript* that reality may well be a system for God, but not for us.[13] Onto-theo-logy points to a self-presence, an absolute foundation, a closure

---

[13] Soren Kierkegaard, *Concluding Unscientific Postscript to Philosophical Fragments*, trans. Howard V. and Edna H. Hong (Princeton: Princeton University Press, 1992), Vol. 1, 118.

and unity of meaning, but it does not, in its authentically Christian forms, purport to be or to possess any of this. It refuses both the Hegelian inference that if this perfection is real, we must be its embodiment here and now, and the postmodern inference that since we are not such an embodiment, this perfection is unreal. This is because postmodernism and Hegel have a deep, if often overlooked, affinity. Neither is able to entertain the possibility of a real difference between the human and the divine. Unlike the theologies of Anselm and Aquinas, both treat the human as absolute.

All of this implies that the difference between the God of the philosophers and the God "before whom David made music and danced" (97, 101) may not be as great as our Jansenist friend, Blaise Heidegger, would lead us to believe. This is one of the most helpful insights, I believe, to be found in Richardson's paper. It is not likely that David was inspired to sing and dance by meditations on "that which cannot be conceived not to exist" or on the God of Israel as *Ipsum Esse Subsistens*, though I think it possible that Anselm and Aquinas had as deep an experience of the divine presence from these activities as David did from singing and dancing. My point is simply that in both cases the sense of divine presence is qualified, is less than the sheer presence that the Bible describes as seeing God face to face and philosophers have tried to describe as either immediacy or totality.

Ricoeur says that the believing soul is "an unhappy consciousness; for him, unity, conciliation, and reconciliation are things to be *spoken of* and *acted out*, precisely because they are not *given* . . ."[14] I believe this applies to religion as celebration as much as to religion as confession. The kinship of our onto-theologians and Heidegger's dancing David is expressed, I think, in this parallelism between *speaking of* and *acting out* that which is not given. So far as the speaking is concerned, the real differences between narrative, liturgy, and metaphysics do not make a difference in this context. Short of experiences that radically transcend the conditions of our present being-in-the-world, whether they be mystical or eschatological, religion is at once naïve and sentimental, the experience of presence and absence inseparably intertwined. There is something of an acoustic illusion about contemporary claims to have discovered this chiasm.

With help from Richardson, Lacan came upon the scene as the possibility of a non-traditional reading of the silence of St. Thomas. The result, it seems to me, has been twofold. First, Lacan fails to throw fresh light on the situation because the analogy between therapeutic and onto-theo-logical destitution is not very convincing. Second, in recognizing this we have been forcefully

---

[14] Paul Ricoeur, *The Symbolism of Evil*, trans. Emerson Buchanan (New York: Harper and Row, 1967), 167-68.

reminded of the difference between onto-theologies of the Hegelian sort, which merit the epithet "metaphysics of presence," and onto-theologies of the authentically Christian sort, which do not.

I want to suggest, however, that Lacan's suggestion that a certain "destitution" is at work in Thomas' "like straw" may have more (and different) truth to it than he suspects. Toward the end of his essay, as part of his argument against Lacan that religion is not a repression of the real, Richardson finds at "the center of the Christian religious experience . . . 'a crucified Christ: to the Jews an obstacle they cannot get over, to the gentiles foolishness'" (100-101; 1 *Cor.* 1:23); and he remembers that the Paul who wrote these words also said, "I am crucified with Christ . . ." (*Gal.* 2:20). I want to suggest that these themes, rather than Lacan's bad analogy, might point us to an alternative reading of the famous words, "like straw."

Is it possible that when Thomas speaks to Reginald of "what has now been revealed to me," he points to a specifically Christian and not generically theistic experience? Might it have been the meaning of Christ and not the essence of God that generated "the loss of the metaphysical structures that had allowed him to speak and write intelligibly about God . . ." (101)? Might it have been, to be more specific, the meaning of the life and death of Jesus, rather than his resurrection and ascension as the Christ that suddenly dawned upon him, Jesus in his lowliness rather than Christ in his glory?[15] Might it have been a realization of what Jesus had done for him and of the call to become himself an *imitatio Christi* that silenced his speculative pen?

Objection 1. But Thomas was well acquainted with the gospel narratives about the life and death of Jesus and could hardly have spoken about them as "what has now been revealed to me."

Obj. 2. But there is no evidence to support this view, and there is a longstanding tradition to the contrary. You haven't proved your case.

Obj. 3. Even if the light of the cross had shined into Thomas' life in a new way, what reason is there to think that the result would be the abandonment of systematic theology?

Reply Obj. 1. As Hegel never tires of reminding us, the familiar, just because it is familiar, may dwell beside us without being really understood. To be familiar with the narratives about Jesus' life and death is one thing. To be seized by the import of this story is quite another.

---

[15] Kierkegaard makes this distinction crucial to his understanding of Christianity in *Practice in Christianity*, trans. Howard V. and Edna H. Hong (Princeton: Princeton University Press, 1991. See especially 24, 36, 108. Contrary to widespread opinion, it is this book more than any other, including the *Postscript*, that gives Kierkegaard's deepest understanding of the meaning of Christian faith.

Reply Obj. 2. The only evidence I know to support the suggestion I am making is the fact that it was while he was writing on Penance that Thomas gave up on writing.[16] This is anything but conclusive evidence, although it seems to me that there is no more and possibly less evidence in support of the traditional view. Still, to the charge that I have not proved my case I would plead guilty if I were trying to prove a case, which I am not. I am rather inviting us to entertain a possibility, which means that the question is not so much how it was with Thomas as how it will be with us.

What I am posing might be called the Bonaventure question. Is it possible, as Bonaventure tried so assiduously to do, to unite St. Francis with Alexander of Hales by developing a speculative metaphysics that would never lose sight of the life and death of Jesus? Or is it the impossibility of this task that was revealed to Thomas (or which became clear in the light of what was revealed)?

Reply Obj. 3. As long as the answer to the Bonaventure question remains open, and I shall not try to close it, no definitive reply to the third objection can be given. But it is possible to sketch a path that is open to reflective faith, even if it is not clearly necessary. When the light of the cross shines into our lives in a certain way, it dawns on us that the question of how we live in its shadow is more important than making good our theoretical escape from the shadows of Plato's cave. The latter task, just to the degree that it offers us the mastery of knowledge, suddenly loses its all-consuming importance in relation to the possibility of seeking to become like the suffering servant. Whether theory in any form can survive the dawning of such a light is a question we cannot afford to be finished with too quickly.

---

[16] James Weisheipl, O.P., *Friar Thomas D'Aquino: His Life, Thought, and Work*, 321.

Aquinas and Heidegger:
Personal Esse, Truth, and Imagination

Robert E. Wood

The theme I want to address is the interrelation of the notions of truth, imagination and being. Our exploration will attempt to look at the relevant phenomena through the eyes of two thinkers: Thomas Aquinas and Martin Heidegger. Beginning with a relatively comprehensive exposition of Heidegger on the notions involved, we will go on to present a preliminary exposition of Aquinas. We will then shift into an interpretive attempt to read Aquinas through Heidegger so as to develop a kind of fusion of horizons between the two thinkers. [1]

I

Heidegger claims to think the ground of metaphysics in a level of truth which is said to found the traditional and Thomistic notion of correpondence: *aletheia* founds *orthotes*. [2] *Aletheia* articulates the being of human reality, *Dasein*, as Being-in-the-world. Being-in-the-world is beyond subjectivism, is the way in which the being of things draws near or recedes by being the way the whole opens up as providing the framework of meaning for the beings that appear. [3] Being-in-the-world is indwelling, lived inhabitance, and has its own mode of thinking given primordial expression in the arts. [4] To that extent,

---

[1] For a fuller discussion of both thinkers and a delineation of the context within which I approach them and others, see my *A Path into Metaphysics: Phenomenological, Hermeneutical and Dialogical Studies* (New York: SUNY Press, 1990).

[2] Martin Heidegger, "On the Essence of Truth" in D. Krell ed., *Martin Heidegger: Basic Writings* (New York: Harper and Row, 1977), 117ff.

[3] Martin Heidegger, *Being and Time*, trans. J. Macquarrie and E. Robinson (New York: Harper and Row, 1962), 78ff and 249.

[4] Martin Heidegger, "The Origin of the Work of Art," in *Poetry, Language and Thought*, trans. A. Hofstadter, (New York: Harper and Row, 1971), 48ff.

imagination has a certain primacy in understanding human existence and the modes of exposure of the totality corresponding to it. Thinking at this level is appreciative thinking, thanking rooted in the *thanc*, the heart, non-sentimentally understood as the unified center of human existence which allows things and persons to draw near within the totality of significance.[5]

The peculiarity of what Heidegger is after can be clarified by his distinction, paralleling the distinction between *orthotes* and *aletheia*, between two modes of thinking, what he calls *representative-calculative thinking*, requiring the peculiar gifts of mathematician or scientist or philosopher who operate at the level of what we have come to call "intellect," and *meditative thinking*, which belongs to humankind as such and which operates in terms of the "heart." The latter mode of thinking is appreciative thinking that indwells in things so that they are allowed to draw near and place their claim upon us. If the former is grasping and conquestive, the latter learns to "let things be," i.e. be manifest in the claim they lay upon us.[6]

What is at stake for Heidegger is thinking the ground of metaphysics, for *Dasein* is the being for whom Being is disclosed.[7] For traditional philosophy thinking the ground of metaphysics is a meaningless effort since metaphysics is precisely the discipline whose task it is to think the ultimate ground, beyond which there can be no further ground: metaphysics thinks being itself.[8] Heidegger, on the contrary, claims that metaphysics takes place under the pall of *the forgottenness of Being*.[9] Again, a meaningless claim for traditional philosophy: metaphysics is precisely the thinking of being qua being, in contradistinction to other disciplines which think being qua quantified or qua biologically constituted and the like.[10] But Heidegger has transformed the question of the meaning of Being: he retains the traditional idea that Being is ultimate, but he denies the traditional idea that metaphysics thinks the ultimate. Heidegger claims that there is an ultimate which metaphysics does not think. Metaphysics thinks in the sphere of what has come out of concealment but does not think unconcealment itself—something which, Heidegger remarks,

---

[5] Martin Heidegger, *Discourse on Thinking*, trans. J. Anderson and E. Freund (New York: Harper and Row, 1962); cf. also *What Is Called Thinking?*, trans. J. Glenn Gray (New York: Harper and Row, 1968), 138ff.

[6] Martin Heidegger, *Discourse on Thinking*, 54-6.

[7] Martin Heidegger, *Being and Time*, 32-35.

[8] Aristotle, *Metaphysics*, IV, 1003a17.

[9] Martin Heidegger, *Introduction to Metaphysics*, trans. R. Manheim (New Haven, Connecticut: Yale University Press, 1959), 18, 19, 25.

[10] Thomas Aquinas, *Commentary on Boethius'* De Trinitate, ed. B. Decker (Leiden: Brill, 1965), qs. V-VI and ST., I, 85, 1, ad 2.

may contain "a hitherto unnoticed hint concerning the nature of *esse*."[11] In thinking what has come out of concealment, metaphysics formulates propositions whose correspondence with what shows itself can be checked. For metaphysics, then, truth is *orthotes*, correctness, correspondence. For Heidegger, thinking of Being is thinking of the granting of the sphere of unconcealment. This entails the thesis that the sphere of unconcealment is not identical for every epoch. But that also entails thinking concealment and thus mystery.[12] The experience of truth as unconcealment contains a negation.[13] What is granted, the sphere of unconcealment, conceals what grants.

Part of Heidegger's evidence for the epochal character of metaphysics is the history of metaphysics. Unlike other sciences such as mathematics or physics, there is no single agreed upon science of metaphysics. Though each school claims to have achieved *the* metaphysics, none have succeeded in persuading other schools to that effect. Heidegger's contention is that something else is operative, beyond the argumentative and constructive power of each metaphysic: that which grants the peculiarity of a metaphysic, the peculiar opening out of a space of meaning within which that metaphysic operates, the coming to pass of the emergence of Heraclitean Logos, the gathering which bestows meaning both chronologically and ontologically prior to the emergence of logic.[14]

Heidegger's second published book, *Kant and the Problem of Metaphysics*, suggests that the root of metaphysics is the imagination.[15] Here Heidegger compares Kant's two editions of his *Critique of Pure Reason*, claiming that in the first edition Kant was moving toward the problem of the imagination as at the root of metaphysics, while in the second edition he backed away from that consideration.[16] Kant's central problem, the possibility of metaphysics, was, as in the case of Descartes, provoked by the marked contrast between stability and progress in mathematics (but also in logic and, since Descartes's time, in mathematical physics) and the continuing wrangling that characterizes the history of metaphysics from its inception to the present day.[17]

[11] "The Way Back Into the Ground of Metaphysics," in Walter Kaufmann ed., *Existentialism from Dostoevsky to Sartre* (Cleveland: World Publishing, 1956), 211.

[12] "On the Essence of Truth," *Martin Heidegger: Basic Writings*, 132ff.

[13] Martin Heidegger, *Parmenides*, trans. A. Schuwer and R. Rojcewicz (Bloomington: Indiana University Press, 1993), 16.

[14] Martin Heidegger, *Introduction to Metaphysics*, 120ff, 128ff, 170.

[15] Martin Heidegger, *Kant and the Problem of Metaphysics*, trans. J. Churchill (Bloomington, Indiana: Indiana University Press, 1962).

[16] *Ibid.*, 166ff.

[17] Kant, *Prolegomena to Any Future Metaphysics*, trans. Carus, revised by J. Ellington, (Indianapolis: Hackett, 1977), 1ff, 25, 38ff; Descartes, *Discourse on Method*, trans. D. Cress , (Indianapolis: Hackett, 1980), 4-5.

Heidegger gives an exposition of Kant's treatment of the relation of sensation as reception to understanding as spontaneity, where, initially, sensation provides the data which understanding conceptualizes. The bridge between the two is the function of transcendental imagination which provides the schemata linking the two roots together.[18] Understanding occurs in terms of a three-fold and simultaneously occuring synthesis: the synthesis of apprehension in sensibility, the synthesis of reproduction in imagination, and the synthesis of recognition in the concept. In his interpretation, Heidegger links the three with present, past and future orientations respectively, and finds the unity of the three in the transcendental unity of apperception, the "I think" which, he claims, is identical with originary temporality.[19] Transcendental imagination, temporality and self-awareness coalesce as *Dasein*, as human reality. *Dasein* is a process which, opening up the meaning of Being within which things can appear over-against awareness *as* something, founds subjectivity and objectivity. Heidegger maintains that this function is more primordial than the split between sensibility and understanding, viewed in the tradition as lower and higher faculties, but also between individual and community—though *Dasein* is "in every case mine."[20] A determinate opening out of the whole of being which is granted us in each epoch and in the tradition as a whole establishes the relation between individual and community and, simultaneously, the relation between intellect and sensibility.

The Kant-book's suggestion that the imagination plays a key role in the fundamental configuration of the whole that dominates each epoch implies that the role of metaphor cuts more deeply into the work of intellect than its traditional peripheral assignment would claim. In his "Dialogue with a Japanese" Heidegger speaks of the imagination operating in a twofold direction. On the one hand it is inclined to scatter itself in all directions; but on the other hand, it performs a fundamental gathering that opens up the spheres of thought.[21] Here we see a convergence with his interpretation of Heraclitean *logos*. In his later thought, the gathering is the coming to presence of the authentic thing, the *Ding* as assembly of the fourfold: earth and sky, mortals and immortals.[22] Here is the sphere of operation for poetry as the linguistic ground of all the arts.[23] Through poetic thinking things are allowed to draw near and human beings learn to

[18] Martin Heidegger, *Kant and the Problem of Metaphysics*, 93-118, 144-177.

[19] *Ibid.*, 178ff.   [20] Martin Heidegger, *Being and Time*, 67.

[21] Martin Heidegger, *Discourse on Thinking*,

[22] "The Thing" in Martin Heidegger, "The Origin of the Work of Art," in *Poetry, Language and Thought*, 174.

[23] "The Origin of the Work of Art" in Martin Heidegger, *Poetry, Language and Thought*, 72ff.

dwell rather than, on the one hand, to slide along the surface in everyday adjustment or, on the other, to master, whether conceptually-logically or, following therefrom, technologically.[24]

We might consult the history of science for a paradigm of epochal thinking operative at a less encompassing level than the opening out of a view of the whole but displaying some important features relevant to understanding Heidegger's basic thesis. Heidegger presents a view parallel to that of Whitehead and made popular more recently by Thomas Kuhn.[25] For Heidegger, natural science operates out of a fundamental projection of the groundplan of nature: it determines ahead of time what is to count as nature. So we see a fundamental paradigm shift from an Aristotelian to a Newtonian view of nature. Instead of Aristotelian natures each seeking their natural ends within a hierarchy of natures, we have a single Nature, indifferent to value, composed of atoms contained within empty space and time moving according to invariant mechanical laws.[26] Nature is imagined differently, a new view is created and thereby a new demand laid upon thought. It holds sway insofar as it allows operations of exploration to occur within its confines. The projection of nature in modern natural science is essentially tied to the ability to control: it is, in essence, technological.[27]

But the scientific world operates within the more encompassing lifeworld which is a cultural world that allows for possibilities of operation, including but also encompassing scientific operation within its confines. It contains a projection of the fundamental groundplan of the whole as a sphere of thinking, acting and feeling. It too changes over time within a culture and differs from culture to culture. For Heidegger such projection is the primordial work of imagination.

But he sees a continuity in the projection of the meaning of being in the Western tradition. Beginning with the Greeks, Western thought has operated under a two-fold unthought approach to Being. On the one hand, Being is conceived of as standing presence, dominated by the Now;[28] on the other hand, Being is thought from the angle of production.[29] In ordinary Greek, the

[24] Martin Heidegger, *The Question Concerning Technology*, trans. W. Lovitt (New York: Harper and Row, 1977), 17-20.

[25] Alfred North Whitehead, *Adventures in Ideas* (New York: Free Press, 1967), 155ff *et passim*; Thomas Kuhn, *The Structure of Scientific Revolutions*, 2nd ed. (Chicago: The University of Chicago Press, 1970).

[26] Martin Heidegger, *What Is a Thing?*, trans. F. Wieck and J. Glenn Gray (Chicago: Regnery, 1967), 80ff.

[27] Martin Heidegger, *The Question Concerning Technology*, 119.

[28] Martin Heidegger, *Introduction to Metaphysics*, 202-206.

[29] Martin Heidegger, *Basic Problem of Phenomenology*, trans. A. Hofstadter (Bloomington, Indiana: Indiana University Press, 1992), 99ff.

term *pragmata*, that which has been done, is one of the dominant terms for things—as is the Latin *facta*, that which has been done. In Plato, both these meanings—standing presence and producedness—coalesce in the notion expressed by the terms *eidos* and *idea* as the unchanging and universal face things present to what we have come to call intellect which thinks of archetypes in accordance with which the *demiourgos* mythically fashions things.[30] The *ousia* of things is their participation in eternal Forms which are productive patterns. In Aristotle, beings thought in terms of the four causes are thought from the perspective of a productive process in which an agent imposes a form upon matter for a purpose. Agency imposing form for a purpose is then read into the nature which agency so operative presupposes.[31] And in Hebrew-Christian thought productive agency is again the primary metaphor, only the Aristotelian hyletic presupposition which is always *hypokeimenon*, always lying there beneath formative activity, is itself viewed as produced—though now "from nothing."[32]

For Heidegger, then, it would seem that imagination grants both a sphere for human dwelling and the unthought metaphors that factually guide metaphysical construction. Imagination so conceived is closely linked to the notion of the heart that underlies the split between understanding and sensibility and between theory and practice.

II

We move now to a treatment of Aquinas. In the opening question of *De Veritate*, truth is spoken of in three ways: in its basis in the things themselves, in the correspondence of the intellect to things, and in the manifestness or showing of things.[33] In a later Thomistic way of speaking, correspondence is thought of in three directions: logical truth is correspondence between our judgments and things; practical truth is correspondence between things and our concepts; ontological truth is correspondence between things and their Divine Ideas.[34] In the first case, failure is error; in the second case, botched activity; in the third, monstrosity or evil.

One has to think this correspondence in terms of our mode of access, and thus the mode of manifestness of the things in question. Whatever is received

---

[30] *Timaeus*, 28ff.   [31] *Physics*, II, 1-3, 192b8ff.

[32] Martin Heidegger, *Basic Problem of Phenomenology*, 118.

[33] *De Veritate*, I, 1.

[34] Cf. for example Robert J. Kreyche, *First Philosophy* (New York: Holt, Rinehart and Winston, 1959), 183ff.

[35] *ST*, I, 12, 4 and 84, 1.   [36] *ST*, I, 76, 5.   [37] *ST*, I, 84, 7 and 85, 1 and 2.

is received according to the mode of the recipient.[35] Since we do not have an intuitive intellect, we must be receptively related to what is to be known.[36] Such receptivity is rooted in sensibility which is linked to things affecting us at a certain limited level as related to the needs of our organism. Imagination retains sensations and links them by association into phantasms, which are more orchestrated appearances than sensations, enriched through time.[37] Intellect actively operates upon the given as so limited to construct concepts, whose combinations in judgment have to be checked against what is initially presented in sensation.[38] But this process, according to Aquinas, never penetrates to the essential principles, so that logical truth remains essentially incomplete and ontological truth is finally unavailable to us. We do not know the essential principles of even so simple a thing as a fly;[39] and, indeed, regarding God, we know best when we know that we do not know.[40]

These declarations do not express an absolute agnosticism, since we do know modes of manifestation and what can be derived therefrom—and these are known as continuous with the wholeness of things in the wholeness of Being. The latter is presented as goal for our natural striving as intellectual beings but is never attained to as goal, at least in this life. Discursive intellect begins with the notion of Being[41] and with the sensorily given (correlated with the manifestness of our own interiority as organically and metaphysically desirous). It must construct its understanding, and in this the work of the imagination is indispensible.

Aquinas' formal treatment of the imagination is restricted to a part of an article on the distinction of the internal senses.[42] Following Avicenna, Aquinas lists as internal senses *sensus communis, phantasia, imaginatio, vis estimativa* and *memoria*. He appeals to the general principle that powers are distinguished by objects. *Sensus communis* operates in conjunction with the external senses in the work of apprehension. It is the single root of the soul's external sensory powers[43] by which we are able to compare the intentions of each of the senses and be aware that we are performing the particular sensory act.[44] It is thus a mode of self-presence, of awareness of awareness. Aquinas reduces Avicenna's *phantasia* to *imaginatio*, having the function of retaining intentions received from the external senses. The *vis estimativa* or instinct (a term expressive of contrast with intellect but positively uninformative in itself, merely pointing

---

[38] Cf. *ST*, I, 16, 2 and 17, 3.

[39] *Commentary on Aristotle's* De Anima I, 1, no. 15; *Disputed Questions on Spiritual Creatures,* 11, ad 3; *On Truth,* 4, 1, ad 8.

[40] *On the Power of God*, 7, 5, ad 14.   [41] *De Veritate*, I, 1.   [42] *ST*, I, 78, 4.

[43] *Ibid.,* ad 1.   [44] *Ibid.,* ad 2.

to the future of the study of animal behavior)—estimative sense perceives intentions of beneficiality or harmfulness not received through specific senses, and the *memoria* retains such intentions. The latter seems an odd way to treat memory, but it underscores a tendency to recall what is related to our perceived needs and to forget what is not: we do not remember everything but, for the most part, what has pertinence. Live memory, as distinct from mechanical recording, essentially involves forgetting. In human beings, the estimative is transformed or subsumed under intellectual activity as *ratio particularis* or *vis cogitativa* which is said to compare individual intentions—a function already assigned to *sensus communis*. Under similar relation to intellect, imagination in human beings is able to create imaginary forms. This is apparently the power Avicenna called *phantasy*.

With this brief explication of Aquinas' treatment of the internal senses, I want next to provide an interpretation which moves toward a "fusion of horizons" with the movement of Heidegger's thought.

III

Having divided the interior senses, it is necessary to relate them. It would, I think, not do violence to Aquinas here to view the power of sensation as such, i.e., the *sensus communis*, not only as the root of the external senses, but also as the root of the internal senses. Retention of intentions, pressed further along Husserlian-Derridian lines, is essential for any appearance to occur, so that "imagination" with its "storehouse" function is involved in the initial sensory appearance.[45] But the recognitional aspect in the appearance of things also requires the entry of the longer-term past into the present: the recognitional appearance involves a gestalting process, a configuration of the *sensa*. This is perhaps what Aquinas means by the *phantasm*. It is not clear to me whether this is the work of the imagination, of the common sense, of cogitative power or of the three together. But as Aquinas remarks, the imaginative work of combining and separating is an act of the composite.[46] The term 'phantasm' is rooted in *phainomai*, I appear. It is that which makes configurational appearance possible. The terms "species" and *intentio* in this context underscore the dimension of appearance insofar as *species* is itself appearance, manifestness,

---

[45] Cf. Edmund Husserl, *Phenomenology of Internal Time-Consciousness*, trans. J. Churchill (Bloomington, Indiana: Indiana University Press, 1964), especially 50ff; Jacques Derrida, *Edmund Husserl's* Origin of Geometry: *An Introduction*, trans. J. Leavey (Lincoln: University of Nebraska Press, 1989), especially, 57ff and 134ff.

[46] *ST*, I, 84, 6, ad 2.

and *intentio* is the transcendence of itself by awareness dwelling in the manifestness of the bodily given other.

But in the human case, appearing is not simply a configuration tied to appetite and functioning without the further elaboration of thought. Thought enters into the constitution of appearing by reason of association with what we know from other sources: thought provides recognition of what is sensorily presented now and imaginatively gathered from the past. In so doing, thought anticipates the future of fuller disclosure. Furthermore, the way thought anticipates is tied essentially to what we want to be and thus to how we make our fundamental choices.

In living our lives, though general principles are crucial, equally crucial is that they be applied to the changing contexts of experience—thus particular reason, comparing individual intentions. Particular reason, we suggest, is, in us, the active phase of imagination. Here one has to gain a comprehensive sense of the concrete context; one has to have gathered up and retained a richness of concrete experience— and this is the work of imagination. One has also to be able to enter imaginatively into the lives of others in order to act prudently in relation to how things appear from the others' mode of being-in-the-world. This is, indeed, one of the presuppositions of rhetoric, an essential aspect of political prudence. One has to be able to come to terms creatively with novel situations and for this one must be able to project alternative ways of acting. It is the arts, I would claim, that advance these capacities.

One problem with a faculty analysis is the tendency to substantialize and separate the faculties. There is no human imagination—or, for that matter, human sensation—without human intellect. The construction of models, the imaginative construction of a work of art, the opening out of a world for human dwelling are sensory-imaginative-intellectual operations, or, as Aquinas has it, the operation of the composite. Rather than speaking of "the intellect" doing this and "the imagination" doing that, it would be better to speak of doing something intelligently or imaginatively where it is a matter of emphasis within a totalistically functioning field of awareness.

The expression "particular reason" becomes problematic and appears as an oxymoron with the initial determination of intellect as the faculty of the universal over against the individual. But perhaps we are systematically misled in these matters by this initial determination. One could work here at our fusion of horizons between Heidegger and Aquinas via an interpretation of the notion of *intellectus agens* as orientation toward being as a whole.[47] Through our

---

[47] Cf. Karl Rahner, *Spirit in the World*, trans. W. Dych (New York: Herder and Herder, 1968), 132ff. Aquinas' treatment of *intellectus agens* is found in *ST*, I, 79, 3-5 and *SCG*, II, 76-78.

orientation toward the whole via the notion of being ("being in a way all things"),[48] abstraction of form is rendered possible since intellect is always already beyond the here and now of sensation and emptily with the whole. Abstraction from the sensory involves locating the sensorily given within the whole of space and time, for we know the universal to apply any time and any place. Then space and time, in a way, must be given apriori. And, as Kant noted, space and time are not originally concepts but individual wholes (about which we can also form concepts), furnishing the essential frame of sensibility, since everything which appears sensorily appears in space and time given as indeterminately surrounding any empirically given spans of space and time.[49] Space and time are thus linked essentially to the operative power of imagination which, as particular reason, compares individual intentions appearing within space and time.

And intellect, though initially discriminated from sensation through its apprehension of abstract universality, is nonetheless, because of its orientation toward being, referred to the concrete wholeness of each thing wherein alone, for Aquinas, being is found. *Imagination* functions generally in grounding both abstraction and conversion, the latter of which gives access not simply to abstract intelligibility but to concrete *esse*, so that to know being truly and completely, a conversion to phantasms is essential.[50] Further, in reflecting upon itself, self as intellect is present to its own individual *esse*,[51] for it is not individuality that is incompatible with intellect but only materiality.[52] But of course the psychophysical self is not intellect, so that concrete self-understanding is, in a way, like the understanding of another, something essentially on the way. In any case, the mind's orientation toward being, which includes absolutely everything in its scope, grounds Aristotle's observation that *nous* apprehends *both* the universal principle and the ultimate particular.[53]

The orientation toward the whole, characteristic of mind, also makes freedom of choice possible,[54] and choice involves concrete alternatives disclosed by a creative employment of imagination. Human beings create institutions, art-forms and scientific models that both expand and mirror (within the limits of the disclosive power of the models) the character of concrete *esse*. Understanding a person involves imaginative entry into his/her world, for his/her being is a mode of being-in-that-world as a variation on the general theme of belonging to intersecting sets of common worlds. Understanding both common worlds

---

[48] *Commentary on Aristotle's* De Anima, III, 8, 431b 21.
[49] Immanuel Kant, *Critique of Pure Reason*, B37/A23ff.
[50] *ST*, I, 84, 7.   [51] *Ibid.,* I, 85, 2.   [52] *Ibid.,* I, 86, 1.
[53] *Nicomachean Ethics*, VI, 1143b.   [54] *ST*, I, 82, 2.   [55] *Ibid.,* I, 32, 1, ad 2.

and individual persons is a matter of learning to grasp particularized *Gestalten* within which general principles operate. Understanding the being of human reality is not fulfilled unless it terminates in such imaginatively configurated *Gestalten*.

Because of the creative power of imagination in constructing a lifeworld, common sense in its functioning as fundamental orientation in the life-world is essentially historical. And both its general structure and the declarations of ontological fixity arising out of the Aristotelian tradition still remain dashboard manifestations in relation to the essential being of any encounterable entities and of our very selves which remain deep wells of mystery.

Likewise because of the creative power of imagination vis-a-vis the sensorily given other, the natural sciences operate to "save the appearances."[55] This means that there are alternative construals possible for understanding—and that means linking together in a coherent way—our observations and inferences. Alternative construals at one level involve imaginative models. Models are, in Thomistic terms, phantasms which, in Heideggerian terms, allow things to appear in a certain way. There is an objectivity to the appearance, a non-arbitrariness to the model-construction, but also an historical relativity in the whole project. We advance in our understanding of nature; but still do not know the final constitutive principles, the essence, of even the simplest of things, even a common fly—though, as someone properly remarked, "I know one when I see one." Functionally we are able to abstract "phenomenal essences," constancies in ways things have of appearing expressively within the circle of sensation. We thus are always possessed of an essential "dashboard realism."[56] One can work at the progressive uncovering of principles-for-us, but things-in-themselves remain deep wells of mystery to which we may also gear our explicit attention. That is what Heidegger has chosen to do.

But there is a further consideration: through artistic disclosure things and persons are "brought near," and we gain a deepened sense of the mystery of their being in the whole. Jacques Maritain, the patron of this society, is one who has gone quite far in this direction, in developing access to *esse* which is more than grasping a system of essences whose link to individual existence is acknowledged through the judgment. On the one hand he stressed "the intuition of being" as a kind of spiritual sense, an enhanced awareness of being-outside-nothing, to which Heidegger's moment of vision in the realization of Being-toward-death is a concrete path.[57] On the other hand, Maritain gave significant

---

[56] This is a modification of Owen Barfield's felicitous expression in *Saving the Appearances: An Essay in Idolatry* (New York: Harcourt, Brace and World), 28-35.

[57] Jacques Maritain, *Preface to Metaphysics: Seven Lectures on Being* (New York: Mentor,

attention to artistic creation and the apprehension of the concrete individual *esse* of human subjectivity involved therein.

In spite of Maritain's deliberate intent to be a "paleo-Thomist," right from the beginning of *Creative Intuition in Art and Poetry* we are placed in a different spiritual landscape than that of Aquinas. The author announces that poetry is "intercommunication between the inner being of things and the inner being of the human Self which is a kind of divination,"[58] while for Thomas poetry is *infima veritas,* lower truth useful for communicating to the uneducated.[59]

Of course, for Maritain this does nothing to alter the fundamental metaphysical framework within which his explorations are located and which he seeks to develop. But for Heidegger, the deepening of our understanding of personal *esse* through the arts is involved in epochal shifts in our understanding of what he calls the onto-theo-logical framework within which alternative metaphysical construals emerge. For Heidegger what does seem to remain fixed is the fundamental structure of *Dasein*. And what is most important to notice is that this is not merely a matter of a Kantian apriori, at least insofar as, through his conception of the apriori, Kant sets up the realm of appearance in such a way that we cannot gain access to things-in-themselves.[60] For Heidegger, on the contrary, the realm of appearance *is* the disclosure (as well as the simultaneous concealing) of things-in-themselves.[61] Where Heidegger differs from Aquinas is in his claim to the perspectivity of the way in which that disclosure occurs.

In understanding Aquinas himself on this matter, it is essential to come to terms with the two agnostic disclaimers to which we have already called attention: that we do not know the essence of any creature, not even something so simple as a fly; and that we know best about God when we know that we do not know about God. The latter fits in with his late declaration, apparently based on some mystical experience, that all he has written is straw.[62] All three declarations point to common ground with Heidegger: that whatever truth-claims we make take place within the finite conditions of human cognitive structure. All *aletheia,* all unconcealment of entities, takes place within the hidden

---

1962), 48-64 and *Existence and the Existent,* trans. Lewis Galantiere and Gerald B. Phelan (New York: Doubleday, 1957), 28ff.

[58] Jacques Maritain, *Creative Intuition in Art and Poetry* (Princeton: Princeton University Press, 1977), 3.

[59] *ST,* I, 1, 9.

[60] Immanuel Kant, *Critique of Pure Reason,* B45/A30 and B295/A236ff.

[61] Martin Heidegger, *Being and Time,* 51-55 and 249.

[62] Cf. James Weisheipl, O.P., *Friar Thomas d'Aquino,* (Garden City, N.Y.: Doubleday, 1974), 321ff for the sources.

background of the *lethe*, the essentially concealed to which, nonetheless, we as humans, via the notion of being, are essentially related. The sense of the *lethe* is the essential mystical sensibility, the sense of mystery that provokes the essential awe which gives rise to and sustains philosophy as the question of the meaning of Being.[63] But the dominance of logic in the tradition and the dominating thrust of modern science tend to move us away from the sustaining ground of awe into the realm of cognitive and practical mastery. It is in the arts that such awe gains essential expression, provided art is not understood as surface decoration provoking fine feelings.

Philosophy and art ontologically understood are rooted in the structure of *Dasein* as sensorily grounded, culturally mediated reference to the whole whose center lies in the thoughtful heart and whose correlate is the coming to presence of unfathomable mystery surrounding the least thing. Its vehicle of expression is the fundamental work of the imagination, which grants the sphere of encompassing dwelling, the derivative sphere of philosophic thinking, and the even more derivative sphere of scientific-technological thinking that currently has us in its grips. Heidegger's thoughtful approach to the ground of metaphysics has changed the terms of philosophic discussion and reopened the question of the relation between philosophy, science and the arts. In so doing, it holds much common ground with Aquinas, but invites a different look at the role of the arts which runs parallel with the work of Jacques Maritain.

---

[63] Martin Heidegger, *What Is Philosophy?* trans. S. Kluback and J. Wilde (New York: Twayne, 1958), 78-85.

Epilogue

Preserving our Memory

Curtis L. Hancock

The essays in *Postmodernism and Christian Philosophy* acquaint us with the main outlines of postmodern philosophy and diagnose its strengths and weaknesses. Additionally, the book has special value in that it asks about the genesis of postmodernism, which naturally encourages many contributors to examine contrasts between postmodern philosophers and earlier thinkers, even ancient and medieval ones. As a result, this volume adds to our stock of knowledge about the history of philosophy. This epilogue will complement the efforts of these earlier essays by reflecting specifically on the relationship between postmodern thought and modern philosophy (especially seventeenth and eighteenth-century thinkers), a discussion that will also emphasize the need to keep our memory about the history of philosophy supple and intact.

Preserving our memory is not as easy as it may seem, for among the many currents that flow through the history of philosophy is the stream of *Lethe*. Philosophers quench their thirst at these waters at their own peril. Yet so chronic is their visit to this spring that forgetfulness and its consequences seem to be central features of the history of philosophy. The whys and wherefores of philosophical amnesia so fascinated Étienne Gilson that he was inspired to write one of the twentieth-century's great books on the history of philosophy: *The Unity of Philosophical Experience*, wherein he argues that sometimes philosophers, having forgotten their own ancestry, will credit to themselves philosophical views that really define an earlier time. What is only imitation, a given age may mistake for novelty. Were Gilson alive, he would appeal to this observation to correct a misplaced nostalgia that often seizes certain writers commenting on postmodernism. While none of the contributors to *Postmodernism and Christian Philosophy* suffers from this blinding nostalgia, authors elsewhere often succumb to the sentiment. This epilogue supports the historically sensitive philosophical work of the present volume by challenging these authors. I refer to writers who long to reclaim modern philosophy, "the age of reason," which they regard as the halcyon era in the history of philosophy, a time when knowledge and value were the goals of philosophy and when the human mind was considered adequate to attain them. This attitude for these writers is prescriptive: "if we could but retrieve the principles and methods of modernism," they say, "we could escape from our postmodern malaise; if we could recover the confidence of a Descartes, a Hume, or a Kant, then all would be right for philosophy again."

The reason that such comments would pique Gilson's historically sensitive antennae is that he knew that the principles and methods of the most influential modern philosophers—Descartes, Hume, and Kant—are really the same in kind as the views of "mainstream" contemporary philosophers. James Marsh in his fine article aptly characterizes postmodernism as an assault on rationality. But studies on postmodernism should also acknowledge that modernism itself, perhaps unwittingly, had already begun that assault. Accordingly, modernism does not really offer an alternative to postmodernism. In terms of philosophical content, these two periods are of the same cloth.[1] The age of reason, in spite of its intentions, was the unhappy progenitor of subjectivism: an intellectual calamity which led ineluctably to skepticism and nihilism, so descriptive of the postmodern malaise. Since the modern philosophers operate within the same limits and according to the same assumptions as the postmodernists, to escape the postmodern cul-de-sac will require finding an exit different from any pathway charted by modernist thinkers. The early prophets of postmodernism—writers such as Nietzsche and Heidegger—were right in judging that modern philosophy was itself *proto*-postmodern; that modernism would eventually crash into the rock of twentieth-century irrationalism. If there is a difference between the two periods, it is largely rhetorical: the postmodernists are more self-conscious and honest about the limitations of their own principles. Contemporary skeptics no longer harbor the illusion that the philosophical assumptions on which modern philosophers based their work can sustain an awareness of reality and objective value. The postmodernists, no longer cowled by philosophical proprieties, have been so impolite as to question whether in fact modern philosophers were not wearing a mask.[2] They

---

[1] This position has been intriguingly argued by Theodore Young in his provocative essay, "Secular Gnosticism and Classical Realism," *The Modern Age*, Winter, 1995, 124-134.

[2] Descartes himself admits to wearing a mask in his "Cogitationes privatae" (see entry for January, 1619): "Just as actors, who are advised against appearing on the stage with a blush on their face, put on a mask, I too enter, with a mask on, the theater of the world in which I have so far lived as a spectator" (*Oeuvres de Descartes*, 10:213). This cryptic remark has been interpreted by Stanley Jaki in *Angels, Apes, and Men* to mean that Descartes masqueraded at being a human, flesh-and-bone, philosopher, when, in fact, his philosophy presumed that his mind was

have exposed the charade, charging the modernists with having professed to be, perhaps unwittingly, what they were not: philosophers committed to the efficacy of reason and the attainment of truth. To Gilson, who looked to ancient and medieval philosophers as his mentors and who had few allegiances either to the fashions of modernism or to the trends of postmodernism, this assessment would seem uncontroversial. To his Thomistic kinsmen who still retain their memories, I suppose this summation is likewise obvious. But I fear that there are yet some thinkers who stubbornly cling to the belief that modern philosophy is different in kind from postmodernism and that a return to modernism is a remedy to postmodernism. Perhaps in this epilogue I can disabuse them of their stubborness by refreshing their memories; perhaps the antidote of *anamnesis,* even if administered in a small dose (which is all I can offer here), will help them to see that our hope is in vain if its object is to restore modernist solutions to our postmodernist problems.

In two of his most engaging works, *Three Reformers* and *The Dream of Descartes,* Jacques Maritain explained in unequivocal terms that the seeds of skepticism and nihilism which would bring modernism to its close were planted in the philosophy of René Descartes. We cannot return to Descartes' way of philosophizing, Maritain insists, without again commiting the "great French sin" of subjectivism. This sin is more akin to an angelic fall than to mere human error, for, according to Descartes, man's knowledge is like that of the pure spirits: innate, intuitive, and independent of things. This last characteristic does not prevent Descartes from advocating that the mind knows real existents. For Descartes, once a clear and distinct idea is grasped, it discloses an essence that presumably puts the mind in contact with real things. But, of course, this *apriorism* is naive. It is an excuse for angelism. In reality, Descartes' severance of the intellect from things condemns the human mind to have only its own contents as its objects. While Descartes envisions an epistemology assured of contact with reality, his own assumptions destine his philosophy in fact for solipsism. The intellect's ideas are not that by which things are known; instead they are the objects, the termini, of knowledge itself. Since ideas do not originate

---

really angelic. This illusion, however, bankrupted reason. Since the human mind is constrained to know things by means of the senses, a limitation the angels do not suffer, then Descartes' theatrics condemn him to dire epistemic errors (see my comments on Descartes below). Peter Redpath, in a stirring forthcoming work, *Cartesian Nightmare: Wisdom's Odyssey from Philosophy to Psychotheology,* explains that Descartes' impersonation of the angels requires him to invent a new art of rhetoric which he mistakes as philosophy, a criticism having parallels in Maritain's *The Dream of Descartes,* where he accuses the Father of Modern Philosophy of being only an "ideosopher," rather than a philosopher.

in knowledge of things, they are innate. But Descartes is unable to show that this innateness conforms to reality. This ironically shows just how unlike an angel Descartes' philosopher really is. An angel's mind is directly illumined by reality; whereas the mind of Descartes' philosopher is a lamp illuminating nothing but itself. When Descartes abandoned the mind's conformity with reality as the starting-point of philosophy, he initiated a new measure of intelligence: to think *more geometrico demonstrata*; to exercise thought's reflection on itself as the aim of philosophical inquiry, perfectly exemplified in mathematics. Descartes' legacy would make the principal worry of philosophy consistency of thinking and not contact with reality. Rather than elevating man to an angel, Cartesianism in fact debases man by bankrupting his intellect. Such an impoverished angel strikes one as an imposter. Descartes is not only impersonating an angel but a philosopher too, Maritain charges, for a philosopher that can only reflect on the contents of his own mind is a philosopher in name only. Descartes' "philosophy" might be better named an "ideosophy," thinking about thinking, taking ideas, rather than things, as the objects of knowledge.

After Descartes, philosophical culture responds predictably. The angelic pretense is soon found out. Before long, man is stripped of the title of pure spirit; in fact, he is denied spirit at all. In time the assumption prevails that man is only a body. The angel's mathematicism of spirit becomes mechanism and manipulation of quantities. Clear and distinct ideas are just atomistic elements in a stream of consciousness. Clarity and distinctness become arbitrary; consistency of thinking becomes a chimera, a cultural bias. Hence, the tragic product of Descartes' pursuit of truth ends in skepticism; his optimism about a science and morals that befits an angel ends in a technology and a nihilism that threaten to make the fallen "angel" now less than human. The dream of Descartes becomes a nightmare.

This proto-postmodern disruption of intellect is only compounded by Descartes' descendants, most notably David Hume and Immanuel Kant. In spite of Hume's vaunted empiricism, he has his own taste for apriorism. His prized assumption—that whatever is separable in thought is distinguishable in fact—generates his doubts about causality, since, if the concept of "cause" is distinct from the notion of "effect," then cause can be denied of effect without contradiction. Accordingly, he commits metaphysics, ever so dependent on causality, to the flames. Without the order of causation, Hume's philosophy devolves into phenomenalism, abandoning even Descartes' *cogito*. The self is dissolved along with the intellect's grasp of anything beyond mere sensation. Man is by no means an angel. He has become an animal. Not even science can survive Humean skepticism: laws of nature and predictability are swept aside once causality is dismissed as mere habit, a characteristic of the mind, which itself is just a rather loosely organized collection of perceptions.

Moreover, morality as traditionally understood is also swept away by Hume's assumption because, if existence or fact can be logically separated from the notion of value, there is no requirement that acquaintance with facts informs us about good or bad, right or wrong. Never mind that the assumption— "whatever is separable in thought is separable in reality"—is arbitrary. Nowhere does Hume attempt to prove it. It nonetheless serves the Enlightenment well, appearing to sweep away at once metaphysics and objective ethics. These results have proved highly influential. In fact, Hume's assumption, especially its fact/ value implication, Nietzsche takes as axiomatic at the dawn of postmodernism.

Kant's reputation as one who salvages Hume from the ruins of skepticism and restores some certainty to experience has received much press in histories of philosophy. However, Kant's achievement is undermined by the nagging subjectivism which seizes his effort to overcome skepticism. Even Kant has to admit that belief in the external world is still the scandal of philosophy. His philosophy, which makes "reality" itself just a category of the mind (along with "actuality" and "existence"!) cannot bridge the gulf between subject and *noumenon*. His latent Cartesianism can give us at best only a phenomenal world, a condition for the intellect which someone once described as the "solipsistic cyclorama." Even Kant's admission that knowledge begins in sense-perception is so qualified as to nullify any step toward realism. For Kant sensation is (using the language of classic realism) only the occasion, not the cause, of knowledge. External things in themselves are not known or involved in the processes of cognition. The forms of sensibility structure sensuousness but offer no contact with extramental sense objects in themselves. The transcendental aesthetic can only provide the possibility of sensations structured by the *a priori* forms of space and time, something akin to Mill's *phaneron*, but it cannot furnish extramental reality. Nor can Kant's later efforts to give us contact with reality through morality or teleology succeed, for the very arguments he constructs to bridge the gulf between the phenomenal and the *noumenal* rely precisely on those categories that he explained earlier are constrained to structure subjective experience only. Once awakened Kantian-style from our dogmatic slumbers, we can only continue to ride the solipsistic carousel.[3]

---

[3] For a lucid account of how Kant's suppositions drive us to solipsism and to postmodernist consequences, see Raymond Dennehy, "The Philosophical Catbird Seat: A Defense of Maritain's *Philosophia Perennis*," in *The Future of Thomism*, editors Deal W. Hudson and Dennis Wm. Moran (Notre Dame, Indiana: The University of Notre Dame Press, 1992), 65-76.

My comments are brief (as befits an epilogue) but sufficient. I offer only the reminder that the heart and soul of modern philosophy—which is Cartesian rationalism, Humean phenomenalism, and Kantian transcendentalism—will not give us back reality or the mind's sufficiency to understand it, the twofold loss which describes the lament of postmodernism. Hence, so long as postmodernists look to modern philosophers for solutions, they will be engaged in a pointless task. Modern philosophy gives us no solvent to dissolve the bonds of postmodernism.

Is there, then, no escape? Fortunately, egress is available because philosophy does not begin with Descartes. There is another more salutary tradition to which the philosopher can turn, a tradition which can offer a solution because it rests on a philosophy of the human person radically different from that of the modernists. According to this more agreeable account, the human mind is not a detached intellect sorting among its own contents for knowledge. Instead, man is a rational animal situated in a world informed by ordinary experience, reflection on which is this philosophy's starting-point. This is a philosophy that does not lock itself into a vicious circle looking for a presuppositionless beginning. The capacity for knowledge is not something to be proved in advance. To offer that proof is already to suppose it. Instead, the alternative is to liberate and exercise the philosopher's genuine critical powers by letting experience of actual, extramental things provide the source of philosophical reflection. It is not presuppositionless, but it is critical because it recognizes at the outset that the Cartesian alternative is a march down a blind alley. Accordingly, this is a tradition that does not begin with angelism, the hubris that leads to the disastrous consequences with which postmodernism now grapples. It is better to recover a tradition in which man is neither an angel nor an animal. Instead, he is a rational knower, but one of flesh-and-blood, situated in history and culture and humbly dependent on sensory awareness of actual things as the content-giving causes of knowledge.

This is the tradition of philosophical realism that harks back to Plato and Aristotle. Gilson labeled it the "Western Creed," and he believed that the health of Western Civilization depends on keeping it. If this vision has defined the West, then it is no surprise that as the West has lost its grip on this ideal it has imperiled its own existence.[4] That Creed flourished among the ancient Greeks and afterward was supported by certain medieval philosophers who recognized

---

[4] My concluding remarks draw significantly from Peter Redpath's recent provocative essay, "The New World Disorder: A Crisis of Philosophical Identity," *Contemporary Philosophy*, December, 1994, 19-24. This work presages certain conclusions that Redpath will discuss at length in *Cartesian Nightmare*.

that reason and faith rightly support one another and that the rational health of the human mind is necessary for the integrity of the faith itself. But the Western Creed began to erode when Descartes initiated the proto-postmodern malaise. There is of course no going back now to embrace the Western Creed in just the way the Greeks or the Medievals did. We must accept, perhaps with a touch of irony, an important historical truth: however much modern philosophy has failed us, we ourselves are a product of modern times. But this does not mean that no retrieval of the Western Creed is possible. Recovery of an alternative pre-modern tradition is possible even if it must be adapted, perhaps paradoxically, to our own time, which is imprinted significantly with the legacy of modernism. We are ourselves modern peoples and we must live in and for the age into which we are born. Still, we can restore to health the Western Creed and let it define our culture in a way *analogous* to what it meant for the Greeks and the High Scholastics.

Near the end of *The Unity of Philosophical Experience* Gilson asks whether "a social order begotten by a common faith in the value of certain principles [can] keep on living when all faith in these principles is lost?" This is an important question to ask as postmodernism threatens the survival of the Western Creed. The essays in *Postmodernism and Christian Philosophy* help us better appreciate the momentousness of Gilson's question and give us the opportunity to reflect on ways to rejuvenate our Western Creed and thereby initiate the era of *post*-postmodern philosophy.

Contributors

BENEDICT M. ASHLEY, O.P., is Professor Emeritus of Aquinas Institute of Theology, St. Louis. He is a memeber of the American Catholic Philosophical Association, the Catholic Theological Society, and the American Maritain Association, and has published *Theologies of the Body: Humanist and Christian* (1985), *Spiritual Direction in the Dominican Tradition* (1995), *Justice in the Church: Gender and Participation* (in press), and with Kevin O'Rourke, *Ethics of Health Care* (2nd ed., 1994), and *Health Care Ethics: A Theological Approach* (4th ed., in press).

DON T. ASSELIN, an Associate Professor of Philosophy at Hillsdale College in Michigan, has written several reviews and scholarly articles on Maritain. He is the author of the book *Human Nature and Eudaimonia in Aristotle*. He also has published in the areas of ethics, medical ethics and the philosophy of religion.

MICHAEL BAUR, Assistant Professor in the School of Philosophy at The Catholic University of America, received his Ph.D. from the University of Toronto. He is currently pursuing legal studies at Harvard Law School and is working on a translation of J.G. Fichte's *Foundations of Natural Right* for Cambridge University Press.

DAVID B. BURRELL, C.S.C., is currently Theodore Hesburgh Professor in Philosophy and Theology at the University of Notre Dame, and has been working since 1982 in comparative issues in philosophical theology in Judaism, Christianity, and Islam, as evidenced in *Knowing the Unknowable God: Ibn-Sina, Maimonides, Aquinas* (Notre Dame, 1986) and *Freedom and Creation in Three Traditions* (Notre Dame, 1993).

ROMAN T. CIAPALO is Associate Professor of Philosophy at Loras College, Dubuque, Iowa, and Director of the Loras College "Classical Philosophy Lecture Series," which he established in the Spring of 1990. He received his Ph.D. in philosophy from Loyola University of Chicago. He has lectured nationally and

288

internationally in New Delhi, Bratislava, and Ukraine. He has been the recipient (1991) of a Fulbright-Hays Summer Seminar Grant and in 1993-94 was a Fulbright Lecturer in Ukraine. He has published articles on Neoplatonism and is currently working on a translation into English of the collected works of the 18th century Ukrainian philosopher, Hryhorij Skovoroda.

JOHN DEELY is Professor of Philosophy at Loras College, Dubuque, Iowa. He has been a Fulbright Scholar to Brazil and, most recently, Mexico. He is one of the leading authorities in the field of semiotics, and has published numerous articles and books, among them *The Human Use Of Signs or Elements of Anthroposemiosis* and *New Beginnings: Early Modern Philosophy and Postmodern Thought*. In addition, he has published (The University of California Press) the critical bilingual edition of *Tractatus de Signis: The Semiotic of John Poinsot*.

JUDE P. DOUGHERTY is Dean of the School of Philosophy of The Catholic University of America and editor of *The Review of Metaphysics*. He has written extensively on social and political topics and regularly lectures on issues confronting the philosophy of law and the philosophy of religion.

CURTIS L. HANCOCK is Professor of Philosophy at Rockhurst College, Kansas City, Missouri. He is co-author of *How Should I Live?*, a book on ethics, and co-editor of *Freedom Virtue, and the Common Good*, a book on political philosophy also produced by the American Maritain Association. He is currently the vice president of that association and is associate editor of *Contemporary Philosophy*. He has published articles on Plotinus and Maritain and on topics pertaining to political philosophy and ethics.

THOMAS HIBBS is Associate Professor of Philosophy at Boston College. He earned his B.A. at the University of Dallas in 1982, and a year later was awarded the M.A. He received his Ph.D. from Notre Dame in 1987. He is the author of a book forthcoming from the University of Notre Dame Press: *Dialectic and Narrative in Aquinas: An Interpretation of the Summa Contra Gentiles*.

GREGORY J. KERR, is an Assistant Professor of Philosophy at Allentown College of St. Francis de Sales in Center Valley, Pennsylvania. He is editor of *The Maritain Notebook*, the newsletter of the American Maritain Association and has written chronicles of past meetings of the AMA for both *Notes et Documents* and *Vera Lex*.

JOHN F. X. KNASAS is Professor of Philosophy in the Center for Thomistic Studies at the University of St. Thomas, Houston. He is the authour of *The Preface to Thomistic Metaphysics: A Contribution of the Neo-Thomist Debate on the Start of*

Metaphysics and of many articles on Thomistic metaphysical concerns that appear in *The Thomist, The Modern Schoolman, The American Philosophical Quarterly, Divus Thomas, Doctor Communis* and *Angelicum*. He is the editor of *Jacques Maritain: The Man and His Metaphysics* and more recently *Thomistic Papers VI* which contains assessments of Gerald McCool's *From Unity to Pluralism: The Internal Evolution of Thomism*.

JOSEPH W. KOTERSKI, S.J., (Ph.D., St. Louis University, 1982) teaches in the department of philosophy at Fordham University and is the Editor-in-Chief of *The International Philosophical Quarterly*. His research interests include medieval philosophy and the relation of religion to culture.

JAMES MARSH is Professor of Philosophy at Fordham University, teaches and writes in the areas of 19th century Continental Philosophy, phenomenology, hermeneutics, critical theory, and Lonergan, and has published over fifty articles and four books, the last one being *Critique, Action, and Liberation*.

MATTHEW S. PUGH holds a B.A. in philosophy from Florida State University, an M.A. in history from Ohio State University, and a Ph.D. in philosophy from Fordham University. He is currently Assistant Professor of Philosophy at the University of St. Thomas, in Houston, Texas, and a member of its Center for Thomistic Studies. Dr. Pugh's interests lie in the area of Thomist metaphysics and epistemology, particularly as interpreted by Jacques Maritain. Ongoing research projects include examining the relationship between the philosophies of Bergson and Maritain on the intuition of being, and problems in the epistemology of the basic judgement of existence.

GREGORY M. REICHBERG has taught at the Catholic University of America, and at Fordham University, where he is presently Associate Professor of Philosophy. After predoctoral studies in France at the Université de Toulouse and the Centre Indépendent de Recherche Philosophique, he received his Ph.D. in philosophy from Emory University in 1990. He has published articles on the ethics of knowing, philosophical issues in theology, and the philosophy of science.

ROBERT ROYAL is the Vice President for Research and Olin Fellow in Religion and Society at the Ethics and Public Policy Center (Washington, D.C.). He is author of *1492 and All That: Political Manipulations of History* and co-editor with George Weigel of *Building the Free Society: Democracy, Capitalism and Catholic Social Teaching*, and with Virgil Nemoianu of *Play, Literature and Religion: Essays in Cultural Intertextuality*.

JAMES V. SCHALL, S.J., is a Professor in the Department of Government at Georgetown University. He has taught in the Gregorian University in Rome and at the University of San Francisco. He has written sixteen books, among which are *Another Sort of Learning; Unexpected Meditations Late in the XXth Century; Reason, Revolution and the Foundations of Political Philosophy;* and *Redeeming the Time.*

ROSALIND SMITH EDMAN is an Assistant Professor of Theology at Allentown College of St. Francis de Sales, Center Valley, PA. She presently teaches a Values Seminar focusing on contemporary woman in the context of Christian Humanism. Professional memberships include the American Maritain Association, College Theology Society, and the Catholic Theological Society of America.

BRENDAN SWEETMAN is Assistant Professor of Philosophy at Rockhurst College, Kansas City, Missouri. He is a native of Ireland and was educated at University College, Dublin, and at the University of Southern California, in Los Angeles, where he obtained his Ph.D. He is co-editor of an anthology in the philosophy of religion, *Contemporary Perspectives on Religious Epistemology* (Oxford University Press, 1992). He has published and presented several papers on the philosophy of Gabriel Marcel, and on recent Continental Philosophy. He is a member of the Executive Committee of the Gabriel Marcel Society.

JOSEPH M. DE TORRE, M.A., Ph.D. (Angelicum) holds the SEASFI Professorial Chair of Social and Political Philosophy at the Manila based Center for Research and Communication, where he has been teaching since 1970. He has published more than twenty books and many articles. He is a member of the Fellowship of Catholic Scholars, the American Catholic Philosophical Association, the American Maritain Association, the Society of Catholic Social Scientists, and the Royal Institute of Philosophy.

MEROLD WESTPHAL is Professor of Philosophy at Fordham University. In addition to two books on Hegel, he is the author of *Kierkegaard's Critique of Reason and Society; God, Guilt, and Death: An Existential Phenomenology of Religion,* and *Suspicion and Faith: The Religious Uses of Modern Atheism.*

ROBERT E. WOOD is Professor of Philosophy at the University of Dallas. He is a past (1995) president of the American Catholic Philosophical Association and editor of *American Catholic Philosophical Quarterly.* He has written *Martin Buber's Ontology; A Path into Metaphysics: Phenomenological, Hermeneutical and Dialogical Studies,* and is currently completing a work on *Approaches to Aesthetics.*

Index